THE BUSINES
SUSTAINABLE DEVELOPMENT
IN AFRICA

Human Rights, Partnerships, Alternative Business Models

EDITORS:
Ralph Hamann
Stu Woolman
Courtenay Sprague

Unisa Press, Pretoria
United Nations University Press, Tokyo, New York, Paris

© 2008 University of South Africa
First edition, first impression

Published in Africa by
Unisa Press
University of South Africa
P O Box 392, 0003 UNISA
ISBN 978-1-86888-527-5

and in association with
GTZ–Gesellschaft für Technische Zusammenarbeit
Centre for Cooperation with the Private Sector
P O Box 13732
Hatfield 0028
Pretoria
South Africa

Published in North America and Asia by
United Nations University Press
United Nations University
53–70 Jingumae 5-chome
Shibuya-ku
Tokyo 150–8925
Japan
ISBN 978-92-808-1168-1

Cover design: Yolanda Booyzen
Page design: Doris Hyman
Editor: Bridget Theron
Typesetting: Compleat
Printed in the United States of America

The views expressed in this publication are those of the authors and do not necessarily reflect the views of the United Nations University.

Library of Congress Cataloging-in-Publication Data

The business of sustainable development in Africa : human rights, partnerships, alternative business models / editors, Ralph Hamann, Stu Woolman, Courtenay Sprague.
    p. cm.
  Includes bibliographical references and index.
  ISBN 978-9280811681 (pbk.)
  1. Sustainable development--Africa. 2. Social responsibility of business--Africa. 3. Human rights--Africa. 4. Business ethics--Africa. I. Hamann, Ralph. II. Woolman, Stu. III. Sprague, Courtenay.
  HC800.Z9E53618 2008
  338.96'07--dc22
                          2008043603

THE BUSINESS OF
SUSTAINABLE DEVELOPMENT
IN AFRICA

CONTENTS

FOREWORD
BY
ELLEN KALLINOWSKY

The United Nations (UN) Global Compact is the world's largest corporate citizenship initiative. It brings companies together with UN agencies, labour and civil society to support universal environmental and social principles. The Global Compact's ten principles (described in more detail in the first chapter of this book) are meant to trigger and guide responsible business behaviour at the level of the individual company, as well as collective action between companies. In this way, the private sector – in partnership with other social actors – works towards a more sustainable and inclusive global economy.

In 2005, Africa's development became more prominent on the international agenda through initiatives such as the Commission for Africa. The Global Compact used this momentum to invite its participants to put Africa high on their corporate citizenship agenda and to engage in learning, dialogue and partnerships that are relevant to the African continent.

In November 2006, representatives of business, civil society, UN organisations and government gathered for the Global Compact 4th International Learning Forum Meeting in Ghana. The objectives of the meeting were to share lessons learned and explore opportunities for co-operation on major topics related to corporate citizenship in Africa: business and human rights, business in zones of conflict, business and community engagement, collective action against corruption, and partnerships for development.

Facilitation of learning at the meeting was supported by a range of specially prepared case studies of relevant managerial experiences. These case studies and related discussions at the Ghana conference have contributed significantly to this book. To make the book even more relevant to the African context, additional case studies of innovative business models that relate to 'bottom-of-the-pyramid' strategies have been included.

I wish to thank Ralph Hamann and his colleagues for their excellent editorial work and introductory chapters, the case study authors for their dedication and insight, and the company managers for committing themselves to long interviews and scrutiny so that their experiences could be shared. A personal 'thank you' goes to Girum Bahri, who has been a pillar of support throughout the entire process. Last but not least, I wish to thank the German Ministry for Economic Cooperation and Development and the Gesellschaft für Technische Zusammenarbeit (GTZ – the German development agency) for their generous financial support.

It is my hope that this publication will help managers around the world and especially in Africa to shape their decision-making processes towards responsible and sustainable business engagement.

ELLEN KALLINOWSKY
Global Compact Regional Learning Forum
GTZ Centre for Cooperation with the Private Sector / PPP
Pretoria, November 2007

FOREWORD
BY
DERICK DE JONGH

This book is a vital contribution to the corporate citizenship debate in Africa and beyond. It will contribute to a much needed deepening of academic integrity in the field of corporate citizenship, linked to practical relevance for decision-makers in business and other organisations. Our vision at the Centre for Corporate Citizenship at the University of South Africa is 'Business in Service of Humanity'. We believe that the only way to achieve this 'end game' is to build individual and institutional capacity for sustainable business and social cohesion.

The reason why this book is so important is indicated in its title. The 'business of sustainable development' is complex and challenging. The book contextualises the role of business in development from an African perspective and offers clarity through alternative views and real-life examples. The book's strength therefore lies in its practical demonstration through case studies combined with conceptual reasoning. It highlights and celebrates the tension and positive energy between business objectives and sustainable development objectives through critical reflection and alternative paradigms. Also noteworthy is the healthy interplay between the concepts in Part 1 and the case studies in Part 2 of the book. The book will challenge you with new concepts and practical innovation, whether you are a student, an academic or a business person.

Being good corporate citizens is not an abstract issue. It requires constant, critical reflection on the purpose of business. The Globally Responsible Leadership Initiative – hosted by the UN Global Compact in conjunction with the European Foundation for Management Development – advocates a revised definition of the purpose of business, and it seeks to respond to the question, How do we create a new generation of globally responsible leaders? This book is part of the response to this question and it will play an important role in advancing globally responsible leadership.

With great appreciation,

DERICK DE JONGH
Centre for Corporate Citizenship
University of South Africa (UNISA)
Pretoria, November 2007

PROLOGUE:
PURPOSE AND SCOPE
OF THIS BOOK

> Never before in human history has a single generation witnessed such explosive change. It seems self-evident, therefore, that the policies we adopt, the decisions we make, and the strategies we pursue over the next decade or two will determine the future of our species and the trajectory of the planet for the foreseeable future. That is an awesome responsibility, to say the least. It is also a huge opportunity.[1]

This book is about enhancing the contribution of business to sustainable development in sub-Saharan Africa, with an emphasis on both challenges and opportunities. Sub-Saharan Africa is confronted with many of the world's most pressing problems. Over 40% of the population continue to live in extreme poverty. It is the only region in the world where the proportion of extremely poor people increased during the final decades of the previous century. (The proportion has been decreasing more recently.)[2] The overarching imperative to support Africa's poor in their quest for better livelihoods, human rights and environmental integrity – in short, sustainable development – is a huge challenge, and the business community, ranging from small companies to multinational corporations, has an important role to play. The purpose of this book is to contribute to a better understanding of this role and its implications for decision-makers in business, as well as, to some extent, government and civil society.

The term sustainable development is increasingly ubiquitous, so much so that some people feel it is becoming devoid of any real meaning. However, it is still highly relevant in that it connotes the need for significant, rapid change at various levels – also in business organisations – if we are to meet 'the needs of the present without compromising the ability of future generations to meet their own needs'.[3] Its key premise is that all economic activity is contingent and dependent on the social and natural systems in which it takes place. Economic activity that undermines the integrity and resilience of communities and ecosystems is not only creating increased hardship for those already struggling with ill-health and poverty, but it is also sowing the seeds of its own destruction. Two key requirements of sustainable development are innovation and fairness – they are necessary because they allow society to continuously create and better share prosperity within the carrying capacity of the natural environment. The creation and distribution of wealth, of course, is fundamentally linked to the role of business in society.

Although the literature on the relationship between business and society has a long history, this theme is becoming much more prominent and vital. It is also particularly pertinent in Africa, where a key sustainable development challenge is increasing economic prosperity. A growing, thriving private sector, increased entrepreneurship and an enabling business environment are widely accepted as important objectives in their own right. However, economic development per se should not be our only goal. Companies that contribute unimpeded to human rights abuses, environmental pollution or anti-competitive practices will take Africa backwards. The role of business organisations, ranging from small, survivalist enterprises to multinational corporations, is thus at the heart of the moral and economic imperative that is sustainable development in Africa.

The expectation that companies can indeed make proactive contributions to sustainable development is linked to a range of terms – we will be using corporate citizenship, corporate social responsibility (CSR), and others where appropriate. In many quarters, CSR is still associated with outdated notions of philanthropy, but we use these terms much more broadly with an emphasis on core business practices. Here we are not concerned so much with how companies spend a proportion of their profits for worthy causes, but rather with how they make those profits (or perhaps losses) in the first place. Definitions will be considered in more detail in Chapter 1 and in any case terminology should not hold us up unduly. The key point is that corporate citizenship is fundamentally about core business strategy and its implementation, and it involves increasingly complex responsibilities and possible dilemmas for business decision-makers, as well as new opportunities. This strategic approach is vital because it enhances the business case for contributing to sustainable development and it increases the reach and effectiveness of such efforts. As argued by prominent management scholars Michael Porter and Mark Kramer,

> The fact is, the prevailing approaches to CSR are so fragmented and so disconnected from business and strategy as to obscure many of the greatest opportunities for companies to benefit society. If, instead, corporations were to analyze their prospects for social responsibility using the same frameworks that guide their core business choices, they would discover that CSR can be much more than a cost, a constraint, or a charitable deed – it can be a source of opportunity, innovation, and competitive advantage.[4]

Hence, much depends on how managers and facilitators approach these issues. Innovative, proactive approaches can turn responsibilities and challenges into opportunities. Creative thinking, innovation and partnerships can give rise to new business models that meet developmental needs, while generating consistent financial returns.

Furthermore, we consider corporate citizenship not only from an organisational perspective focused on companies themselves, but also, where appropriate, from a broader analytical perspective that considers the role of supply chains, government policies, civil society groups and other features of what business scholars like Stuart Hart call the 'ecology of commerce'. Facilitating seamless transitions between these various levels of analysis is an important skill not only for researchers – management scholars, in particular, are often criticised for their focus on the business firm only[5] – but also one that deserves fostering among business practitioners, particularly in corporate citizenship matters.

The book's target audience is broad. It is aimed at managers and students (especially those in business organisations or in business-related courses), as well as those with scholarly interests in related fields, such as management, law or development studies. Hence we have tried to balance the needs and interests of these different types of readers, on the premise that a combination of practical and theoretical relevance is important for business managers and others who face complex challenges and need to know how to respond to them better. Similarly, we have backed up the theoretical chapters (Part 1) with case studies that give an African contextual flavour to these debates (Part 2).

This book is, however, not primarily a 'how to' guide to corporate citizenship management, although some managerial implications are considered where appropriate.[6] It does not take for granted the role of profit maximisation as a guiding vision for business or the need for unfettered free markets – two key notions commonly associated with traditional MBA programmes that have been cogently criticised by eminent management scholars such as Harry Mintzberg and Sumantra Goshal.[7] As noted by Nobel laureate, Joseph Stiglitz:

> Today, there is a mismatch between social and private returns. Unless they are closely aligned, the market system cannot work well.[8]

Where appropriate, the book introduces perspectives that are critical of the role of business and especially of multinational corporations and their claims of being good citizens when in fact they have much to answer for. Such perspectives are an important aspect of the corporate citizenship debate and they also contribute to the learning process within business organisations. Though this book argues that business decision-makers can make important contributions to sustainable development, I want to stress at the outset that such contributions can only be effective in the long term as part of a suite of efforts by a broader range of role-players, including civil society and governments. Much depends on our ability to shape the public sector context in which companies operate, from local to global levels.[9]

There is a recurring emphasis in this book on learning. For business, government and civil society, learning is vital. To accept this is to acknowledge that we do not have all the answers and that not only 'best practice' examples provide learning opportunities. Indeed, perhaps the most telling lessons come from individuals or companies confronted with difficult situations or dilemmas, where it is hard to know how to 'do the right thing'. Once decisions are made and actions taken, we have an opportunity to learn with the benefit of hindsight. Making good use of such opportunities is one of the primary purposes of the case studies in Part 2 of this book.

Within the overarching topic of corporate citizenship and the role of business in Africa's development, the book has three guiding themes. Each theme has a dedicated introductory chapter in Part 1 and is illustrated by five (and in one instance six) case studies in Part 2.

The first theme is human rights. We ask the question: How can business decision-makers best respond to human rights dilemmas in the often challenging African business environment? There are often no easy answers to the vexing questions facing managers who want to act ethically and with integrity.[10] For a start, where do we draw the line when it comes to deciding what a company is responsible for? Do we include the activities of its business partners or even the host government? State organisations are normally expected to ensure that the interests of poor and vulnerable people are safeguarded and to mediate between different rights and interests, but in many parts of Africa these organisations are constrained or ineffective. In such circumstances, the sole pursuit of profits for the company can have a very detrimental impact on people and the environment – as well as on the long-term prospects of the company. Furthermore, companies may become obliged to act as mediators and guarantors of the public interest – a role for which most managers are ill-equipped.

Companies are finding themselves in increasingly complex webs of cause-and-effect relationships and interactions between diverse role-players. Business decision-makers can no longer afford to focus solely on their business models or their immediate partners in the value chain, because too many other factors and players may have a significant impact on the business process and the way it affects society. The complexity and unpredictability of the business environment is particularly manifest in many African countries, because of the emerging nature of their economies. Institutional frameworks that provide legal certainties and ensure trust between anonymous parties – crucial conditions for economic growth [11] – are in many instances still developing, even in relatively prosperous South Africa (as discussed in a number of cases in this book). In the worst cases, violent conflict is prevalent or looming, and the implications of this are illustrated incisively in the two case studies set in the eastern DRC (Democratic Republic of the Congo). In others, countries and communities are struggling to recover after years of war. Doing business in such circumstances is often difficult and dangerous, which makes sticking to one's principles more complex, as well as urgent. Of course, difficult business contexts are found elsewhere, too, so in Part 2 of the book we have included a case study from Brazil to illustrate the significant challenges linked to land ownership, and how they have been responded to in an innovative manner by a pulp and paper company.

The second theme is the role of partnerships and collaboration between business, government and civil society in achieving sustainable development objectives. Partnership, both its rhetoric and its practice, has become increasingly prominent in the debates about corporate citizenship and sustainable development in general. The guiding principle is 'collaborative advantage', or the expectation that business, government and civil society organisations can achieve their objectives more effectively through strategic alliances in which each party contributes its unique strengths and resources. Arguably many of the challenges facing companies in Africa and elsewhere, such as the burgeoning informal settlements, or crime and corruption, often require careful, strategic collaboration, because they are too large and complex for any one organisation to deal with by itself. But government, business and civil society often have little experience of working together, so such collaboration initiatives have their own array of difficulties.

Furthermore, like corporate citizenship, the notion of partnership is controversial. Critics highlight risks such as the possible undue influence of business on public sector decision-making and the erosion of representative democracy. Such concerns need to be considered carefully, so that the effectiveness and accountability of collaborative initiatives can be enhanced and their broader role in achieving sustainable development objectives assessed. However, partnerships come in many varieties, and the different types are likely to involve different approaches to implementation and evaluation. Chapter 3 provides a typology of initiatives, based on their objectives and levels of institutionalisation, and the corresponding case studies in Part 2 illustrate not only the diversity of partnerships, but also the crucial and complex role local history and context play in motivating and circumscribing these partnerships and determining how feasible and effective they will be.

The third theme is the way alternative business models can be used to help meet sustainable development objectives. In many ways this is an entirely different approach that goes well beyond the mainstream views of corporate citizenship. Rather than integrating social and environmental objectives into existing business models, this approach takes the achievement of these objectives as a point of departure. What is innovative about such initiatives is the way the achievement of social objectives is often premised upon an entrepreneurial business model that provides financial returns at the same time and thus ensures the enterprise's long-term, independent financial viability.

Related notions such as social entrepreneurship are linked to a broader emphasis on identifying and supporting market-based, entrepreneurial solutions to such problems as poverty, ill-health and environmental degradation. Here we see dedicated programmes by international development agencies, and business leaders and educators showing increasing interest in the notion of 'the fortune at the base of the pyramid', a concept popularised by Prahalad and Hart.[12] Chapter 4 is devoted to this concept, noting some of the tensions between developmental objectives and the continuing pressures for short-term financial returns. These tensions are well illustrated in the case study of one of Hewlett Packard's initiatives in this field.

Perhaps the most exciting innovations linking social and business objectives are those we see coming from smaller companies that can integrate social objectives decisively into their organisational purpose and strategy, and can then also respond flexibly to the opportunities identified by their leaders. The case studies of Honey Care and E+Co illustrate this potential, as well as some of the challenges it entails. But we also see some larger corporations demonstrating this kind of courageous entrepreneurship that seeks to link profits to social well-being, as illustrated in the case study of Aspen Pharmacare's supply of low-cost generic medicines to the South African population.

The three overarching themes were chosen on the basis of their particular relevance in the African context, although of course they are also apposite in other regions. The first two themes, human rights and partnership, were especially prominent during the UN Global Compact International Learning Forum Meeting that was held in Ghana in November 2006, which provided many of the case studies and some of the inspiration for this book. The third theme, alternative business models, was added in response to an increasing interest in such initiatives and their potential for sustainable development in Africa. Crucially, the three themes are closely interrelated. For instance, many companies facing human rights challenges, or social entrepreneurs with an innovative business model, have found that collaborating with other sectors is an effective and efficient strategy. There is therefore a good deal of thematic overlap among the case studies in Part 2.

This book's focus on these particular themes does not of course mean that other aspects of corporate citizenship are less important. The themes of labour rights and environmental management, for instance, are also vital and they present business managers with many dilemmas, in Africa and elsewhere. The various aspects of corporate citizenship are interlinked and interdependent in diverse ways. For instance, many environmental concerns are also human rights concerns, given the devastating effects that pollution or land degradation can have on poor people's livelihoods.[13] These links between the environment, human rights, and sustainable development are made particularly explicit in some of the case studies, such as the VidaGas effort to provide Liquid Petroleum Gas to clinics and households in northern Mozambique.

Many of the case studies are drawn from the UN Global Compact meeting in Ghana, mentioned above. Most of these were written by independent case authors in collaboration with the relevant representatives of the companies or initiatives concerned. The rest have more eclectic origins. They include cases from postgraduate research projects (Rustenburg mining and HP i-Community), cases that were part of a UNDP (United Nations Development Programme) study on enterprise initiatives targeting the base of the pyramid (VidaGas and Aspen Pharmacare), and cases recently published for the Ivey School of Business (Honey Care Africa and E+Co). The case studies are thus not uniform in terms of style or analysis. Some are predominantly descriptive, others include more theoretical discussion. The case studies also vary in the degree to which they are critical of corporate practices and this variance is one of the important tensions underlying the concept and material of this book. The case studies are united, however, by the overall aim of providing ample material for reflection by the reader or for discussion in a group or class – the editors have therefore added a few questions for reflection or discussion at the end of each case study.[14]

Finally, I would like to thank:

- The authors of the case studies, who have all been wonderfully engaged and committed to this project;
- My former colleagues at the Unisa Centre for Corporate Citizenship and the UN Global Compact Learning Forum for Sub-Saharan Africa, in particular Derick de Jongh, Ellen Kallinowsky, and Girum Bahri;
- The Gesellschaft fuer Technische Zusammenarbeit (GTZ), TrustAfrica, and the Environmental Evaluation Unit (EEU) at the University of Cape Town for financial and in-kind support. At the EEU, I am particular grateful to Fahdelah Hartley and Ntombovuyo Madlokazi for their help;
- Di Kilpert and Bridget Theron for their excellent and speedy editing; Beth Le Roux, Sharon Boshoff, Lindsey Morton, Doris Hyman and their colleagues at UNISA Press for their care and oversight; and Yolanda Booyzen for the wonderful cover design;
- My family for putting up with my long working hours during the Cape Town winter.

RALPH HAMANN
Cape Town, May 2008

Notes

1 S. Hart, *Capitalism at the Crossroads: The Unlimited Business Opportunities in Solving the World's Most Difficult Problems* (Upper Saddle River: Wharton School Publishing, 2004), xxxvi.

2 Extreme poverty is the most severe form of poverty, in which people cannot meet basic needs such as food, shelter or health care. It was defined by the World Bank and others as the percentage of people living on less than about US$1 a day, measured in terms of 1993 purchasing power parity. But in 2008 this threshold was moved by World Bank researchers to US$1.25 (relative to 2005 purchasing power in the US), with the result that the number and proportion of people considered to be extremely poor increased significantly (from less than 1 billion to 1.4bn worldwide). For an overview of poverty trends worldwide, see annual publications by the United Nations on progress on the Millennium Development Goals, which are available via http://www.un.org (e.g., United Nations, *The Millennium Development Goals Report 2007* (New York: United Nations, 2007)), similar regular reports by the World Bank (available via http://www.worldbank.org), and J. Sachs, *The End of Poverty: How we can Make it Happen in our Lifetime* (London: Penguin, 2005). Note that though this book's title and some of its sections refer to Africa, we are primarily concerned with sub-Saharan Africa.

3 This is part of the famous 'Brundtland' definition of sustainable development – see United Nations Report of the World Commission on Environment and Development: General Assembly Resolution 42/187, 11 December 1987. For introductory materials on the concept and debates surrounding sustainable development, see for instance http://www.iisd.org/sd (accessed July 2007). For a general overview, see R. W. Kates, T. M. Parris and A. A. Leiserowitz, 'What is sustainable development? Goals, indicators, values, and practice', *Environment* 47, 3 (2005): 8–21. For a progressive policy statement on what sustainable development means at a national level, I recommend South Africa's

recently adopted National Framework for Sustainable Development, available via http://www. environment.gov.za (accessed September 2008).

4 M. E. Porter and M. R. Kramer, 'Strategy & Society: The Link Between Competitive Advantage and Corporate Social Responsibility', *Harvard Business Review*, (December 2006): 1.

5 For such a critique from within organisational scholarship, see for instance, N. Lee and J. Hassard, 'Organization Unbound: Actor-Network Theory, Research Strategy and Institutional Flexibility', *Organization*, 6, 3 (1999): 391–404; for a perspective from geography, see P. O'Neill, 'Where is the Corporation in the Geographical World?' *Progress in Human Geography*, 27, 6 (2003): 677–80.

6 There are a number of such guide-books, some of which are introduced briefly in Part 1 of this book. In particular, see C. Fussler, A. Cramer, and S. van der Vegt, *Raising the Bar: Creating Value with the United Nations Global Compact* (Sheffield: Greenleaf Publishing, 2004).

7 See, for instance, S. Ghoshal, 'Bad Management Theories are Destroying Good Management Practices', *Academy of Management Learning & Education*, 4, 1 (2005): 75–91.

8 J. Stiglitz, 'Poor hit hardest by global lesson in market failure', *Business Day*, 10 July 2008: 9.

9 These overarching arguments are introduced in R. Hamann, 'Can business make decisive contributions to development? Towards a research agenda on corporate citizenship and beyond', *Development Southern Africa*, 23(2) (2006): 175-195.

10 See also W. Visser, M. McIntosh and C. Middleton, eds, *Corporate Citizenship in Africa: Lessons from the Past; Paths to the Future* (Sheffield: Greenleaf, 2006).

11 D. C. North, 'Economic Performance through Time', *American Economic Review*, 84, 3 (2004): 359–68.

12 See, for instance, C. K. Prahalad and S. Hart, 'The Fortune at the Bottom of the Pyramid', *Strategy and Business*, 26 (2002): 2–14.

13 Also note the direct links between human rights and the environment in international agreements and national legislation (see, for instance, section 25 of the Universal Declaration of Human Rights or article 24 of the South African Constitution, which guarantees the right to an environment that is not harmful to health or well-being).

14 Note that due to the case studies' eclectic origin and diverse styles we do not lay claim to an overarching sampling strategy that would facilitate more rigorous case comparison (see K. Eisenhardt, 'Building Theory from Case Study Research', *Academy of Management Review*, 14, 4 (1989): 532–50). In our introductory chapters in Part 1, we draw on other research that is based on rigorous methodology, including both qualitative and quantitative approaches, but when we refer to the case studies in Part 2 it is primarily for the purpose of illustration or exploration.

CHAPTER 1

Introducing corporate citizenship

RALPH HAMANN

This chapter provides a broad introduction to corporate citizenship. First, it describes the increasingly prominent expectation that companies adopt more wide-ranging, explicit responsibilities than previously. Second, it looks at ways of defining corporate citizenship, particularly in Africa, where the context may require different priorities and approaches. Third, it considers some controversies surrounding corporate citizenship, taking into account liberal and radical critiques, and suggests a middle way. It discusses the 'business case' for corporate citizenship and its limitations. Finally, it describes some generic challenges faced by companies in implementing corporate citizenship policies.

A new role for business in sustainable development?

The relationship between business and society, and the way this is circumscribed by ethics and institutions, has long been a subject of debate.[1] Adam Smith, often called the father of modern economics, emphasised how economic transactions were premised on a range of ethical assumptions and foundations.[2] At least since Smith's days, establishing an institutional context in which business activity, broadly speaking, can enhance social outcomes has been a key objective and legitimating foundation for the development of modern states.

In much of Africa, this interplay between ethics, states and markets has historically been characterised by colonialism and slavery. Traditional institutions that previously created a balance between personal wealth creation and collective benefit have to a large extent been dissipated or distorted by systematic colonial subjugation and 'divide-and-rule' tactics, and this legacy persists in the difficulties African states have experienced since independence.[3] There is thus an uneasy tension between the contemporary notion of corporate citizenship and the origins of some of the first truly multinational corporations – such as the British and Dutch East India Companies, which were founded on the systematic exploitation of African slaves and primary resources.

1

Yet even in the days of the East India Companies, questions were being asked about their social responsibilities – by Smith himself, among others – and this arguably contributed to their demise. The history and political economy of corporate citizenship is fascinating,[4] but the point being made here is that questions about the social responsibility of businesses have long been asked, even if they were not situated in debates about 'sustainable development', as they are currently. So is there really a new, socially responsible role for business in sustainable development? The answer is yes, to the extent that there are now increasingly prominent demands and expectations that business leaders contribute more comprehensively to broader social objectives than they used to, and that many of the largest companies seem keen to adopt these expanding responsibilities, at least rhetorically.

The increasingly mainstream and high-level expectation that business can and should contribute to sustainable development is perhaps best illustrated in the primary multilateral agreements on sustainable development and related issues. Already in 1992, a key document of the first Earth Summit in Rio de Janeiro, Brazil, argued that 'the policies and operations of business and industry, including transnational corporations, can play a major role in reducing impacts on resource use and the environment'.[5]

There is thus a call for a growing private sector that will provide more 'employment and livelihood opportunities',[6] and over and above this there are increasing expectations that business leaders should contribute decisively to sustainable development by changing their strategies and decisions. Perhaps the most prominent expression of this is the UN Global Compact, an initiative of the UN Secretary-General, described in more detail below, which argues: 'By taking a principle-based approach to business, companies can help to ensure that sustainable development is achieved and that the benefits of globalization are shared more widely.'[7] Such expectations are also raised with particular reference to Africa's development. The Commission for Africa advises: 'Businesses must sign up to leading codes of good social and environmental conduct, including on corruption and transparency, and focus their efforts on coordinated action to tackle poverty – working in partnership with each other, with donors, with national governments, and with civil society, including trades unions.'[8]

This image of business as contributor to development is supported by parts of the business community, led by major multinational companies. In particular, the World Business Council for Sustainable Development (WBCSD) has been at the forefront of efforts to argue the business case for sustainable development and to propose mechanisms for implementing this contribution. In a report focused on the Millennium Development Goals (MDGs), the WBCSD says: 'Business is good for development and development is good for business.'[9] What motivated companies to join this group? Writing in 2002, three of the WBCSD's main founders explain:

> Some business leaders were drawn to the concept as they realised that not only was it not anti-growth but also it called for serious economic growth to meet the needs of the current population. Also, some warmed to the idea as they compared the issues involved in sustaining the planet with those involved in sustaining a corporation. Both require balancing acts between managing for the long term and managing for the short term.[10]

The increasing interest among governments, business and civil society in corporate citizenship has produced a wide array of initiatives or guidelines. Among the first were the Sullivan

Principles, which were established in 1977 in response to concerns about US corporations' investments in apartheid South Africa. They obliged their signatories to ensure fair labour practices and oppose racial segregation in their operations in South Africa, and they have since been re-branded as the Global Sullivan Principles.[11]

Increasing calls for companies to provide reliable and timely information about their environmental and social performance led to the establishment and rapid growth of the Global Reporting Initiative (GRI), a 'long-term, multi-stakeholder, international process whose mission it is to develop and disseminate globally applicable *Sustainability Reporting Guidelines…* for voluntary use by organisations for reporting on the economic, environmental and social dimensions of their activities, products, and services'.[12] Initiatives such as the GRI emphasise their voluntary nature. But in the context of repeated criticism of voluntary initiatives by many non-governmental organisations (NGOs) (to be discussed in more detail below), it is notable that some governments, such as those of France and Australia, have promulgated legislation requiring increased transparency on social and environmental issues.[13]

Other initiatives have more direct government involvement in their implementation. One of the most prominent of these is the OECD (Organization for Economic Cooperation and Development) Guidelines on Multinational Enterprises, which were first developed in 1976 and revised in 2000. These guidelines pertain, among other things, to disclosure of information, employment relations, environmental management, bribery, competition and consumer interests, and are 'the only multilaterally endorsed and comprehensive rules that governments have negotiated, in which they commit themselves to help solve problems arising in corporations'.[14] Signatory governments commit themselves to establishing National Contact Points that will investigate complaints about violation of these rules.

There is also an increasing array of standards, most notably those of the International Organisation for Standardisation (ISO). The ISO 14000 series focuses on corporate environmental management systems, promoting continual improvement without specifying actual standards of performance. Social issues are not given much consideration, though there is reference to stakeholder engagement. This series has been an important guide for companies in Africa, many of which have become certified in connection with international supply chain and consumer expectations. The ISO's breadth and legitimacy also contribute to the interest devoted to the current development of ISO 26000, a social responsibility guidance standard due for release in 2008 or 2009. This will not prescribe a formal management system, but will provide guidance on specific issues and suggest how organisations can address them. Nevertheless there are concerns that it may become a de facto performance standard in international supply chains, thereby increasing pressure on businesses, especially small and medium enterprises in Africa.[15]

In addition to such universal standards, there are a number of sector-specific standards and certification systems. These include, for instance, the certification systems of the Forest Stewardship Council and the Marine Stewardship Council, the chemical industry's Responsible Care programme, and the Kimberley Process, which seeks to counter the trade in 'blood diamonds'. Key drivers of such initiatives commonly include customers and retailers in developed countries. In those industries with international supply chains and high levels of consumer choice, such programmes have enjoyed relatively high prominence among companies operating in many African countries.

3

Other market-based initiatives focus on the role of investors as potential drivers of sustainable business practices, particularly in the form of socially responsible investment (SRI) funds. These include the Dow Jones Sustainability Index in the US and the FTSE4Good in the UK. In South Africa, the Johannesburg Securities Exchange launched its JSE Socially Responsible Investment Index in 2004, the first of its kind in the developing world.[16] An important role has also been played by corporate governance and risk management guidelines, which are often included in the larger stock exchanges' listing requirements. So, for instance, the JSE in South Africa requires adherence to core components of the internationally respected King 2 Report on Corporate Governance in South Africa, published in 2002 (and currently being updated), and the Nigerian Stock Exchange has a code on corporate governance adopted in 2004, though the latter makes less explicit reference to issues such as corporate citizenship and sustainability reporting than the JSE.[17]

Arguably the most prominent corporate citizenship initiative is the UN Global Compact, first proposed in 1999 by UN Secretary-General Kofi Annan at the World Economic Forum. According to the Global Compact website:

> Through the power of collective action, the Global Compact seeks to promote responsible corporate citizenship so that business can be part of the solution to the challenges of globalisation. In this way, the private sector – in partnership with other social actors – can help realize the Secretary-General's vision: a more sustainable and inclusive global economy. The Global Compact is a purely voluntary initiative with two objectives: Mainstream the ten principles in business activities around the world [and] catalyse actions in support of UN goals...[18]

The ten principles of the Global Compact are listed in Box 1. Its 4000 signatory organisations (as of mid 2007) – mostly multinational corporations, but also including universities and even municipalities – commit themselves to complying with the Global Compact principles and furthering the objectives of the United Nations. Importantly, both commitments go beyond compliance to embrace proactive efforts in pursuit of sustainable development. As signatories, companies also commit themselves to submitting 'Communication on Progress' reports and participating in the various initiatives of the Global Compact, such as the Regional Learning Forum that organised the event in Ghana where many of this book's case studies were first presented.

In response to critics of the Global Compact, who emphasise the lack of enforcement or monitoring of signatories' adherence to the principles, one of the architects of the Global Compact argues as follows:

> The Global Compact has explicitly adopted a learning approach to inducing corporate change, as opposed to a regulatory approach; and it comprises a network form of organization, as opposed to the traditional hierarchic/bureaucratic form. These distinctive (and, for the UN, unusual) features lead the Compact's critics seriously to underestimate its potential, while its supporters may hold excessive expectations of what it can deliver... The hope and expectation is that good practices will help drive out bad ones through the power of dialogue, transparency, advocacy and competition.[19]

There are many who doubt the power of dialogue and transparency for driving out bad corporate practices. This is discussed in more detail below. Yet the Global Compact remains one of the key points of reference for business managers and others grappling with corporate citizenship.

Box 1: The UN Global Compact principles

The Global Compact asks companies to embrace, support and enact, within their sphere of influence, a set of core values in the areas of human rights, labour standards, the environment and anti-corruption:

Human rights
- Principle 1: Businesses should support and respect the protection of internationally proclaimed human rights; and
- Principle 2: make sure that they are not complicit in human rights abuses.

Labour standards
- Principle 3: Businesses should uphold the freedom of association and the effective recognition of the right to collective bargaining;
- Principle 4: the elimination of all forms of forced and compulsory labour;
- Principle 5: the effective abolition of child labour; and
- Principle 6: the elimination of discrimination in respect of employment and occupation.

Environment
- Principle 7: Businesses should support a precautionary approach to environmental challenges;
- Principle 8: undertake initiatives to promote greater environmental responsibility; and
- Principle 9: encourage the development and diffusion of environmentally friendly technologies.

Anti-corruption
- Principle 10: Businesses should work against all forms of corruption, including extortion and bribery.

Source: http://www.unglobalcompact.org (accessed July 2007).

In many African countries, such as Malawi and Mozambique, it provides a crucial introduction to corporate citizenship principles and ideas, where many business managers have yet to be confronted with corporate citizenship initiatives.[20] It also provides an important platform for convening multi-stakeholder discussion and negotiation on issues ranging from human rights to corruption. For instance, when confronted with allegations that ABB's operations in the Sudan were contributing to the human rights abuses in that country, ABB managers realised that the Global Compact could provide a vital, legitimate platform to invite other companies, civil society organisations and – most crucially – the national government, to a discussion on how human rights concerns are affecting the country's socio-economic development.[21] One

5

of the case studies in this book shows a similar role being played by the Global Compact in facilitating multi-stakeholder deliberations on curbing corruption in Malawi.

The current proliferation of initiatives dealing with various aspects of corporate citizenship is proving a headache for many business managers. They are confused and even overwhelmed, and there is much talk of 'code fatigue'. However, the reality is that the number of key initiatives that have proven their pertinence and established legitimacy among diverse stakeholder groups (even though they might continue to be controversial) is relatively small. Furthermore there are important differences between them, and many of them complement each other. For instance, among other things the GRI represents a useful complement to the UN Global Compact, because it allows companies to report comprehensively on their performance regarding adherence to the Global Compact's ten principles. The most prominent initiatives – especially the GRI, the Global Compact and the soon to be issued ISO26000 guidelines – have explicit agreements in place to build these complementarities and synergies.

Defining corporate citizenship

Corporate responsibilities

As noted above, some of the tenets of corporate citizenship have been on people's minds for as long as they have created formal groups for the purpose of economic activity. Whereas 'corporate citizenship' is a term that has only become commonly used relatively recently, systematic efforts to define 'corporate social responsibility' (CSR) have a longer history, especially in the North American management literature. Archie Carroll attributes the first explicit consideration of CSR to Howard Bowen, who defined it in his 1953 book, *Social Responsibilities of the Businessman,* as 'the obligations of businessmen to pursue those policies, to make those decisions, or to follow those lines of action which are desirable in terms of the objectives and values of our society'.[22]

In the 1970s, in response to society's concerns about increasingly powerful corporations, a tiered model of CSR was developed, culminating in Carroll's well-known pyramid model (see Figure 1), which illustrates his observation that '[t]he social responsibility of business encompasses the economic, legal, ethical, and discretionary expectations that society has of organisations at a given point in time'.[23] The pyramid notion implies that economic responsibilities are the foundation on which all the others rest – 'economic performance undergirds all else'. Above these, in ascending sequence, are the legal, ethical and discretionary responsibilities. However, Carroll explains that business 'should not fulfil these in sequential fashion'; rather, that 'each is to be fulfilled at all times'.[24]

In a later version, Carroll describes the economic and legal responsibilities in terms of what is *required*, the ethical ones as what is *expected*, and the discretionary or philanthropic ones as what is *desired*.[25] Similarly, Klaus Leisinger, the special advisor on the Global Compact to the UN Secretary-General in 2005/6, describes 'must', 'ought to' and 'can' dimensions of corporate responsibility (see Figure 2), based on the work of German sociologist Ralf Dahrendorf.[26] Leisinger's 'ought to' dimension encompasses applying best practice norms in circumstances where state legislation is weak or lacks enforcement, and striving to enhance the social and environmental performance, even of third parties for (instance, in the supply chain). Somewhere

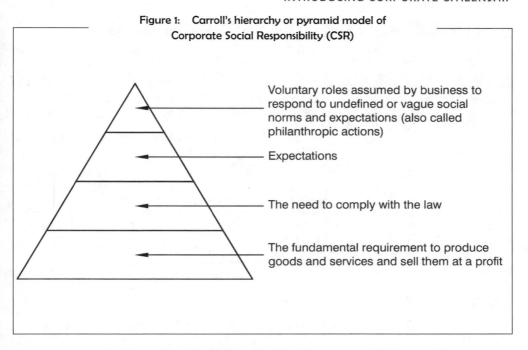

Figure 1: Carroll's hierarchy or pyramid model of Corporate Social Responsibility (CSR)

Voluntary roles assumed by business to respond to undefined or vague social norms and expectations (also called philanthropic actions)

Expectations

The need to comply with the law

The fundamental requirement to produce goods and services and sell them at a profit

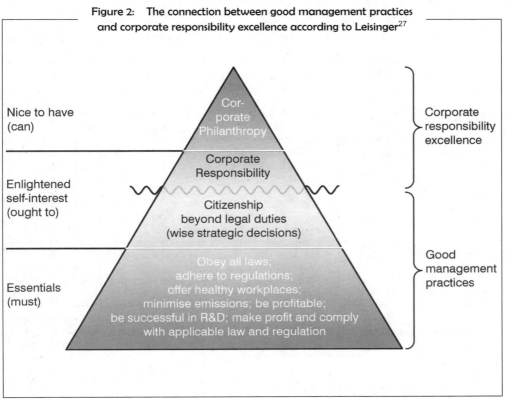

Figure 2: The connection between good management practices and corporate responsibility excellence according to Leisinger[27]

Nice to have (can)

Enlightened self-interest (ought to)

Essentials (must)

Cor-porate Philanthropy

Corporate Responsibility

Citizenship beyond legal duties (wise strategic decisions)

Obey all laws; adhere to regulations; offer healthy workplaces; minimise emissions; be profitable; be successful in R&D; make profit and comply with applicable law and regulation

Corporate responsibility excellence

Good management practices

Table 1:   An overview of South Africa's generic Broad-Based Black Economic Empowerment scorecard

Scorecard component	Focus areas include consideration of (among other things)
Ownership (20%)	• The nature of the exercisable voting rights in the hands of black people • The nature of the economic interest of black people in the enterprise • The level of involvement of black people in ownership of the enterprise through employee ownership schemes, broad-based ownership schemes and co-operatives
Management control (10%)	• The nature of the exercisable voting rights of black Board members • The number of black executive directors • The level of representation of blacks in senior top management • The number of black independent non-executive directors
Employment equity (10%)	• The level of representation of black employees in senior, middle and junior management • The number of black disabled employees as a percentage of all employees
Skills development (20%)	• The level of skills development expenditure on specified learning programmes for black employees • The number of black employees participating in defined learnerships as a percentage of total employees
Preferential procurement (20%)	• The level of B-BBEE procurement spend from all recognised B-BBEE suppliers as a percentage of total procurement spend • The level of B-BBEE procurement spend on suppliers that are 50% black-owned and suppliers that are 30% owned by black women, as a percentage of total procurement spend
Enterprise development (10%)	• The level of the average annual value of all enterprise development contributions and sector specific programmes made by the enterprise as a percentage of a defined target relating to profit and turnover
Socio-economic development initiatives (10%)	• The level of the average annual value of all socio-economic development contributions made by the enterprise as a percentage of a defined target relating to profit and turnover

Source: DTI (Department of Trade and Industry), General Notice 112 of 2007, 'Codes of Good Practice on Black Economic Empowerment Act (9 February 2007)'.

within this range of ethical responsibilities lies the 'responsibility frontier' (the wavy line) between good management practices and corporate responsibility excellence. The position of this frontier 'remains the prerogative of informed top management'.[28]

Because Carroll's pyramid model is one of the best known approaches to defining CSR, it has been subjected to numerous adaptations and critiques. Wayne Visser argues that it requires substantial revision if adapted to the African context, suggesting that in Africa a dominant interpretation of CSR is in terms of philanthropic activities, so the discretionary aspects of CSR are often more important here than the legal and ethical ones.[29] This, he argues, is because the socio-economic development needs in many parts of Africa are 'so great that philanthropy is an expected norm', and because CSR in general 'is still in an early stage of maturity'. Legal responsibilities, on the other hand, are seen to represent less pressure for good conduct, because the legal infrastructure is often poorly developed and 'many African countries are also behind the developed world in terms of incorporating human rights and other issues relevant to CSR into their legislation'.[30]

Visser does not back up his critique with empirical research, though there are other studies that support it at least partially. For instance, my research on mining companies in South Africa found that most corporate managers interpret CSR as so-called corporate social investment activities – or philanthropic contributions towards services such as education, health and welfare – and that the emphasis on this philanthropy sidelined more important changes to companies' core business practices.[31] However, contrary to Visser's argument, my South African research suggests that the most influential driver of recent changes in companies' policies and practices has been the government's new regulatory framework.

Notwithstanding Visser's critique, Carroll's pyramid model is highly relevant in Africa at least in terms of its *normative* application, that is, as a yardstick of what the social responsibilities of business *should* be. For a start, Carroll's definition explicitly includes legal responsibilities, in contrast to those who emphasise the voluntary nature of CSR, such as the European Commission in its 2001 green paper on CSR.[32] As Visser points out, the lack of government policy and its enforcement may be a reason why legal compliance is seen as a relatively low priority for companies from a *descriptive* perspective. But the prevalence of this perception should not detract from the important role that regulations *should* play. With particular reference to East African countries, Mumo Kivuitu and his colleagues suggest that '[t]he limited capacity of regulators and inspectorates means that compliance with even basic legislation can be in effect voluntary'.[33] Hence, especially in the African context, CSR cannot be seen as merely 'beyond compliance', but needs to focus on 'towards compliance' as well.

Further, in the context of the debates about the developmental role of the state and continued efforts to remedy the ills of the colonial and apartheid legacies, many African governments are seeking to define a social role for companies more proactively than is catered for in the European Commission definition of CSR mentioned above (though note that this can also be said of many European national governments, such as Norway). This is illustrated for instance in the South African debate about black economic empowerment (BEE), which has parallels in other African countries, such as the Nigerian government's 'Local Content' policies. BEE requirements are stipulated on a 'balanced scorecard' (see Table 1) and South African companies are obliged to improve their scores if they want to do business with the government (which is by far the country's largest procurer of goods and services) or obtain licences (such as mining or fishing licences). As shown in Table 1, one of the elements of the BEE scorecard is preferential procurement, which means that a company needs to show that it is procuring goods and services from companies that are complying with the BEE requirements. This ensures that significant pressure to comply with BEE requirements is filtered down the supply chain.

Though there are noteworthy critiques of BEE and its implementation in South Africa,[34] it can be argued that it represents a negotiated definition of what CSR means in this country – at least in part – with the state playing a strong role in defining and enforcing it.[35] The broader implication is that corporate citizenship cannot be seen as purely a voluntary effort by business but that complying with the spirit of government policies and regulations is a crucial component. Rather than sidelining the role of governments by emphasising business voluntarism, this role ought to be integrated and strengthened in enhancing corporate citizenship.

Perhaps the more significant critique of Carroll's pyramid is its simplicity, in that it 'does not adequately address the problem of what should happen when two or more responsibilities are in conflict'.[36] Visser highlights this point with an example especially pertinent in much of Africa:

> In an African context, such conflicts and contradictions [between the levels in Carroll's pyramid] tend to be the norm, rather than the exception – how to reconcile job creation and environmental protection, short term profitability and Aids treatment costs, oppressive regimes and transparent governance, economic empowerment and social investment? And in reality, the interconnections between Carroll's four levels are so blurred as to [make these levels] seem artificial or even irrelevant. For example, is the issue of Aids treatment primarily an economic responsibility (given the medium to long term effects on the workforce and economy), or is it ethical (because Aids sufferers have basic human rights), or is it philanthropic (it is not an occupational disease, so surely treatment amounts to charity)?[37]

CSR as social cost accounting and transparency

Parallel to the efforts by Carroll and others to identify and, to some extent, prioritise different corporate social responsibilities, there has been a long-standing emphasis on business organisations' accountability for their negative impacts. This emphasis is also in line with more critical assessments of the role of business in society, and with the growing convergence between the debates on CSR and those on sustainable development and the attendant quest for performance indicators, and it is particularly noticeable in industries with significant direct social and environmental impacts. So, for instance, Alyson Warhurst and Paul Mitchell define CSR in mining as 'the internalisation by the company of the social and environmental effects of its operations through pro-active pollution prevention and social impact assessment so that harm is anticipated and avoided and benefits are optimised'.[38]

The social cost accounting perspective has led to the development of new accounting frameworks that seek to introduce social and environmental criteria into corporations' accounting practices. Such frameworks have a dual purpose: first, to achieve internal management objectives; and second, to help the company achieve and maintain legitimacy among its stakeholders. More broadly, this perspective emphasises the transformative potential of increased transparency. Stuart Hart illustrates this with a US example:

Passed in 1998… the Toxic Release Inventory (TRI) in the US received relatively little attention in its early days. This seemingly innocuous provision required only that manu-facturers disclose their use, storage, transport, and disposal of more than 300 toxic chem-icals (all of which were perfectly legal at the time). Much to everyone's surprise, this data… became an important new source of information for activist groups, the media, and third-party analysts to track corporate environmental performance… The TRI also provided, for the first time, a metric for corporate and facility managers to track their own firms' performance and benchmark it against competitors. What gets measured gets done. Ten years later, toxic emissions in the United States had been reduced by more than 60 percent, even though the US economy boomed during the 1990s.[39]

From a company perspective, the most widely used and systematic mechanism for publicly re-porting on sustainable development impacts is, of course, sustainability reporting. Though this practice has come a long way from the initial discussions in the 1970s on social accounting to the current prominence of the GRI,[40] most companies' reports are arguably still not very effec-tive in explaining actual impacts on stakeholders, especially for the company as a whole. The first problem here is the tension between universal guidelines – epitomised by the GRI – and companies' diverse and complex local contexts. Attempts are therefore being made to augment high-level indicator systems with more participatory methods involving local stakeholders.[41]

More fundamental critiques of corporate sustainability reports involve claims of 'green-washing', or the intentional provision of misinformation to suggest the company is environ-mentally responsible.[42] Despite the advances made through the GRI, many NGOs continue to view corporate sustainability reports negatively with regard to their 'credibility and suf-ficiency'.[43] To some extent, the increasing scrutiny of corporate activity by a global network of NGOs, linked to local activists and making effective use of the media and the Internet, argu-ably increases the pressure on companies to become more transparent. Yet there is considerable scope for enhancing this involvement of civil society in company-level impact appraisals, not only to increase the local legitimacy of the indicators used, but also to increase accountability and trust.[44] One of the most striking examples of such an approach was a study on the impacts of Unilever on poverty in Indonesia conducted jointly by the company and Oxfam.

Enter corporate citizenship

This growing emphasis on joint initiatives between companies and civil society organisations to increase companies' accountability already goes well beyond Carroll's definition of CSR. So, whereas many use the term 'corporate citizenship' interchangeably with 'CSR' (and indeed some of the authors do so in parts of this book), Andrew Crane and Dirk Matten identify an extended view of corporate citizenship that goes beyond the above definitions of CSR.[45] Their definition emphasises the concept of 'citizenship', which relates to the rights and responsi-bilities of members of a community. Although corporations are not 'real' citizens, they are juristic persons and powerful actors in society, so they arguably have duties to respect, uphold and further the social, civil and political rights of citizens. This duty is all the more pertinent because 'the failure of governments to fulfil some of their traditional functions, coupled with the rise in corporate power, has meant that corporations have increasingly taken on a political role in society'.[46]

This expanded view of corporate citizenship is defined as 'the corporate function for administering citizenship rights for individuals'.[47] These citizenship rights are social, civil and political. The following are examples of these rights and the company's consequent responsibilities:

- *Social rights* include, for instance, the right to education, health care or aspects of welfare. As Crane and Matten point out, 'in developing countries where governments simply cannot (and very often do not want to) afford a welfare state... improving working conditions in sweatshops, ensuring employees a living wage, providing schools, medical centres and roads, or even providing financial support for the schooling of child labourers are all activities in which corporations... have engaged under the label of corporate citizenship'.

- *Civil rights* generally refer to, among others, the right to be protected from abuse by third parties, especially the state, and they include the right to a fair trial and freedom of speech. Crane and Matten mention the example of Shell in Nigeria to show that 'corporations might play a crucial role in either discouraging (as Shell [has done]) or encouraging governments to live up to their responsibility in this arena of citizenship'.

- *Political rights* allow individuals to participate in political processes, including the right to vote or to be voted into office. Here, corporate citizenship provides citizens with a means to effect change by making corporations prime targets of campaigners and advocacy groups.[48]

Crane and Matten's definition of corporate citizenship is useful because it begins to see the corporation in its broader socio-political context (alluded to at the beginning of this chapter), and because it provides a link to the crucial role of human rights in these discussions (the topic of Chapter 2). It is also a useful platform for discussing the stakeholder model of CSR, the subject of the next section.

The stakeholder model

The need to define companies' social responsibilities more clearly has led many scholars and practitioners to conclude that rather than identify responsibilities to society in general, it is perhaps better to consider companies' responsibilities to their *stakeholders*. Clarkson provides the following definition:

> Stakeholders are persons or groups that have, or claim, ownership, rights, or interests in a corporation and its activities, past, present, or future. Such claimed rights or interests are the result of transactions with, or actions taken by, the corporation, and may be legal or moral, individual or collective. Stakeholders with similar interests, claims, or rights can be classified as belonging to the same group: employees, shareholders, customers, and so on.[49]

Two types of stakeholder are identified, though they are not clearly delineated. *Primary stakeholders* are those whose continuing participation is vital to the corporation, or those who have direct and well-established legal claims on a corporation's resources.[50] Groups that would satisfy both criteria include shareholders, creditors, employees and government. Depending on the circumstances, customers and local communities may fulfil the first requirement, but not the second. *Secondary stakeholders* are those groups that are affected by the corporation but not essential to its survival, or that do not have legal claims but rather rely on non-binding or ethical obligations.

Figure 3 represents graphically the kinds of stakeholders that may be relevant to, say, a publicly-listed mining company, including the ways they might seek to influence the company. The stakeholders are tentatively aligned according to geographic scale and their likely status as primary or secondary stakeholders. Bear in mind, however, that this status cannot be clearly assigned as it depends on the circumstances. As mentioned, for instance, a local community group may not have a contractual relationship with a company (i.e. a legal claim on it), but can nevertheless exert significant influence through protest or other means.

Clarkson describes the stakeholder model as a fundamentally different perspective on the role and objectives of a corporation. It sees the corporation as 'a system of primary stakeholder groups, a complex set of relationships between and among interest groups with different rights, objectives, expectations, and responsibilities'.[51] Because the corporation depends on the continued participation of the primary stakeholders, its success will depend on the degree to which the primary stakeholders – not just the shareholders – are provided with 'wealth, value, or satisfaction'.

> This means that managers must resolve the inevitable conflicts between primary interest groups over the distribution of the increased wealth and value created by the corporation. Resolving conflicting interests fairly requires ethical judgement and choices.[52]

The stakeholder model is popular because it is based on a more manageable definition of the scope of CSR: companies are no longer responsible for vague notions of the good society, but must rather respond to specific issues raised by stakeholder groups, which can generally be identified relatively easily. The model allows for a more precise assessment of the outcomes of corporate activity, and it has been used to provide advice on managerial practice.[53] Perhaps most significantly, it emphasises relationships as a key principle:

> Corporate citizenship really means developing mutually beneficial, interactive and trusting relationships between the company and its many stakeholders… through the implementation of the company's strategies and operating practices. In this sense, being a good corporate citizen means treating all of a company's stakeholders (and the natural environment) with dignity and respect, being aware of the company's impacts on stakeholders and working collaboratively with them when appropriate to achieve mutually desired results.[54]

Corporate citizenship as a contribution to improved governance

There are, however, a few problems with the stakeholder model. One is that it focuses almost exclusively on the relationship between the company and the stakeholders. In other words, it implies neutral relationships between the stakeholders. But stakeholders and stakeholder groups, particularly the local ones, are in fact embedded in a complex web of relationships. Furthermore, it puts the company in the centre of these relationships, which potentially sidelines important processes that are outside the immediate ambit of the company but which nevertheless play a crucial role in an effective corporate citizenship strategy. Consequently,

Figure 3: A model of company stakeholders and their means of influence on company governance

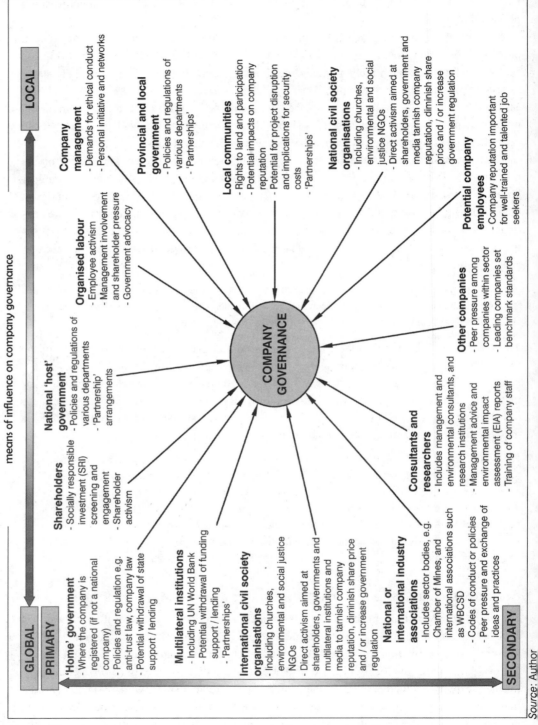

Source: Author

it often places insufficient emphasis on the role of power in the relationships between the company and its stakeholders, as well as between the various stakeholders.

The model in Figure 4 is a response to these problems, suggesting a complex set of relationships between a company and various local stakeholders.[55] It depicts the company as an inherent component of a local governance system. This system is characterised by the rights, interests, roles and interrelations of various organisations and institutions, which are shown in the oval enclosed by a broken line. It encompasses the local development context, summarised here by reference to the sustainable livelihoods framework, which categorises the resources, or 'capitals' – financial, social, human, physical, and natural – available to households to construct livelihoods for their members (see also Case 6, Figure 1). This is important because local governance is determined by the development opportunities or challenges faced at the local level. The relationship between local groups will be influenced by the way individuals and groups relate to these development issues. Seeing a company as a participant and contributor to this governance system is a variant of Crane and Matten's political interpretation of corporate citizenship mentioned above.

The model proposes four primary categories of groups or organisations at the local level that are commonly encountered in Africa (though there are likely to be others). These are local government; traditional institutions and authorities; other civil society groups, such as NGOs or community-based organisations; and the corporations present in the area. Although this model focuses on the local stakeholders, others whose origins are international or who are operating on an international scale – such as international NGOs – may also be pertinent in this local system, especially in the case of large, high-profile or even controversial projects. The organisational or institutional categories are shown in squares that are also enclosed by broken lines, to indicate that they are defined subjectively and that there is often some overlap between them, depending on the local context. The arrows between the categories indicate formal or informal interactions, such as communication pathways or resource transfers.

This local governance system cannot be easily influenced by decisive actions by any one group within the local system, including a corporation. The relationships implied in Figure 4 are path-dependent: the opportunities offered or constraints imposed by the local governance system depend on what happened in the past. This history is manifest in the relationships between organisations and institutions, and in the way the stakeholders see each other and how much they trust each other. Proverbially speaking, it takes years for trust to be created, but only a moment for it to be destroyed.

In some instances, weak and inefficient local government organisations, conflict between elected, state-centric government and traditional authorities, historical distrust or resentment of large, possibly multinational companies and growing expectations of them because of local political agendas, all coalesce to contribute to vicious cycles of interaction. Such patterns are characterised by low collaboration potential and high levels of unpredictability. In these circumstances especially, traditional corporate citizenship activities based on unilateral company actions or engaging stakeholders independently of each other are unlikely to meet their objectives. Instead, a more proactive involvement in moving local governance towards accountability and inclusiveness is often necessary.

A key outcome of seeing corporate citizenship in terms of local governance complexity, therefore, is that it dampens expectations of what can be achieved by unilateral corporate

Figure 4   Schematic model of corporate presence as part of the
local governance system in Africa

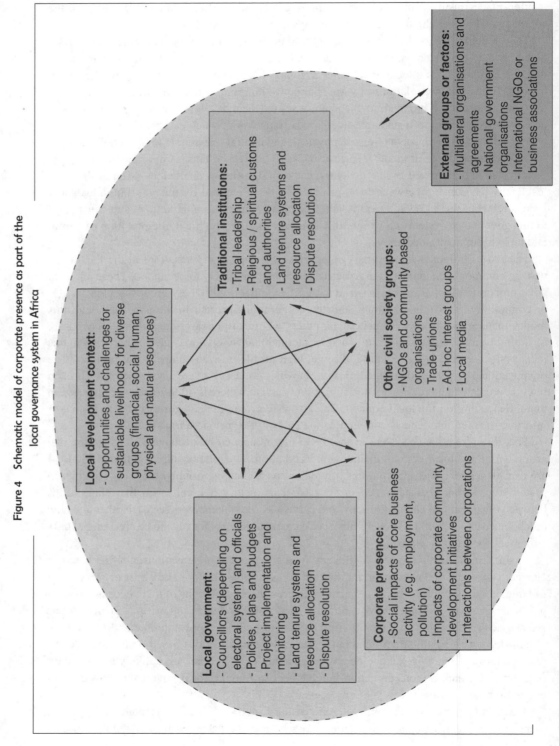

Local development context:
- Opportunities and challenges for sustainable livelihoods for diverse groups (financial, social, human, physical and natural resources)

Traditional institutions:
- Tribal leadership
- Religious / spiritual customs and authorities
- Land tenure systems and resource allocation
- Dispute resolution

External groups or factors:
- Multilateral organisations and agreements
- National government organisations
- International NGOs or business associations

Other civil society groups:
- NGOs and community based organisations
- Trade unions
- Ad hoc interest groups
- Local media

Local government:
- Councillors (depending on electoral system) and officials
- Policies, plans and budgets
- Project implementation and monitoring
- Land tenure systems and resource allocation
- Dispute resolution

Corporate presence:
- Social impacts of core business activity (e.g. employment, pollution)
- Impacts of corporate community development initiatives
- Interactions between corporations

actions. Rather, proactive and creative approaches are often necessary to develop and foster local collaboration arrangements. Collaboration is a gradual, self-organising process in which successive steps depend on prior agreements and commitments and the final outcomes cannot be predetermined. (In the terminology of complexity theory, this is referred to as an 'emergent' process.) In other words, establishing collaboration arrangements requires much time, dedication and creativity from the company. But it is arguably the most efficient, long-lasting and sometimes the only way of implementing corporate citizenship principles at the local level. This is illustrated in Cases 7 and 8 in this book.

Corporate citizenship as an opportunity and new purpose for business

Some of Africa's socio-economic challenges may present innovative companies with new business opportunities. The quest for innovative products or services that benefit the poor is at the frontier of corporate citizenship, despite seldom being described as such. Most prominently, C.K. Prahalad and Stuart Hart argue that large corporations can make substantial profits in marketing to the poor at the 'bottom of the pyramid':

> Contrary to popular assumptions, the poor can be a very profitable market – especially if MNCs [multinational corporations] change their business models. Specifically, [the poor are] not a market that allows for the traditional pursuit of high margins; instead, profits are driven by volume and capital efficiency.[56]

This notion is popular with big business. The WBCSD says leading companies are 'offering clear development benefits through investing in new ideas designed to create opportunities for the poor', and mentions Eskom's efforts at affirmative procurement and support for small businesses and Vodafone's use of mobile phones to extend access to financial services to the poor.[57] An example of a much smaller but particularly innovative exploitation of a business opportunity is the provision of streetlights in Nairobi by an advertising company in Kenya that asked companies to pay for those lights that would carry their advertisements – lights that are furthermore erected by street children.[58]

The concept of the bottom of the pyramid (which is not to be confused with Carroll's pyramid model of CSR mentioned above) is discussed in more detail in Chapter 4, but it is worthwhile briefly considering the extent to which MNCs are able and willing to 'change their business models'. Considering the persistent pressures for short-term returns to shareholders, epitomised by quarterly reports, it is fair to suggest that innovative business models that effectively cater for the poor may remain a sideshow to 'business as usual', at least for large, listed corporations. Allen White, the former head of the Global Reporting Initiative, argues that the corporate citizenship debate focuses too much on peripheral elements of corporate activity and neglects core elements such as company law and fiduciary duties to shareholders.[59] This is as yet uncharted territory and there are also crucial opportunities for investigating the philosophy, practicalities and feasibility of revising the purpose of business to place greater emphasis on value-based principles, longer time frames and the interests of a broader array of stakeholders.

Tensions and controversies

The view that big business is motivated and able to make decisive contributions to sustainable development is controversial. There are essentially two main sources of critique, which, though they share some characteristics, come from contrasting vantage points with opposing assumptions and diverging interpretations of sustainable development. The first critique is that of the liberal economists, who are superficially more likely to believe that a corporation operating within the law in a competitive market is inherently contributing to sustainable development because it is contributing to the most efficient and effective allocation of resources. The second is that of the radical economists or advocacy groups, who believe the ideal free market conditions assumed by the liberal economists are far from the current reality and that, generally speaking, corporations *detract* from sustainable development because in their quest for profits they seek to externalise the costs to society (for example by decreasing real wages) and the environment (for example by causing air and water pollution).

Somewhere between these stereotypes lies a range of arguments that companies' effects on sustainable development are not inherently positive or negative, but rather depend on the strategies the companies use and the decisions they take, and on the institutional context in which they operate. Concepts such as corporate citizenship or CSR can thus be interpreted in terms of the incentives and mechanisms that companies can choose in order to contribute to rather than detract from sustainable development. These arguments are summed up in the form of some representative quotes in Figure 5.

The liberal critique and some counter-arguments (including the business case for corporate citizenship)

The liberal economists' concern is that business decision-makers are not mandated or capacitated to devote attention and resources to anything other than the company's core purpose of making money. The most well-known statement to this effect was Nobel laureate Milton Friedman's argument in 1970 that 'the social responsibility of business is to increase its profits'.[60] More recent proponents of this view include David Henderson, former chief economist at the OECD, who argues: 'The case against CSR is... that it would make people in general poorer by weakening the performance of business enterprises in their primary role.'[61] In 2005, *The Economist* weighed in along similar lines in its editorial for a theme issue on this topic:

> All things considered, there is much to be said for leaving social and economic policy to governments. They, at least, are accountable to voters. Managers lack the time for such endeavours, or should do. Lately they have found it a struggle even to discharge their obligations to shareholders, the people who are paying their wages. If they want to make the world a better place – a commendable aim, to be sure – let them concentrate for the time being on that.[62]

These various criticisms of the notion that business decision-makers have objectives over and above the profit motive are distilled by Margolis and Walsh into two central concerns.[63] *Misappropriation* is seen to occur when decision-makers 'divert resources from their rightful claimants, whether these be the firm's owners [in the case of public companies, their shareholders] or, sometimes, their employees'. *Misallocation*, it is argued by CSR critics, occurs

Figure 5: Perspectives on the role of big business in sustainable development

Liberal economists' critique of corporate social responsibility (CSR):	Calls for corporate citizenship / CSR:	Radical economists' / activists' critique of CSR:
'There is one and only one social responsibility of business – to use its resources and engage in activities designed to increase its profits so long as it stays within the rules of the game, which is to say, engages in open and free competition without deception or fraud.' (Friedman, 1970) 'The case against CSR is… that it would make people in general poorer by weakening the performance of business enterprises in their primary role.' (Henderson, 2005)	'By taking a principle-based approach to business, companies can help to ensure that sustainable development is achieved and that the benefits of globalization are shared more widely.' (UN Global Compact, 2005)	'Corporations' profits depend to a disturbing extent on their ability to use their extraordinary economic power to extract huge subsidies from the larger society.' (Korten, 2001) 'CSR is a completely inadequate response to the sometimes devastating impact that multinational companies can have in an ever more globalised world – and… it is actually used to mask that impact.' (Christian Aid, 2004)

Source: Author, using quotes from various sources.[64]

when business decision-makers are distracted from what they are good at – making money for the company's owners – by doing what they are generally not good at, or at least not as good as public servants ought to be.

CSR proponents have made diverse responses to these criticisms from liberal economists (also known as contractarian criticisms). In many instances, these have involved arguments about what is called the 'business case' for sustainable development or CSR – that is, that contributing to social objectives will also benefit a company's financial performance. Indeed, in the North American academic literature there is a long history of studies that aim to identify a correlation between companies' social performance and their financial performance. For instance, Margolis and Walsh surveyed 127 studies on this topic published between 1972 and 2002. They write that 'a simple compilation of [these studies'] findings suggests that there is a positive association, and certainly very little evidence of a negative association, between a company's social performance and its financial performance'. [65] However, they also note that these various studies are plagued by diverse methodological shortcomings, so the debate over the business case remains unresolved.

The other concern about this literature is that it focuses almost exclusively on North American and, to a lesser extent, European companies. Studies on the business case in the African context mostly rely on case studies or anecdotal evidence. A recent study of mining companies in South Africa argues that the business case cannot be relied on and that much depends on companies' institutional context, especially the regulatory environment.[66] An earlier study, conducted by the IFC and others, considers anecdotal evidence from around the world, including Africa (see Table 2). This study is noteworthy for its analysis of the way various aspects of CSR are likely to have varying relationships with different aspects of a firm's financial performance. In particular, it suggests that environmental performance dimensions have generally a stronger impact on financial performance than, say, human rights issues.[67]

The key concern, however, is that the business case alone is not a sufficient motivation for responsible business practices: 'While there is a strong "business case" for respecting human rights, companies are obliged to respect human rights at all times, not just when it suits them.'[68] In many instances, such arguments have been made on ethical grounds. Nobel laureate Amartya Sen, for example, has argued that the conventional view of economic self-interest as the primary or even the only motivation for business is out of place, noting that economic transactions themselves rely to a large extent on social norms and values.[69]

A further response to the liberal economists' critique of CSR is to focus on the changing context in which companies find themselves. Friedman himself emphasised that the business manager's responsibility is generally 'to make as much money as possible *while conforming to the basic rules of the society, both those embodied in law and those embodied in ethical custom*' (emphasis added).[70] These rules of the society are bound to change, including legal requirements and ethical custom, and it may be argued that the current emphasis on CSR and business contributions to development and respect for human rights is part of a broader shift that has taken place since 1970.

Hence, over and above economic and ethical arguments focused at the level of the business organisation, the liberal economists' critique of CSR can be rebutted on the grounds that it presupposes a 'well-ordered, strong governance context, where whole system needs such as law and order, social justice and conservation, and market failure issues such as monopoly and externalities are relatively well controlled'.[71] Such conditions are rare, if they exist at all, particularly in Africa. In the context of globalisation, the power of nation states is widely perceived to be diminishing relative to that of big companies in the wake of technological developments and global trade connections, as well as many governments' quest to attract foreign direct investment. The World Economic Forum, for instance, states that:

> In the face of high levels of insecurity and poverty, the backlash against globalization,
> and mistrust of big business, there is growing pressure on business leaders and their

Table 2: Examples of the business case for corporate citizenship in Africa, according to IFC *et al.*

Example	Business case
Investments in prevention, treatment and care of HIV/AIDS by companies operating in southern Africa (such as Eskom) have led to reduced incidence, and also improved workers' quality of life.	Reductions in the cost of benefit payments, employee training, overtime and casual wages, insurance premiums, supervision and management, increases in productivity and employee motivation, and retention of trained employees.
Fairtrade chocolate, which provides a market for initiatives such as Kuapa Kokoo, a cooperative involving 35 000 farmers in Ghana farming according to social and environmental principles.	The Fairtrade movement is based on consumers' willingness to pay a premium on products that are produced with high social and environmental standards, thereby providing more secure income to the cooperative's members.
During the 1980s and early 1990s, UK-based company Thor Chemicals' mercury reprocessing plant in South Africa had severe pollution and health impacts on employees, including the death of two workers in 1993.	The company's blatant pollution and health offences prompted numerous protest and legal actions. Business partners discontinued their relationship with the company. In 1993, the company and three of its directors were charged by the South African state (though charges were dropped after the payment of a small fine). In 1994 the plant was closed down by the government. The company was subsequently sued both in South Africa and the UK, with settlement payments totalling over \$3 million.
The Nairobi based Serena Group of Hotels has built a number of lodges and tented camps in East Africa. It has implemented extensive environmental management, community involvement and enterprise development programmes.	The acceptance of the Group's activities among local populations has significantly reduced the incidence of theft. The Group has also won a prestigious 'Green Globe' award, thereby improving its reputation in the travel industry. Sensitive siting, protection of resources, and good community relations add to its visitors' ecotourism experience.
In an electrification project involving ABB, a transmission line was re-routed to minimise social impacts, significantly decreasing the number of people to be resettled. The company and its partners have also established a social committee to facilitate interaction with affected communities and to implement social investment projects.	Resettlement costs were significantly reduced since there were fewer people to be moved. The social committee and related initiatives also reduced the potential for community grievance and protest, which might have led to project delays and various extra costs.

Source: Adapted from International Finance Corporation, SustainAbility, and Instituto Ethos, The Business Case in Emerging Economies (Washington: International Finance Corporation, 2002).

companies to deliver wider societal value. This calls for effective management of the company's wider impacts on and contributions to society, making appropriate use of stakeholder engagement.[72]

There is now also a greater awareness of the complex interrelationships between socio-economic and natural systems – as manifested in climate change, for instance – which are further evidence of the limitations of the traditional reliance on the nation state to respond to such problems. Not only do these complex sustainable development challenges transcend the borders of nation states, they often require collaboration between different role-players in society, including business. This makes it difficult to see a clear dividing line between government and business responsibilities. In sum, the liberal economists' critique of corporate citizenship is arguably rendered inapplicable by widespread poverty and illiteracy, weak and corrupt national governments and struggling multilateral bodies, monopolisation and growing concentration of economic power, and increasingly complex and interconnected social and natural systems.

The radical critique and a middle way

At the other end of the spectrum, consistent criticism of CSR or corporate citizenship has come from radical economists and advocacy NGOs, who see it as empty, harmful rhetoric. They argue that business leaders' emphasis on voluntary corporate *responsibility* initiatives is a means to pre-empt or limit mandatory government regulations to ensure corporate *accountability* that would make corporations answerable for the negative consequences of their actions:

> Business... has consistently used CSR to block attempts to establish the mandatory international regulation of companies' activities. Its basic argument is that CSR shows how committed corporations already are to behaving responsibly and that introducing mandatory regulation could destroy this good will. Business leaders are also constantly saying that regulation is bad for their profits – the two statements are, of course, not unconnected.[73]

Activist NGOs are not the only ones to have raised such concerns. Analysts and academics of diverse persuasions have agreed that there is a danger of CSR becoming dominated by companies' public relations departments. Even prominent business management scholars, such as Michael Porter, lament the precedence of image over substance in the approach of most companies to CSR.[74]

> A critical view of CSR emphasizes the need to consider underlying motivations for business to embrace and perpetuate the CSR concept. These may relate to accommodation – the implementation of cosmetic changes to business practice in order to preclude bigger changes – and legitimization – the influence by business over popular and policy-related discourse in order to define what questions may be asked and what answers are feasible.[75]

When companies' motivations for sustainability reporting are more to do with maintaining legitimacy and controlling stakeholders than with being accountable to those stakeholders and curbing unsustainable trends, this not only has detrimental effects on the credibility of the corporate citizenship movement, it may also have perverse side-effects: 'The purchase of the

Figure 6:   A cartoon popular during the World Summit on
Sustainable Development in Johannesburg, 2002

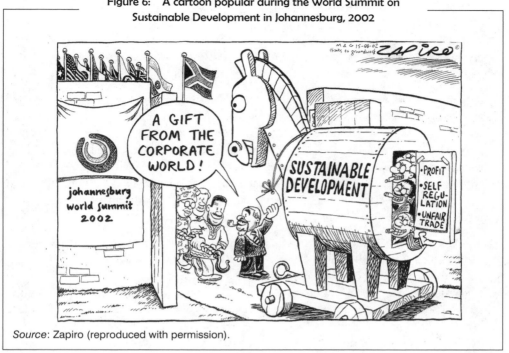

Source: Zapiro (reproduced with permission).

"commodity of compliance" sufficient to shift the risk of liability and loss, in certain firms, may result in decreased levels of care by senior managers.'[76]

The critical view of big business under the rubric of corporate accountability featured prominently at the World Summit on Sustainable Development (WSSD), in particular. Common reference was made to 'greenwash': 'It is often the world's most polluting corporations that have developed the most sophisticated techniques to communicate their message of corporate environmentalism.'[77] A related term was 'bluewash' – the concern that the legitimacy of the United Nations itself was being co-opted by big business interests. During the WSSD, this notion was captured in a popular cartoon, shown in Figure 6.

Craig Bennett, of Friends of the Earth International, explained one of the main concerns of NGOs: 'For every company that sincerely implements its CSR policies, there are hundreds who greenwash, and for each of these there are hundreds more who don't even bother with that.'[78] To thwart greenwash and, more importantly, raise the social and environmental performance of recalcitrant companies, NGOs have demanded more effective and targeted government intervention, including the guarantee of human rights, rights to a clean and healthy environment, access to justice, access to information, and public disclosure of pertinent information. Cases of litigation against corporate wrong-doing have been highlighted to emphasise the need for stricter regulation and liability, including the demand for an International Convention on Corporate Accountability that would impose explicit '*duties* on corporations with respect to social and environmental matters'[79] (see Box 2).

Box 2: Cases of litigation against mining companies in South Africa

The final report of the South African Truth and Reconciliation Commission (TRC) (established to investigate, inter alia, human rights abuses during apartheid) recommended that big business should pay reparations to apartheid victims.

On the one hand, this was received with great concern by business, the business media and investment analysts. On the other, the TRC's findings provided substantial impetus to litigation, in which many companies, including multinational companies based elsewhere, stand accused of having knowingly gained from or supported unjust apartheid policies, primarily as they related to labour laws. The Apartheid Claims Taskforce (ACT) and Jubilee 2000 South Africa initiated separate legal proceedings in the United States, arguing that the accused firms 'knowingly propped up the apartheid state and made huge profits by doing so'.[80]

The best known litigation against mining companies that operated in South Africa is that in which about 7 500 South Africans with asbestos-related diseases sued UK-based company Cape plc before UK courts. This set a vital precedent because the House of Lords decided against the applicability of the *forum non conveniens* rule on the basis that 'in South Africa in all probability the claimants would not be able to obtain the professional representation and the expert evidence that would be essential to justice in the case'.[81] In addition, UK laws allowed the claimants substantially higher compensation rewards. The Cape plc claimants won a large out-of-court settlement in early 2002, but the company failed to honour the settlement and pay its first instalment in mid 2002 due to the threat of insolvency. (Indeed, a concern raised by human rights lawyers is that companies faced with significant claims against them are prone to file for bankruptcy.)[82]

Parallel to the Cape plc litigation, asbestosis sufferers sued Gencor in South Africa. Gencor had controlled a number of asbestos mines at one stage. One implication of this case was that Gencor was prohibited from unbundling its 46% share in Impala Platinum (which comprised Gencor's main worth) prior to the case being settled. Furthermore, Gencor was added as a co-defendant in the Cape plc case, partly because of Cape plc's apparent inability to honour its settlement. Eventually, an out-of-court agreement was reached in mid 2003, in which both Cape plc and Gencor were to pay a once-off contribution to a trust fund that would support the critically ill.

Source: Adapted from R. Hamann, 'Corporate Social Responsibility in Mining in South Africa' (PhD thesis, University of East Anglia, 2004).

It is apparent that the activist NGOs and radical critics have very different perspectives on the role of business than the business leaders and others who are espousing corporate citizenship principles and initiatives such as the UN Global Compact. The polarisation of the debate between CSR protagonists (in business and elsewhere) and anti-CSR activists may prevent the acknowledgement of strengths or weaknesses in the arguments in each of the respective camps. So, for instance, while the pro-CSR business lobby is arguably correct to emphasise the potentially important role of private sector investment and innovation in sustainable development, it often pays insufficient attention to the negative social and environmental impacts of such investments, especially the indirect or cumulative impacts. Conversely, while the activists play an important role in highlighting human rights or environmental infringements by insensitive companies, arguing for stricter government rules and their enforcement, they arguably pay insufficient attention to the potential for market forces and voluntary initiatives to achieve improved social and environmental outcomes.

Of course, the characterisation of these two camps is in many ways a caricature. There are already many initiatives and organisations that create something approaching a middle way between these contrasting perspectives. This middle way consists of a more differentiated assessment of the current role of business in sustainable development, in that it is both a contributor to and a detractor from sustainable pathways, and much depends on the strategies adopted and decisions taken by business leaders and the broader institutional context in which business operates. Governments have a crucial role to play in making this institutional context more amenable, for instance by ensuring that costs to the environment are factored into prices (including measures such as carbon taxes) – indeed this is a principle on which progressive business representatives and radical critics of business are beginning to agree.[83] Governments can also play a more active role in supporting voluntary initiatives by business, while at the same time expanding legal measures to enhance corporate accountability and to provide redress for people who have been harmed by corporate activities.[84]

There is also a need for greater multilateral efforts to encourage corporate responsibility, as well as enforce corporate accountability. The OECD Guidelines on Multinational Enterprises, mentioned above, are an important initiative in this regard, not only because they are among the most comprehensive guidelines for responsible business conduct, but because they involve government agencies in their implementation through what are called National Contact Points that probe allegations of misconduct. A further key initiative has been the UN Commission on Human Rights publication in 2002 of a draft report entitled *Responsibilities of Transnational Corporations and Other Business Enterprises with Regard to Human Rights* and the subsequent work of the Special Representative of the UN Secretary-General on business and human rights – this is discussed in more detail in Chapter 2. There is arguably a strong business case for international frameworks on corporate citizenship with some legal standing, which would 'raise the common standard of practice and ensure greater benefit for all'.[85]

Finally, the role of NGOs is increasingly vital, but they need to improve their efforts at practising what they preach in terms of accountability, stakeholder dialogue and legitimacy. They should also develop a more differentiated view of business that goes beyond black-and-white caricatures, while bearing in mind that both criticism and collaboration are often necessary to achieve genuine changes in companies' strategies and systems. This notion of 'critical cooperation'[86] is also apposite to business decision-makers, who need to acknowledge that going into partnership with government or civil-society groups does not make the company immune to criticism. They need to learn to face challenges and criticism in an open and courageous manner, and it must be shown that mistakes are acknowledged and that lessons are being learnt from them. These issues are considered in more depth in Chapter 3.

Putting corporate citizenship into practice

An increasingly wide variety of guidelines and tools for implementing corporate citizenship principles within company management are being produced. While many of them deal with particular aspects or sectors, such as human rights management or assessing conflict related risks in the extractives sector,[87] the most widely used ones provide companies with advice on implementing corporate citizenship in general. They generally seek to be relevant to companies of different sizes and in different sectors, and they have in common an emphasis on continuous improvement, based on the so-called Deming cycle that was developed for quality management, a cycle that consists of identifying progressively rising targets and implementing corresponding strategies, implementation systems and monitoring. The Deming cycle is used in, for instance, the ISO 14000 series of environmental management systems, mentioned above, the Sigma framework,[88] and the UN Global Compact Performance Model. The last mentioned is of particular interest because a number of case studies in Part 2 of this book explicitly refer to this model (in particular Case 3, about Global Alumina). This model, shown in Figure 7 and described in Box 3, focuses on diverse enabling factors and the kind of results that are to be achieved and monitored.

Much is to be gained by corporate leaders and decision-makers – and their companies' stakeholders – from a thorough engagement with the recommendations of the Global Compact Performance Model. But management guidelines will only take a company so far. For a start, the earlier discussion of definitions of corporate citizenship is pertinent because, as noted, many business leaders in Africa still emphasise its philanthropic aspects. This view is a fundamental barrier to implementing corporate citizenship in its more comprehensive form.

Though philanthropic support for worthy causes is a welcome contribution, particularly in the areas of education and health, it is an easy target for criticism because by itself it does not affect the way companies go about their business. As a CSR manager in a prominent mining company in South Africa notes:

> The view that CSR is primarily CSI [corporate social investment, or philanthropy] is a result of how things were structured, in the sense that businesses thought that they needed to pay what some people referred to as blood money, but it never needed to be part of the business processes. So in order to operate, they needed to do some charity work or CSI, but it has never been key to their own business strategy.

Despite the various initiatives that emphasise a broader approach to corporate citizenship, many CEOs in Africa are still prone to point to their charitable foundations or similar departments when asked about corporate citizenship. A lack of integration into core business is apparent in the way some companies call themselves good corporate citizens, with reference to their education and health programmes, while at the same time continuing to ignore some of the negative consequences of their core business activities.

Yet the habit of confusing philanthropy with corporate citizenship is not only prevalent in Africa. In an influential article published in the *Harvard Business Review*, Porter and Kramer highlight the need to develop more strategic approaches to CSR, beyond the current emphasis on philanthropy and stakeholder engagement.[89] They argue that such a strategic approach needs to identify and focus on the points of intersection between a company's core business and

Figure 7: The UN Global Compact Performance Model

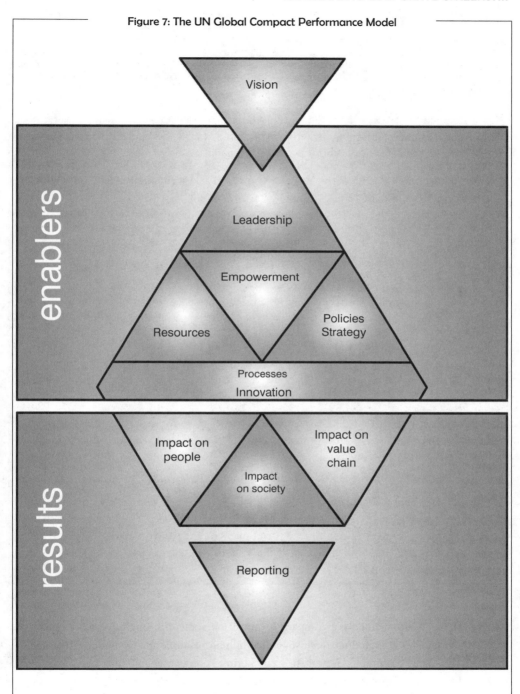

Source: C. Fussler, A. Cramer and S. van der Vegt, *Raising the Bar: Creating Value with the United Nations Global Compact* (Sheffield: Greenleaf Publishing, 2004).

Box 3: Overview of key components of the UN Global Compact Performance Model

The upper box in the model (see Figure 7) represents the enablers of corporate citizenship. The key components here are:

The company's *vision* – 'a shared ambition of a highly desirable end-state' – ought to take into account also society at large. 'The redefining of the boundaries of the company... is at the heart of the corporate citizenship debate.'

Effective *leadership* is necessary to prioritise issues and it requires 'being in tune with the accepted codes and culture of their social environment'.

Empowerment entails stimulating and nurturing the creativity of each employee, and it includes the need for effective training, dialogue between various levels of the organisation, and establishing an appropriate recruitment profile.

Policies and strategies are the core of company management system and they need to reflect the commitments made to corporate citizenship, also with a view to identifying and obtaining competitive advantages on the basis of these commitments.

Though engagement in the Global Compact does not require large *resources*, 'any system of vision, policies and strategy will only be as good as the means to implement it'. The key resources are time, knowledge, technology, material assets and financial resources.

Process management has become a fundamental feature of the corporate citizenship field through its emphasis on continuous improvement, an important aspect of which is *innovation*: 'Innovation is to bridge two conflicting realities with a new behaviour that generates value and that can be implemented.'

Overall this model emphasises the role of stakeholder engagement and partnership: 'Stakeholders and partnerships... are signs of a new paradigm that sees success in managing complex changes through the association of interdependent actors with a shared purpose, real accountability in parts of the system and a real stake in the success or failure of the endeavour.'

society. These points include the company's impact on society through everyday operations across its value chain, including for instance its human resource management, procurement, and logistics. They also include the firm's competitive context, such as the need to enhance high-quality inputs (for instance, human resources or physical infrastructure) or fair and open competition and transparency.

Integrating business and social needs takes more than good intentions and strong leadership. It requires adjustments in organization, reporting relationships, and incentives. Few

The lower box shows the results achieved through continuous improvement of the company's enablers. These require monitoring, evaluation and reporting:

Impact on employees: Respecting the basic rights of workers reduces costs (e.g. with regard to health and safety) and improves productivity (e.g. through enhanced employee participation in policy- and decision-making). 'Employees do not just expect material advantages from their job, but rather an enhancement of meaning and community in their lives.'

Impact on value chain: It is important to understand how customers perceive issues related to corporate citizenship as this will influence their purchasing behaviour. It is also important for companies to better understand how they can influence suppliers and contractors so that they improve their social and environmental performance.

Impact on society: Assessing and managing a company's impact on society is complex and fraught with tensions. One of these difficulties is assessing the boundaries of a company's responsibilities up or down the supply chain. Another is the tension of conflicting expectations – while the term 'sustainable development' confuses some people because of its simultaneous emphasis on growth and limits, it ought to be seen rather as a requirement for creative thinking and innovation. Finally, there is the concern about a company's ability to make a difference when the broader framework conditions – market pricing, weak governments, etc. – present such powerful countervailing forces.

Reporting: Despite frustrations with regard to corporate sustainability reports when it is said that 'few read them and fewer believe them', the model emphasises the need for reporting because this helps fulfil the Global Compact commitments, by facilitating continuous improvement and allowing for benchmarking and informed dialogue with stakeholders

Source: C. Fussler, A. Cramer, and S. van der Vegt, *Raising the Bar: Creating Value with the United Nations Global Compact* (Sheffield: Greenleaf Publishing, 2004).

companies have engaged operating management in processes that identify and prioritize social issues based on their salience to business operations and their importance to the company's competitive context. Even fewer have unified their philanthropy with the management of their CSR efforts, much less sought to embed a social dimension into their core value proposition. Doing these things requires a far different approach to both CSR and philanthropy than the one prevalent today. Companies must shift from a fragmented, defensive posture to an integrated, affirmative approach. The focus must move away from an emphasis on image to an emphasis on substance.[90]

Top level commitment is crucial in devising and implementing a strategic approach to corporate citizenship. A quick, if somewhat superficial test of this commitment, is to consider the extent to which social and environmental issues are reflected in performance assessment measures for operational management. To illustrate, it is striking that in 2004 only one mining company with significant operations in southern Africa had a comprehensive, systematic process in place for including both environmental and social criteria in the performance appraisals of mine managers.[91]

The potential contradiction between rhetoric and practice or, in the words of Porter and Kramer, between image and substance, is the primary concern of critics who label corporate citizenship a 'greenwash' strategy, as discussed above. These critics argue that the gap between corporate policy and its implementation is inevitable or even intentional. An alternative interpretation, more common among company representatives, is to point out the complexity of implementing corporate citizenship in often difficult circumstances. These representatives commonly refer to 'the steep learning curve' that they are on, both personally and as organisations. They are prone to point out the challenge of generating the necessary buy-in from all pertinent employees, especially if these employees have a background in technical professions with little inclination towards 'soft issues'. A related problem they identify is the challenge of creating management systems that effectively coordinate the diverse and interrelated elements of sustainable development. Anglo American's sustainable development manager says that:

> Integration and coordination remain the biggest challenge, given that implementing the various sustainable development policies is too big for any one individual. No one could drive this broad-ranging agenda individually. So we need to find out how best to integrate, and also when it's okay to let [different line departments] operate in parallel.[92]

Another challenge for many companies is that implementation of policy objectives is often hampered by 'turf wars' between departments, lack of coordination, multiple and overlapping reporting and performance management systems, and limited capacity (and the resulting reliance on external consultants).

Company representatives also emphasise the complexities and contradictions encountered in the quest for sustainable development, which make it difficult to implement CSR policies. As the CSR manager of a mining company pertinently asked: 'For example, we have a mine… that cannot pay for environmental standards but provides 6 000 jobs – what do you do, close it down?' Similar dilemmas are a significant feature in many of the case studies in Part 2 of this book. These experiences show that there are no stock responses to such problems, but much depends on the willingness of decision-makers to consider all options, think creatively, engage with all stakeholders, and acknowledge and redeem previous mistakes.

To add a further level of complexity, achieving corporate citizenship objectives is often outside the ambit of firms acting independently. Crucial efforts are under way to take a sector-based approach, because different sectors face different challenges and opportunities, and many of these can best be dealt with collectively. In South Africa, the National Business Initiative is one such collective effort[93] and Cases 9 and 10 in Part 2 of this book provide further examples.

Over and above collective business action, for companies to achieve corporate citizenship objectives, whether individually or collectively, often requires collaboration with stakeholders, including the state and civil society organisations. For instance, mining companies in

South Africa, Kenya, Mali and elsewhere are realising that they can deal effectively with the pressing social problems around many of their mines only by systematically helping to enhance local governance and local economic development planning, in collaboration with local government, NGOs and others (as considered in the section above on local governance). Such collaboration is of course often difficult to achieve, given the various priorities and capacities of these different role players. Partnerships and cross-sector collaboration are discussed in more detail in Chapter 3, and a number of cases in Part 2 provide illustrative examples.

Conclusion

This chapter has assessed, in broad terms, some of the main issues of corporate citizenship: the public's expectations of companies; how to define the concept, particularly in Africa; and the controversies it generates. It has suggested that enlightened self-interest, ethics, and changed environmental and institutional contexts mitigate the liberal economists' critiques of corporate citizenship. It described the business case for corporate citizenship as important but not to be relied upon. The chapter also considered the radical critiques of corporate citizenship, suggesting a middle way between anti-CSR activists and CSR protagonists. Finally, it has outlined some of the difficulties companies face when they try to put corporate citizenship into practice.

Many of the case studies that follow in Part 2 show that the arguments and tensions over how to define and implement corporate citizenship are not confined to academia, but are something companies themselves have to deal with when working on their own strategies and policies (as in the case of Sasol – Case 1) or when confronted with dilemmas (as in the case of mining companies' problems with informal settlements – Case study 7). Taken as a whole, the case studies show that the requirements for more effective business contributions to sustainable development can go beyond a company's own commitments, strategies and management systems, and that what is needed is broad commitment to changing the institutional context of business, and to innovative collaboration between companies and stakeholders.

Notes

1   Institutions have been defined as the 'rules of the game' in a particular socio-economic context. See, for instance, D.C. North, 'Economic Performance through Time', *American Economic Review*, 84, 3 (2004): 359–368.

2   A. Sen, 'Economics, Business Principles, and Moral Sentiments', in G. Enderle, ed., *International Business Ethics: Challenges and Approaches* (Notre Dame: The University of Notre Dame Press, 1999).

3   See, for instance, M. Mamdani, *Citizen and Subject: Contemporary Africa and the Legacy of Late Colonialism* (Princeton: Princeton University Press, 1996).

4   For such a discussion in the South African context, see D. Fig, ed., *Staking their Claim: Corporate Social and Environmental Responsibility in South Africa* (Pietermaritzburg: University of KwaZulu-Natal Press, 2007).

5   UN, *Agenda 21* (New York: United Nations, 1992), available via http://www.un.org/esa/sustdev/documents/agenda21

6   Ibid.

7   http://www.unglobalcompact.org, (accessed September 2005).

8   Commission for Africa, *Our Common Interest: Report of the Commission for Africa* (London: Commission for Africa, 2005), 74.

9   WBCSD (World Business Council for Sustainable Development), *Business for Development: Business Solutions in Support of the Millennium Development Goals* (Geneva: World Business Council for Sustainable Development, 2005), 6.

10   C.O. Holliday, S. Schmidheiny and P. Watts, *Walking the Talk: The Business Case for Sustainable Development* (Sheffield: Greenleaf Publishing, 2002).

11   See http://globalsullivanprinciples.org (accessed July 2007).

12   See http://www.globalreporting.org (accessed July 2007).

13   A. Kolk, 'Trends in Sustainability Reporting by the Fortune Global 250', *Business Strategy and the Environment*, 12, 5 (2003): 279–291.

14   TUAC-OECD (Trade Union Advisory Committee to the Organisation for Economic Co-operation and Development) *The OECD Guidelines on Multinationals: A User's Guide* (Paris: TUAC-OECD, 2002), 2, see also www.oecd.org.

15   R. Hamann, T. Azagbue, P. Kapelus and A. Hein, 'Universalising Corporate Social Responsibility? South African Challenges to the International Organization for Standardization's New Social Responsibility Standard', *Business and Society Review*, 110, 1 (2005): 1–19.

16   See, respectively, http://www.sustainability-index.com; http://www.ftse.com/ftse4good/index.jsp; and http://www.jse.co.za/sri. For a discussion of the latter and its impact on socially responsible investment in South Africa, see D. Sonnenberg and R. Hamann, 'The JSE Socially Responsible Investment Index and the State of Sustainability Reporting in South Africa', *Development Southern Africa*, 23, 2 (2006): 305–320.

17   G.J. Rossouw, 'Business Ethics and Corporate Governance in Africa', *Business & Society*, 44, 1 (2005): 94–106; B. Ahunwan, 'Corporate Governance in Nigeria', *Journal of Business Ethics*, 37 (2002): 269–287.

18   http://www.unglobalcompact.org

19   J. Ruggie, 'The Theory and Practice of Learning Networks: Corporate Social Responsibility and the Global Compact', *Journal of Corporate Citizenship*, 5 (2002): 28, 32.

20   L. Rieth, M. Zimmer, R. Hamann and J. Hanks, 'The UN Global Compact in Sub-Sahara Africa: Regionalisation and Effectiveness', *Journal of Corporate Citizenship*, 28 (2007): 99–112.

21   ABB in the Sudan case study for the Global Compact International Learning Forum Meeting, Ghana, 2006.

22   Quoted in A.B. Carroll, 'Corporate Social Responsibility: Evolution of a Definitional Construct', *Business & Society*, 38, 3 (1999), 270.

23   A.B. Carroll, 'A Three-Dimensional Conceptual Model of Corporate Social Performance', *Academy of Management Review*, 4 (1979), 500.

24   Carroll, 'Corporate Social Responsibility', 289.

25   A.B. Carroll, 'Managing Ethically with Global Stakeholders: A Present and Future Challenge', *Academy of Management Executive*, 18, 2 (2004): 114–120.

26   K. Leisinger, 'Capitalism with a Human Face: The UN Global Compact', *Journal of Corporate Citizenship*, 28(2007): 113–132.

27   Ibid.

28   Ibid.

29   W. Visser, 'Revisiting Carroll's CSR Pyramid: An African Perspective', in E.R. Pedersen and M. Huniche, eds, *Corporate Citizenship in Developing Countries* (Copenhagen: Copenhagen Business School, 2006).

30   Ibid., 40–42.

31   R. Hamann, 'Corporate Social Responsibility, Partnerships, and Institutional Change: The Case of Mining Companies in South Africa', *Natural Resources Forum*, 28, 4 (2004): 278–290.

32   In its 2001 Green Paper, the European Commission defines CSR as 'a concept whereby companies integrate social and environmental concerns in their business operations and in their interactions with their stakeholders on a voluntary basis': European Commission, *Promoting a European*

Framework for Corporate Social Responsibility – Green Paper (Luxembourg: Office for Official Publications of the European Communities, 2001), 4.

33   M. Kivuitu, K. Yambayamba and T. Fox, *How can Corporate Social Responsibility Deliver in Africa? Insights from Kenya and Zambia* (London: IIED, 2005), 3.

34   For instance, see S. Ponte, S. Roberts and L. van Sittert, 'Black Economic Empowerment, Business and the State in South Africa', *Development and Change*, 38, 5 (2007): 933–955.

35   R. Hamann, S. Khagram and S. Rohan, 'South Africa's Charter Approach to Socio-Economic Transformation: Collaborative Governance or Hardball Bargaining?', *Journal of Southern African Studies*, 34, 1 (2008): 21–37.

36   A. Crane and D. Matten, *Business Ethics: A European Perspective* (Oxford: Oxford University Press, 2003), 44.

37   Visser, 'Revisiting Carroll's CSR Pyramid', 47.

38   A. Warhurst and P. Mitchell, 'Corporate social responsibility and the case of the Summitville mine', *Resources Policy,* 26 (2000): 91-102, 92.

39   S. Hart, *Capitalism at the Crossroads: The Unlimited Business Opportunities in Solving the World's Most Difficult Problems* (Upper Saddle River: Wharton School Publishing, 2004), 10-11.

40   With regard to the former, see R.W Estes, *Corporate Social Accounting* (New York: Wiley, 1976). On the GRI, see http://www.globalreporting.org.

41   A. Chamaret, M. O'Connor and G. Recoche, 'Top-Down/Bottom-Up Approach for Developing Sustainable Development Indicators for Mining: Application to the Arlit Uranium Mines (Niger)', *International Journal of Sustainable Development*, 10, 1/2 (2007): 161–174.

42   See, for instance, K. Bruno and J. Karliner, *earthsummit.biz: The Corporate Takeover of Sustainable Development* (Oakland, CA: Food First Books, 2002); W.S Laufer, 'Social Accountability and Corporate Greenwashing', *Journal of Business Ethics*, 43 (2003): 253–261.

43   B. O'Dwyer, J. Unerman and E. Hession, 'User Needs in Sustainability Reporting: Perspectives of Stakeholders in Ireland', *European Accounting Review*, 14, 4 (2005): 759–787.

44   See J. Clay, *Exploring the Links Between International Business and Poverty Reduction: A Case Study of Unilever in Indonesia* (Oxford: Oxfam GB, Novib Oxfam Netherlands and Unilever, 2005).

45   Crane and Matten, *Business Ethics*.

46   Ibid., 68.

47   Ibid., 69.

48   Ibid., 69.

49   M.B.E. Clarkson, 'A Stakeholder Framework for Analysing and Evaluating Corporate Social Performance', *Academy of Management Review*, 20, 1 (1995), 106.

50   For the first criterion, see ibid., for the second, see T. Jones, 'Instrumental Stakeholder Theory: A Synthesis of Ethics and Economics', *Academy of Management Review*, 20, 2 (1995): 404–437.

51   Clarkson, 'A Stakeholder Framework', 107.

52   Ibid., 107 and 113

53   See, for instance, S.A. Waddock, C. Bodwell, and S.B. Graves, 'Responsibility: The New Business Imperative', *Academy of Management Executive*, 16, 2 (2002): 132–150.

54   S.A. Waddock, Editorial, *Journal of Corporate Citizenship*, 9, 1 (2003), 3.

55   R. Hamann, D. Sonnenberg, A. Mackenzie, P. Kapelus and P. Hollesen, 'Local governance as complex system: Lessons from mining in South Africa, Mali and Zambia', *Journal of Corporate Citizenship*, 18 (2005): 65.

56   C.K. Prahalad and S. Hart, *The Fortune at the Bottom of the Pyramid. Strategy+Business*, 26 (2002), 5.

57   WBCSD, *Business for Development*, 7.

58   See http://www.adopt-a-light.com (accessed July 2007).

59   L.A. White, 'Lost in translation? The future of corporate social responsibility', *Journal of Corporate Citizenship*, 16 (2004): 19–24.

60   Friedman, 'The Social Responsibility of Business'.

61 D. Henderson, 'The Role of Business in the World Today', *Journal of Corporate Citizenship*, 17 (2005), 30–32.

62 *The Economist*, 22 January 2005, 11.

63 J.D Margolis and J.P. Walsh, 'Misery Loves Companies: Rethinking Social Initiatives by Business', *Administrative Science Quarterly*, 48 (2003): 268–305.

64 See M. Friedman, 'The Social Responsibility of Business is to Increase its Profits', *New York Times Magazine*, 13 September 1970; http://www.unglobalcompact.org, (accessed September 2005); D.C. Korten, 'The Responsibility of Business to the Whole', in R. Starkey and R. Welford, eds, *The Earthscan Reader in Business and Sustainable Development* (London: Earthscan, 2001); Christian Aid, *Behind the Mask: The Real Face of Corporate Social Responsibility* (London: Christian Aid, 2004).

65 Ibid., 278.

66 Hamann, 'Corporate Social Responsibility'.

67 International Finance Corporation, *SustainAbility, and Instituto Ethos, The Business Case in Emerging Economies* (Washington: International Finance Corporation, 2002).

68 C. Avery, 'The Difference between CSR and Human Rights', *Corporate Citizenship Briefing*, 89 (August/ September 2006), 4.

69 Sen, 'Economics, Business Principles'.

70 Friedman, 'The Social Responsibility of Business'.

71 C. Marsden, 'The New Corporate Citizenship of Big Business: Part of the Solution to Sustainability?', *Business and Society Review*, 105, 1 (2000): 9–25.

72 Quoted in N.C. Smith, 'Corporate Social Responsibility: Whether or How?', *California Management Review*, 45, 4 (2003), 54.

73 Christian Aid, *Behind the Mask*, 4.

74 M.E. Porter and M.R. Kramer, 'Strategy and Society: The Link Between Competitive Advantage and Corporate Social Responsibility', *Harvard Business Review*, (December 2006): 1–14.

75 R. Hamann and N. Acutt, 'How Should Civil Society (and the Government) Respond to "Corporate Social Responsibility?" A Critique of Business Motivations and the Potential for Partnerships', *Development Southern Africa*, 20, 2 (2003), 255.

76 Laufer, 'Social Accountability and Corporate Greenwashing', 257.

77 Friends of the Earth International (FoEI), *Towards Binding Corporate Accountability* (London: FoEI, 2002).

78 C. Bennett, Friends of the Earth International, presentation to Corporate Accountability Week, Johannesburg, 20 August 2002.

79 FoEI, *Towards Binding Corporate Accountability*, 1; emphasis in original.

80 A representative of the claimants, quoted in *Business Day* 13 November 2002, 2.

81 H. Ward, *Corporate Accountability in Search of a Treaty? Some Insights from Foreign Direct Liability* (London: The Royal Institute of International Affairs, 2002), 8.

82 R.M. Meeran, 'Cape plc: South African Mine Workers' Quest for Justice', *International Journal of Occupational and Environmental Health*, 9 (2003): 218–229.

83 For instance, see Holliday *et al.*, *Walking the Talk* ; and Korten, 'The Responsibility of Business to the Whole'.

84 On public policy measures to support corporate responsibility, see, for instance, T. Fox, 'Corporate Social Responsibility and development: In quest of an agenda', *Development*, 47, 3 (2004): 29–36. On the evolving expectations for states to protect citizens from corporate abuse and to ensure redress, see United Nations, 'Protect, Respect, and Remedy: a Framework for Business and Human Rights: Report of the Special Representative of the Secretary-General on the issue of human rights and transnational corporations and other business enterprises, John Ruggie' (New York: UN, 2008).

85 J. Bendell, ed., *Terms of Endearment: Business, NGOs and Sustainable Development* (Sheffield: Greenleaf Publishing, 2000), 251.

86 J. Covey and L.D. Brown, Critical Cooperation: An Alternative Form of Civil Society – Business Engagement (Boston: Institute for Development Research, 2001).

87   See, for instance, the Guide to Human Rights Impact Assessment and Management (Road-Testing Draft, June 2007) published by the International Business Leaders Forum and International Finance Corporation (available via http://www.iblf.org); or *Conflict-Sensitive Business Practice: Guidance for Extractive Industries* (London: International Alert, 2005).

88   http://www.projectsigma.co.uk (accessed July 2007).

89   Porter and Kramer, 'Strategy and Society'.

90   Ibid., 12-13.

91   The company was BHP Billiton, according to Hamann, 'Corporate Social Responsibility'. This study was focused on South Africa, but the point pertains to the rest of the region. It would be worthwhile investigating the degree to which this has changed in recent years.

92   K. Ireton, interview with author, Johannesburg, 27 November 2002.

93   A. Fourie and T. Eloff, 'The Case for Collective Business Action to Achieve Systems Change: Exploring the Contributions Made by the Private Sector to the Social, Economic and Political Transformation Process in South Africa', *Journal of Corporate Citizenship*, 18 (2005): 39–48.

CHAPTER 2

Truly enlightened self-interest:
Business, human rights and the UN Global Compact

STU WOOLMAN

It is not from the benevolence of the butcher, the brewer, or the baker, that we expect our dinner, but from regard to their own interest. We address ourselves, not to their humanity but to their self-love.

Adam Smith, *The Wealth of Nations* (1776)

How selfish soever man may be supposed, there are evidently some principles in his nature, which interest him in the fortunes of others, and render their happiness necessary to him, though he derives nothing from it, except the pleasure of seeing it. Of this kind is pity or compassion, the emotion we feel for the misery of others, when we either see it, or are made to conceive it in a very lively manner.

Adam Smith, *The Theory of Moral Sentiments* (1759)

Principle 1: Businesses should support and respect the protection of internationally proclaimed human rights within their sphere of influence; and

Principle 2: Businesses should make sure that they are not complicit in human rights abuses.

United Nations Global Compact

Introduction

'Greed is good' remarked Gordon Gecko early on in the movie *Wall Street*. For many, that remains the abiding creed of doing business, whether one works in a well-heeled investment bank or in something comparable to Tony Soprano's waste management consulting firm.

But 'greed is good' is not the only view on the relationship between business and ethics. Adam Smith articulated a vision of social relations in which no economy, let alone a capitalist economy, could get off the ground unless it was underpinned by a community in which most citizens placed a significant degree of trust, faith, loyalty, and confidence in their fellow citizens. As *The Theory of Moral Sentiments* makes clear, what differentiates human beings from other sentient creatures is our capacity for empathy: an understanding that others possess dreams, aspirations and desires much like our own. The butcher and the baker who feature in *The Wealth of Nations* can pursue their enlightened self-interest only against the background of a community of relative equals who are willing and able to cooperate with one another over a large range of endeavours.

And so it is with most businesses. Although we cannot attribute such emotions as empathy to a large corporation, most corporations, like most natural persons, prefer to act against a background of mutual trust, loyalty and confidence. They, like their human counterparts, know that they can only act effectively, over the long term, when fairness and the rule of law lie at the core of a community's system of justice.[1]

Kofi Annan recognised these features of capitalist economies when he introduced the United Nations Global Compact in 1999. He wrote:

> National markets are held together by shared values. In the face of economic transition and insecurity, people know that if the worst comes to the worst, they can rely on the expectation that certain minimum standards will prevail. But in the global market, people do not yet have that confidence. Until they do have it, the global economy will be fragile and vulnerable – vulnerable to backlash from all the 'isms' of our post-cold-war world: protectionism; populism; nationalism; ethnic chauvinism; fanaticism; and terrorism.
>
> What all those 'isms' have in common is that they exploit the insecurity and misery of people who feel threatened or victimised by the global market. The more wretched and insecure people there are, the more those 'isms' will continue to gain ground. What we have to do is find a way of embedding the global market in a network of shared values. I hope I have suggested some practical ways for us to set about doing just that.[2]

What Annan recognised is that the globalisation of capitalism had outstripped the ability of the Canadian butcher and the Burmese baker to recognise one another – from opposite sides of the planet – as members of the same community and thus as individuals entitled to the same degree of trust, loyalty, compassion, justice and fairness in their day-to-day interactions. In the absence of a sense of sympathy, the world economy and the global community has become a 'fragile' place indeed.

Annan's recipe for the construction of an international economic community in which the Canadian butcher and the Burmese baker are able to pursue their self-interest while also investing the social capital necessary to sustain that international community, embraces what the United Nations calls the 'Global Compact'. This compact of ten principles is intended to ensure that businesses do not forget that a community based upon compassion and care is, ultimately, the necessary precondition for successful business itself. The alternative is too bleak to consider: a war of all against all in which the majority of humanity is exploited in the service of those few individuals and corporations that have access to the levers of political, legal, military and economic power. If Hobbes' *Leviathan* (1651) – and almost 400 years of social contract theory – signalled a theoretical break from the justifications for monarchy, oligarchy and plutocracy, then the UN Global Compact and an array of post WWII domestic constitutions signal a break – albeit nascent – from the standard justifications for globalisation and the relatively unfettered power wielded by multinational corporations.

The 10 principles for the Global Compact are drawn from a broad array of existing international human rights documents: the Universal Declaration of Human Rights (1948); the International Covenant of Civil and Political Rights (1967); the International Covenant of Economic, Cultural and Social Rights (1967); the Rio Declaration on Environment and Development (1992); the International Labour Organisation's Fundamental Principles and Rights at Work (1998); and the UN Convention Against Corruption (2003).[3] Despite this impressive pedigree, the status of the United Nations Global Compact remains uncertain: and it is that uncertainty which drives the analysis in remainder of this chapter. As we shall see, questions of accountability and enforcement, the softness of international law, the application of international treaties to non-state actors, the extension of such terms as 'complicity' and 'sphere of influence', the ability of the international community and corporations themselves to monitor human rights compliance in zones of conflict or weak and ineffective political governance, continue to dog the Compact.

Questions about the Compact

Accountability and enforcement

The Global Compact, as it is currently constructed, is an entirely 'voluntary' exercise. No business is required to sign on to its principles. And no legal enforcement mechanisms exist to ensure that signatories in fact comply with the Compact.[4]

The absence of clear mechanisms for accountability attracts criticism from all sides. As Oliver Williams notes:

> US company reluctance to join the Compact centers on the accountability issue. In an environment of increasing skepticism, without a traditional accountability structure or monitoring as part of the Global Compact, its legitimacy will be in question.[5]

The ethical commitment of the businesses that sign on to the document may have their bona fides queried if the document cannot be 'legally' enforced.

Despite the UN Compact's absence of legal enforcement mechanisms, the majority of US firms are concerned that by signing on to the document, they *will* be bound *legally* to the terms it contains by virtue of domestic or municipal laws that echo the Compact's principles. Such concerns are not unwarranted. In *Marc Kasky v Nike*, the California Supreme Court effectively permitted an activist to sue a company where that company allegedly offered a false depiction of the manner in which it conducts its business.[6] The refusal of the US Supreme Court to review the ruling led to a settlement in which Nike agreed to pay US$1.5 million to the Fair Labour Association. *Kasky* stands for the proposition that a company that claims to be committed to the UN Global Compact – and makes a public record of that commitment – could open itself up to litigation in a domestic tribunal. Given the litigious nature of the American justice system, a US company might well ask what benefits accrue from an entirely 'voluntary' system that might lead to costly litigation and a tainted public image.[7]

Others view the Compact as a public relations document without substance. Those persons or organisations holding this view come from two discrete camps. The first camp consists of scholars who would like to see a Compact that enables one to measure in objective terms the principles to which the companies adhere.[8] The second camp consists of social activists already critical of economic globalisation and who therefore tend to view the Compact as just another institution designed to cover-up the pernicious effects of global capitalism.

Both views have merit. But they also overlook the Compact's obvious virtues – virtues that actually serve the sceptic's agendas. For NGOs and other activists, the Compact provides a mechanism that enables them to pressure firms to function as 'better corporate citizens'.[9] Indeed, non-governmental organisations (NGOs) and other organs of civil society can, employing the Compact, use its principles to build a political culture – national and international – committed to the common good, and thus to dignity, civility, health, fair labour relations, environmental protection, and non-corrupt political practices. With respect to sceptical scholars, it is possible that they protest too much. When companies provide more accurate quantitative data as to the costs of doing business in terms of the Compact and rich qualitative data in terms of the relationships formed and cultivated in an effort to make good the promise of the Compact, economists and sociologists will then possess the requisite tools to measure the social impact of compliance with the Compact. Indeed, I would contend that most multinationals – as publicly held companies – have an obligation to shareholders to provide such data given that these expenses have an effect on the bottom line. Moreover, recent experience with respect to the response of social movements and capital to companies doing business in 'criminal jurisdictions' – e.g. the forced withdrawal of companies from apartheid South Africa, the pressure on De Beers to ensure that they do not traffic in blood diamonds purloined from weak states – suggests that companies have a pecuniary interest in compliance with the Compact.

However, what both sets of sceptics miss is the need to create a set of conditions that do not yet exist: a background of trust, loyalty, care and compassion in the conduct of transnational business.[10] As one Compact official remarks:

> The Global Compact is not designed as a code of conduct. Rather it is a means to serve as
> a [frame] of reference to stimulate best practices and to bring about convergence around
> universally shared values.[11]

Application to non-state actors

The Compact must be viewed as part of an extended effort to inspire multinational corporations to view themselves as members of the communities in which they do business and thus as actors that have duties to the other members of those communities. So when Louis Henkin, a primary architect of the international human rights regime, pens the following stirring words about corporate accountability, those words must be placed in the appropriate aspirational context:

> Every individual includes juridical persons. Every individual and every organ of society
> excludes no one, no company, no market, no cyberspace. The Universal Declaration applies to them all.[12]

The critical distinction that Henkin glosses over is the distinction between ethics and law.[13] As John Ruggie notes: 'The Declaration's aspirations and moral claims were addressed, and apply, to all humanity ... But that does not equate to legally binding effect.'[14]

As I have noted above, international treaties and conventions are generally understood to bind particular kinds of signatories – *states* – to the terms of the document. Most human rights documents do not contemplate their direct application to non-state actors.

It helps, as Donaldson writes, to make three distinctions between the kinds of duties that might apply to non-state actors such as corporations operating under international covenants:

1. Refraining from depriving people of the object of a right.

2. Protecting (in some instances) the right from being deprived.

3. Restoring some good to people whose rights have been violated.[15]

For example, a pharmaceutical company, under international law, will rarely be made responsible for protecting individuals from the violations of others. However, the question of accountability shifts when the violations are alleged to have occurred as a result of the corporation's actions. We might be inclined – even in the absence of clear international law – to say: (a) that a pharmaceutical company may never take medicines from the diseased (duty class number 1); (b) that circumstances *might* exist under which a pharmaceutical company would be obliged to protect people from contracting a disease or dying from a disease (duty class number 2); that a pharmaceutical does *not* have an ongoing obligation to provide medicines to all persons who suffer from a disease for which they have some agent that might be a palliative or a cure (duty class number 3). However, it is important to note that Donaldson's examples of the distinction between obligations that a multinational corporation might have to discharge and might not have to discharge are just that: examples. A meaningful international regulatory framework remains to be worked out.

Again: the Compact is voluntary. However, unlike other human rights documents, its objects are no longer limited to relationships between sovereign states and their citizens. Its very purpose, *its achievement*, is to extend the application of human rights norms to relationships between corporations and citizens. So although the Compact currently lacks meaningful enforcement mechanisms, it clearly contemplates the application of its norms to non-state actors.

That the UN Compact might be viewed as a test run for norms that have substantially greater bite with respect to non-state actors is evident from the current draft of 'Norms on the Responsibilities of Transnational Corporations and Other Business Enterprises with regards to Human Rights' ('Norms').[16] As David Weissbrodt notes:

> While the Norms apply to all companies, they are not legally binding ... Eventually, of course, the Norms could be considered what international law scholars call soft law and could also provide the basis for drafting a human rights treaty on corporate social responsibility ... The ... final notable attribute of the norms is that they endeavor to include five basic implementation procedures and anticipate that other techniques and processes may later supplement them. First, the Norms anticipate that companies will adopt their own internal rules of operation, to assure the protections set forth in this instrument. Second,

the Norms indicate that businesses are expected to assess their major activities in light of its provisions. Third, compliance with the Norms is subject to monitoring that is independent, transparent, and includes input from relevant stakeholders. Fourth, if companies violate the Norms and cause damage, the Norms call for compensation, return of property, or other reparations. And fifth … the Norms call upon governments to establish a framework for the application of the Norms.[17]

Although the Norms have met with significant resistance from state and non-state actors alike, they suggest the likely direction of future international efforts to bring the practices of multinational companies and domestic businesses into line with existing human rights norms.[18]

Complicity and sphere of influence

Corporations are rarely themselves responsible for the most egregious forms of human rights abuse. The accusation most often levelled against businesses is that they have been complicit with state or military abuses of human rights.

The UN commentary on the draft Norms – 'The Global Compact and Human Rights: Understanding Sphere of Influence and Complicity: OHCHR Briefing Paper' – defines 'complicity' as follows:

> The responsibility on business entities to 'make sure they are not complicit in human rights abuses' similarly raises complex issues. Corporations often act with other partners in joint ventures or with national and local governments which could lead to allegations of complicity if the partner itself has abused human rights. One definition of 'complicity' states that a company is complicit in human rights abuses if it authorizes, tolerates, or knowingly ignores human rights abuses committed by an entity associated with it, or if the company knowingly provides practical assistance or encouragement that has a substantial effect on the perpetration of human rights abuse.
>
> Four situations illustrate where an allegation of complicity might arise against a company. First, when the company actively assists, directly or indirectly, in human rights violations committed by others; second, when the company is in a partnership with a Government and could reasonably foresee, or subsequently obtains knowledge, that the Government is likely to commit abuses in carrying out the agreement; third, when the company benefits from human rights violations even if it does not positively assist or cause them; and fourth, when the company is silent or inactive in the face of violations.[19]

Although the Norms go on to note that although the specific duty 'in each of these situations might not always be clear', that such duties exist is recognised, unequivocally, under international law.[20]

Perhaps the best known example of corporate complicity were the findings at the Nuremburg Trials that Adolf Krupp and his 9 co-conspirators had, through the use of slave labour, engaged in gross violations of human rights during the Nazi regime and throughout Nazi-occupied Europe.[21] All 10 received prison sentences: Krupp himself was sentenced to 12 years. The findings against Krupp were hardly unique. Twenty four directors of the IG Farben Industry 'were convicted for using slave labour, for designing and producing poison gas used in the concentration camps.'[22] More recently, as David Weissbrodt writes:

> The UN Panel of Experts on the Illegal Exploitation of Natural Resources and Other Forms of Wealth of the Democratic Republic of Congo identified more than eighty companies from developed nations that exploited Congolese resources during the war. Some of those companies have used forced labour; others have facilitated the transfer of weapons to the warring parties that have been implicated in committing war crimes.[23]

It is important to note, however, that the UN Panel lacked legal standing and that its report has not, at the time of writing, led to any convictions.

While the term 'complicity' may well have 50 years of international and domestic jurisprudence behind it, the notion of 'sphere of influence' is not as well-established. John Ruggie's 2007 report on the draft 'Norms on the Responsibilities of Transnational Corporations and Other Business Enterprises with regards to Human Rights' acknowledges that 'sphere of influence' is a non-legal concept that has as yet not been authoritatively defined. However, Ruggie's 2007 Report then goes on to suggest how 'sphere of influence' might come to be understood:

> [T]he 'sphere of influence' of a business entity tends to include the individuals to whom it has a certain political, contractual, economic or geographic proximity. Every business entity, whatever its size, will have a sphere of influence; the larger it is, the larger the sphere of influence is likely to be. It is relevant to note that the Global Compact asks participating business entities to embrace, support and enact, within their sphere of influence, its ten principles ... The notion of 'sphere of influence' could be useful in clarifying the extent to which business entities should 'support' human rights and 'make sure they are not complicit in human rights abuses' by setting limits on responsibilities according to a business entity's power to act. Importantly, 'sphere of influence' could help clarify the boundaries of responsibilities of business entities in relation to other entities in the supply chain such as subsidiaries, agents, suppliers and buyers by guiding an assessment of the degree of influence that one company exerts over a partner in its contractual relationship – and therefore the extent to which it is responsible for the acts or omissions or a subsidiary or a partner down the supply chain. At the same time, 'sphere of influence' should help draw the boundaries between the responsibilities of business and the obligations on States so that business entities do not take on the policing role of Government. Finally, the notion of 'sphere of influence' could ensure that smaller business entities are not forced to undertake over-burdensome human rights responsibilities, but only responsibilities towards people within their limited sphere of influence.[24]

Despite its rather recent vintage, the phrase 'sphere of influence' has already featured in a complaint laid against a company in terms of the UN Global Compact. In *Compliance Complaint, Nordea's International Corporate Social Responsibility and Human Rights Obligations*, the Centre for Human Rights and Environment charged that Nordea's financial support to the Oy Metsä-Botnia project in the construction of the Orion pulp mill in Uruguay implicates Nordea and constitutes Nordea's complicity in:

- the violation of international human rights and international environmental law;

- the violation of the United Nations Global Compact;

- the violation of the United Nations Statement by Financial Institutions on the Environment and Sustainable Development (UNEPFI);

- violations to the UN Human Rights Norms for Transnational Corporations;

- the violation of the principles and standards set out by the Guidelines for Multinational Enterprises of the Organization for Economic Co-operation and Development (OECD);
- the violation of International Labour Organisation (ILO) Conventions;
- the violation of the Universal Declaration on Human Rights;
- the violations to International Financial Corporation (IFC) Environmental and Social Safeguard Policy OP 4.01, and the IFC's Disclosure Policy;
- the violation of national laws in Uruguay; and
- the violation of international bilateral law as established by the Uruguay River Treaty.[25]

In particular, Nordea and its partners were charged with refusing to consult with a popular movement known as the opposition group Environmental Assembly of Gualeguaychú – a local association created in response to and in opposition to the projects within the companies' sphere of interest. How broad is that 'sphere of interest'? The complaint recognises that the large-scale pulp production in question will affect not only significant portions of Uruguay, but neighbouring portions of Argentina along the Uruguay River. To buttress its claim that the 'sphere of the companies' influence' extends beyond Uruguay's borders, the Centre notes 'that Argentina has decided to take the case to the International Court of Justice in the Hague, and ground its complaint on violations to the Uruguay River Treaty.'[26] Whatever the term 'sphere of influence' comes to mean over time, it seems reasonable to conclude, as do the complainants above, that it is not limited by national or political boundaries. 'Sphere of influence' must mean the geographical area or the operational area – and the human rights of all parties within that area – affected by the activities of the companies in question.[27]

Hard law, soft law and guidelines for conducting business in a manner consistent with human rights

That much of the law around the human rights obligations of business appears amorphous does not mean that we are, 60 years after the UN Declaration of Human Rights, operating without discernable standards to assess corporate behaviour. When it comes to hard law, the Nuremburg Trials, the Rome Treaty and the International Criminal Court suggest that corporations cannot rely upon their status as non-state actors to avoid charges of: Genocide; Slavery; Murder or causing disappearances of individuals; Torture or other cruel, inhuman or degrading treatment or punishment; Prolonged arbitrary detention; Systematic racial discrimination; Consistent patterns of gross violations of human rights.[28] Brew and Ermaster note that four additional obligations *should* – but do not yet unequivocally – bind corporations. Brew and Ermaster, like Donaldson, contend that corporations should, where possible, (1) avoid violating peoples' rights; (2) prevent others from violating peoples' rights; (3) act to provide access to entitlements enshrined in peoples' rights; (4) use education systems and public information to inform individuals of their rights.[29] These nascent obligations – which abound in the academic literature and international instruments – constitute soft law.[30]

Soft law, as John Ruggie points out, is just that, soft. He writes:

> Soft law is 'soft' in the sense that it does not by itself create legally binding obligations. It derives its normative force through recognition of social expectations by states and other key actors. States may turn to soft law for several reasons: to chart possible future

directions for, and fill gaps in, the international legal order when they are not yet able or willing to take firmer measures; where they conclude that legally binding mechanisms are not the best tool to address a particular issue; or in some instances to avoid having more binding measures gain political momentum.[31]

Ruggie identifies the following mechanisms as soft law that might, over time, harden into more enforceable forms of customary international law: ILO Tripartite Declaration of Principles Concerning Multinational Enterprises and Social Policy; OECD Guidelines for Multinational Enterprises; the Kimberley Process Certification Scheme (Kimberley) to stem the flow of conflict diamonds; and the Extractive Industries Transparency Initiative (EITI).[32]

Given the lack of unanimity on the culpability of corporations for human rights violations and the lack of effective mechanisms for international enforcement of these rights, we must expect that a long period of volunteerism will proceed a time in which corporations are regularly brought to book for violations of human rights – especially those violations that occur in weak zones of political governance. In addition to the UN Global Compact, actors such as the International Finance Corporation and International Business Leaders Forum have created various guides for corporations that wish to follow a 'systematic methodology for identifying, evaluating and managing the human rights impacts and consequences of any business operation or project.'[33] The IFC and IBLF guidelines suggest the following steps:

> Conduct an initial appraisal on the need for a dedicated human rights impact assessment; (2) Assemble the information required to understand the context within which the project will operate; (3) Determine the current human rights baseline or status quo of the project; (4) Verify the human rights issues through engagement with relevant stakeholders; (5) Assess the actual and potential human rights impacts of the project; (6) Prepare conclusions and recommendations; (7) Eliminate or mitigate negative impacts and promote positive impacts by integrating human rights management into the overall project management plan; (8) Monitor, evaluate and report on the project in operation.[34]

As our case studies reflect, some major multinationals are employing just such criteria to assess their prospective business operations in weak or conflict-ridden governance zones.

Transnational business conducted under civil war, internecine conflict and weak and ineffective political governance

Many of the case studies in this book were undertaken in countries plagued by cross-border wars, internecine conflict and weak political governance. As Brew and Ermaster observe:

> Countries [in the midst of civil strife or] with weak government often have poor human rights records also, because of their lack of capacity to administer law and justice. Operating effectively in either a controversial state or a weak governance zone will bring particular pressures on the management of the business operation or project, requiring well-informed experience, skills and resources to maintain standards and reduce risks.

It is worth asking, however, whether risk management is the right way to think about doing business in places that are so politically compromised. While Brew and Ermaster suggest that multinationals are not particularly responsible generally for the political machinations of the governments in the countries in which they operate, Kathryn Gordon argues that the opposite might be true:

> Multinational enterprises, through the payments they make to troubled countries, can play an inadvertent role in their problems by providing funding and stakes for conflict. This is a particularly challenging issue for corporate responsibility because most of the problems arise from lack of 'government responsibility' in these host countries and, in particular, from poor public governance (budget systems, government transparency and accountability, protections of civil and political rights).[35]

Gordon contends, in sum, that large transnational corporations, by paying taxes and being good corporate citizens, may actually prop up illegitimate regimes. The costs of a transnational company's presence, on the whole, might actually outweigh the benefits that flow to the local community in which a company exercises the greatest influence. Under conditions of civil strife and unaccountable government, foreign direct investment may not only fail to be an unalloyed good; it may actually result in consequences far more deleterious than would obtain in its absence.[36]

Gordon's charges have some merit. But as several of the case studies in this work indicate, the constructive engagement of companies with employees, local communities and representatives of the state often work to improve the human rights conditions within a company's area of operation. Gordon's words are, perhaps, best viewed as a warning against Pollyanna-ish pronouncements about the capacity – or the willingness – of corporations to dramatically alter the existing political, social and economic conditions of the communities and countries within which they operate.

Case studies and the Compact

Generalisations are difficult when the circumstances under which the businesses surveyed vary to such a large degree. That said, a few themes repeatedly surface in the five cases found in the human rights section in Part 2 of this book.

Companies such as Pharmakina and AngloGold Ashanti lead rather Manichean existences in the war-torn environments in which they operate. No one doubts the intestinal fortitude required to keep a business going amidst such strife, the good intentions of current management, and the clear benefits of the companies' presence to many members of their respective communities. However, Pharmakina and AngloGold Ashanti still offer somewhat grim reminders of the limited capacity of corporations to create a human rights culture in war-torn environments. In AngloGold Ashanti, the company admitted to having provided monetary support and logistical assistance to a local militia responsible for ongoing civil strife in the Democratic Republic of Congo ('DRC'). In Pharmakina, the company denied that any monetary remittances had been offered to local rebels, but admitted that other forms of assistance were a necessary part of doing business in an area of the DRC that operated without effective governance. No analysis of 'the business of sustainable development' in failed or chaotic states can afford to look at their subjects solely through the rose-coloured glasses of 'community empowerment'.

Global Alumina is fortunate that its bauxite operations exist in Guinea – and not in the neighbouring war-torn nations of Liberia, Sierra Leone and Ivory Coast. However, even Global

Alumina understands that its business, not far removed from some of the worst conflicts on the continent, is not immune from the ethical risks that attach to the weak governance in Guinea and the potential for corruption that attaches to a major investment in an impoverished land.

However, all three companies have not only invested money in the DRC and Guinea: they have also invested time and effort in the communities within which their operations take place. This community investment is, perhaps, the most significant contribution Pharmakina, Anglo-Gold Ashanti and Global Alumina have made to creating the kind of international economic community that Smith and Annan have envisaged.

For Pharmakina, the primary investment takes the form of paying a living wage, a health care system for its employees and direct family members, and the provision of malaria medicines and ARVs for members of the local community. In a part of the world where just surviving is a noble fight, Pharmakina's contributions to the well-being of the community in which it is situated cannot be underestimated.

AngloGold Ashanti has focused more of its attention on local stakeholder engagement. AngloGold Ashanti has set up a community forum to act as a body to engage directly with the company. Twenty-three different community groupings, from women's groups to indigenous pygmy groups, are represented. The hope is that the community forum will initiate community development projects with the support of the company and will oversee their implementation and management. By providing a forum that determines how foreign donor aid is disbursed and how monies for health care, education, and infrastructure development are spent, Anglo-Gold Ashanti creates the space and the support for meaningful self-governance.

Global Alumina, in accord with the Equator Principles and World Bank Guidelines, developed a Resettlement Action Plan (RAP) through long and careful deliberations with the surrounding community. As a result, Global Alumina's public consultations have produced a long-term integrated and sustainable socio-economic development plan that will engage almost every aspect of local community life: administrative organisation, environmental safety, land tenure regimes and normal economic activities such as agriculture and animal husbandry.

These three cases suggest that while it is essential for international businesses to discuss and to protect 'human rights', it is perhaps even more important that such businesses first create an environment where such rights can be meaningfully asserted. All three cases suggest that consultative forums are essential both for the economic development of communities within the companies' spheres of influence and for the creation of political institutions that allow for meaningful self-governance. For only when a community possesses the material conditions of existence and a voice to articulate its concerns can we truly start to discuss the implementation of the finer points of the Compact.

VCP and Sasol offer a substantially different picture of the relationship between business and the communities of which their businesses are a part. VCP developed a business model tailored to the specific needs of the community in which it wished to expand. The company created a more favourable environment for business growth by providing or facilitating novel livelihood opportunities for the rural poor – easy terms of credit, purchase guarantees, and free technical assistance. It also engaged oppositional social movements – representatives of the landless and the disposed. VCP's innovative programmes and its good faith disarmed much of the local resistance to its plans for large scale pulp production. Finally, VCP engaged both government and civil society actors (such as universities with a long term interest in the stability of the region) regarding the viability of staking the regions stability to the long term production of pulp and paper.

Sasol has, from the vantage point of the Compact's promoters, taken steps that appear to be proactive rather than reactive. It has not simply created a code of ethics – modelled on the Compact and other international documents – that dictate the conditions under which the company will invest in a given country and its obligations to the communities in which its operations exist. Many companies have such codes. SASOL's management appears to be using the code both to alter corporate culture and to assist the company's assessment of future investment opportunities. Sasol's use of its code in Mozambique suggests it understands that its long term interests lie in a sustained sympathy for and engagement with the communities with which its businesses are inextricably linked.

The five case studies in this section may provide too small a cohort from which to draw meaningful conclusions. They do support a number of initial observations. First. While companies may consider their pecuniary interests first, the reality of doing business in areas with weak or contested governance oblige, if not force, companies to consider the direct and the indirect effects of their operations on the communities in which they operate.[37] Second. The human rights of the Compact are abstractions: the human rights of the communities within which Pharmakina, AngloGold Ashanti, Global Alumina, VCP and Sasol operate are quite tangible. Making good on the promise of the Compact requires more than paying mere lip service to Principles 1 and 2: it requires listening to and responding to the lived realities of the people most deeply effected by a new investment. Listening means more than just hearing. It means negotiating the terms under which a business and a community can both flourish; it means investing not just economic capital, but social capital in persons who may exist only on the margins of an enterprise; its means seeing others not merely as a cost of doing business, but as individuals to whom we owe a duty of care. Third. The UN Compact assumes, at least tacitly, the existence of governments that will share the responsibility for safeguarding the welfare of their citizens. In many parts of Africa, such conditions do not obtain. Doing business in Africa, while remaining committed to the goals of the UN Compact, requires the recognition on the part of all parties that the principles of the Compact remain largely aspirational. And yet, as the five case studies demonstrate, those aspirations are altering both the way business is being done and the commitment of many transnational corporations to the often poor and embattled communities of which they are a part.

Notes

1 Of course, the system of justice to which I refer need not be as thick as the welfare state justification found in John Rawl's *A Theory of Justice* (Belknap: Cambridge: 1991), the social democratic vision propounded in Michael Walzer's *Spheres of Justice* (New York: Basic Books, 1985) or the radical reconstruction of the polity on offer in Karl Marx's *Das Kapital* (New York: LW Schmidt, 1867). See also M. Sandel *Liberalism and the Limits of Justice* (Cambridge: Cambridge University Press, 1998). However while many businesses may do quite well under fascist, exploitative corporate regimes – e.g. Nazi Germany or contemporary China – most businesses thrive – and know that they will do better – in systems in which courts dispense justice relatively even-handedly and the broader community believes – falsely or not – that the underlying mechanisms of distributive justice generate reasonably legitimate outcomes.

2   'Secretary-General Proposes Global Compact on Human Rights, Labour, Environment, in Address to World Economic Forum in Davos' (31 January 1999); UN Press Release Sg/Sm/6881 (1 February 1999). For commentary on this speech and the Compact, see S. Tester and G. Kell, *The United Nations and Business* (New York: St Martin's Press, 2000), 51. For a good overview of the Compact, see D. Cassel, 'Human Rights and Business Responsibilities in the Global Marketplace', *Business Ethics Quarterly,* 11, 2 (2000): 261.

3   The universe of international covenants and accords that apply to business is likely exhausted by the following list: Universal Declaration of Human Rights, http://www.unhchr.ch/udhr/index.htm; International Covenant on Economic, Social and Cultural Rights, http://www.ohchr.org/english/law/cescr.htm; International Covenant on Civil and Political Rights, http://www.ohchr.org/english/law/ccpr.htm; Optional Protocol to the International Covenant on Civil and Political Rights, http://www.ohchr.org/english/law/ccpr-one.htm; Second Optional Protocol to the International Covenant on Civil and Political Rights, aiming at the elimination of the death penalty, http://www.ohchr.org/english/law/ccpr-death.htm; International Convention on the Elimination of All Forms of Racial Discrimination, http://www.ohchr.org/english/law/cerd.htm; Convention on the Elimination of All Forms of Discrimination against Women, http://www.ohchr.org/english/law/cedaw.htm; Convention against Torture and Other Cruel, Inhuman or Degrading Treatment or Punishment, http://www.ohchr.org/english/law/cat.htm; Convention on the Rights of the Child, http://www.ohchr.org/english/law/crc.htm; Convention on the Rights of Persons with Disabilities, http://www.un.org/disabilities/convention/conventionfull.shtml; United Nations Convention against Corruption, http://www.unodc.org/unodc/crime_convention_corruption.html; United Nations Declaration on the Rights of Indigenous Peoples, http://www.ohchr.org/english/issues/indigenous/declaration.htm; Basic Principles on the Use of Force and Firearms by Law Enforcement Officials, http://www.ohchr.org/english/law/firearms.htm; Code of Conduct for Law Enforcement Officials, http://www.ohchr.org/english/law/codeofconduct.htm; United Nations Global Compact, *The Ten Principles*, http://www.unglobalcompact.org/AboutTheGC/TheTenPrinciples/index.html; UN Millennium Development Goals, http://www.un.org/ millenniumgoals/Appendix 1; United Nations Economic and Social Council, *Economic, Social and Cultural Rights: Norms on the Responsibilities of Transnational Corporations and other Business Enterprises with Regard to Human Rights*, http://www.unhchr.ch; Tripartite Declaration of Principles concerning Multinational Enterprise, http://www.ilo.org/public/english/employment/multi/download/english.pdf; ILO Declaration on Fundamental Principles and Rights at Work, http://www.ilo.org/dyn/declaris/; Forced Labour Convention, 1930, http://www.itcilo.it/actrav/english/common/C029.html; C87 Freedom of Association and Protection of the Right to Organise Convention, 1948, http://www.itcilo.it/actrav/english/ common/C087.html C98; Right to Organise and Collective Bargaining Convention, 1949, http://www.itcilo. it/actrav/english/common/C098.html; C100 Equal Remuneration Convention, 1951, http://www.itcilo.it/actrav/english/common/C100.html; C105 Abolition of Forced Labour Convention, 1957, http://www.itcilo.it/actrav/english/common/C105.html; C111 Discrimination (Employment and Occupation) Convention, 1958, http://www.itcilo.it/actrav/english/common/C111.html; C138 Minimum Age Convention, 1973, http://www.itcilo.it/actrav/english/common/C138.html; C169 Indigenous and Tribal Peoples Convention, 1989, http://www.ilo.org/ilolex/cgi-lex/convde.pl?C169; C182 Worst Forms of Child Labour Convention, 1999, http://www.itcilo.it/actrav/english/common/C182.html; Amnesty International, *Human Rights Principles for Companies*, http://web.amnesty.org/library/index/engACT700011998?open&of=eng-398; Business Leaders Initiative on Human Rights, http://www.blihr.org/Caux; Round Table, Principles for Business, http://www.cauxroundtable.org/principles.html; Danish Institute for Human Rights, Human Rights Compliance Assessment, http://www.humanrightsbusiness.org/040; Dow Jones Sustainability Indexes, http://www.sustainability-indexes.com/; European Parliament, Code of Conduct for European Enterprises, http://198.170.85.29/European-Parliament-Code.htm; FTSE, FTSE4Good Index Series, http://www.ftse.com/Indices/FTSE4Good_Index_Series/index.jsp; Global Reporting Initiative http://www.globalreporting.org/ReportingFramework/; Global Sullivan Principles of Social Responsibility, http://globalsullivan-principles.org/principles.htm; International Institute for Sustainable Development, *ISO Corporate Social Responsibility* (CSR) Standards, http://www.iisd.org/standards/csr.asp; Organisation for Economic Co-operation and Development, *Guidelines for Multinational Enterprises*, http://www.oecd; Social Accountability International, *Social Accountability 8000 Standard,* http://www.sa-intl.org/index.

4   In an exhaustive study of what could be gleaned from the Sullivan Principles in South Africa and employed global codes today, one key finding was that 'an independent oversight monitoring function is an absolute necessity': S.P. Sethi and O.F. Williams, 'Creating and Implementing Global Codes of Conduct: An Assessment of the Sullivan Principles as a Role Model for Developing International Codes of Conduct – Lessons Learned and Unlearned', *Business and Society Review*, 105, 2 (2000), 187. Of course, the Compact is not entirely without mechanisms to ensure some degree of accountability. The 'Communication on Progress' requirement is one such example. However, the point remains: the Communication is not a genuine enforcement mechanism.

5   O.F. Williams 'The UN Global Compact: The Challenge and the Promise', *Business Ethics Quarterly*, 14, 4 (2004), 755, 757.

6   *Nike v Kasky* 539 US 654 (2003). See also L. Girion, 'Nike Settle Lawsuit over Labor Claims', *Los Angeles Times*, 13 September 2003, C1. Similar negligence claims have been brought in both English and Australian courts. See *Lubbe v Cape PLC* [2000] 4 ALL ER 268; *Connelly v RTC* [1998] AC 854; *Dagi and Orrs v BHP and OkTedi Mining Ltd (No 2)* [1997] 1 VR 428.

7   See J. Nolan, 'The United Nations Compact with Business: Hindering or Helping the Protection of Human Rights?, *Queensland Law Journal*, 24 (2005), 451, 454: 'Support for stronger notions of corporate accountability is ... evidenced by a new wave of litigation against companies alleged to have violated human rights or environmental obligations ... [T]he Alien Torts Claims Act (ATCA) ... was passed by the United States Congress in 1789 and provides [federal] District Courts with jurisdiction over violations of the "law of nations". In the modern era, [US] courts have allowed foreign victims to address egregious human rights violations'. More recently, the ATCA has been used against corporations that have allegedly been knowingly complicit in human rights violations. See also S. Joseph, *Corporations and Transnational Human Rights Litigation* (Oxford: Hart Publishing, 2004). Litigation against Walmart for alleged false representations made with regard to its compliance with its code of conduct has recently been initiated under California's Unfair Business Practices Act. The complaint alleges that Walmart failed to adhere to its own code of conduct – incorporated into its contracts with foreign suppliers – with respect to how those foreign suppliers would treat their workers. See <http://www.laborrights.org/projects/corporate/walmart/WalmartComplaint091305.pdf>.

8   S.P. Sethi writes: 'The Global Compact ... provides a venue for opportunistic companies to make grandiose statements of corporate citizenship without worrying about being called to account for their actions.' S.P. Sethi, 'Global Compact is Another Exercise in Futility', *The Financial Express*, 8 September 2003, available at http://www.financialexpress.com/fe_full_story.php?contentid=41523. See also S.P. Sethi, *Setting Global Standards: Guidelines for Creating Codes of Conduct in Multinational Corporations* (Hoboken: Wiley Press, 2003).

9   Williams, 'UN Global Compact', 761, citing letter by Louise Frechette, deputy secretary-general of the United Nations, of 3 June 2003, responding to the officers of Oxfam, Amnesty International, Lawyers Committee for Human Rights, and Human Rights Watch.

10 Mary Robinson, former United Nation's high commissioner for human rights, and a supporter of the Compact, writes: 'Can you imagine doing business in a society where your business cannot own property or is at risk of having property removed without proper redress? Can you imagine doing business in a society where education is not available to all? Will you be able to find sufficient skilled resources both now and in the years to come? Will your workforce have the diversity that brings both creativity and an empathy and understanding of the customer?': M. Robinson, 'The Business Case for Human Rights, Visions of Ethical Business', *The Financial Times*, London, 1998, 14–15. Robinson further contends that while economic activities can take place without a commitment to human rights, the absence of a well-established regime of human rights creates, for all business, a set of risks that, ultimately, will result in unsustainable operations. For a critique of Robinson's position and the UN's efforts, see S. Arkani and R. Theobald, 'Corporate Involvement in Human Rights: Is It Any of Their Business?', *Business Ethics: A European Review*, 14, 3 (2005), 190.

11 Tester and Kell *The United Nations and Business*, 53.

12 L. Henkin, 'The Universal Declaration at 50 and the Challenge of Global Markets', *Brooklyn Journal of International Law*, 17 (1999), 25.

13 Indeed, the UNHRC's most recent General Comment, 3, para. 8, notes that the ICCPRs treaty obligations 'do not …have direct horizontal effect as a matter of international law'. The treaty only binds non-state actors to the extent that its provisions have been made a part of enforceable municipal law.

14 J. Ruggie, 'Business and Human Rights: Mapping International Standards of Responsibility and Accountability for Corporate Acts', Report of the Special Representative of the Secretary-General (SRSG) on the Issue of Human Rights and Transnational Corporations and Other Business Enterprises' Implementation of General Assembly Resolution 60/251 of 15 March 2006, Human Rights Council, A/HRC/4/035 (February 2007) ('Business and Human Rights') at para. 45. See also M. Wright and A. Lehr, 'Business Recognition of Human Rights: Global Patterns, Regional and Sectoral Variations', Mandate of the Special Representative of the Secretary-General on Human Rights and Transnational Corporations and Other Business Enterprises (February 2007).

15 See T. Donaldson, *The Ethics of International Business* (New York: Oxford University Press, 1989); T. Donaldson, 'The Perils of Multinationals' Largess', *Business Ethics Quarterly,* 4, 3 (1994), 367.

16 Norms on the Responsibilities of Transnational Corporations and Other Business Enterprises with regards to Human Rights (UN Doc. E/CN.4/Sub.2/2003/12/Rev.2, 26 August 2003) (hereafter 'Norms').

17 D. Weissbrodt, 'Business and Human Rights', *Cincinnati Law Review,* 74 (2005), 55, 67. For a full account of the drafting of the Norms, see D. Weissbrodt and M. Kruger, 'Norms on the Responsibilities of Transnational Corporations and Other Business Enterprises with regard to Human Rights', *American Journal of International Law,* 97, 4 (2003), 901. See also E. Morgera, 'The UN and Corporate Environmental Responsibility: Between International Regulation and Partnerships', *RECIEL,* 15, 1 (2006), 93; C.F. Hillemanns, 'UN Norms on the Responsibility of Transnational Corporations and Other Business Enterprises with Regard to Human Rights', *German Law Journal,* 10, 4 (2003), 1065; D. Weissbrodt, *Principles Relating to the Human Rights Conduct of Companies* (UN Doc. E/CN.4/Sub.2/2000/WG. 2/WP.1, 25 May 2000).

18 See Office of the High Commission on Human Rights, 'The Global Compact and Human Rights: Understanding Sphere of Influence and Complicity: OHCHR Briefing Paper', Sub-Commission on the Promotion and Protection of Human Rights, Economic and Social Council, Report on the Human Rights on the Responsibilities of Transnational Corporations and Related Business Enterprises with regard to Human Rights GENERAL, E/CN.4/2005/91 (15 February 2005) (hereafter '*Commentary*'). This commentary on the Norms reads, in relevant part, as follows: 18. The draft 'Norms on the Responsibilities of Transnational Corporations and Other Business Enterprises with regard to Human Rights' (hereafter 'draft Norms') attempt to impose direct responsibilities on business entities as a means of achieving comprehensive protection of all human rights – civil, cultural, economic, political and social – relevant to the activities of business. The draft Norms identify specific human rights relevant to the activities of business, such as the right to equal opportunity and non-discrimination, the right to security of persons, the rights of workers, and refers to the rights of particular groups such as indigenous peoples. The draft Norms also set out responsibilities of business enterprises in relation to environmental protection and consumer protection. As an initiative of a United Nations expert body, the draft seeks wide territorial coverage. It also seeks broad company coverage as appears from the reference in its title to 'transnational corporations and other business enterprises'. The draft envisages a range of implementation mechanisms of both a promotional and protective character such as self-reporting and external verification. The Commission has indicated that the draft Norms contain 'useful elements and ideas for consideration by the Commission' but, as a draft proposal, it has no legal standing. 19. The draft Norms is an attempt in filling the gap in understanding the expectations on business in relation to human rights. However, the consultation process revealed a wide range of opinions amongst stakeholders on the value and content of the draft. Employer groups, many states and some businesses were critical of the draft while non-governmental organisations and some states and businesses as well as individual stakeholders such as academics, lawyers and consultants were supportive. *Commentary,* paras 18–19. According to Amnesty International, the Norms, properly understood, require 'that businesses refrain from activities that directly or indirectly violate human rights or benefit from human rights violations, and to use due diligence in avoiding harm'. Amnesty International, *The UN Human Rights Norms for Business: Towards Legal Accountability* (New York: Amnesty International, 2004), 14.

19 *Commentary* at paras. 33–34.

20 The *UN Commentary* notes that at international criminal law, a finding of complicity requires proof of three elements: (1) a crime must have been committed; (2) the accomplice must contribute in a direct and substantial way to the crime; and (3) the accomplice must have had intent or knowledge or was reckless with regard to the commission of the crime. See also International Peace Academy and Fafo AIS, *Business and International Crimes: Assessing the Liability of Business Entities for Grave Violations of International Law,* (New York: UN International Peace Academy, 2004), 23.

21 *United States v Krupp, 9 Trials of War Criminals before the Nuremberg Military Tribunals under Council Law* No. 10 (1950). For a recent validation of the Nuremberg Court's definition of and finding of 'complicity', see *Doe v Unocal Corporation,* 110 F Supp 2d 1294, 1310 (CD Cal 2000) affirmed 395 F3rd 392 (9th Circuit 2002). The Tribunal found the defendants guilty of employing slave labour because their will was not overpowered by the Third Reich 'but instead coincide[d] with the will of those from whom the alleged compulsion emanate[d] … Krupp … had manifested not only its willingness but its ardent desire to employ forced labour.'

22 Weissbrodt, *Principles Relating to the Human Rights Conduct,* 56, citing *US v Krauch, 8 Trials Before the Nuremberg Military Tribunals Under Control Council Law* No. 10 (1952).

23 Weissbrodt, *Principles Relating to the Human Rights Conduct,* 57. See also A. Clapham and S. Jerbi, 'Categories of Corporate Complicity in Human Rights Abuses', *Hastings International & Comparative Law Review,* 24 (2001), 339: 'In the field of human rights, there are growing expectations that corporations should do everything in their power to promote universal human rights standards, even in conflict situations where governance structures have broken down.'

24 Ruggie, 'Business and Human Rights', paras 37–38.

25 *Compliance Complaint, Nordea's International Corporate Social Responsibility and Human Rights Obligations in its Role as Lead Arranger for Oy Metsä-Botnia in Uruguay* (6 February 2006) (hereafter *Nordea Compliance Complaint*).

26 Ibid., 3.

27 Brew and Ersmarker identify four distinct spheres of influence: '(1) The company's core business – where the company will have most direct control and can put in place the necessary management procedures; (2) Between the company and its business partners – where the level of direct control will vary depending on the nature of the relationship, but where at least strong influence can and should be exerted to ensure that human rights violations do not arise. Any formal documentation of the business relationship should specifically refer to expected performance on human rights; (3) Between the company and the community in which it operates – where the level of influence and control will depend on a range of economic, social and environmental factors; (4) Between the company and national government organisations – where influence is likely to be more applicable than control, and where a range of economic, social and environmental issues will be central to the outcome.' P. Brew and C. Ersmarker *Guide to Human Rights Impact Assessment and Management: Road-Testing Draft* (UN Global Compact: New York, 2007), 15. They contend that a company invariably has less influence as the relationship in question moves away from its core business. John Ruggie, in his 2008 UN Report, offers this important distinction on the meaning of spheres of influence: 'To begin with, sphere of influence conflates two very different meanings of influence: one is impact, where the company's activities or relationships are causing human rights harm; the other is whatever leverage a company may have over actors that are causing harm. The first falls squarely within the responsibility to respect; the second may only do so in particular circumstances … Anchoring corporate responsibility in the second meaning of influence requires assuming, in moral philosophy terms, that "can implies ought". But companies cannot be held responsible for the human rights impacts of every entity over which they may have some influence, because this would include cases in which they were not a causal agent, direct or indirect, of the harm in question. Nor is it desirable to have companies act whenever they have influence, particularly over governments. Asking companies to support human rights voluntarily where they have influence is one thing; but attributing responsibility to them on that basis alone is quite another.' J. Ruggie, 'Protect, Respect and Remedy: a Framework for Business and Human Rights: Report of the Special Representative of the Secretary-General on the Issue of Human Rights and Transnational Corporations and Other Business Enterprises' Human Rights Council Eighth Session Agenda Item 3, Promotion and Protection of All Human Rights, Civil, Political, Economic, Social & Cultural Rights, Including The Right To Development, A/Hrc/8/5 (7 April 2008) (hereafter Ruggie, '2008 UN Report'), paras 68 and 69.

28 Brew and Ersmarker, *Road-Testing Draft*, 82.

29 Ibid.

30 John Ruggie's 2008 UN Report characterises these 'soft' obligations in terms of 'respect': 'To respect rights essentially means not to infringe on the rights of others – put simply, to do no harm. Because companies can affect virtually all internationally recognised rights, they should consider the responsibility to respect in relation to all such rights, although some may require greater attention in particular contexts. There are situations in which companies may have additional responsibilities – for example, where they perform certain public functions, or because they have undertaken additional commitments voluntarily. But the responsibility to respect is the baseline expectation for all companies in all situations'. (Ruggie, 2008 UN Report, para. 24.)

31 J. Ruggie, 'Business and Human Rights: Mapping International Standards of Responsibility and Accountability for Corporate Acts', Report of the Special Representative of the Secretary-General (SRSG) on the Issue of Human Rights and Transnational Corporations and Other Business Enterprises Implementation of General Assembly Resolution 60/251 of 15 March 2006, Human Rights Council, A/HRC/4/035 (9 February 2007), para. 45.

32 Ibid., paras 47, 48 and 51, citing in support of these soft and novel approaches to international regulation the interventions made in the symposium on 'Global Governance and Global Administrative Law in the International Legal Order', *European Journal of International Law,* 17 (February 2006).

33 Brew and Ersmarker, *Road-Testing Draft,* 22.

34 Ibid.

35 K. Gordon *Multinational Enterprises in Situations of Violent Conflict and Widespread Human Rights Abuses* (Paris, Organisation for Economic Co-operation and Development, 2002).

36 Gordon further contends: 'This [study] suggests that multinational enterprises can play indirect (and inadvertent) roles in the logic of violence and human rights as the taxes and royalties they pay enter extremely weak frameworks for public governance ... Violence is a feature of all societies, but its prevalence varies. Some societies show relatively high levels of what might be called "random" violence. Organised violence, at least in its modern forms, requires considerable capital equipment, specialised personnel and significant organisational, technological and financial capabilities. In most countries, governments are generally effective in securing both *de facto* and *de jure* control of the use of force by armies and police forces. Thus, recourse to force in many countries tends to be focused on law enforcement and defence. It is also reasonably subject to accountability and control through political and social processes. In contrast, in ... troubled societies ... large scale, organised violence and coercion –directed by governments or by tribes or ethnic or religious groups – is used for many political and economic purposes (to eliminate or silence dissent, to force people to work, to obtain access to goods, services or assets).' Some empirical studies offer insights into the causes of internal conflict and war. One study published by the World Bank – Collier and Hoeffler – look at two alternative views of the motives for civil war or other forms of violent internal conflict. 'On Economic Causes of Civil War' 50 *Oxford. Economic Papers* (1998): 563-573. The first views civil strife as arising out of grievances or hatreds associated with ethnic, religious or other forms of social division. The second, economic view regards civil strife as being motivated by a desire to alter the allocation of economic resources ... The findings of this study are as follows: Despite the attention given to ethnic and religious fragmentation as sources of conflict, these variables do not have statistically significant effects, once economic variables are accounted for. In other words, the presence of ethnic or religious divisions within a country is not found to be an independent risk factor that increases the probability of civil strife. These conclusions do not imply that ethnic, tribal or religious tensions are irrelevant to conflict, but they do underscore the importance of the role of economic forces – which may interact with social factors – in heightening the risk of conflict. An empirical study by finds that high endowments of 'fuel and ore' resources tends to be associated with higher levels of corruption. Many of the transnational companies examined in this text are involved in the extraction of natural resources. Gordon's conclusions cast something of a pall over the notion that any investment – even an investment that equals the GNP of a host nation – is necessarily a good investment. C. Leite and J. Weidmann, 'Does Mother Nature Corrupt? Natural Resources, Corruption, and Economic Growth' (June 1999). IMF Working Paper No. 99/85, available at SSRN: http://ssrn.com/abstract=259928.

37 See *OECD Risk Awareness Tool for Multinational Enterprises in Weak Governance Zones* (Paris: Organisation for Economic Cooperation and Development, 2006), 11 (available via http://www. oecd.org/ dataoecd/26/21/36885821.pdf): 'Weak governance zones are defined as investment environments in which governments cannot or will not assume their roles in protecting rights (including property rights), providing basic public services (e.g. social programmes, infrastructure development, law enforcement and prudential surveillance) and ensuring that public sector management is efficient and effective. These "government failures" lead to broader failures in political, economic and civic institutions that are referred to as weak governance. The broader institutional failures create situations which pose many ethical dilemmas and challenges for companies. As companies themselves often note, weak governance zones represent some of the world's most difficult investment environments. In addition to the usual financial and business risks encountered in all investment environments, weak governance zones pose ethical dilemmas and present risks that stem directly from government failure – e.g. widespread solicitation, extortion, endemic crime and violent conflict, abuses by security forces, forced labour and violations of the rule of law.'

CHAPTER 3

Partnerships and cross-sector collaboration

RALPH HAMANN & FLEUR BOULOGNE[1]

The emergence of partnerships for sustainable development

A notable issue that comes up in the debates over corporate citizenship and sustainable development is cross-sector partnership, or collaboration between role-players from business, government and civil society on the basis of common interests, focused on achieving joint objectives. Calls for such partnerships have been a feature of key sustainable development conferences, including the Rio Earth Summit in 1992 and the Johannesburg World Summit on Sustainable Development (WSSD) in 2002. Indeed, during the WSSD, partnerships were identified and agreed upon as a complement to the formal inter-governmental agreements (as what are called 'Type 2' agreements). The Millennium Development Goals (MDGs) also explicitly call for a partnership for sustainable development, and Sir Mark Moody-Stuart, chairman of Anglo American and prominent participant in the WBCSD (see Chapter 1), goes so far as to argue that 'All the best examples of the application of principles of sustainable development involve partnership'.[2]

Partnerships exist on different scales and take different forms, but they have in common the expectation that the participants can achieve their objectives more effectively and efficiently by making strategic alliances with others rather than acting independently. This has also been referred to as 'collaborative advantage'.[3] This advantage is gained by pooling complementary resources and sharing risks and rewards in the joint undertaking.[4] Of course, the partnerships considered in this chapter are those in which there is an emphasis, even if implicit, not just on the interests of the partners, but on those of broader society in the pursuit of sustainable development. Though many commentators exclude public-private partnerships (PPPs) from such discussion – perhaps because traditionally they have a focus on relatively straightforward infrastructure projects and the like – we include them because their purpose is providing public goods.

Further defining characteristics of partnerships, broadly speaking, are that they are based on the partners' voluntary participation and they are 'horizontally organised, maintaining the partners' autonomy'.[5] The principle is that all partners have some measure of influence when it comes to making joint decisions about the partnership's objectives and procedures. This means that partnerships are characterised, at least in principle, by a greater degree of flexibility and openness than traditional mechanisms dominated by either public or private sector organisations. Whereas contracts can still play a role in some partnerships (especially infrastructure PPPs – as discussed in more detail below), the notion of partnership implies some measure of ongoing negotiation and adaptation. This, it is hoped, allows partnership initiatives to adapt to the changing needs and objectives of the process and its context, and it also facilitates greater learning among participants and others.[6]

Some commentators argue that the definition of partnerships excludes 'market transactions'.[7] However, this is too restrictive, because many partnership initiatives may involve commercial mechanisms in their implementation. For instance, PPPs in infrastructure provision may involve a tendering process. Even much more informal collaborative arrangements may apply commercial mechanisms in order to enhance their viability and support sustainable development objectives. To illustrate, the case study on emerging small-scale enterprises in Zanzibar (Case 6) is an example of diverse role-players in both the public and private sectors contributing complementary resources and sharing risks and rewards (which may be defined broadly) over a longer period than is usual in standard short-term commercial contracts.

Though of course collaboration and partnerships have a long history,[8] they are becoming increasingly popular in areas of policy-making and implementation that were previously the domain of the state or the market only, in particular infrastructure, health, education and the environment. In the United Kingdom, for instance, the Tony Blair government committed £35.5 billion for 563 private finance initiatives, in which private sector funding and management were to be leveraged in public sector projects (especially in infrastructure, health and education) based on long-term contracts. In the United States similar arrangements have often focused on urban renewal and downtown economic development.[9] Referring to more open-ended, public policy partnerships between multinational corporations and the United Nations (UN), Jens Martens notes, '[t]here is hardly any multinational corporation on the Fortune 500 list which does not run a partnership project with a UN organisation'.[10]

The driving forces behind this increasing interest in partnerships work at two levels. The first level is the particular circumstances: the prospective partners see compelling incentives for getting together to achieve their specific objectives. Setting up and maintaining an effective partnership arrangement can mean significant transaction costs, but the potential benefits are seen to outweigh these costs. In particular, partnerships can leverage contributions and resources from the various participants and coordinate their allocation effectively, and they can also spread risks. An effective pooling of resources and risks can improve developmental outcomes at comparatively low costs to individual participants – this reliance on 'complementary core competencies'[11] is discussed in more detail below. Furthermore, engaging in partnerships can improve the relationships between the participants, leading to higher levels of trust and better channels of communication and thereby enhancing the participants' reputation and social capital. Given the broader incentives and drivers for engaging in sustainable development, as discussed in Chapter 1, a company may therefore see partnership as an effective means to achieve corporate citizenship objectives.[12]

The second level is the broader interests of society: the proliferation of partnerships can be interpreted as part of a broader shift in governance, or the process of giving 'direction to society'[13] through the interplay between government, business and civil society. Indeed, partnerships are sometimes seen as a new model of governance, variously referred to as 'new' or 'collaborative' governance, among other terms.[14] New governance can be defined as the shift of policy- and decision-making power and responsibility from the state towards more dispersed, collaborative networks of social actors. As noted by Peter Utting,

> The confrontational politics of earlier decades, which had pitted a pro-regulation and redistributive lobby against TNCs [transnational corporations], lost momentum as governments, business and multilateral organisations alike, as well as an increasing number of NGOs, embraced ideas of 'partnership' and 'co-regulation' in which different actors or stakeholders would work together to find ways of minimising the environmental and social costs of economic growth and modernisation.[15]

In particular, it has been argued that partnerships are being established as a response to gaps or deficits in traditional governance models, especially with regard to the limited – and some argue declining – ability of states to devise and implement rules in the increasingly global and complex interactions between social, economic and environmental systems. Thorsten Benner and his colleagues talk of *operational* and *participatory* gaps in global governance, though their arguments can be adapted to apply at the national and local levels, as well.

To explain what they mean by 'operational' governance gap, they refer firstly to the 'asymmetry between the territorially bounded nature of the nation-state and the transnational nature of many of today's key problems'.[16] Air pollution and climate change, or illegal migration and the slave trade, for instance, are problems beyond the ambit of nation states because they cut across national boundaries. They refer secondly to the temporal asymmetry that results from the incapacity of bureaucratic and political systems to respond simultaneously to the need for increasingly quick decision-making, on the one hand, and to the long-term time horizons required by intergenerational equity,[17] on the other. Thirdly, they refer to the fact that 'the complexity of public policy issues is steadily increasing, contributing to growing knowledge and information asymmetries'.[18] Hence existing governance structures are challenged with the need to integrate knowledge and information from different disciplines, encompassing environmental, cultural and technological systems, among others, as well as across different sectors of society. And fourthly, Benner *et al.* argue that the international integration of trade driven by the World Trade Organisation (WTO), among others, is at odds with a comparatively less effective integration on issues related to the environment and human rights. They relate this to the perceived need for governments, especially in developing countries, to provide a favourable environment for foreign investment, with less risk of ad hoc government intervention in the market.[19]

These operational governance gaps are complemented by 'participatory' gaps. Here, participation means people's involvement in economic activity and their enjoyment of the fruits thereof, and their taking part in decision-making that affects them. The biggest participatory gap, therefore, is the growing inequality between what Wolfgang Sachs calls the 'globalised rich' – those who have access to the global economy and political influence – and the 'loca-lised poor' – those who are largely excluded from the global economy but are nevertheless influenced, often negatively, by global economic and environmental developments.[20] In terms of political influence, the participation gap is furthermore characterised by a decreased role for national legislatures, especially in transnational policy making, and a concomitant increase in the numbers of vocal non-governmental organisations that are demanding more influence on policy-making both at national and international levels (though arguably such NGOs are more prominent in developed countries and themselves often face criticism related to lacking accountability).

The above describes gaps in global governance, but increasing territorial, temporal, knowl-edge and participation asymmetries mean there are also gaps in local and national governance. For instance, there is the need to integrate knowledge across disciplinary boundaries and to help local people participate more in decisions that affect them. These are key sustainability challenges at the local level across Africa, and these generic challenges are compounded by more particular ones. For a start, many local, provincial and national government organisations in Africa are hampered by significant shortfalls in human and financial resources. This affects the quality of policy making and implementation. Of course, this is not unique to Africa,[21] but policy implementation is a particularly pressing challenge in many African countries.

Government institutions in many parts of Africa are further constrained by continued challenges to their legitimacy. These challenges, which themselves have varying degrees of legitimacy, range from legal challenges or protest action in places where executive leaders are perceived to be abusing their powers (such as Zimbabwe) to continued civil strife, violence and human rights abuses by both rebel and government forces in places such as the east of the Democratic Republic of the Congo (DRC). Throughout much of Africa, the legitimacy of formal government – particularly at the local level – is often challenged by traditional leadership structures. In most African countries, formal and traditional governance structures exist side by side on the basis of either tacit or, as in the case of South Africa, explicit rules of mutual cooperation, though this relationship often becomes strained when there is a significant change, such as a large-scale mining or industrial investment.

In summary, therefore, the variety of governance gaps, ranging from generic, global ones to more particular, local ones has meant there has been an increase in partnerships. Such 'net-works that bring together state actors… civil society and business on an issue basis have been one of the innovative responses to the perceived need for innovation in governance'[22] at local, national and international levels.

However, the partnership phenomenon is not without controversy. On the one hand many commentators refer to the growth in partnership initiatives as a desirable or even inevitable process, emphasising that partnerships – if set up judiciously – hold much promise for solving problems where traditional methods have proven inadequate:

> Recent years [have] seen an extraordinary growth of the number, size and scope of part-nerships as vehicles to deliver public services or address more complex public policy issues such as the digital divide and climate change. Indeed, partnerships are emerging as the institutional 'pathway of choice' across an extraordinary range of activities… With this trend, the matter of [partnerships'] effective governance and the manner in which they can be held to account is, equally, becoming a mainstream issue.[23]

On the other hand there are commentators who are much more sceptical about this recent enthusiasm for partnerships. Referring in particular to 'global partnerships' involving the UN, the private sector and others, Jens Martens sounds a warning that may apply to partnerships more broadly as well:

> The new models, despite their image of greater flexibility and efficiency, bring their own serious risks and side effects. To go along with the trend uncritically might be in the interests of powerful business lobbies whose influence over shaping global policy can grow through such models, but not in the interests of the affected people. The core question... should therefore not be – how can partnership models of this type be strengthened or their management improved? The core question should instead be – how can global problems be solved in a framework of democratic multilateralism, and what role do models of cooperation between public and private actors play in this process? Experience so far suggests that this role can and should only be a very limited one.[24]

The opportunities and strengths of partnerships and their weaknesses and risks are considered in more detail below. First, we argue that much depends on the type of partnership. Though most partnership initiatives are multifaceted and constantly evolving, it is possible to distinguish broad types, and it is likely that different criteria for success or failure and different implementation guidelines apply to the various types. Next, we consider in more detail the incentives for partnerships and the implementation challenges they face, with an emphasis on balancing power, rights and interests. We then consider the way partnerships are evaluated, in terms of both their effectiveness and their accountability, and we look at some of the main criticisms of partnerships, alluded to in the quote from Jens Martens above. Finally, we provide a brief overview of the case studies in this book in the light of the preceding discussion.

Types and diversity of partnerships

Since partnership arrangements come in many kinds and entail diverse challenges and opportunities, there have been numerous attempts at developing a typology or categorisation of partnerships. For a start, analysts have distinguished between initiatives on the basis of the main constituent parties: *co-management arrangements* between the state and civil society; *public-private partnerships* between the state and the private sector; *private-social partnerships* between the private sector and civil society; and *tri-sector partnerships* involving all three sectors (see Figure 1). Given the focus of this book, the partnerships that are subject of this chapter are primarily those involving business, with an emphasis on both public-private partnerships (PPPs) and tri-sector partnerships (also referred to as multi-stakeholder partnerships – MSPs). PPPs and MSPs are often characterised by different objectives, institutional forms and geographic scale – the key differentiation features that we will now use to establish a typology of partnerships.

Most attempts to develop a typology of partnerships have focused, at least in part, on the primary purpose or function of the initiatives in question. For instance, Martens suggests five types: advocacy, standard-setting, financing, implementation and coordination.[25] Zadek and Radovich suggest three condensed versions of these five: *service* partnerships, which entail the delivery of public services and infrastructure (such as water or transport infrastructure) by business in pursuit of profit; *resourcing* partnerships, which involve the mobilisation of public

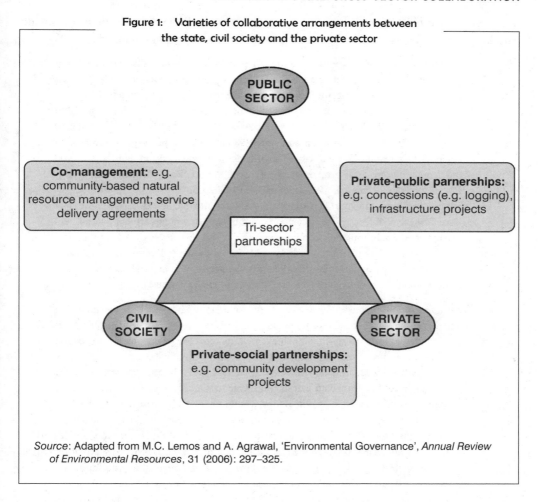

Figure 1: Varieties of collaborative arrangements between the state, civil society and the private sector

PUBLIC SECTOR

Co-management: e.g. community-based natural resource management; service delivery agreements

Tri-sector partnerships

Private-public parnerships: e.g. concessions (e.g. logging), infrastructure projects

CIVIL SOCIETY

PRIVATE SECTOR

Private-social partnerships: e.g. community development projects

Source: Adapted from M.C. Lemos and A. Agrawal, 'Environmental Governance', *Annual Review of Environmental Resources*, 31 (2006): 297–325.

and private resources to address public goals; and *rule-setting* initiatives, which are meant to develop and advocate for rules, such as anti-corruption codes or human rights principles for businesses. These authors point out that 'importantly, there is a growing convergence between these three forms as, for example, resourcing partnerships become *de facto* rule-setters, and rule-setters take on increasingly commercial approaches to sustainability'.[26]

There are thus inherent limits to the usefulness of such categories, especially if they become quite narrow or specific. So, rather than develop a complex and detailed set of categories, we suggest a simplified and synthesised version of the categories mentioned above, based on two axes.[27] The first is the extent to which the purpose and objectives of the partnership are clearly defined and measurable. The second is the extent to which the institutional structure of the partnership is formalised, ranging from a legal contract that imposes binding obligations on the participants, to more informal arrangements such as a memorandum of understanding or tacit agreements within social networks. Based on a cursory review of a wide array of partnership initiatives in southern Africa, we have found that relative to these two axes there are boradly speaking two main clusters – or types – of partnerships, as shown in Figure 2:[28]

1   *Rule-setting and advocacy partnerships.* These focus predominantly on establishing and adopting rules and standards. They create a guiding or facilitative framework for action, rather than affecting action per se. They seek to respond to a problem that defies resolution through government or multilateral policy – that is, they respond to a governance gap, as described above. Partners in such initiatives invest significant time and effort in coming to an agreement about what the problem is and how to solve it. As a result, their purpose is open-ended and emergent, in that the outcome (and sometimes even the problem to be addressed) is not clearly defined at the outset. Because of this open-endedness, such initiatives are not very formal in terms of institutional structure, in part because they need to be flexible and in part because they have few clear objectives or financial commitments to which partners can be held accountable. Such initiatives can be established at all levels, ranging from the local to the global. They often take the form of MSPs (as shown in Figure 1), because it is often civil society organisations that identify the need for a partnership, and because of the commonly perceived need for balance and representation.

2   *Implementation partnerships.* These are predominantly about facilitating, financing and managing action to achieve particular, tangible objectives. Because the objectives are well defined and because their achievement requires the leveraging and allocation of financial resources, these initiatives have a formal institutional structure, commonly involving a binding legal agreement. Such initiatives can also be established at all levels, but due to the formal, legal nature of such agreements, they are more common at local or national levels. This predisposition to formal contracts also gives rise to the prevalence of PPPs in this type of initiative, with a common focus on local-level implementation.

    PPPs generally involve the private sector on the basis of the profit motive, with risk and reward shared between the private and public sectors. There are usually legal contracts specifying roles and responsibilities for all participants, and because they often involve public expenditure or expose the public sector to risk, they are generally established either implicitly or explicitly within dedicated national policy frameworks.[29] Though PPPs are often criticised, especially by labour unions, for being inefficient and contrary to public benefit and for focusing on the loss of jobs in what is perceived as little more than straightforward privatisation, PPPs are enjoying significant support from many African governments as a means to attract private sector funding and implementation capacity in the provision of public services.[30]

Again, these definitions represent two idealised types – broad trends rather than definite categories. According to Zadek and Radovich, many initiatives are likely to be explicitly or implicitly hybrid forms whose aim is both to establish rules or principles and to facilitate tangible action to support these. However, perhaps it is more accurate to speak of bifurcated partnership structures. For instance, a common pattern is that a particular partnership may be most well known as a strategic negotiation forum with relatively informal institutionalisation, but it will hive off smaller, more focused and formalised initiatives to allow for local-level implementation. To illustrate this, Box 1 shows some examples of partnership initiatives active in South Africa and Figure 3 shows how they are placed in the typology.

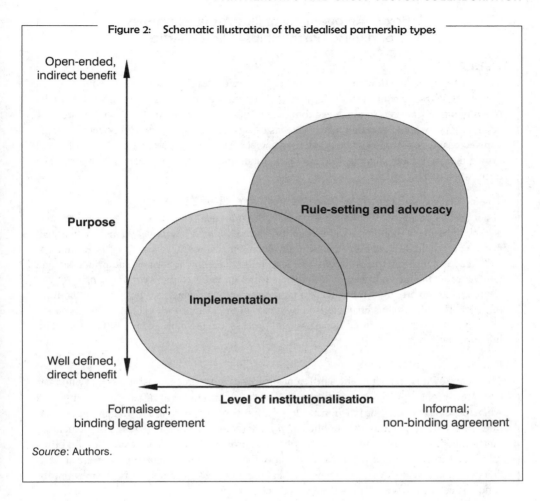

Figure 2: Schematic illustration of the idealised partnership types

Open-ended, indirect benefit

Purpose

Rule-setting and advocacy

Implementation

Well defined, direct benefit

Level of institutionalisation

Formalised; binding legal agreement

Informal; non-binding agreement

Source: Authors.

The opportunity and challenge of partnerships from a business perspective

From the perspective of the corporate citizenship debates described in Chapter 1, partnership may be seen as the culmination of a progression from individual, commonly reactive company initiatives to more proactive, collective and collaborative efforts in conjunction with NGOs, government agencies and others (see Figures 4 and 5).

For companies seeking to demonstrate their corporate citizenship commitment, partnerships hold the promise of a more efficient and effective way to comply with legal requirements and to respond to stakeholder expectations. With a focus on mining companies, it has been argued that 'tri-sector partnerships are, in essence, a new form of strategic alliance [that] can result in more manageable costs and risks for the company, increased effectiveness of actions

61

Box 1: An overview of illustrative examples
of diverse partnerships in South Africa

NEDLAC

The founding declaration of the National Economic Development and Labour Council (NEDLAC) was signed in 1995 by government, organised business and organised labour. Its overarching objective is to make economic decision-making more inclusive and to promote economic growth and social equity by means of 'social dialogue' between government, organised business, organised labour and civil society. There is a national act (No. 35 of 1994) providing for its establishment, but there is no binding agreement between participants. (See http://www.nedlac.org.za)

The Grabouw Sustainable Development Initiative (SDI)

Grabouw is a small town in the Western Cape, South Africa (close to Cape Town) characterised by high levels of poverty and inequality. The SDI aimed to facilitate a more integrated, participatory and sustainability-focused development planning process, premised on a Social Accord deliberated upon by an inclusive multi-stakeholder forum. The principles and guidelines of this accord have been translated into an integrated development plan for the town, linked to particular implementation projects, some of which are proposed in the form of PPPs. The SDI is thus characterised by a two-pronged approach encompassing both the open-ended, loosely structured Social Accord process and the more formal PPPs focused on implementation.

Cape Town Partnership

The Cape Town Partnership unites different spheres of government, businesses and a number of not-for-profit organisations with the aim of developing, managing and promoting (and where necessary upgrading) the inner-city of Cape Town. Its core is a development facilitation agency striving to mobilise public and private sectors in coordinating and implementing multi-dimensional development programmes and projects. It is another example of a bifurcated partnership. Certain elements are strongly focused on implementation (and are embedded in formal service level agreements); others focus on creating a facilitative framework for action. (See http://www.capetownpartnership.co.za)

EU Water Initiative (EUWI)

This Type II partnership was launched at the World Summit for Sustainable Development (WSSD) in Johannesburg in 2002. EUWI's dual approach facilitates the formulation of an overarching strategy for achieving global water and sanitation targets and objectives, and it simultaneously enables the development of regional (and thematic) programmes (one of the regional programmes is specifically focused on Africa). Within these sub-programmes specific projects are being implemented or supported – one example is the establishment of a transboundary river basin management organisation for the Volta River. (See http://www. euwi.net)

Renewable Energy and Energy Efficiency Partnership (REEEP)

REEEP was also established in 2002 as a WSSD Type II partnership. It supports policy and regulatory initiatives for clean energy and facilitates financing for sustainable energy projects. Backed by more than 200 national governments, businesses, development banks and NGOs, the partnership aims to accelerate the integration of renewables and to advocate energy efficiency to reduce greenhouse gas emissions. There are eight regional secretariats and more than 3 500 members. The partnership has funded more than 50 projects in 44 countries, addressing market barriers to clean energy in the developing world and economies in transition. Potential projects are identified through regular 'calls for proposals' and an international selection procedure. Becoming a REEEP partner entails commitment to the REEEP mission statement, but does not include further obligations. While the individual implementation projects are clearly defined and formalised, the overall REEEP partnership has a more informal structure and strategic objectives. In South Africa, one of the initiatives supported by REEEP is Kuyasa, a project developing innovative finance mechanisms that enable poor households to obtain renewable and energy efficient technologies such as solar water heaters, ceiling insulation and compact fluorescent light bulbs. (See http://www.reeep.org)

Build, Operate, Train, Transfer (BoTT)

BoTT was a water partnership in four of the poorest provinces in South Africa (Northern Cape, Eastern Cape, KwaZulu-Natal and Mpumalanga). It was set up as a PPP between the Department for Water Affairs and Forestry (DWAF) and four private sector consortia, and it ended in 2001. One of the key principles of the partnership was that sustainability could only be achieved by actively involving local communities and local government in all stages of the project's life cycle. The partnership focused on the delivery of water and sanitation infrastructure. Its objective was to hand over the responsibility for the infrastructure to local authorities (and communities) when the partnership ended, but this transition proved problematic in a number of cases. BoTT was supported by an international programme focused on partnerships in water and sanitation. (See http://bpd-waterandsanitation.org)

Gautrain

The Gautrain is an 80km Mass Rapid Transit railway system under construction in Gauteng Province, South Africa, that will ultimately link Johannesburg, Pretoria (Tshwane metropolitan area), and OR Tambo International Airport. It is hoped that this railway will relieve the traffic congestion in the Johannesburg–Pretoria traffic corridor and offer commuters a viable alternative to road transport. Established as a PPP between the provincial government and a private sector consortium, it is the largest such long-term contract in Africa, and the second largest PPP project of its kind in the world. (See http://www.gautrain.co.za)

Cape Action for People and the Environment (C.A.P.E.)

The primary focus of C.A.P.E. is on biodiversity and conservation. It is a programme of the South African government, with support from international donors, to protect the rich biological heritage of the Cape Floristic Region. A memorandum of understanding was signed in 2001. C.A.P.E. seeks to unlock the economic potential of land and marine resources through focused investment in the development of key resources, while conserving nature and ensuring that all people benefit. The private sector (mainly private landowners and agricultural producers) is involved in a number of conservation initiatives and stewardship programmes, and there are also affiliated programmes with business, such as the Biodiversity and Wine Initiative. (See http://www.capeaction.org.za)

Sources: Adapted from various documents and websites.

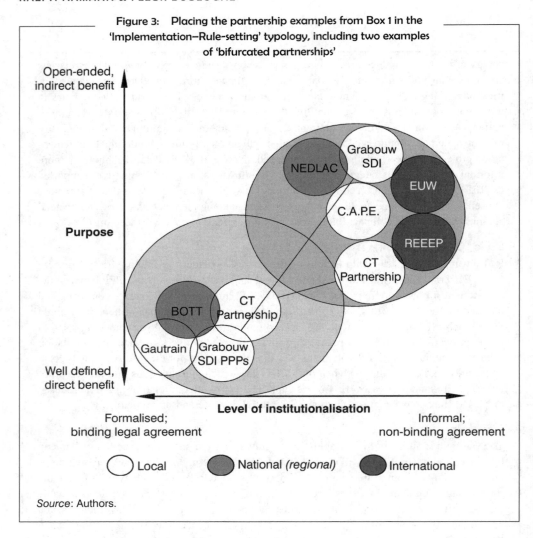

Figure 3: Placing the partnership examples from Box 1 in the 'Implementation–Rule-setting' typology, including two examples of 'bifurcated partnerships'

Source: Authors.

in the community and reduced long-term dependence of communities on the company'.[32] The key principle is 'complementary core competencies', whereby the capabilities and resources of the company are combined with those of other sectors for maximum effect, allowing each participant to concentrate on their strengths.

To take an example, if the purpose is to contribute to local economic development around a mining company's operation, the mining company should concentrate on doing what it does best, such as providing engineering services and project management skills. In the context of a partnership, these capabilities can be used to maximum effect, as they complement and are guided by the input and resources of the other partners. So, for instance, the government may provide a regional planning framework and bulk infrastructure, local communities may supply labour and building materials, and NGOs may provide expertise and external auditing. This principle is illustrated in Figure 6.

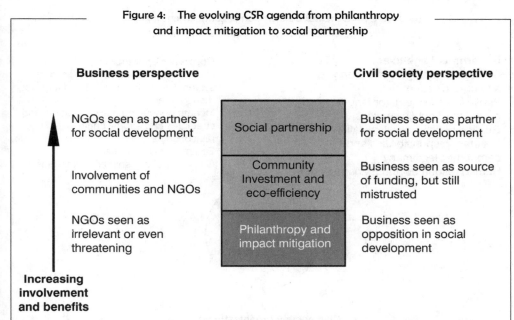

Figure 4:   The evolving CSR agenda from philanthropy
and impact mitigation to social partnership

Business perspective   **Civil society perspective**

NGOs seen as partners for social development	Social partnership	Business seen as partner for social development
Involvement of communities and NGOs	Community Investment and eco-efficiency	Business seen as source of funding, but still mistrusted
NGOs seen as irrelevant or even threatening	Philanthropy and impact mitigation	Business seen as opposition in social development

**Increasing
involvement
and benefits**

Source: R. Hamann, 'Mining Companies' Role in Sustainable Development: The "Why" and
"How" of Corporate Social Responsibility from a Business Perspective', *Development Southern Africa*, 20, 2 (2003): 237–254; adapted from Pinney (2001) and O'Riordan (2001).

Figure 5:   Progression of CSR from individual companies'
philanthropic action to collective multi-stakeholder action[31]

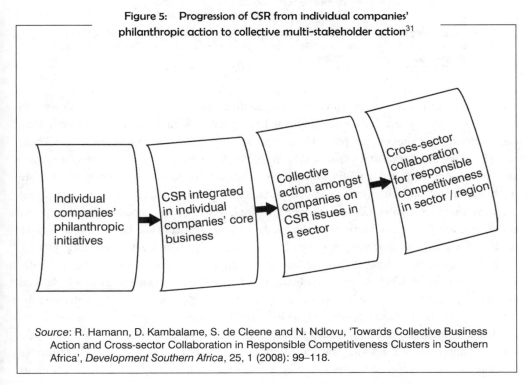

Individual companies' philanthropic initiatives

CSR integrated in individual companies' core business

Collective action amongst companies on CSR issues in a sector

Cross-sector collaboration for responsible competitiveness in sector / region

Source: R. Hamann, D. Kambalame, S. de Cleene and N. Ndlovu, 'Towards Collective Business
Action and Cross-sector Collaboration in Responsible Competitiveness Clusters in Southern
Africa', *Development Southern Africa*, 25, 1 (2008): 99–118.

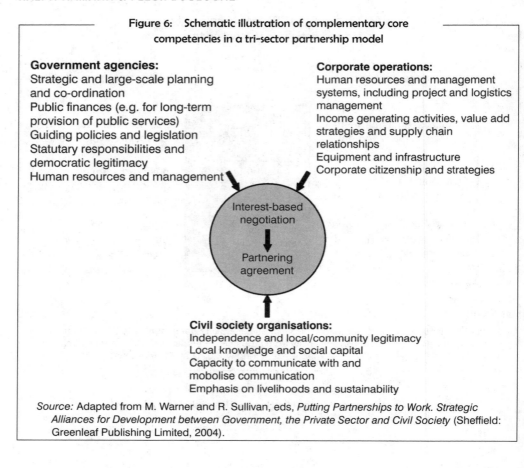

Figure 6: Schematic illustration of complementary core competencies in a tri-sector partnership model

Government agencies:
Strategic and large-scale planning and co-ordination
Public finances (e.g. for long-term provision of public services)
Guiding policies and legislation
Statutory responsibilities and democratic legitimacy
Human resources and management

Corporate operations:
Human resources and management systems, including project and logistics management
Income generating activities, value add strategies and supply chain relationships
Equipment and infrastructure
Corporate citizenship and strategies

Interest-based negotiation

Partnering agreement

Civil society organisations:
Independence and local/community legitimacy
Local knowledge and social capital
Capacity to communicate with and mobolise communication
Emphasis on livelihoods and sustainability

Source: Adapted from M. Warner and R. Sullivan, eds, *Putting Partnerships to Work. Strategic Alliances for Development between Government, the Private Sector and Civil Society* (Sheffield: Greenleaf Publishing Limited, 2004).

Case studies of tri-sector partnerships involving mining companies, government organisations and civil society suggest that – when implemented sincerely, with the necessary commitment, and in the right context – the partnership approach may have substantial benefits.[33] These include higher developmental impacts, in terms of tangible results such as infrastructure provision, training or land access, with comparatively low costs for participants. These, in turn, are likely to improve the participating company's reputation. Further, the case studies suggest that local communities involved in such partnerships are likely to be less dependent on the mining company, due to increased participation in the development process and higher levels of skills development. This is particularly important in the context of mine decommissioning. Finally, the case study authors argue that partnerships lead to improved relationships between key role-players, with higher levels of trust and better channels of communication. This is beneficial to company–community relations, since successful partnerships have arguably enhanced the company's 'social licence to operate' at the local level and diminished the risk to investment.

Box 2 summarises one of the case studies mentioned above on the implementation of a tri-sector approach to facilitating the closure of a large gold mine in Indonesia. It illustrates how the partnership approach was identified as possibly the only way to escape acrimonious

Box 2: The tri-sector partnership applied by Kelian Equatorial Mining, Indonesia

The Kelian Equatorial Mining (KEM) gold mine in East Kalimantan (owned primarily by Rio Tinto) was due to close down operations in 2004. The company understood that in order to manage the many significant and complex social and environmental issues related to mine closure, such as community dependency and dam safety, it was important to involve all relevant stakeholders, and hence it initiated a tri-sector partnership. However, early attempts to implement such a partnership were hampered by the troubled relationship between KEM and local stakeholders, which centred mainly on grievances about land compensation. It was therefore necessary first to implement a dedicated and mutually agreed upon grievance resolution process. The dispute did not need to be resolved entirely, but what was required was the initiation of a sincere and respected process that all parties believed would eventually redress their grievances. This allowed all the stakeholders to come together – guided by an external facilitator – to explore and design the partnership structure.

The result was the Mine Closure Steering Committee (MCSC), whose constitution, objectives and consensus-based decision-making rules were formalised in the MCSC Charter. Within two years, this partnership elicited the buy-in of all the relevant stakeholders and created an accountable and transparent framework for making consensus-based decisions. This allowed for the collective ownership of decisions and actions taken with respect to mine closure. This is particularly significant, considering the highly dynamic and difficult operating environment faced by the company. The case study therefore shows that partnership may be an effective, even necessary, approach in challenging circumstances, but that it cannot be implemented half-heartedly. Far-reaching commitments were required particularly from the company in order to gain the trust and buy-in from other stakeholders. Other success factors include:

- the assistance of external, trusted facilitators;
- dedication early in the process to negotiating and determining jointly agreed upon processes and decision-making principles;
- demonstrated commitment from top-level stakeholder representatives; and
- persistent dedication to involving local stakeholders and supporting stakeholder representatives in their role as intermediaries for their constituents.

Source: Adapted from R. Hamann, 'Kelian Equatorial Mining, Indonesia: Mine Closure', in M. Warner and R. Sullivan, eds, *Putting Partnerships to Work: Strategic Alliances for Development*

and damaging conflict between the company and local communities and NGOs. It also suggests key success factors, including high-level commitment and joint decision-making on the procedures and outcomes of the partnership. Implementation challenges and success factors are discussed in more detail in the next section.

Balancing power, rights and interests

Common practical challenges to the partnering process are an inadequate understanding by the potential partners' representatives of what the parties could offer each other; an unwillingness to modify or compromise; ineffective attempts to institutionalise the partnership within the participating organisations; and insufficient orientation of newcomers to the partnership.[34] Even where common interests can be identified, the partners' culture, working methods and organisational objectives are often very different. Such differences may also be apparent in the representatives of these sectors and organisations. The kind of communication between people that underlies effective partnership cannot be taken for granted.

Partnerships are no panacea. In particular, they may require certain circumstances and conditions. According to one critic, the notion of partnership assumes that 'both parties are relatively equal in their power and access to resources', an assumption that is rarely justified.[35] Others maintain that a balance of power is not necessary, arguing that the partnership need only benefit each partner more than is possible by any other means: 'The parties do not have to be equal in power – but they do have to recognise each other as capable of imposing significant costs or providing valuable benefits.'[36] Most agree, however, that partnerships cannot succeed if companies misuse their considerable financial or human resources, or their undue influence over government officials, to systematically enhance their bargaining position.

One sensitive issue here is the relationship between the company (or companies) and the state. Partnerships may be set up in circumstances where state institutions are weak; yet control, facilitation and monitoring of the partnering and development process need to be secured by the legitimacy of the state. Hence it has been argued that companies have to learn to 'lead from behind' by providing resources and building capacity for the state to play an active managerial role, while at the same time 'taking a back seat' when accepting benefits or credit.[37] This argument is illustrated in Case Study 7 in this book, and is discussed in more detail below.

More fundamentally, the critical view of corporate citizenship discussed in Chapter 1 points to the fear that partnerships may provide certain limited benefits to some civil society groups, but at the cost of obstructing more far-reaching, structural changes. In a survey of ten cases of collaboration between civil society organisations (CSOs) and businesses in Brazil, India, and South Africa, Ashman argues that 'CSOs and businesses reap mutual benefits from collaboration, but CSOs tend to shoulder more of the costs'.[38] In particular, the limited economic gains that local citizens in poor countries may gain from partnerships should not detract from the necessary political empowerment that would ensure more sustainable livelihoods.

Given these competing incentives, how should civil society engage with business? Should it oppose what it sees as corporate abuses, or should it engage in partnerships? One answer that is also instructive for companies' approach to partnership is – both! Covey and Brown propose the term 'critical cooperation' to argue that 'the possibilities of productive engagement between civil society and business are greatly expanded as we learn more about how to manage not just cooperation *or* conflict, but cooperation *and* conflict in the same relationship' (original emphasis).[39] Such relationships may occur when both parties have significant converging and conflicting interests, and when both manage to go beyond settling their disputes by means of *power* or *rights*, and design ways of negotiating on the basis of *interests*.

The concept of interest-based (or principled) negotiation was introduced by Fisher and Ury in their ground-breaking book, *Getting to Yes*. They argue that bargaining on the basis of entrenched positions does not produce optimal outcomes because more attention is paid to positions than underlying interests. It is also inefficient because opponents tend to start with extreme positions, and it strains the ongoing relationship between the parties. Their alternative – principled negotiation – requires negotiators to, inter alia, 'focus on interests, not positions', to 'invent options for mutual gain' and 'insist on objective criteria' for the process and outcomes of decision making.[40] This approach is the basis of the following four requisite conditions for partnerships:[41]

1 *Balancing power asymmetries*: Fisher and Ury interpret power as follows: 'The relative negotiating power of two parties depends primarily upon how attractive to each is the option of not reaching agreement.'[42] Identifying and developing the Best Alternative to a Negotiated Agreement, or BATNA, will help potential partners decide when collaboration with other parties is advantageous. That is, collaboration should only be pursued if it will provide benefits greater than would be gained by alternative strategies. Identifying these strategies and understanding their implications will thus improve the negotiating position of each partner, especially the weaker ones. This may mean taking into account not only negotiation based on common interests but also strategies involving rights and power (see Figure 7).

2 *Acknowledging critical rights*: Critical rights need to be explicitly acknowledged by all parties in order for the negotiation to find solutions that go beyond statutory requirements. In some instances, the threat of litigation may be an important negotiation tactic for civil society groups. Such options are part of the 'objective criteria' that facilitate the choice of options independent of the will of either of the negotiating parties.[43] These criteria should be based on a shared or agreed set of norms and standards for process (procedural rights) and outcomes (substantive rights). All parties must therefore be clear about, and agree upon the objectives and procedures for their interaction.

3 *Negotiating both converging and conflicting interests*: Interest-based negotiation is premised on the goal of finding creative solutions that respond to underlying interests, and these need to be identified and made explicit by the negotiating parties. An awareness of each party's interests makes it possible to identify 'options for mutual gain'. However, negotiations should not only emphasise the search for shared interests. Making conflicting interests explicit allows for a better understanding of the partnership in the context of the ongoing relationship between the parties, and this includes a continuing appraisal of whether the partnership is benefiting each participant's interests.

4 *Managing relations with stakeholder constituencies*: The negotiators need to bear in mind and be responsive to the interests and perspectives of their stakeholder constituencies. This is especially important where there has been a history of conflict or mistrust between civil society and business, or where stakeholder groups are characterised

by much diversity. Managing conflict *within* stakeholder groups is therefore a crucial component of managing conflict *between* groups. This issue of the internal accountability of partners and is discussed in more detail below.

Evaluating partnerships

Evaluation criteria

Broadly speaking, there are two overarching, interrelated criteria for evaluating partnerships: effectiveness and accountability. Effectiveness is an instrumental measure for assessing whether partnerships achieve what they are established to achieve, and whether they do so in a cost-effective manner. It takes into consideration the opportunity costs – that is, it compares the effectiveness of a partnership with the effectiveness of achieving its objectives by alternative means, if indeed there are any. Accountability is a political and procedural measure for ensuring that partnerships are fair and inclusive. Partnerships need to be accountable to those affected by them, particularly the poorest and most vulnerable.

Effectiveness and accountability are interrelated because the latter also involves accounting for a partnership's broader impacts (as discussed in more detail below), and because the former is hypothetically dependent on the latter. So for instance, Zadek and Radovich suggest: 'Improved governance and accountability of partnerships enhances performance, and governance aligned to accountability to those impacted by partnerships will enhance development outcomes.'[44]

There are two levels at which a particular partnership may be evaluated. The first is from the perspective of a partner organisation. Here the focus is probably on the effectiveness criterion. Such an evaluation is likely to take the form of a cost-benefit analysis.[45] Assessing benefits means looking at the extent to which the organisation's explicit and implicit objectives for the partnership are being or have been achieved, as well as ancillary or unexpected benefits, including increases in knowledge and social capital, and improved reputation. The costs may include the financial and in-kind contributions to the partnership, staff costs, and possible negative effects on reputation, or broader sustainable development indicators, especially if the partnership does not go as planned. Also to be considered are the opportunity costs, as mentioned above.

The second level of evaluation is of the partnership itself. At this level, the key measure of effectiveness is the impact of the initiative as a whole. Here a significant body of experience and literature on development impact evaluation can be drawn on. For a start, such an evaluation ought to consider the extent to which the explicit objectives of the partnership have been achieved or are likely to be achieved. How far this is feasible will, of course, depend on how clearly and explicitly the objectives are defined. Hodge and Greve point out that 'vague partnership goals are typical'.[46] The 'implementation' type of partnership discussed above is by definition more likely to have tangible and clearly defined objectives, so impact evaluation in these cases is likely to be a more exact science. To evaluate partnerships focused on rule-setting and advocacy, it may be necessary to include an appraisal of the partnership's *outcomes* (such as organisational commitments) and *outputs* (such as changes in behaviour), as intermediary steps towards assessing actual *impacts* or goal attainment.[47]

Figure 7:   A strategic approach to partnerships*

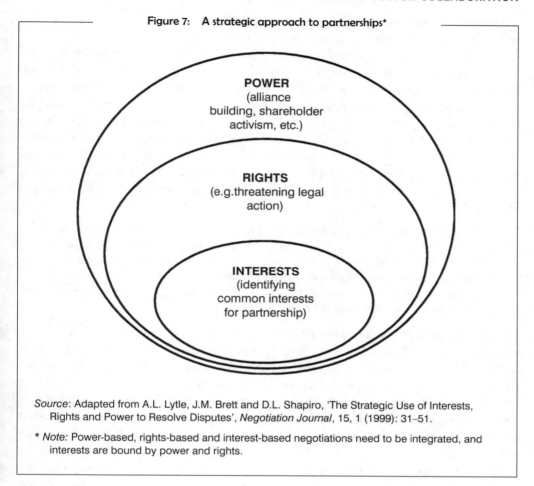

Source: Adapted from A.L. Lytle, J.M. Brett and D.L. Shapiro, 'The Strategic Use of Interests, Rights and Power to Resolve Disputes', *Negotiation Journal*, 15, 1 (1999): 31–51.

* *Note:* Power-based, rights-based and interest-based negotiations need to be integrated, and interests are bound by power and rights.

Of course, in assessing impacts it is necessary to consider not just how far the partnership's objectives are or are likely to be achieved, but also ancillary or unintended, possibly negative, outcomes. In short, the broader impact of the partnership needs to be assessed not just with regard to the objectives of the initiative and the partners involved, but also with the broader, universally agreed principles and standards of sustainable development (as codified in various international agreements, such as Agenda 21 and the Universal Declaration of Human Rights).

The challenge here is that the partnership may be assessed on the basis of issues that were not explicitly on its agenda. For instance, parties involved in a partnership focused on biodiversity conservation may resent being criticised for its unintended (and unconsidered) effects on the livelihoods of farm-workers. However, given the overarching objective of facilitating partnerships for sustainable development, and also because of the involvement of public bodies and finances in such initiatives, some measure of integrated, transparent and universally agreed upon appraisal will be crucial. A related challenge is the need to evaluate a partnership in terms of its opportunity cost. However, in the light of the discussion above that identified partnerships as a response to various governance gaps – particularly in the case of rule-setting and advocacy partnerships – it is often unclear whether there are in fact feasible alternatives, so this may be an unrealistic expectation with regard to evaluation.

If a partnership initiative demonstrates that it is effectively solving the problems it set out to solve, then this is a crucial contribution to what political scientists call its 'output-oriented' legitimacy.[48] Explicitly demonstrating this problem-solving capability is what Benner *et al.* refer to as a partnership's 'accountability for outcomes'.[49] In this view, effectiveness and accountability are directly linked. However, there are other elements of accountability that add important evaluative criteria. Benner *et al.* define these as the accountability of the *actors* involved in a partnership, on the one hand, and the accountability of the partnership *process*, on the other. Both of these depend on peer pressure, public reputation, market incentives, and financial agreements or contractual arrangements. Regarding *actor* accountability, Benner *et al.* argue that

> Networks can only be as legitimate as the actors involved. If the actors in networks do not live up to basic criteria of accountability and transparency, the network itself cannot either. Therefore it is of foremost importance to ensure the individual accountability of participants in networks. In this context peer accountability and public reputational accountability are the most important mechanisms… Transparency is key here. Internal procedures and structures have to be open to scrutiny.[50]

Most organisations involved in partnerships have some kind of organisational accountability measures in place. These are most explicit, in principle at least, in the case of government organisations. Organisational accountability in the case of private sector companies was discussed at some length in Chapter 1 with reference to initiatives such as the Global Reporting Initiative (GRI). Although, traditionally, civil society organisations have been less targeted on accountability issues, they are increasingly expected to enhance their own levels of internal accountability, as illustrated, for instance, by the development of a dedicated NGO-focused set of GRI guidelines.[51]

It is reasonable to expect well-established organisations to have formal accountability structures and to put out regular reports, but obviously less reasonable to expect these of poor or fledgling NGOs or community-based organisations that become involved in partnerships. As the example of the partnership in Indonesia (Box 2) showed, in such cases the proactive support of civil society or community groups by more established organisations may be crucial for making the partnership work. Such support should focus on building internal accountability mechanisms, through which, for example, community representatives are enabled and required to engage directly with their constituency. For the other partners, this is important because it will enhance the effectiveness of the partnership (through improved information exchange) and its legitimacy (through improved buy-in from the affected local constituencies).

Process accountability refers to the procedural aspects of the partnership and the extent to which they are transparent to the initiative's stakeholders and the broader public. Transparency is – again – the key requirement that will catalyse the accountability forces of peer pressure, reputation, market incentives, and financial or legal commitments. For a start, this pertains to how participants in a partnership are identified and selected, and whether the criteria used are openly defined and consistently applied. It also applies to how decisions are made within the partnership and the extent to which each partner's commitment is communicated to a broader audience. In effect, a partnership can be seen as a new organisational form to which many of the accountability measures developed for corporations – stakeholder engagement and sustainability reporting, for instance – also apply.

Evaluations of PPPs

The existing evaluations of partnerships are generally focused on either PPPs or MSPs, as defined above (though it needs to be borne in mind that some commentators use the term PPP broadly, in a manner that includes our definition of MSP). On the basis of an extensive review of the literature on PPPs, Hodge and Greve argue that they have been 'the subject of much rhetorical assessment and commentary' but 'evidence on cost and quality gains for techniques such as the [UK private finance initiatives] seems limited', despite the significant financial commitments involved.[52] This predominance of rhetoric over evidence supports the concern that partnerships, and in particular PPPs, involve a 'language game' through which their proponents seek a veiled, legitimated adoption of strategies that have become unpopular, particularly those closely related to previous privatisation attempts.

So, for instance, the early claim that PPPs would make public services cheaper for the public sector has been discredited. Apart from those arrangements where users are charged (such as toll roads), the ultimate financial liability generally remains with the public sector, though PPPs do make possible smaller payments over a longer time frame. The more important claim – that PPPs provide better value for money than traditional procurement methods – has been supported by a number of studies of the UK experience, but the general, international experience suggests a more mixed and controversial picture. Hodge and Greve use particular examples to suggest that PPPs favour the private partner at the expense of the public sector and citizens (though PPPs in particular sectors, such as road infrastructure, seem less problematic than those in others, such as IT and education). Not only is the effectiveness of PPPs in achieving their objectives variable, there are also concerns about accountability, with the transparency of PPPs limited by high deal complexity, opaque agreements, confidentiality clauses, and the ability of private parties to make strategic threats of bankruptcy in order to diminish or compensate for their risks:

> Governance risks appear to have increased with PPPs... the unavailability of project economic evaluations, the fact that most deals are two-way affairs between government and business without explicitly including citizens, the length of time governments can tie up future governments, the apparent willingness to protect investor returns rather than the public interest, the lack of clarity of commercial arrangements, and the desire of governments to proceed with hasty project construction for political purposes all appear to contribute to this conclusion.[53]

A factor that is perhaps underconsidered in the literature is the way PPPs may contribute to corruption and patronage. In order to prevent corruption and ensure that PPPs do, indeed, represent the public interest throughout their lifespan, the relevant government organisation (be it at local, provincial or national level) needs to have significant capacity in place to define the PPP objectives, identify partners, design the contract and monitor performance, among other things. As noted, PPP contracts are likely to be very complex, particularly because the diverse risk profiles of the partners need to be responded to effectively.

In many African countries this leads to a dilemma because, on the one hand, PPPs are suggested as a way the private sector can help the public sector provide public services, but on the other hand a well-capacitated government is crucial if PPPs are to be effective and accountable. Government efforts to support the identification and implementation of PPPs thus deserve considered attention. In South Africa, for instance, the government has followed the UK example and has established a dedicated PPP Unit in the Treasury. On the basis of existing legislation it has developed a regulatory framework and guidelines for PPPs that are much respected and have been used as a model for other developing countries in Africa and beyond.

The South African experience is thus of some interest to the rest of Africa, particularly with regard to the following points.[54] First, while the PPP Unit's requirements for PPPs are well respected, there are concerns that they are too complex and onerous, with the result that relatively few PPPs are gaining regulatory approval. It is difficult to achieve a balance between regulatory rigour and the need to adapt to local circumstances. One of the PPP Unit's responses to this is to develop a set of process-oriented decision-making guidelines to help municipalities – the key protagonists of many infrastructure PPPs, in particular – comply with the regulatory requirements. These guidelines are also meant to ensure that PPPs are seen as but one of a range of options for public service delivery, and that their feasibility in a particular instance is compared to these other options. The emphasis is hence on PPPs as a means to an end – i.e. effective service delivery – as opposed to seeing them as an end in themselves. However, the PPP Unit itself has been criticised in this regard, because it simultaneously fulfils a regulatory function and advocates for the increased adoption of PPPs as an implementation mechanism, which leads to potential conflicts of interest.[55]

A further point commonly emphasised in the South African debate is the crucial need for improved skills and knowledge about PPP related issues among representatives of the public and private sectors, as well as civil society. The complexity of PPP contracts, for instance, was mentioned above, and this means that the relevant government officials should not only have special legal and financial skills but also a broad understanding of the partners' strategic objectives and operating mechanisms. It is often noted that public and private sector organisations have different organisational cultures, and there is also much distrust between them, so an ability to transcend these cultural divides seems a likely condition for designing and implementing effective and accountable partnerships. Indeed, PPPs have been likened to marriages in need of continued counselling – necessitating particular skills in interest-based negotiation and trust building. Even in large, formal PPPs, in which legal considerations play a dominant role, the success of the partnership is likely to depend on the quality of the underlying relationships and the trust between the parties.

Evaluations of MSPs

Whereas the above section focused on PPPs which involve formal contracts and usually focus on infrastructure or service delivery, this section is a brief overview of existing evaluations of the more informal MSPs that are predisposed to rule-setting and advocacy. As noted above, some of the most prominent MSPs are the 'Type 2' agreements that emanated from the WSSD in Johannesburg in 2002. A recent official UN overview of these initiatives focuses on 'progress in implementation within the broad categories of partnership building / coordination, capacity-building activities, information sharing and pilot projects',[56] but it provides hardly any information about performance as measured against the wider sustainability objectives these partnerships are meant to achieve.

Another study has shown that most Type 2 initiatives are predominantly financed by governments (comprising over 83% of total funding), with only 1% of total finances coming from the private sector (despite there being a sizable role for business in their public relations material).[57] This dominant role for northern governments in particular in Type 2 initiatives contributes to their particular character, with some analysts bemoaning the 'almost invisible... southern civil society involvement'.[58]

With regard to MSPs more broadly, there is a range of assessments, depending also on the particular focus of the evaluation in question, in terms of partnership types, scales and industry sectors. Even if evaluations are broadly focused on similar types of initiatives, the differing samples may well give rise to contradictory assessments. So on the one hand, for instance, an overview of case studies of local level tri-sector partnerships in the extractives industries concludes that such partnerships 'can, under the right conditions, yield better results for communities and for business than alternative approaches to community development'.[59] Arguably, however, this particular sample is skewed towards the explicit objective of demonstrating the value of partnerships – indeed, this quest for 'best practice' examples of MSPs is a common constraint of many existing evaluation exercises.

On the other hand, some studies have contributed to growing scepticism about the effectiveness and accountability of MSPs, broadly speaking. A survey of MSPs in South Africa in 2004, for instance, found that many of the initiatives surveyed were struggling to become institutionalised in a manner that would lead to tangible actions and outcomes.[60] A common concern was that the participants in such initiatives did not share a similar understanding of the objectives or mechanisms of the partnership, and levels of organisational and personal commitment were diverse and variable. A key constraint was the inability to raise funds to sustain the partnership and its activities. In other studies, the financially more powerful position of the business partners leads to their dominating the initiative. For instance, in a study of 10 collaborative initiatives between businesses and civil society organisations, it was found that the latter 'shoulder more of the costs [and] business can dominate collaborative decision-making, with negative results for sustainability'.[61]

This challenge of financial sustainability in MSPs is a recurring concern, leading some to approach partnerships with an explicit emphasis on identifying entrepreneurial links to markets and supply chains. So, for instance, the International Union for the Conservation of Nature (IUCN) and others established the Seed Initiative, or Supporting Entrepreneurs for Environment and Development. Most of the successful partnerships supported by this initiative 'rely on a mix of sources for financing their activities' based on 'innovative and flexible business models that combine the working methods of the private sector and non-governmental organisations'.[62] Nevertheless the most pressing challenge for many initiatives involved in the Seed Initiative remains financial support, and other hurdles it faces are the diverse operating and reporting requirements across the private and non-governmental sectors, and the way investment and grant programmes commonly focus on either business or non-profit projects.

Assessing the impact of partnerships of course becomes more complex at larger scales of analysis, often leading to an even greater emphasis on their *outputs* and *outcomes*, rather than *impacts*. This is perhaps most evident in the opposing assessments of one of the most prominent corporate citizenship initiatives, the UN Global Compact (described in more detail in Chapter 1), a key criticism of which has been that 'there is no assessment mechanism (just corporate self-reports)'.[63] A more optimistic appraisal notes that the Global Compact can play a particularly important role in developing countries such as Malawi and Mozambique, where it is often the first systematic introduction to CSR issues for local role-players and where it can provide a crucial convening platform for cross-sector collaboration at the national level.[64]

MSPs involving the United Nations have been subject to particular controversy. In a wide-ranging review of the literature, Jens Martens argues that the following risks, among others, require careful consideration in such partnerships, and indeed they deserve consideration also in partnerships more broadly, in addition to the points made above:[65]

- There is a danger that partnerships allow companies – in particular multinational corporations – undue influence on political agenda-setting and decision-making. This could be part of a broader trend in which elites increase their influence on governance at the expense of representative democracy.[66] The legitimacy of government organisations (at the local, national or international level) involved in partnerships may also be at risk if some of the other partners are implicated in human rights or environmental abuses.

- Partnerships can distort competition because companies may become partners through an uncompetitive process and can thereafter enjoy unfair advantages, including reputation benefits, access to markets, and influence on government policy. In general, the selection of partners is often based on the discretion of the initiators and their pragmatic considerations and existing relationships. This limits the extent to which they can claim to be truly representative.

- The proliferation of partnerships that focus on particular issues and often emphasise "quick win" solutions may contribute to a fragmented and piecemeal response to sustainable development challenges, instead of more coordinated, comprehensive, and long-term responses. This is also a concern because many partnerships are established and promoted as a replacement for government action, in contrast to the UN guidelines that emphasise that they should rather be complementary.

An overview of the partnership case studies in this book

It should be noted first that partnership is of course also an important feature in many of the case studies in Sections 1 and 3 of Part 2. Among the human rights related case studies, for example, there are the efforts by AngloGold Ashanti (discussed in Case 2, Section 1) to set up, support and participate in a local stakeholder committee that facilitates joint decision-making about local community development in the vicinity of the prospective mine (in a context of lingering mistrust). Such partnership initiatives focused on local community development are increasingly common in the extractives sector and they are also dealt with in the case study of the Magadi Soda Company (Case 8).

Various aspects of partnership are also evident in the case studies in Section 3, on new business models. This is explicitly so in the study of HP's i-Community initiative in South Africa (Case 11), which was labelled a PPP and also illustrated some of the key issues mentioned above, such as the risks arising from a dominant role for the private sector in designing and implementing the partnership. Another, more positive example is that of Honey Care Africa (Case 14), which thrives on a business model that is premised on an innovative partnership between itself, international development agencies and local communities.

This theme of entrepreneurial partnership is most directly dealt with in the case study of women entrepreneurs in Zanzibar (Case 6), which describes the various impediments to women starting their own small-scale businesses and emphasises the role that informal social networks can play in overcoming some of these obstacles. Supporting such small-scale entrepreneurs was identified by a group of international development and conservation agencies as an important mechanism for simultaneously supporting economic development and more sustainable livelihoods and conserving Zanzibar's threatened biodiversity. These efforts were able to tap into social networks among Zanzibari women in support of small-scale enterprises in handicrafts and agriculture, most directly in the form of collective savings and credit groups.

Although the Zanzibar case study considers the role of formal companies only tangentially (making brief reference to some of the local hotels, for instance), it is a useful point of departure in this set of partnership case studies because it illustrates the crucial role of local ownership in the design and implementation of partnership objectives and mechanisms. It also illustrates the role that small-scale entrepreneurs can play as equals in partnerships. Though the international agencies and the government made significant contributions to the process – facilitating market access, capacity building and policy changes – they did not determine the pace of the process, thereby allowing the women cooperatives to identify and implement changes 'that work for them'. The initiatives described in this case study are characterised by a fairly well defined set of overall objectives, but a simultaneous open-endedness with regard to how they are to be achieved. The key participants – i.e. the women cooperatives – have important informal institutions but comparatively few formal, legal arrangements. These characteristics are tentatively represented in the case study's position in Figure 8.

The case study on mining companies in the Rustenburg area in South Africa (Case 7) is situated in a very different milieu. The key protagonists here are the three largest platinum mining companies in the world, and the focus is on their efforts to enhance collaboration among themselves and with other key role-players in the region: the local government, the traditional authority and local community-based organisations. Despite these companies' resources, however, effective and accountable collaboration remains elusive, and the case study's main purpose is to show how difficult and intractable collaboration can be in particular circumstances, even when there is broad agreement that it is necessary. For a start, the companies' managements have long denied any responsibility for the social problems around the mines, exemplified by the informal settlements (so-called squatter camps), which have severe social, environmental, health and security problems. Only relatively recently have the company managers and other role-players acknowledged a shared responsibility for these settlements, motivated also by the realisation that only a collaborative approach has any hope of success. The case study thus demonstrates that sometimes significant groundwork is necessary to ensure that key role-players recognise the need for and make a decisive commitment to collaboration.

The Rustenburg study also shows how the scope for partnerships is affected by the broader institutional context. Over and above lingering mistrust between the mining companies and local communities, for instance, the Rustenburg area is characterised by significant tension between the local government and the traditional authority. Indeed, such tensions are a feature

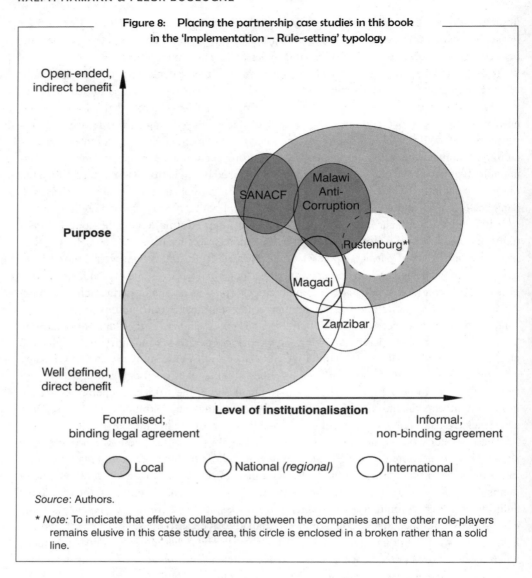

Figure 8: Placing the partnership case studies in this book in the 'Implementation – Rule-setting' typology

Source: Authors.

* *Note:* To indicate that effective collaboration between the companies and the other role-players remains elusive in this case study area, this circle is enclosed in a broken rather than a solid line.

in many parts of Africa, and may well confront company managers who seek collaborative approaches to local development problems.[67] The study suggests that such challenges require that the broader local governance system be the subject of collaborative action, with an important role for the private sector to 'lead from behind'.

The case study on Magadi Soda Company in Kenya (Case 8) illustrates the way collaborative approaches to local challenges can benefit both the company and the local community – it is thus an effective counterpoint to the Rustenburg case study, though admittedly the Rustenburg context is more complex in that it involves more role-players and a larger area. The Magadi case describes the progressive shifts in corporate strategy from a paternalistic approach to a more consultative one, premised on a structured process of community engagement. This, in turn, led to a more integrated approach to local governance, predicated upon the needs of the community rather than those of the company. These shifts have produced benefits for the company as well, including lower transaction costs and improved reputation. Like the Zanzibar case, this case demonstrates the crucial role of local ownership of partnership objectives and decision-making.

Cases 9 and 10 are similar to each other, but rather different to the preceding three. Both are about collaborative approaches to fighting corruption at the national level. Corruption is a key example of challenges that require a collaborative approach. As noted in the Malawi case study, since corruption is a team sport, fighting corruption must involve a team effort. Both case studies illustrate the importance of generating sufficient commitment to the initiatives among key role-players, especially business leaders – and the difficulty of doing so. This also highlights the need for effective associations to represent and advocate among the business community – hence one of the key constraints in the early stages of the South African National Anti-Corruption Forum was the absence of a business association that represented all companies in the country. Sufficient buy-in from business leaders is also crucial because – in the language of game theory – a threshold number of participants needs to commit to the agreements with a view to obtaining their long-term benefits, even if this means accepting short-term disadvantages. Otherwise there will be too many defectors motivated by the short-term benefits of defection (in this case, obtaining contracts through corrupt means, for example) and the initiative will fail.

There are also some important parallels between these two anti-corruption initiatives and Cases 7 and 8 on the efforts of mining companies in local community development. All four cases illustrate companies' incentives to contribute to improved governance, whether at the local or the national level, and they show how collaborative approaches are likely to be the only feasible and effective way to deal with such challenges.

To conclude, Figure 8 suggests how most of the case studies included in this book could be characterised primarily by relatively informal forms of institutionalisation. In other words, there are no binding contracts making participants accountable. They thus do not represent the full spectrum of possible partnership types provided for in Figure 2. However, the anti-corruption initiatives are notable for their relatively detailed memoranda of understanding or statements of principle, through which they seek to engage participants in the long-term collaboration 'game' alluded to above. The Zanzibar case, meanwhile, involves relatively few formal agreements, but there is much reliance on informal institutions. All in all, the case studies in this book suggest that diversity and complexity are defining characteristics of partnerships and local context plays a crucial role. To understand the diversity, complexity and context-specific nature of partnerships, more research is called for to consider a larger number of initiatives across the spectrum of purpose, institutionalisation and geographical scale.

Notes

1   We are grateful to Vanessa Sannier for insightful comments on an earlier draft of this chapter.
2   Quoted in Business Partners for Development, *Putting Partnering to Work* (London: Business Partners for Development, 2002), 9.

3   C. Huxham and S. Vangen, 'Leadership in the Shaping and Implementation of Collaboration Agendas: How Things Happen in a (Not Quite) Joined-up World', *Academy of Management Journal*, 43, 6 (2000): 1159–1175.

4   PPPs have been defined as 'cooperation of some sort of durability between public and private actors in which they jointly develop products and services and share risks, costs, and resources which are connected with these products': see H. van Ham and J. Koppenjan, 'Building Public-Private Partnerships: Assessing and Managing Risks in Port Development', *Public Management Review*, 4, 1 (2001), 598.

5   I. Kaul, 'Exploring the Policy Space between Markets and States: Global Public Private Partnerships', in I. Kaul and P. Conceicao, eds, *The New Public Finance* (Oxford: Oxford University Press, 2006), 222, quoted in J. Martens, *Multistakeholder Partnerships – Future Models of Multilateralism?* (Berlin: Friedrich-Ebert-Stiftung, 2007), 20. Note that these characteristics were described with a focus on partnerships with global scope, but in our view they are also relevant to partnerships that are active at smaller scales.

6   T. Benner, W.H. Reinicke and J. Martin Witte, 'Multisectoral Networks in Global Governance: Towards a Pluralistic System of Accountability', *Government and Opposition*, 39, 2 (2004): 191–210; J.G. Ruggie, 'The Theory and Practice of Learning Networks: Corporate Social Responsibility and the Global Compact', *Journal of Corporate Citizenship*, 5 (2002): 27–36.

7   See for example S. Zadek and S. Radovich, *Governing Collaborative Governance: Enhancing Development Outcomes by Improving Partnership Governance and Accountability* (Cambridge, MA: John F. Kennedy School of Government, Harvard University, 2006), 5.

8   G.A. Hodge and C. Greve, 'Public-Private Partnerships: An International Performance Review', *Public Administration Review*, (May/June 2007): 545–558.

9   Ibid.

10 Martens, *Multistakeholder Partnerships*, 20.

11 Business Partners for Development, *Putting Partnering to Work*, 8.

12 On the benefits of the partnership approach to corporate protagonists, see Ibid; also R. Hamann, 'Mining Companies' Role in Sustainable Development: The 'Why' and 'How' of Corporate Social Responsibility from a Business Perspective', *Development Southern Africa*, 20, 2 (2003): 237–254; M. Warner and R. Sullivan, eds, *Putting Partnerships to Work. Strategic Alliances for Development between Government, the Private Sector and Civil Society* (Sheffield: Greenleaf Publishing Limited, 2004); and A. Warhurst, 'Corporate Citizenship and Corporate Social Investment: Drivers of Tri-Sector Partnerships', *Journal of Corporate Citizenship*, 1 (2001): 57–73.

13 See R.A.W. Rhodes, *Understanding Governance. Policy Networks, Governance, Reflexivity and Accountability* (Buckingham: Open University Press, 1997).

14 The term 'new governance' is defined in R.A.W. Rhodes, 'New Governance: Governing without Government', *Political Studies*, 44, 4 (1996): 652–667; it is applied in the context of corporate citizenship in J. Moon, 'Business Social Responsibility and New Governance', *Government and Opposition*, 37, 3 (2002): 385-408. 'Collaborative governance' is a term discussed in J.D. Donahue, *On Collaborative Governance* (Massachusetts: Harvard University, 2004). Related terms include 'multi-layered governance' and 'network governance'. For the former, see J.A. Scholte, 'Globalisation, Governance, and Corporate Citizenship', *Journal of Corporate Citizenship*, 1 (2001): 15 –23; for the latter see Ruggie, 'The Theory and Practice'.

15 P. Utting, *Business Responsibility for Sustainable Development* (Geneva: United Nations Research Institute for Social Development, 2000), 6.

16 Benner *et al.,* 'Multisectoral Networks', 193.

17 Intergenerational equity is a crucial aspect of sustainable development, in that – according to the famous Brundtland definition – sustainable development 'meets the needs of the present without compromising the ability of future generations to meet their own needs'. See United Nations Report of the World Commission on Environment and Development: General Assembly Resolution 42/187, 11 December 1987.

18 Ibid., 194.

19   See, for instance, P. Carmody, 'Between Globalisation and (Post) Apartheid: the Political Economy of Restructuring in South Africa', *Journal of Southern African Studies*, 28, 2 (2002): 255–275; and Scholte, 'Globalisation, Governance, and Corporate Citizenship'.

20   W. Sachs, *Rio+10 and the North-South Divide* (Berlin: Heinrich Boell Stiftung, 2001).

21   For instance, Jens Martens mentions the implementation and funding gap in global governance: governments often struggle to implement policies or agreements, because of a lack of know-how, tools, financial resources or political will. See Martens, *Multistakeholder Partnerships,* 33.

22   Benner *et al.*, 'Multisectoral Networks', 195.

23   Zadek and Radovich, *Governing Collaborative Governance*, 2.

24   Martens, *Multistakeholder Partnerships*, 62.

25   Ibid., 21.

26   Zadek and Radovich, *Governing Collaborative Governance*, 9.

27   These axes closely resemble concepts and diagrams developed by Darian Stibbe of The Partnering Initiative at the International Business Leaders Forum (personal communication), see http://thepart-neringinitiative.org

28   For a similar two-pronged typology, see Benner *et al.*, 'Multisectoral Networks'. Paul Kapelus (personal communication) also describes these two broad types, referring to the first as 'soft' and the second as 'hard'.

29   The South African Treasury notes, for instance, 'South African law defines a PPP as a contract between a public sector institution/municipality and a private party, in which the private party assumes substantial financial, technical and operational risk in the design, financing, building and operation of a project'. See http://www.ppp.gov.za

30   Staying with the South African experience, PPPs have become quite prominent in particular areas (especially in infrastructure projects), with significant support from the government. For instance, the Finance minister, Trevor Manuel is quoted as commending PPPs because, 'the public gets better more cost-effective services; the private sector gets new business opportunities – both are in the interests of the nation'. See http://www.engineeringnews.co.za/eng/features/ppp/?show=69403. This is part of an international trend: 'We are certainly now drowning in promises by governments around the world that PPPs will provide public sector services more cheaply and quickly, with reduced pressure on government budgets'. See Hodge and Greve, 'Public-Private Partnerships', 549.

31   R. Hamann, D. Kambalame, S. de Cleene and N. Ndlovu, 'Towards Collective Business Action and Cross-sector Collaboration in Responsible Competitiveness Clusters in Southern Africa', *Development Southern Africa*, 25, 1 (2008, forthcoming).

32   Warner and Sullivan, *Putting Partnerships to Work*, 17.

33   Business Partners for Development, *Putting Partnering to Work*, 3.

34   Ibid.,16.

35   S.B. Banerjee, 'Corporate Citizenship and Indigenous Stakeholders: Exploring a New Dynamic of Organisational-Stakeholder Relationships', *Journal of Corporate Citizenship*, 1 (2000), 45.

36   J. Covey and L.D. Brown, *Critical Cooperation: An Alternative Form of Civil Society – Business Engagement* (Boston: Institute for Development Research, 2001), 8.

37   Paul Kapelus (personal communication); see also R. Hamann, D. Sonnenberg, A. Mackenzie, P. Kapelus and P. Hollesen, 'Local Governance as Complex System: Lessons from Mining in South Africa, Mali, and Zambia', *Journal of Corporate Citizenship*, 18 (2005): 61–73.

38   D. Ashman, 'Civil Society Collaboration with Business: Bringing Empowerment Back in', *World Development*, 29, 7 (2001), 1097.

39   Covey and Brown, *Critical Cooperation*.

40   R. Fisher, and W. Ury, *Getting to Yes: Negotiating Agreement without Giving in* (Boston: Houghton Mifflin Company, 1981), 11–12.

41   Covey and Brown, *Critical Cooperation*.

42   Fisher and Ury, *Getting to Yes*, 106.

43   Ibid.

44 Zadek and Radovich, *Governing Collaborative Governance*, 4. See also Benner *et al.*, 'Multisectoral Networks'.

45 The basic outline of such a cost benefit analysis is well summarised in diagrams provided by Darian Stibbe (personal communication).

46 Hodge and Greve, 'Public-Private Partnerships', 548.

47 For an application of these different categories of development impact evaluation in the context of corporate citizenship and partnerships, see L. Rieth, M. Zimmer, R. Hamann and J. Hanks, 'The UN Global Compact in Sub-Sahara Africa: Decentralisation and Effectiveness', *Journal of Corporate Citizenship*, 28 (2007).

48 F. Scharpf, *Governing in Europe: Effective and Democratic?* (Oxford: Oxford University Press, 1999), 2.

49 Benner *et al.*, 'Multisectoral Networks', 204.

50 Ibid., 200–201. Note that Benner *et al.* are referring particularly to what they call global 'multisectoral public policy networks' – in terms of organisational form, these are generally akin to what we have characterised as 'rule-setting / advocacy' networks in the previous section – but the points they make about accountability are nevertheless appropriate to a broader range of initiatives.

51 See http://www.globalreporting.org

52 Hodge and Greve, 'Public-Private Partnerships', 549.

53 Ibid.

54 These points are based on a number of interviews conducted with diverse informants during 2007, as well as participation in various workshops.

55 Note that this is not just a South African concern, but has been highlighted in places such as the UK as well. See for example Hodge and Greve, 'Public-Private Partnerships'.

56 United Nations, Partnerships for Sustainable Development: Report of the Secretary-General (New York: United Nations, 2006), 1.

57 T.N Hale and D.L. Mauzerall, 'Thinking Globally and Acting Locally: Can the Johannesburg Partnerships Coordinate Action on Sustainable Development?', *Journal of Environment & Development*, 13, 3 (2004): 220–239.

58 A. Steward, and T. Gray, 'The Authenticity of "Type Two" Multi-stakeholder Partnerships for Water and Sanitation in Africa: When is a Stakeholder a Partner?', *Environmental Politics*, 15, 3 (2006), 375.

59 Warner and Sullivan, *Putting Partnerships to Work*, 262.

60 African Institute of Corporate Citizenship, *A Preliminary Audit of Tri-Sector Partnerships in South Africa* (Report prepared for the South African Department of Environmental Affairs and Tourism, 2004).

61 Ashman, 'Civil Society Collaboration with Business', 1097.

62 J. Steets, *The Seed Initiative Partnership Report 2006* (Gland: The Seed Initiative, 2006), 7.

63 A. Chatterji and D. Levine, 'Breaking Down the Wall of Codes: Evaluating Non-Financial Performance Measurement', *California Management Review*, 48, 2 (2006), 32.

64 Rieth *et al.*, 'The UN Global Compact in Sub-Sahara Africa'.

65 Martens, *Multistakeholder Partnerships*.

66 It is worth considering the caveat, however, that 'it is the existing degree of democracy... against which [public policy] networks should be evaluated': see Benner et al., 'Multisectoral Networks', 206. On the other hand, critics may retort that increasing reliance on partnerships may pre-empt the progressive realisation of more democratic forms of governance.

67 See, for instance, Hamann *et al.*, 'Local Governance as Complex System'.

Alternative approaches
to reaching the bottom of the pyramid

COURTENAY SPRAGUE[1]

> All of us are prisoners of our own socialization. The lenses through which we perceive the world are colored by our own ideology, experiences, and established management practices.[2]

Chapter 4 has two chief aims. First, C. K. Prahalad's framework for tackling the problem of poverty will be considered against the backdrop of the dominant approach to addressing this phenomenon. Second, the findings of a set of six field-based case studies will be explored. This chapter will articulate where our case conclusions differ from Prahalad's vision of the perceived role and motivations of multinational firms. It will, at the same time, reveal the limits of corporate social responsibility for Bottom of the Pyramid (BOP) enterprises. The chapter's main thesis is this: Prahalad's approach to reaching the poor was – in the main – a top-down approach to reaching the bottom, the poorest of the poor. This set of cases shows that a bottom-up approach to BOP entrepreneurship makes more sense: enabling the poor to tap into existing markets themselves without relying on fickle multinational companies. The cases offer some insight into how we might throw off the shackles that bind us to the old business models and ways of thinking – for the benefit of the poorest among us.

Dominant approaches to poverty alleviation[3] vs Prahalad

This book investigates the role of business in upholding human rights and ethical commitments, and its responsibility in advancing development on sustainable terms. To the extent that the larger issues or questions raised in these pages do not have one final answer or solution, they can be said to constitute puzzles. The pieces of these puzzles do not fit together easily, and a neat, elegant solution has not yet been forthcoming.

Thomas Kuhn, a physicist and philosopher of science, refers to 'puzzle-solving' to explain the role of science in addressing particular problems where solutions have remained elusive.[4]

Kuhn states that some examples of scientific practice, which include law, theory and application, 'provide models from which spring particular coherent traditions'. If exercises in puzzle solving are successful, and if they share two special achievements, then Kuhn calls them 'paradigms'.[5] The two achievements? Those sufficiently unprecedented to attract a stalwart group of adherents; and those sufficiently open-ended to still leave 'all sorts of problems' for the next group of practitioners to resolve.[6]

'Puzzle-solving'

Development and the poor

Current discourse on development and the poor features two primary puzzles. The first is composed of pieces that embrace development, economic growth, the poor, and other relational factors that inhibit or constrain development, with a view to improving the welfare and livelihoods of poorer populations.[7] Most of the poor live in 58 countries, an estimated 70% in Africa and the remainder in Central Asia. From the early 1990s, more than four billion people in the developing world have begun to move out of the depths of poverty, some of them very rapidly. But the countries in which the poorest live have barely grown at all since the 1970s.[8] Over the last several decades, one camp has trumpeted its views on how to solve this puzzle. Unlike Prahalad, it has not been particularly keen to leverage business for development. The value of philanthropy and aid to assist the poor is held by many. This can be called the Jeffrey Sachs view because he has been one of the most vocal in calling for aid to support poverty alleviation.[9]

But the reliance on aid, cash-strapped governments, and NGOs has not increased the well-being of poor people on a large scale. Most experts agree that there must be another, better way to advance development and reduce poverty. Indeed, most experts and non-experts (though not all) do not quibble with the 'why' of development but with the 'how'. Many academics and professionals have spent their careers figuring out how to solve this puzzle.[10] But development is a complex process and clear-cut solutions have remained elusive.

Business and the poor

The second puzzle is one that comprises 'business and the poor' and how their relationship should be characterised, and for some, maximised. This puzzle includes elements such as corporate social responsibility (CSR), corporate social investment (CSI), corporate citizenship, ethics, human rights and labour rights.[11] The central questions herein revolve around the role of business in upholding labour standards, increasing employment, and uplifting poor communities through CSI programmes. This puzzle often has business and the poor pitted against one another like David and Goliath. It raises challenging questions about fairness. At the same time it asks salient questions about power and responsibility – much of what this book is about.[12]

This second puzzle has been dominated by differing groups. Some claim that the 'use of the cloak of social responsibility, and the nonsense spoken in its name by influential and prestigious businessmen, does clearly harm the foundations of a free society' (this, the Milton Friedman view, is discussed by Ralph Hamann in Chapter 1).[13] The detractors claim that business has an ethical responsibility to employees and communities (that are impacted by its operations) to invest in those communities in a socially responsible way. This group often advocates the triple-bottom-line approach. The United Nations Global Compact is a well-known supporter of corporate governance in the global South, as is Mervyn King, chairman of the King Committee on Corporate Governance in South Africa.[14]

The emphasis on the ethical duty of companies has emerged in response to a grim historical record including the Bhopal and Love Canal disasters, where injury, illness and death resulted directly from corporate negligence.[15] One anecdote is perhaps illustrative of the broader tension. Clive Crook, a former deputy editor for *The Economist* is quoted as saying: 'for the past few decades I have been collecting movies that cast Big Business in a good light... Well... strictly speaking, I should say, I don't yet have an actual collection, because in 30 years I haven't been able to find one. (If you know of an instance, I'd love to hear from you. There might be a prize.)' [16]

A simple proposition

C. K. Prahalad, a professor of Corporate Strategy and International Business at the University of Michigan (USA), looked at the two puzzles and noticed the overlap. To the conventional theory that business exploits the poor, and that business and development are fundamentally in conflict, he saw untapped possibility. In response, he supplied an alternate theory.

In Prahalad's view, this new or shifting paradigm begins with a simple proposition: if we start thinking of the poor as 'resilient and creative entrepreneurs and value-conscious consumers, a whole new world of opportunity will open up'.[17] But in 1997, the world was not yet ready. Prahalad and Stuart Hart produced a working paper titled 'The Strategies for the Bottom of the Pyramid' but no one would publish it. Prahalad recalls: 'Not a single journal would accept the article for publication. It was too radical. Reviewers thought it did not follow the work of developmental economists. Nobody noticed that we were offering an alternative to the traditional wisdom'.[18]

Five years later, Prahalad and Hart succeeded in publishing the piece in *Strategy + Business*. This was the initial blueprint for Prahalad's 2004 book.[19] In that first article, Prahalad and Hart offer Exhibit 1, a triangle with four tiers (see Figure 1). Tier four is the market under scrutiny. These consumers have an income of less than US$1,500 per year; they are the lowest tier; the bottom – or the base – of the pyramid. The BOP add up to four billion in numbers, and they reside in some of the fastest growing, most attractive economies in the world. Prahalad and Hart referred to the BOP as 'the invisible opportunity'.[20] What, if anything, had changed?

Investment destinations and the poor

Prahalad and Hart laid bare a number of assumptions that the top 200 multinational corporations (MNCs) share with regard to tier four, and they explained the fallacy of this orthodoxy, calling for its re-examination. Most of these assumptions can be grouped around the ability and willingness of the poor to pay for quality products, services and technology.[21] MNCs have now begun to envisage profits in regions such as China, India and Africa. Asia now houses half the world's people (think half the world's 'consumers'), together with half the world's fastest

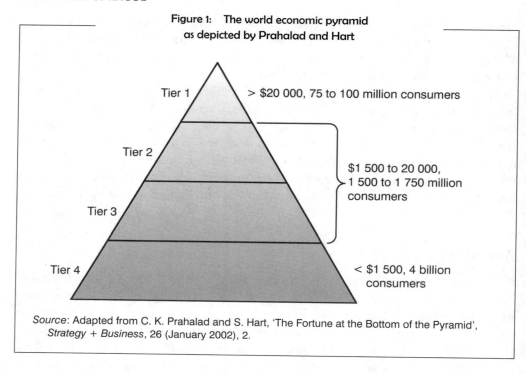

Figure 1:   The world economic pyramid
as depicted by Prahalad and Hart

Tier 1   > $20 000, 75 to 100 million consumers

Tier 2

$1 500 to 20 000,
1 500 to 1 750 million
consumers

Tier 3

Tier 4   < $1 500, 4 billion
consumers

Source: Adapted from C. K. Prahalad and S. Hart, 'The Fortune at the Bottom of the Pyramid',
Strategy + Business, 26 (January 2002), 2.

growing economies. Resource-rich nations in Africa are attracting much more investment than they did 30 years ago.[22]

The World Bank stated in 2000 that Africa has 'enormous unexploited potential in resource-based sectors and in processing and manufacturing. It also has hidden growth reserves in its people – including the potential of its women, who now provide more than half of the region's labour force'.[23] Africa is appealing, not just for its natural resources, but because of its potential customer base. Even the sceptic George Ayittey admitted in *The Economist* of 21 August 2007: 'Africa could well be the next and final frontier for roaring market-based capitalism'.[24] Currently there is indeed fierce competition to do business with Africa.

The two investment destinations just cited – Asia and Africa – are composed primarily of poor people. There has long been a prevailing perception that the poor do not comprise a viable market; that they have not taken part in the so-called global economy; and, that they have no buying power. But in this regard there has been a signal change. The poor – who have often been seen merely as disadvantaged 'victims' requiring assistance in the form of corporate social investment programmes or from governments and NGOs – are willing to pay, and willing to pay more than their middle class counterparts, for essential goods and services:

Across the world the story is the same – poor consumers pay more than rich consumers for basic services. In Mumbai, slum-dwellers in Dharavi pay 1.2 times more for rice, 10 times more for medicine and 3.5 times more for water than do middle class people living at the other end of the city on Bhulabhai Desai Road.[25]

The low-income residents of Dharavi also pay 600% to 1,000% in interest to secure credit from moneylenders. A commercial bank could charge much less and still make a sizeable profit.[26] The so-called 'poverty penalty' is the result of local monopolies, inadequate access, poor distribution, and strong traditional brokers. It suggests that the poor pay five to 25 times what the rich pay for the same services.[27] As one author put it: 'if you break the economic and physical bottlenecks of distribution you can reach huge, previously neglected markets... millions of small sales can, in aggregate, add up to big profits'.[28] In purchasing power parity (PPP) terms, the Indian economy alone is worth US$3 trillion. Nine developing countries, including China, Brazil, South Africa, India and Mexico, constitute 90% of the developing world, with a GDP in PPP terms worth US$12.5 trillion – larger than the combined GDP of Japan, Germany, France, Italy and the United Kingdom in PPP terms.[29] Dharavi households, like other consumers, will spend their money on items that seem like luxury goods (85% own television sets and 75% own a blender and a pressure cooker).[30]

A new approach?

Compared with other thinkers, Prahalad views the role of business in addressing poverty, especially multinational corporations, as prominent – indeed essential. Here was another novel notion that would challenge the existing puzzles: business, and big business, blamed by some for many social ills including birth defects and cancers linked to emissions of pesticides and chemicals (in cases mentioned such as Bhopal) may actually be good for our health and development.[31] A leading business school syllabus captures this altered mindset: 'Once perceived as part of the problem, business is increasingly (even grudgingly in some circles) admired for its dynamism, its market-discipline, its incentives for efficiency and innovation, and its economically self-sustaining character'.[32]

Prahalad was also able to back his claims with data: 12 cases appear in his book. Another seven cases are documented in online videos and reports. As you read this, he has a case-writing team of 23 BOP researchers, mainly University of Michigan students or graduates, who are working away like a pack of beavers to produce even more results. And, he is involved in a series of UNDP global initiatives, which includes a minimum of 50 BOP-style cases. Like Kuhn's first criterion for a paradigm, Prahalad had instant followers, loyal adherents who began to test his ideas. His publication had a lightning rod effect. Business school professors took up the ideas with interest. His book was enthusiastically endorsed by Bill Gates and Madeleine Albright,[33] and received a number of awards.[34] Suddenly this professor based in sleepy Ann Arbor, Michigan had gained a cult following. Like Kuhn's second criterion (leaving all sorts of problems), Prahalad still left a number of open questions for exploration by other students and practitioners.[35]

Considering Prahalad's proposition and re-formulation

The cases in this section offer a window into that world – the alternative paradigm. They comprise a small, but not insignificant, sample. Similar studies are underway which will add to the evidence base. For instance, the United Nations Development Programme for the last decade has focused on CSR and initiatives such as the Global Compact. The last five to seven years have seen an evolution in the thinking of the UNDP. One of the milestones in this evolution was the UNDP's Commission on the Private Sector and Development. Co-chaired by the prime minister of Canada, Paul Martin, together with Ernesto Zedillo, former president of Mexico, this commission was established in 2003. Prahalad was one of its members. The aim of the commission was to identify and address the legal, financial and structural obstacles that impede the expansion of the 'indigenous private sector' in developing countries – and to generate growth for the poorest regions and communities in those countries. The commission focused on creating domestic employment and wealth, and tapping into local entrepreneurial talent. A landmark report resulted: *Unleashing Entrepreneurship: Making Business Work for the Poor*. From that report, which promised additional reports (in characteristic UN fashion), the UNDP subsequently began to focus on the poor (vis-à-vis the private sector), against the backdrop of increasing globalisation and its often detrimental impacts on those without a living wage, without property, and without access to credit.

The UNDP put together a subsequent initiative, of which this author was part. Initially called Making Business Work for the MDGs it used the language of Prahalad in the conceptual approaches and frameworks, such as his 'BOP Heat Map' and 'BOP approaches'.[36] However, the focus of this report, which was undergirded by 50 field-based case studies presenting real world experience, was on southern-based entrepreneurs and written by researchers who were primarily based in the southern hemisphere. With this mounting knowledge, data and experience drawn from different disciplines, the UNDP has distanced itself from Prahalad's language and taken up the language of 'Growing Inclusive Markets'.[37] Its report, *Creating Value for All: Strategies for Doing Business with the Poor,* was launched on 24 June 2008. How much the current initiative and report owe intellectually to Prahalad is a matter of debate. What is clear is that UNDP is using the vast UN family of 23 international agencies and UN staff in 185 countries,[38] to create bridges between the international financial institutions, the private sector and entrepreneurs in developing countries. Its development agenda is specifically focused on achieving the Millennium Development Goals (MDGs) through private sector involvement. The halfway point for the MDGs was July 2007, and the pressure is on.[39]

The take-away

Prahalad saw business as a vehicle for development and economic change on a revolutionary scale. Other, slightly different initiatives to address poverty through enterprise, such as 'making markets work for the poor' led by the World Bank, were also attempted. But they did not take off on a large scale because the Bank and the International Monetary Fund have not been viewed by developing country governments and the poor as credible partners.[40] The effects of structural adjustment programmes, which critics claimed led to economic stagnation, decreased wages, and cuts in social programmes to finance external debt, meant a further retreat to the ideological bases long held by the public, private and NGO sectors.

Prahalad called into question the powerful perceptions that multinational corporations held toward the bottom of the pyramid. To make the BOP enterprise attractive to jaded business leaders, he used planks taken from both dominant paradigms – he used the logic of profits and he appealed to the social responsibility of business leaders. To the sceptics who said business and development are fundamentally mismatched, he appealed to their sense of social responsibility. To the nay-sayers who said business exists to make profits, he focused on the business case. In so doing, he fought his detractors by using arguments that he adapted to their own ideologies. Whether he has succeeded in fully convincing them of the merits of BOP enter-prise, remains to be seen. However, his emphasis – and the major distinction of the Prahalad approach – was on large firms seeking to open new markets in low-income sectors.

The cases

Three observations

Our cases reveal a number of key findings and insights. They also offer six opportunities to reflect on whether Prahalad's framework stands up under scrutiny and whether shifts in think-ing are warranted.

Firstly, the focal point for Prahalad was using multinational corporations as a vehicle to engage the BOP and to tap into BOP markets such that large firms would create products and services ideally suited for the poor. The way he presented it was as a largely top-down approach to reaching the bottom. The key finding of the cases demonstrates that a bottom-up approach to reaching entrepreneurs and consumers at the bottom of the pyramid makes more sense: enabling the poor to tap into existing markets themselves without relying on fickle MNCs. Honey Care and E+Co demonstrate that if you have some financial resources, you can use people on the ground, local staff of companies or NGOs, to begin a business venture. A multinational is not required; and the resources and bureaucracy of a multinational are not es-sential. Hence, BOP enterprise does not have to occur via the gateway of a MNC. For example, one of the weaknesses identified by critics of Prahalad's work is that the obstacles faced by poor consumers are massive, and he did not always have satisfactory answers to some of the greatest barriers. For example, as one critic rightly noted: 'companies cannot simply apply top-of-the-pyramid marketing and distribution strategies, but rather must incorporate completely new tactics to reach the BOP'.[41]

Secondly, our case studies demonstrate that such new tactics are readily available. In Honey Care, for example, local entrepreneurs are used to target poor consumers, and they rely on existing social networks to develop distribution channels. In the VidaGás case, Fundação para o Desenvolvimento da Comunidade (FDC – a community foundation) uses social networks (comprised mainly of women, as they do most of the cooking and cleaning in this region) to spread the word in the local communities of northern Mozambique that the stoves, powered by liquefied petroleum gas (LPG) are safe, efficient, clean and superior to using wood or kerosene for cooking.

Thirdly, there is the not-so-small challenge of partnership (see Chapter 3 for further dis-cussion). BOP entrepreneurs and companies must collaborate much more intimately and intensively than with top-of-the-pyramid markets, as our cases illustrate. Much of the time governments or NGOs are involved. Prahalad acknowledges the role and presence of other actors but he does not acknowledge the wailing and gnashing of teeth, the energy-intensive and time-consuming nature of working in partnership. Prahalad remains somewhat vague when it comes to overcoming these impediments.[42] The VidaGás case shows that these partnerships can be brokered among northern and southern NGOs and developing country governments to good effect: a Seattle-based NGO raises capital while the Maputo-based NGO uses specialised local knowledge of BOP consumers to explain why they should switch from kerosene stoves to those powered by liquefied petroleum gas sold by VidaGás. The Ministry of Health has a memorandum of understanding with these NGOs to power health clinics in northern Mozambique with LPG.

Applying the theory to the problem

Of the cases in this section, all are company ventures that began with a dual business and social purpose. Most (but not all) began with a viable business plan. All the companies investigated by our case authors operate their businesses in poorer regions of the world in developing countries, primarily in sub-Saharan Africa. For two-thirds of these companies, their employees are poor and their consumers are poor. They are the base of the pyramid. Each of these companies serves the poor through their core business offering, be it a product or service. For BOP enterprises (or any profit-minded initiative) to be successful a company should become revenue-generating and financially viable and sustainable – and the time period for this depends on how much capital you have (or are willing to part with), the expectations of owners and shareholders, and the industry sector and type of business.

So what does success look like for a BOP company? In viewing the company case studies in this section, we found the presence of the following four elements in a 'formula' that could be considered successful.

1 Overcoming regulatory hurdles and start-up costs

One must consider that countries in Africa have infrastructural and human capacity constraints that are unlike those in the industrialised world. Mozambique ranks 135th out of 178 countries in terms of the World Bank's annual *Ease of Doing Business* survey for 2008 (an improvement from 140th in 2007). The World Bank estimates that specific business procedures take 113 days in Mozambique – compared to an average of 16 days in the OECD countries.[43] These legal, bureaucratic hurdles are mind-numbing. BOP ventures are meant to take root in some countries where a small transaction can be likened to a Herculean feat, such as extracting a molar from a hungry lion with one's bare hands. (Try getting a legal title in Sudan.) According to the 2008 *Ease of Doing Business* survey, India ranks 120th (from 132nd last year), and South Africa ranks 35th. Kenya stands at 72nd place (from 82nd in 2007); Uganda at 118th; and Tanzania in 130th place. The Democratic Republic of the Congo ranks in last place at 178th. Getting going in these contexts is an achievement in itself. All of the companies in our sample met this criterion.

2 Employing problem-based innovation

Levels and types of innovation are a characteristic feature of all of the case studies. This set of companies, whether they prove to be successful or not over the longer term, have innovation embedded in their DNA. They illustrate the entrepreneurship taking place up and down the African continent. There is a thrilling array of problem-solving activity that is moving these entrepreneurs and their employees and associates from subsistence to the next level through business models that seek social good and not solely profits. The business owners profiled in this section reveal a willingness to take the necessary risks; to adapt to market conditions; to identify profit making ventures while developing their own conceptions of how their businesses can serve communities. These include farmers in East Africa, producers and consumers of alternative energy in Mozambique, Ghana, Senegal and South Africa, and disabled miners. To meet this criterion, a company must be able to take a social or environmental problem and devise some kind of innovation to overcome it. VidaGás and E +Co both did this successfully with alternative energy solutions. Aspen did so with generic medicines. Stitch Wise came up with safety equipment to solve the problem of the large number of mining accidents and injuries, and HP promised ongoing IT training to address the problem of computer illiteracy. Honey Care takes the social and economic problem of unprofitable rural farmers and offers the solution of gainful employment through the sale of honey.

3 Achieving a social development impact (with multiple spinoffs)

Each of these companies demonstrated some measurable social benefit, such as employment for a large number of people at the BOP; significant increases in income level for employees (moving them to the next income bracket); creating essential products or providing services that would be consumed by the BOP at affordable prices; or making credit available to allow other BOP entrepreneurs to become business owners.

Stitch Wise produces safety equipment for disabled miners, and provides them with employment and increased income. Honey Care creates jobs and increased incomes to the BOP in East Africa. Aspen supplies low-cost, affordable generic antiretroviral drugs to the poor (and everyone else), and E+Co and VidaGás both sell alternative green fuels that enable poor consumers to avoid environmentally hazardous, unhealthy, conventional fuels. HP offered computer skills to community members in Mogalakwena, South Africa before the project ended. Spinoffs of these ventures are varied, including expanded access to capital and markets to additional BOP; establishing micro-credit initiatives; and building knowledge and capacity.

4 Realising long-term profitability

This criterion creates an immediate filter. Of the six cases in our sample, three definitively met this criterion with the HP case failing; the VidaGás start-up breaking even; and the long-term financial sustainability of Stitch Wise not completely assured. Honey Care, E + Co and Aspen easily met this criterion. Indeed, the body of cases illustrate that grassroots initiatives started by entrepreneurs can, with the right ingredients, allow for financial success, and also be taken to scale. It is still early days but E+Co, Honey Care and Aspen were able to transform their operations and sales to dramatically increase profits and achieve significant economies of scale.

These are, in the main, bottom of the pyramid entrepreneurs solving their own problems. They are movers and shakers: inventors, risk-takers, leaders, and managers; producers of knowledge, products and services. The cases demonstrate how BOP entrepreneurs were able to overcome early structural hurdles in challenging contexts – high risk, high barrier to entry, difficultly accessing capital or credit – to innovate, adapt, and achieve early growth. Most of these companies have creative, determined individuals at the helm who were able to innovate their way out of a web of constraints. All have not achieved unmitigated success, however. One was aborted and two others must still prove their long term viability. The majority of the cases, many of which are already successful, demonstrate enormous growth potential. The criteria outlined above seem to provide a minimum, winning success formula for BOP enterprise. The cases provide additional substantiation that alternative models, called 'Growing

Inclusive Markets', by UNDP, are bearing fruit against a background of complexity, difficulty and resistance.

Going further than Prahalad

These cases reveal a discernable shift – and one that goes further than Prahalad (at least in his early writings on the BOP). What do we mean by this? Prahalad appealed, in part, to the social responsibility of corporations.[44] What we find is that, to be successful, BOP ventures must be fully conceived as for-profit initiatives. The prototype for success that emerges so far is as follows: a business model that is self-sustaining through profits – and one that delivers social benefits to consumers through its core business activities. Social enterprise tacked on as CSR does not yield the same benefits on the face of this evidence, and may in fact be a recipe for failure. Our evidence base is too small to make generalised recommendations at this stage. However, the 50 UNDP case studies previously mentioned do corroborate our findings.[45] If you want to know which is most important – a CSI motive or a business motive, the latter proves critical in ensuring sustainability and success over time. In sum, we differ from Prahalad on the fundamental design of BOP ventures; on what the motivation should be for an MNC to become involved; and how critical it may be to get MNCs involved in the first instance. For Prahalad it is the major way; for us it is just one way.

Conclusion: Shifting paradigms

Much of this book has been devoted to one of the two puzzles previously discussed – that of CSR and its impact on the livelihoods of the poor – with human rights obligations, ethical dilemmas and implications at the fore. At the same time, the cases and conceptual chapters give careful treatment to the role of the business community in addressing poverty against the backdrop of a set of complex challenges.[46] This chapter has sought to consider Prahalad's approach as it relates to our case studies, which inevitably takes us back to our puzzle-solving exercise.

Prahalad refers to the 'dominant logic' by which stakeholders, e.g., governments, international financial institutions, and non-governmental organisations, address social and economic development,[47] observing that we are conditioned by our ideological assumptions. The notion that there are standard ways of doing things and 'best practices' holds true for most fields. As Kuhn notes, '[t]he student generally learns from and is mentored by researchers and practitioners who learned the rudiments of their field from the same concrete models; hence there is little disagreement over fundamentals'.[48] The problem is that the fundamental assumptions of 40 years ago may not yield results today. If we cannot solve these puzzles it may be that our assumptions are flawed; or perhaps the puzzles themselves have changed.

Thomas Kuhn argued that the transition from one successive paradigm to the next occurs via a revolution. Revolution, Kuhn claimed, was the usual route or pattern of mature science. During the eighteenth century, scientists who attempted to derive the observed motion of the moon from Newton's laws of motion and gravitation failed to do so time and again. Kuhn observed that consequently some of them suggested replacing the inverse square law with a law that deviated from it at small distances: 'To do that would have been to change the paradigm, to define a new puzzle, and not to solve the old one'.[49]

The scientists preserved the age-old rules until 1750 when one of them discovered how they could be successfully applied. 'Only a change in the rules of the game could have provided an alternative', Kuhn notes.[50] The facts reveal that the old puzzles may not be solved by continuing to approach these problems in the same way. Our traditional paradigms have led us along particular pathways; the contributions made in this book have served to illuminate the path ahead – to identify entrepreneurial solutions that have addressed the problem of poverty through pro-poor business solutions. Such solutions have been successfully engineered by entrepreneurs in the southern hemisphere, proving effective in particular contexts. Are we poised to re-think the paradigm? The answer is up to you readers to decide. To understand this changing, closely-knit world, to bring greater scrutiny to bear on these problems, is the challenge for practitioners, educators and students alike. Let us get on with the journey.

Notes

1   I thank Laura Bures (International Youth Foundation, formerly of the International Finance Corporation), Martin Hall (University of Cape Town), Kevin McKague (York University), Ralph Hamann (University of Cape Town) and Stu Woolman (University of Pretoria) for their invaluable comments on this chapter.

2   C. K. Prahalad, *The Fortune at the Bottom of the Pyramid: Eradicating Poverty through Profits*, sixth printing (Upper Saddle River, NJ: Wharton School Publishing, Pearson Education, 2006). Prahalad's work was first published in 2004.

3   Poverty alleviation, poverty relief and reduction are used synonymously in the popular and development literature. However, this language is objectionable to some who argue that it is laden with historical baggage, suggesting that the poor are victims requiring financial assistance, people who lack agency or decision-making power over their own lives. Poverty alleviation is often seen as a focus area within the broader scope of social and economic development. However, there is no universal consensus on how poverty should be measured. Some focus on absolute poverty and others on relative poverty. The World Bank considers people earning less than US$1 per day (in 1993 purchasing power parity) to be absolutely poor. Relative poverty can be defined as the minimum economic, social, political and cultural goods needed to maintain an acceptable way of life in a particular society. The European Union defines the relatively poor as persons, families and groups of persons whose resources (material, cultural, social) are so limited as to exclude them from the minimum acceptable way of life in the member state in which they live. From http://www.unescap.org/pdd/publications/urban_poverty/urban_poverty.asp

4   T. Kuhn, *Structure of Scientific Revolutions* (Chicago: University of Chicago Press, 1996), 36. Kuhn was from Ohio, USA. Although he was Harvard-trained (BA, MA, PhD), he wrote his best-known work *Structure of Scientific Revolutions* (1962) at the University of California, Berkeley, and spent most of his professional career at the Massachusetts Institute of Technology and Princeton. He died in 1996.

5   Kuhn, *Structure of Scientific Revolutions*, 10. Kuhn did not coin the phrase 'paradigm' but his work popularised it.

6   Ibid., 12.

7   I have employed the term, 'puzzle solving' as used by Kuhn. However, he may disagree with whether the present problem would constitute a puzzle, as his puzzles must have a solution. There is some debate on whether poverty can be eradicated, with some Christian church leaders arguing that the poor will never stop coming, a not uncontroversial view. 'Though intrinsic value is no criterion for a puzzle, the assured existence of a solution is'. Kuhn, *Structure of Scientific Revolutions*, 36–39.

8   Figures from 'Springing the Traps', *The Economist*, 2 August 2007.

9   I am simplifying the Sachs view for the purposes of illustration. The more nuanced Sachs view may be that poverty requires massive injections of capital and funding to kick-start self-reliance. However, in presentations and talks Sachs gives around the world, and that this author has attended,

his clarion call is for more money and more aid. I thank Martin Hall for his comments on this point. See J. Sachs, *The End of Poverty: Economic Possibilities for Our Time* (New York: Penguin, 2005). Sachs is one of the loudest voices in this camp, and one of the most influential. See 'Springing the Traps', The Economist, 2 August 2007. A chief critic of the Sachs view is William Easterly, who sought to reveal the mockery of the aid business. His study demonstrated that only 1% of €20m of aid sent to Chad actually reached the rural health clinics intended. See W. Easterly, *The White Man's Burden: Why the West's Efforts to Aid the Rest Have Done So Much Ill and So Little Good* (New York: Penguin Books, 2006).

10   On the complex dimensions of development, the following are just some of the most insightful theorists and practitioners. See P. Collier, *The Bottom Billion: Why the Poorest Countries are Failing and What Can Be Done About It* (Oxford: Oxford University Press, 2007); A. Sen, Development as Freedom (New York: Random House, 1999); A. Sen, *Inequality Re-Examined* (Cambridge, MA: Harvard University Press, 1992); M. Nussbaum, *Women and Human Development: The Capabilities Approach* (Cambridge: Cambridge University Press, 2000); H. de Soto, *The Mystery of Capital* (New York: Penguin Books, 2000); D. Landes, *The Wealth and Poverty of Nations, Why Some are So Rich and Some so Poor* (New York: W.W. Norton & Co, 1999); M. Yunus, *Banker to the Poor: Micro-Lending and the Battle Against Poverty* (New York: Perseus Books, 2003); J. Drèze and A. Sen, *The Political Economy of Hunger: Studies in Development Economics* (Oxford: Clarendon Press, 1990); J. Drèze and A. Sen, *Hunger and Public Action* (Oxford: Clarendon Press, 1989); and P. Samuelson, *Welfare Economics* (Cambridge, MA: Harvard University Press, 1983).

11   According to Segel, definitions of CSR are wide-ranging, 'from the narrowest (the imperative of maximising profit for shareowners) to the very broad (managing the social needs of diverse stakeholders for sustainable ends)'. Segel observes: 'Despite its importance to contemporary business environments, there is little agreement on what social responsibility is and how to discharge it'. She asserts that there is a growing acceptance of CSR: 'the crux… being the place and purpose of private institutions in public arenas in so far as these impact on society'. K. Segel, 'State-Corporate Social Development in South Africa: The Role of the State in Advancing Corporate Social Engagement' (PhD thesis, London School of Economics and Political Science, University of London, 2004), 24–25.

12   This puzzle is also one that considers the governance responsibilities and requirements of business toward employees or communities, and the environment near the company's operations.

13   M. Friedman, 'The Social Responsibility of Business is to Increase its Profits', *The New York Times Magazine*, 13 September 1970. Note that the far left critique of CSR is even more sceptical.

14   The King Committee on Corporate Governance, headed by former High Court judge, Mervyn King, incorporated a Code of Corporate Practices and Conduct. It was launched in 1994, the first such code in South Africa, and sought to reform corporate governance in the country. The report was internationally acclaimed, and has become a model for some other African countries. King I championed an integrated approach to good governance in the interests of a wide range of stakeholders. To match legislative developments, the King Committee on Corporate Governance developed a second King Report on Corporate Governance for South Africa in 2002 (King II). King II's contribution is to embody a shift from the single bottom-line (profit for shareholders) to a triple bottom-line, which includes the economic, environmental and social aspects of a company's activities. From Cliffe Dekker's website. The King II Report can be downloaded from http://www.cliffedekker.co.za/literature/corpgov/

15   These two are just the tip of the iceberg. For an update on Bhopal, see T. Satyanand, 'Aftermath of the Bhopal Accident', *Lancet*, 371 (2008), 1900.

16   C. Crook, quoted in 'The Pursuit of Busyness', *The Economist*, 10 April 2007. Available from http://www.the economist.com

17   Prahalad, *The Fortune at the Bottom of the Pyramid*, 1.

18   Ibid., xviii.

19   Ibid. Significantly, the phrase 'bottom of the pyramid' was used first, not by Prahalad, but by former US president Franklin D. Roosevelt. In his radio address of 7 April 1932, titled 'The Forgotten Man', Roosevelt remarked: 'These unhappy times call for the building of plans that rest upon the forgotten, the unorganized but the indispensable units of economic power… that build from the bot-

tom up and not from the top down, that put their faith once more in the forgotten man at the bottom of the economic pyramid'. From http://www.wikipedia.com

20 C. K. Prahalad and S. Hart, 'The Fortune at the Bottom of the Pyramid', *Strategy + Business*, 26 (January 2002), 2.

21 The authors take care to note that of these 200 global MNCs, 82 are US firms, and 41 Japanese. See Prahalad and Hart, 'The Fortune at the Bottom of the Pyramid', 4. Prahalad saw that pieces of the puzzle had shifted; and by 2002 they had. The drivers of this shift have been linked to globalisation, deregulation, privatisation, changing industry boundaries and standards, the tremendous reach and speed of information and communication technology and transport. See M. Castells, 'Toward a Sociology of the Network Society', *Contemporary Sociology*, 29, 5 (2000): 693–699.

22 *The Economist*, 30 August 2007.

23 Quoted in *World Development Indicators* (Washington, DC: World Bank, 2000).

24 G. Ayittey, *Africa Unchained: The Blueprint for Africa's Future* (New York: Palgrave Macmillan, 2005), 2.

25 UNDP, *Unleashing Entrepreneurship* (New York: UNDP, 2004), 7–8.

26 Prahalad, *The Fortune at the Bottom of the Pyramid*, 11.

27 Ibid., 12.

28 See C Anderson, The Long Tail: Why the Future of Business is Selling Less of More (New York: Hyperion, 2006). Anderson is editor in chief of *Wired* magazine, and formerly US business editor at *The Economist*.

29 Prahalad, *The Fortune at the Bottom of the Pyramid*, 10.

30 Ibid.

31 Quoted in Crook, 'The Pursuit of Busyness', Economist.com 10 April 2007.

32 Quoted in Harvard Business School course syllabus on 'Entrepreneurship in the Social Sector'.

33 It was endorsed by Bill Gates, head of Microsoft, Madeleine Albright, former US secretary of state, and Mark Malloch Brown, former administrator of the UNDP.

34 These awards are listed on the back of the 2006 publication of the *Fortune at the Bottom of the Pyramid*. Prahalad also won awards for best book of 2004 by Amazon.com, Fast Company magazine, and was ranked in *The Economist*'s top 25 books that same year.

35 Hart introduces the assumption in *Capitalism at the Crossroads* that BOP will be essential if MNCs are to maintain their profit margins since they have saturated markets in the north and west. His assertion is that BOP must be seen as a corporate strategy with benefits for poorer communities. See S Hart, *Capitalism at the Crossroads* (Upper Saddle River, NJ: Wharton School Publishing, 2007).

36 This language and these conceptual approaches were in evidence when we, as the UNDP group of researchers, met in Paris, 21–22 September 2006.

37 Bruce Jenks of UNDP spoke of the evolution of UNDP's ideas and work in his discussion of the UNDP report at a recent address at the Growing Inclusive Markets Conference in Halifax Canada, 20–21 June 2008.

38 These agencies include, among others, the World Bank/International Finance Corporation (IFC – the private sector arm of the Bank), the International Monetary Fund, the World Health Organisation, the UN Children's Fund (UNICEF) and the UN Population Fund (UNFPA).

39 The basis for this work was, according to Annan, as follows: 'Our experience has shown that a large part of the work for development is about preparing the ground for sufficient private sector activity to provide the jobs and income needed to build a more equitable and prosperous society. Yet the UN has only sporadically tapped the power that can be drawn from engaging the private sector in the work of development'. Cited in K. Annan, 'Background to UNDP Initiative'. Available from http://www.undp.org

40 See J. Stiglitz, *Globalization and its Discontents* (New York: W.W. Norton & Company, 2003). For the leftist critique, see N. Chomsky and R. McChesney, *Profit over People: Neoliberalism and Global Order* (New York: Seven Stories Press, 1998); see also D. Moore, ed., *The World Bank: Development, Poverty, Hegemony* (Durban: University of KwaZulu-Natal Press, 2007).

41 W. Baue, 'Review of the Fortune at the Bottom of the Pyramid: Eradicating Poverty through Profits', 18 November 2004. See http://sknworldwide.net/library/economic/bop/document.2004-11-23.9742739672/

42 Ibid.

43 See the World Bank 'Ease of Doing Business' survey by country, available from http://www. doingbusiness.org.

44 See Prahalad, *The Fortune at the Bottom of the Pyramid* for further discussion on this point.

45 The author is involved in this UNDP initiative, which offers 50 southern case studies along similar lines to the ones in this section of the book, written by authors primarily based in the southern hemisphere. For more information, see http://www.growinginclusivemarkets.org/. See also the UN's ECOSOC Innovation Fair (Innovation and Transformation for Poverty Reduction and Hunger), available from http://www. un.org/ecosoc/innovfair/innovfair.shtml

46 As the prologue to this book states: 'The overarching imperative to support Africa's poor in their quest for better livelihoods, human rights and environmental integrity – in short, sustainable development – is a huge challenge, and the business community, ranging from small companies to multinational corporations, has an important role to play. Contributing to a better understanding of this role and its implications for decision-makers in business, as well as other sectors, is the purpose of this book'.

47 The phrase socio-economic development as it is used throughout this chapter simply means improving the quality of life of people, which can be done through a number of interventions, such as ensuring access to essential services, such as healthcare, housing, water, and electricity.

48 Kuhn, *Structure of Scientific Revolutions*, 10. On this point Brand Magazine astutely observes: 'Part of the problem with the world is that most of us think in ruts. Business and marketing books tend to be just more of what we already know, only in more detail, entrenching us further in our comfort zone. But every now and then comes something that challenges us to review radically the assumptions underlying how we think. The Fortune at the Bottom of the Pyramid is just such a challenge'. See http://www. brandmagazine.co.za.

49 Kuhn, *Structure of Scientific Revolutions*, 41–42.

50 Ibid.

Sasol and petrochemical investment
in developing countries

JONATHON HANKS[1]

Introduction

Principles 1 and 2 of the UN Global Compact call on businesses to support and to respect the protection of internationally proclaimed human rights within their sphere of influence, and urge them to ensure that they are not complicit in human rights abuses. This case study identifies some of the practical implications and dilemmas associated with implementing these principles in the context of large-scale corporate investments in countries where there may be concerns about human rights abuses.

Using Sasol – a South African-based multinational petrochemicals company – as the basis for the review, the study analyses some of the recent thinking about how to interpret and to apply the UNGC Principles. Sasol's experience in managing the human rights aspects of community resettlement activities as part of its Mozambique Natural Gas Project provides a broad background to the study. While Sasol has managed these issues effectively, the study questions whether this experience alone is sufficient to guide the company's current and proposed investments in countries such as Iran, China and Nigeria.

Sasol provides a particularly interesting case study: it operates in the extractive sector (which has one of the worst records for human rights infringements); several of its anticipated investments are joint venture partnerships with governments in countries with recognised poor human rights records; and many of these investments are in a strategic commodity that has a significant impact on the local economy. Collectively, these facts increase Sasol's sphere of influence and its risk of being deemed complicit in government abuses directly or indirectly associated with the project investment.

Sasol: Company profile

Sasol is an integrated oil and gas company with complementary interests in coal extraction and chemicals, and the international development of synthetic-fuel ventures based on its proprietary Fischer-Tropsch (FT) technology. Formed in 1950, Sasol began FT-based production in 1955. It mines coal in South Africa and converts this coal, along with Mozambican natural gas, into fuels and chemical feedstock through its FT technology.

The company has significant chemical manufacturing and marketing operations in South Africa, Europe, the US and Asia. In South Africa it refines imported oil into liquid fuels and retails liquid fuels and lubricants through Sasol convenience centres and Exel service stations. It remains one of South Africa's largest investors in capital projects and skills training, employing upwards of 30 000 people. It is listed on the Johannesburg Securities Exchange (JSE) in South Africa and the New York Stock Exchange in the US.

Sasol has recently embarked on an ambitious programme of international growth, with plans to roll out new gas-to-liquid (GTL) and coal-to-liquid (CTL) projects. In June 2006 its first international GTL plant, the US$1 billion ORYX GTL joint venture, was inaugurated at Ras Laffan in Qatar. With a second GTL plant under construction in Nigeria, discussion underway about possible GTL ventures in Algeria and Australia, and feasibility studies of two CTL plants in China being conducted in the next decade, Sasol is set to become a more significant player in the global energy sector.[2]

Human rights and Sasol's global investment strategy

Stiaan Wandrag, Sasol's recently-appointed corporate sustainable development manager, looks forward to focusing his efforts on one of his key responsibilities: ensuring effective implementation of Sasol's commitment to the principles of the UN Global Compact. While he feels confident that Sasol had the resources, capacity and focus to address the UNGC's labour and environmental principles, Wandrag is concerned about whether the company had a sufficiently systematic approach to safeguarding and promoting human rights. With Sasol's rapid expansion into countries that have dubious rights records, he recognises that this might well become an increasingly material issue for the company.

On his desk, on a pile of newspaper clippings, lies a 160-page report by Human Rights Watch[3] that is highly critical of the activities of a South African listed gold mining company in the Democratic Republic of Congo. Next to this report is a map of the world. The map captures the human rights risk profiles of various countries. Here he circles the countries where Sasol had, or was planning, significant capital investments and technology deployments, including China, India, Iran, Malaysia and Nigeria (see Document 1).

Moving the map aside, he picks up a copy of Sasol's most recent *Regional and Environmental Assessment* report that was due to be submitted to the International Finance Corporation (IFC) as part of their funding conditions for the Mozambique Natural Gas Project. As one of Sasol's first large-scale investments in a foreign country, the project has served as a testing ground for understanding the human rights implications of Sasol international growth plans – and has provided some useful lessons for informing a more structured approach to human rights management in Sasol's project activities.

Human rights and international project investments: Issues and dilemmas

Wandrag swivelled in his chair and looked at what he had written on his whiteboard a few weeks earlier when he had first undertaken to review and to assess Sasol's current approach to safeguarding human rights. In the column on the left were the three key issues he saw as being necessary to ensure meaningful implementation of Sasol's commitment to the human rights principles of the Global Compact:

- clarifying the scope of the 'internationally proclaimed human rights' relevant to Sasol's acitivites;

- understanding the nature and the extent of Sasol's 'sphere of influence'; and

- determining the conditions under which the company might be deemed 'complicit' in human rights abuses.

In the column on the right – under the heading Potential Dilemmas – were four comments he had noted in his discussions with some of his colleagues involved in international project investments:

> It's difficult for us to identify the 'universally applicable' human rights that we should be safeguarding in different countries. Can we go around imposing Western values on everyone?
>
> Surely our responsibility is mainly to comply with the law of the country in which we invest? By doing that we respect the local social, cultural and economic context. Is it our job to tell the government what they should be doing?
>
> It's better for us to be investing in countries rather than not investing in them. By being there, and implementing our human resource policies and practices, we expose others to our way of doing things. And of course we create jobs and promote economic development, which has to be positive for human rights.
>
> Human rights issues have not traditionally been considered as a potential 'show-stopper' in our risk assessment processes. But perhaps they should be?

As he reflected upon these statements, and the different perceptions of the human rights discourse they revealed, he looked forward to the challenges of embedding human rights considerations in a more structured manner in the company's international project management activities. To understand some of these challenges, and the impact of Sasol's current response to them, he turned to review Sasol's experience with the Mozambique Natural Gas Project, one of its first large-scale project investments outside South Africa.

The Mozambique Natural Gas Project: Selected human rights experience

Project background and overview [4]

The economic potential of utilising Mozambique's natural gas resources has been under investigation for many years. Following the conclusion of an Exploration Agreement and a Petroleum Production Agreement covering the Temane and Pande Gas Fields, Sasol, along with its Mozambican affiliate companies, was granted exploration rights in the northern parts of Mozambique's Inhambane Province. In November 2001, the company obtained formal approval from the government of Mozambique to start implementing the NGP. And since the World Bank Group was providing project financing, the company had to comply with detailed safeguard requirements, policies, guidelines and standards relating to the project's safety, health, environmental and social impacts.

The project involves the phased extraction, processing, transportation and utilisation of the natural gas reserves in the Pande and Temane field reservoirs. To date, the project has included the first phase of exploring and developing these gas fields, the establishment of a Central Processing Facility (CPF) at Temane, and the construction of an 865km cross-border pipeline to transport gas from Temane in Mozambique to Secunda in South Africa. It has also entailed the conversion of the Sasol Gas pipeline network supplying customers in South Africa, the conversion of the Sasolburg factory to process gas as its hydrocarbon feedstock, and the conversion of Sasol's Secunda factory to process gas as a supplementary feedstock. Construction of the CPF and the pipeline began in 2002. The first supply of natural gas reached Secunda in February 2004 and the project became commercially operational on 26 March 2004. The second phase of exploration work for the project is ongoing. An onshore seismic programme was completed during the course of 2005 and exploratory drilling began in 2006/2007.

The Natural Gas Project and 'internationally proclaimed human rights'

The Natural Gas Project is a large undertaking. Its various components cover a large portion of central and southern Mozambique. While the project holds significant potential for stimulating economic development in Mozambique and South Africa, it has some unavoidable impacts on the social and economic environment of the region.

Principles 1 and 2 of the Global Compact call on businesses to support and to respect the protection of 'internationally proclaimed human rights' within their 'sphere of influence', and to ensure that they are not 'complicit' in human rights abuses. Crucial to the implementation of these principles is an appreciation of the nature and scope of the human rights requirements that fall within a company's sphere of influence. The *International Bill of Human Rights* provides a useful starting point for understanding what this requirement includes.[5] Some specific practical examples of these rights are provided in Box 1.

Although governments have the primary responsibility for promoting, protecting and fulfilling human rights, the Universal Declaration of Human Rights calls upon 'every individual and every organ of society' to strive to protect and to respect these rights. The exact nature of companies' responsibility for safeguarding these rights remains the subject of some debate.[6]

The Mozambican Natural Gas Project raises a number of readily identifiable human rights issues:

- ensuring non-discrimination in employment practices;
- ensuring that appropriate benefits from the project accrue to affected communities, for example by promoting localisation of labour and local procurement, providing skills development and training opportunities, and implementing focused corporate social investment initiatives;
- minimising any potential negative environmental and occupational health impacts;

- addressing concerns relating to HIV/AIDS; and
- managing issues relating to resettlement and compensation.

Box 1: Internationally proclaimed human rights in Sasol's sphere of influence

Using the International Bill of Human Rights as a reference, listed below are some examples of the expected human rights activities or principles that fall within Sasol's sphere of influence.

Employees

- Implement measures to provide safe and healthy working conditions and environments.
- Provide employees with freedom of association and the right to collective bargaining.
- Promote non-discrimination in personnel management practices.
- Ensure that the company does not directly or indirectly use forced labour or child labour, and undertake appropriate screening and monitoring of suppliers on these issues.
- Pay at least a living wage in countries of operation.

Communities

- Prevent the forcible displacement of individuals, groups or communities, and compensate accordingly in instances of voluntary resettlement.
- Provide work to protect the economic livelihood of local communities.
- Respect the rights of indigenous people and communities.
- Work with local police or security service providers to ensure a common understanding of human rights requirements relating to the use of force, and train security personnel in appropriate practices.
- Provide access to basic health, education and housing for employees and their families, if these are not provided elsewhere.

Environment

- Implement measures designed to minimise the damage of the company's operations to the environment.

Host government

- Respect national sovereignty.
- Be committed to political neutrality.
- Implement training, monitoring and related procedures to prevent bribery and corruption.

Arguably the most significant of these issues relates to the resettlement and compensation of individuals displaced by the project activities. Community resettlement, often a consequence of large-scale infrastructure projects, is a perennial human rights risk in many developing country investments, particularly where these projects are undertaken in partnership with a government party that can impose resettlement requirements.

Resettlement: Managing a potential human rights dilemma in Mozambique

Within Mozambique, the Natural Gas Project requires three primary activities: exploration, gas field development and operation, and pipeline construction and operation. Each of these three activities results in three discrete resettlement programmes. To meet the financing requirements of the IFC, Sasol was obliged to adapt its initial Resettlement Action Plan into a more comprehensive Resettlement Planning and Implementation Programme (RPIP) that complies with relevant World Bank procedures, policies and directives. The RPIP is designed to realise the following primary objectives:

- involuntary resettlement should be avoided where feasible, or minimised, with all viable alternatives explored;
- where it is not feasible to avoid resettlement, such activities should be conceived and executed in a sustainable manner, providing sufficient investment resources to enable the persons displaced by the project to share in project benefits;
- displaced persons should be meaningfully consulted and should have opportunities to participate in planning and implementing resettlement programmes; and
- displaced persons should be assisted in their efforts to improve their livelihoods and standards of living or at least restore them, in real terms, to pre-displacement levels or to levels prevailing before the project began, whichever is higher.

Effective implementation of the RPIP required consultation with government authorities at all levels, from the national government of Mozambique to local traditional authorities. Two key requirements were that a representative Joint Task Force should be established and that the Resettlement Team members should be accompanied by government representatives. In addition, Sasol was required to deploy a full-time Community Liaison Team that would have ongoing discussions with the government and affected communities.

The Mozambique section of the pipeline and the flow lines from the wellheads to the central processing facility needed exclusion zones around them for safety and maintenance. While there is little restriction on agricultural development, settlement within the exclusion zones, other than a small agreed increase, is prohibited. From a human rights perspective, the implementation of these exclusion zones may not unnecessarily restrict the use of land, and must allow those people temporarily affected by construction activities to return to their lands and agricultural practices. It must also provide fair compensation to those people permanently moved as a result of the project.

Monitoring and evaluation programme

Periodic monitoring and evaluation (M&E) is critical for ensuring continuing application of a company's human rights commitments. In this project, M&E reports had to be submitted quarterly for the first two years and twice annually for the following two years. In addition, regular internal audits were required. One external audit per annum is required for a period of five years following the start of the monitoring programme. The outcomes of the M&E programme and the findings of the internal and external audits constitute an important barometer for evaluating the impact of the project on resettlement and human rights issues.

The stated objectives of the M&E programme – which covered homesteads, graves and farming settlements (*machambas*) – were to assess compliance with the following resettlement objectives: to help re-settlers adapt to their new environment; to monitor the effects of resettlement for a period of four years and to take the necessary action to address resettlement related problems should they arise; and to continuously assess the re-establishment of comparable sustainable livelihoods of persons affected by resettlement.

During the M&E assessments, the auditors visited all the households that had been provided with replacement housing, and a selection of those that had been provided with replacement *machambas*. On the basis of these visits, the auditors confirmed that the M&E procedures required by the RPIP had generally been correctly applied. In addition, Sasol's M&E staff were found to be competent, considerate of the affected households that were visited and professional in their approach to them. Although the auditor found that replacement houses had been built according to a specification agreed upon with the Mozambican government, it recommended that Sasol consider improving the insulation and/or ventilation in the houses; which Sasol agreed to do. Finally, the procedures to enable the owners of the replacement *machambas* to participate more effectively during the M&E visits were put into place.

Ensuring transparent communications

Operating in the context of high levels of mistrust of corporations – which, arguably, is particularly understandable in a project of this nature, given the frequent human rights transgressions associated with extractive sector investments in developing countries[7] – a company committed to upholding human rights necessarily needs to be particularly transparent and effective in its communication.

As the operator of the pipeline, Sasol developed a communications plan that was intended to serve as a preventative management tool. In Mozambique, the plan communicated to people the safety aspects of gas transmission and the risks caused by unauthorised activities in the partial protection zone around the pipeline. All relevant authorities and government departments were sent letters to reinforce awareness of the pipeline. In addition, as an aid to planning agricultural and agro-industrial developments, local authorities were supplied with GIS (Geographic Information System) documents that showed the exact location of the pipeline. Colour posters in Portuguese and Tsetswa were created to help villagers better understand the project.

From 2005, Sasol implemented the plan at various levels: national, provincial and local government, village chiefs and community forums. Five route inspectors were appointed, who were responsible for monitoring the integrity of the pipeline and reinforcing local awareness of it. This team liaised with local authorities, traditional leaders and members of local communities along the route as part of their routine pipeline inspections. The community liaison manager visited the district authorities along the route once every two months to discuss any issues relating to the pipeline and the surrounding partial protection zone. This was supplemented by communication campaigns focusing mainly on community groups and schools during the school holiday camps.

Implementation of a focused social investment programme

In addition to the resettlement plan, the M&E activities and the communications programme, a final related activity was the implementation of a strategic social investment programme funded by a separate Social Development Fund (SDF). With IFC assistance this programme involved the development of rigorous procedures in terms of which Sasol identifies, approves, implements and monitors these social investment projects.

An SDF management team has developed a project-specific work methodology aimed at delivering sustainable community projects: defining needs in consultation with members of the affected community; generating solutions that involve the community and provide for environmental issues; approving projects in a manner that ensures good corporate governance; implementing the projects using Sasol's project management experience; and undertaking M&E programmes aimed at ensuring project sustainability.

In Mozambique, Sasol approved an amount of US$800,000 for the 2006 financial year for use in social investment programmes. Approved projects embrace the provision of water, craft training, electrification of a primary school, rehabilitation of cattle-dipping facilities and the construction of a water supply dam. Sasol's Social Development Fund has become involved in the management of HIV/AIDS issues and has decided to support existing NGO initiatives rather than designing stand-alone HIV/AIDS programmes. A joint SDF and NGO programme is located in Magude in Maputo Province and funds have been allocated for this purpose.

Lessons from the Mozambican experience

Reflecting on Sasol's experience in Mozambique, Wandrag identified a number of important things that would have to be done to deal specifically with the human rights challenges arising from its resettlement activities: having a clearly defined set of project commitments relating to resettlement (as detailed in the IFC-mandated Resettlement Planning and Implementation Programme); ensuring provision for a formalised monitoring and evaluation programme that would include periodic assessments and audits by both internal and external auditors; promoting transparency and engagement though the company's structured communications plan; and implementing a strategic corporate social investment programme that would address specific needs identified in consultation with members of the affected community.

This was all very well, thought Wandrag, but to what extent were these activities primarily a function of the project funding requirements stipulated by the IFC? To be sure, while management of many of the safety, health, environmental and human resource aspects of the project would have been addressed as part of Sasol's existing policies and practices, it was evident to Wandrag that the need to comply with World Bank policies as a financing requirement was an overriding additional consideration.

This left him feeling a little unsettled. While these financing requirements are now increasingly seen as the norm for projects of this nature – as reflected by the widespread adoption of the Equator Principles[8] – Wandrag was not sure that this would be sufficient to mitigate potential human rights risks. Some future projects might not be subject to the Equator Principles funding requirements, and even where they were, Wandrag was not convinced that this in itself would be sufficient to ensure effective protection of human rights.

He recalled a recent discussion with one of the newer Sasol executives, who, in commenting on the Mozambique project, had suggested that 'as Sasol gains experience in the international arena, it is moving up the maturity scale; it is no longer focusing predominantly on pure commercial viability (as was largely the case with the Mozambique project), but it is also now beginning to consider issues relating to reputation and image'.

Wandrag looked back at the map on his desk – Human Rights and Business Risk in the Extractive Sector (see Document 1) – and noted that some of the countries where Sasol was contemplating investments had been singled out for various specific human rights violations connected with extractive sector activities. Several of Sasol's anticipated projects are joint venture partnerships with the host country governments of these countries. Many of these investments in strategic commodities would have an important impact on the local economy. It was clear to Wandrag that significant potential reputational challenges and risks lay ahead for Sasol. He was not sure that the company's current approach to human rights was sufficiently structured to address these challenges. The apparent success of the Mozambican project did not allay his concerns.

Human rights and reputational risk: Addressing critical challenges

As Sasol expands its operations into countries that have been criticised for their human rights records, Wandrag recognises that the company needs a structured process to minimise the potential reputational risks associated with its investment activities.

He recognises, however, that implementing such a process would present some significant challenges for the traditional approach to project investment decisions. Some of the questions the company needs to consider are:

- How should one address a potential conflict between 'internationally proclaimed human rights' and the legal (and sometime cultural) context of the country in which one is investing?

- Under what conditions might a company be deemed complicit in human rights abuses?

- Are there certain countries in which investments of any kind should be screened because of the country's human rights record?

Assessing Sasol's current approach to human rights risk management

Sasol currently has no separate policy that *specifically* addresses human rights. Its only stated policy commitment is found in the Sasol Code of Ethics (see Documents 2 and 3). This code, which binds all Sasol businesses, consists of four fundamental ethical principles – responsibility, honesty, fairness and respect – and 15 ethical behavioural standards. In terms of one of these behavioural standards (respect), all Sasol employees are required to 'respect human rights and dignity'. The company's policies and procedures also embrace provisions for: labour and trade union rights; the protection of employee safety and health; environmental management activities; community engagement; and corporate social investment activities. Sasol has recently approved a set of minimum requirements for safety, health and environmental performance that reflect the safeguard policies of the IFC.

A carefully structured process is applied to project assessment and roll-out. All new invest-ment decisions and projects are subject to Sasol's Business Development and Implementation Model (BD&I). The model contains a series of 'decision gates'. At each gate the various risks associated with that project are reviewed. For projects that entail investments in new countries, Sasol undertakes a country-specific risk assessment process that includes a review of potential financial, technical, socio-economic, political and legal risks. The assessment uses a detailed database of around 3,000 potential risks, and the final decision on whether or not to invest is informed by the company's risk-bearing capacity. This risk assessment process is complex and entails both quantitative and qualitative aspects. Sasol is in the process of further refining the model as part of a general global trend that places greater emphasis on more intangible issues associated with the company's reputation.

Some project managers have suggested that in the early days of Sasol's expansion into new regions its risk assessment process focused almost exclusively on a project's commercial and technical viability. However, as the company gained greater experience in the international arena, and improved its understanding of what is expected of global companies, it has gained greater awareness of the need to manage some of the so-called 'non-financial' risks in a more systematic manner. As Africa's largest non-state oil and gas company it acknowledges that it has the potential to play a particularly important role in addressing some of the challenges of effective human rights risk management.

Balancing international norms and local compliance

The challenge of respecting universally-applicable human rights, while at the same time ac-knowledging the specific social, cultural, economic and legal context of the country of opera-tion, can present companies with some significant dilemmas:

- How does one reconcile the dictates of a country's legal sovereignty with what the UN Bill of Rights views as a binding international norm?

- Is it within the remit of the company to get actively involved in contributing to an improved human rights governance framework, or could such activity be construed (however incor-rectly) as undue intervention and influence by the private sector in the policy decisions of the host country government?

Sasol's international growth plans might see the company faced with several dilemmas: man-aging issues of human resources, collective bargaining, and political and religious freedom in Iran and China; voluntary community relocation that may be required in India as a result of a possible petrochemical venture; ensuring appropriate protection of its petroleum interests in Nigeria without precipitating possible human rights abuses (such as the management of security forces); addressing concerns about rights to privacy and non-discrimination in Qatar; and managing concerns about the role and status of women in Islamic countries.

Finding an approach that respects international principles and local custom often requires a nuanced approach to legal sovereignty and universal rights. Recent evidence of the way Sasol strikes such a balance is its response to the locally-imposed requirement that all prospective employees in Qatar take an HIV/AIDS test. A negative result is the precondition for entry into Qatar. Sasol's response to this requirement was to ensure that all prospective employees considering this posting were provided with ample notification of the requirement and given full flexibility to decide whether or not to apply. Sasol offered no judgement about the decision they took, nor did it engage in any action that could be seen as career discrimination on the basis of the decision. By creating such a flexible policy, the company protected rights to privacy and freedom of choice while simultaneously complying with the existing law of Qatar. Finding this balance in the context of some of the other dilemmas that Sasol faces in other regions might not be as easy.

'Complicity' in human rights abuses

While recognising the ultimate responsibility of governments for ensuring that human rights are respected, protected and promoted, the changing operating context for business has prompted the Office of the High Commissioner for Human Rights (OHCHR) to lead efforts to understand and define *corporate* complicity in human rights abuses. An OHCHR briefing paper on human rights suggests that a company is complicit in human rights abuses 'if it authorises, tolerates, or knowingly ignores human rights abuses committed by an entity associated with it, or if the company knowingly provides practical assistance or encouragement that has a substantial effect on the perpetration of human rights abuse'.[9] Citing a court case in the US, the OHCHR goes on to suggest that 'the participation of the company need not actually cause the abuse; rather, the company's assistance or encouragement has to be to a degree that, without such participation, the abuses most probably would not have occurred to the same extent or in the same way'.[10]

In assessing the potential risk of being deemed 'complicit' in human rights abuses, the company needs to consider both the government's involvement in the abuse and the company's proximity to the abuse. To evaluate the host government's involvement in breaches of human rights obligations, the company must assess the extent to which the host government is either *oppressive* (actively endorses the human rights violations), or *ineffective* (is simply incapable of preventing such violation). Such an assessment can be informed by the advice of relevant UN agencies and NGOs such as Amnesty International or Human Rights Watch. Companies are less likely to be found complicit in state breaches of human rights where the breach is the result of ineffective enforcement, rather than deliberate government oppression.

In those countries where the government is seen to be actively committing the human rights abuse, a company needs to ensure that its activities are not closely linked to this abuse. It needs to consider, for example, the company's geographic proximity to the abuse, the potential for the company's products to be used in committing the violation, and whether the company is seen as helping to strengthen the role of civil society or further entrenching the power of the host government.

Screening countries on the basis of their human rights record

An important element of a systematic approach to human rights risk management is to identify those countries where the act of investing in that country will be sufficient, in and of itself, to increase the risk of being complicit in human rights violations. It has been suggested that if a country displays any of the following characteristics, a company should avoid investments in that country:[11]

- it is subject to international sanctions;
- it has been accused of genocide, war crimes and/or crimes against humanity;
- it refuses access to a neutral body such as the International Committee of the Red Cross;
- there has been a clear expression of popular sentiment against any foreign commercial activities.

A systematic human rights risk management process must consider the above issues as part of its existing country risk assessment process. Guidance for identifying such countries is typically available from human rights NGOs and governmental and intergovernmental agencies.

Conclusion: Towards a more systematic approach to human rights

Reflecting on Sasol's current approach to human rights risk management, Wandrag came to the conclusion that while their experience in Mozambique had generally been positive, this outcome did not adequately reflect whether the company was effectively addressing the potential reputational risks associated with its anticipated new investments. Noting the experience of companies such as BP, Total and Shell – each of which had suffered reputational consequences from its perceived complicity in human rights abuses – Wandrag felt that Sasol needed to take a more systematic approach.

Drawing on his review of the recently developed human rights strategies in companies such as BP, Total and Shell, Wandrag began to list the principles he believed should inform a more structured human rights risk management process. His initial list comprised five key principles:

- Provide human rights awareness and training programmes for specifically targeted staff, designed to increase understanding of international human rights obligations, the risks and opportunities these rights present, and the human rights situation in countries where the company has investments or is planning to invest.
- Integrate human rights issues more formally into project and country risk assessments, make provision for accessing regularly updated information to assess the human rights situation in the countries where Sasol is planning operations, and identify the activities of the company most at risk of being deemed complicit in possible rights abuses. In certain defined instances (using the criteria identified earlier) a country's human rights record should constitute a sufficient basis for screening investments in that country.
- Ensure further integration of human rights concerns in company policies and procedures, formalising lines of responsibility for human rights, providing for human rights in procurement and supplier audits, and developing appropriate security procedures, including screening and training of security staff.
- Ensure appropriate consultation and communication on human rights issues, both internally and externally.

- Develop appropriate monitoring and assurance mechanisms, and make use of the Human Rights Compliance Assessment (HRCA) tool.[12]

In developing these principles for the company, Wandrag looked forward to continuing his dialogue with relevant Sasol decision-makers. He was confident he would be able to report good progress regarding Sasol's human rights activities in the company's next sustainable development report.

Document 1: Human rights and business risk in the extractive sector

Document 1, produced by Amnesty International and the Prince of Wales International Business Leaders Forum, illustrates the exposure of various extractive companies in countries where human rights violations are prevalent. The identified violations for each country are not comprehensive, but have been selected on the basis of relevance to corporate risk. These countries are not necessarily the ones with the worst human rights records. Several selected countries have Sasol investments, or are countries that Sasol is investigating with regard to the potential for investments. A number of these investments will be JV partnerships with government bodies.

Document 1: Human rights and business risk in the extractive sector

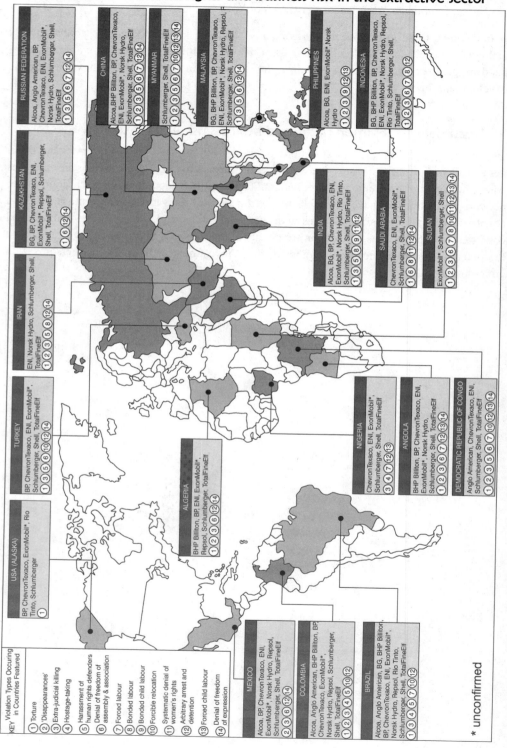

KEY Violation Types Occuring in Countries Featured
1. Torture
2. 'Disappearances'
3. Extra-judicial killing
4. Hostage-taking
5. Harassment of human rights defenders
6. Denial of freedom of assembly & association
7. Forced labour
8. Bonded labour
9. Bonded child labour
10. Forcible relocation
11. Systematic denial of women's rights
12. Arbitrary arrest and detention
13. Forced child labour
14. Denial of freedom of expression

USA (ALASKA)
BP, ChevronTexaco, ExonMobil*, Rio Tinto, Schlumberger
①

MEXICO
Alcoa, BG, ChevronTexaco, ENI, ExonMobil*, Norsk Hydro, Repsol, Schlumberger, Shell, TotalFineElf
② ③ ⑥ ⑫ ⑭

COLOMBIA
Alcoa, Anglo American, BHP Billiton, BP, ChevronTexaco, ExonMobil*, Norsk Hydro, Repsol, Schlumberger, Shell, TotalFineElf
① ② ③ ④ ⑤ ⑫

BRAZIL
Alcoa, Anglo American, BG, BHP Billiton, BP, ChevronTexaco, ENI, ExonMobil*, Norsk Hydro, Repsol, Rio Tinto, Schlumberger, Shell, TotalFineElf
① ③ ④ ⑤ ⑦ ⑩ ⑫

ALGERIA
BHP Billiton, BP, ENI, ExonMobil*, Repsol, Schlumberger, TotalFineElf
① ② ③ ⑥ ⑫ ⑭

TURKEY
BP, ChevronTexaco, ENI, ExonMobil*, Schlumberger, Shell, TotalFineElf
① ③ ⑤ ⑥ ⑩ ⑫ ⑭

IRAN
ENI, Norsk Hydro, Schlumberger, Shell, TotalFineElf
① ② ③ ⑤ ⑧ ⑫ ⑭

KAZAKHSTAN
BG, BP, ChevronTexaco, ENI, ExonMobil*, Repsol, Schlumberger, Shell, TotalFineElf
① ⑥ ⑫ ⑭

RUSSIAN FEDERATION
Alcoa, Anglo American, BP, ChevronTexaco, ENI, ExonMobil*, Norsk Hydro, Schlumberger, Shell, TotalFineElf
① ③ ⑤ ⑥ ⑦ ⑫ ⑭

CHINA
Alcoa, BHP Billiton, BP, ChevronTexaco, ENI, ExonMobil*, Norsk Hydro, Schlumberger, Shell, TotalFineElf
① ② ③ ⑤ ⑥ ⑦ ⑫ ⑭

MYANMAR
Schlumberger, Shell, TotalFineElf
① ② ③ ⑤ ⑥ ⑦ ⑩ ⑫ ⑬ ⑭

MALAYSIA
BG, BHP Billiton, BP, ChevronTexaco, ENI, ExonMobil*, Norsk Hydro, Repsol, Schlumberger, Shell, TotalFineElf
① ③ ⑤ ⑥ ⑫ ⑭

PHILIPPINES
Alcoa, BG, ENI, ExonMobil*, Norsk Hydro
① ② ③ ⑨ ⑬

INDONESIA
BG, BHP Billiton, BP, ChevronTexaco, ENI, ExonMobil*, Norsk Hydro, Repsol, Schlumberger, Shell, TotalFineElf
① ② ③ ⑥ ⑦ ⑧ ⑫

INDIA
Alcoa, BG, BP, ChevronTexaco, ENI, ExonMobil*, Norsk Hydro, Rio Tinto, Schlumberger, Shell, TotalFineElf
① ③ ⑤ ⑧ ⑨ ⑪ ⑫

SAUDI ARABIA
ChevronTexaco, ENI, ExonMobil*, Schlumberger, Shell, TotalFineElf
① ⑥ ⑧ ⑪ ⑫ ⑭

SUDAN
ExonMobil*, Schlumberger, Shell
① ② ③ ⑥ ⑦ ⑧ ⑩ ⑪ ⑫ ⑬ ⑭

NIGERIA
ChevronTexaco, ENI, ExonMobil*, Schlumberger, Shell, TotalFineElf
③ ④ ⑦ ⑫ ⑬

ANGOLA
BHP Billiton, BP, ChevronTexaco, ENI, ExonMobil*, Norsk Hydro, Schlumberger, Shell, TotalFineElf
① ② ③ ⑥ ⑦ ⑫ ⑬ ⑭

DEMOCRATIC REPUBLIC OF CONGO
Anglo American, ChevronTexaco, ENI, Schlumberger, Shell, TotalFineElf
① ② ③ ⑤ ⑥ ⑦ ⑩ ⑬ ⑭

* unconfirmed

Document 2: Sasol's Code of Ethics

1. **Responsibility – We hold ourselves responsible and accountable to our stakeholders for our actions**
- We hold ourselves responsible and accountable to apply Sasol's resources to maximise sustainable returns to Sasol's shareholders.
- We manage Sasol to be a responsible corporate citizen and we are committed to conduct Sasol's business with due regard to the interests of its stakeholders, the environment and its social responsibilities.
- We comply with all applicable legal requirements as a minimum standard.
- We subscribe to effective corporate governance.
- We implement controls to ensure that disclosures in respect of Sasol's business are not misleading and made timely.

2. **Honesty – We are truthful**
- We emphatically reject all forms of dishonesty and do not tolerate dishonest acts such as bribery, corruption, fraud, falsification and misrepresentation.
- We avoid and declare conflicts of interest with Sasol's interests.
- We apply the assets and other resources of Sasol for business purposes only and do not use such assets and other resources for personal benefit unless approved in accordance with an official Sasol group policy.
- We do not misuse our Sasol positions to obtain personal benefits.

3. **Fairness – We treat our stakeholders equitably**
- We treat others as we would like to be treated in similar circumstances.
- We base business decisions on policy, strategy, facts and analysis, and not on irrational emotion, prejudices or other irrelevant factors.

4. **Respect – We acknowledge the rights and dignity of others**
- We respect human rights and dignity.
- We treat our stakeholders with respect.
- We do not discriminate on the basis of factors such as race, religion, gender or sexual orientation.

Document 3: Extract from the Sasol guide to the application of Sasol's Code of Ethics

Respect – We acknowledge the rights and dignity of others

We respect human rights and dignity

- Sasol supports the concept of human rights as contained in the Constitution of the Republic of South Africa and the UN Universal Declaration of Human Rights.

- Sasol respects the rights to life, liberty, security, and the right to be free from slavery, servitude, torture or cruel, inhuman or degrading treatment or punishment.

- Sasol wishes to make a positive and constructive contribution to the reduction and elimination of all forms of forced and compulsory labour. We do not tolerate unacceptable treatment of workers such as exploitation of children, physical punishment, or involuntary servitude. We expect our contractors and customers with whom we do business to uphold the same standards.

- In places where Sasol operates and child labour exists, we will seek to engage in programmes and projects which encourage and facilitate the transition to alternatives to child employment such as apprenticeships, training and further education, and will work constructively with our contractors and suppliers where appropriate.

- Sasol respects people's rights to privacy, in matters relating to family, home, correspondence, reputation and freedom of movement. Sasol also respects people's rights to freedom of thought, conscience and religion, freedom of opinion and expression and association and the right to take part in government.

- Sasol respects the rights to social security and to the economic, social and cultural rights indispensable to human dignity and the free development of each individual's personality.

- High levels of violence and a poor human rights record in some countries are to be condemned, but need not in themselves preclude company investment. Although it is not always easy, it is possible to work securely and in an ethical way in such situations. Sasol supports and respects the protection of internationally recognised human rights within our sphere of influence.

We treat our stakeholders with respect

- Fair business conduct requires that we note and acknowledge the rights of our stakeholders and have an awareness and appreciation of the impact of our decisions on our stakeholders.

We do not discriminate on the basis of factors such as race, religion, gender or sexual orientation

- Sasol respects fundamental rights and freedoms for all, without discrimination on the basis of race, colour, religion, gender, age, language, culture, national origin, citizenship, sexual orientation or disability.

Editors' reflections and questions

1. Sasol is expanding its operations internationally and is considering investing in countries where there have been concerns about the abuse of human rights. These investments include large-scale petrochemical operations, which would involve joint venture partnerships with the host country's government. Company managers recognise that should the company go ahead with these investments it could find that some of the local legislative requirements (relating for example to the establishment of trade union organisations, or the screening of employees on religious grounds) would conflict with stated company policies on freedom of association and non-discrimination. How should such tensions be responded to? Is it possible and desirable to establish a company policy to provide guidance in such instances, and should such a policy be made public? To what extent should the company get involved in lobbying for reform on human rights issues?

2. Sasol's managers also recognise the increased scrutiny that companies are facing from NGOs, as well as the perception that in some instances a company's mere presence in a country is seen as condoning the abuses being committed in that country. The case study recommends a screening process to assess such risks in particular countries prior to investing in them, and it suggests criteria for disqualifying countries for investment. Are these criteria likely to be widely accepted, and to what extent can they be objectively assessed? How should company managers deal with instances where there are disputed assessments of a country's human rights record?

3. Within the company, there are contrasting opinions on the role of human rights in the business. Some are concerned that operating in countries with questionable human rights records is inherently problematic, while others see it as an opportunity to foster universal human rights values in these places. Some reject both positions, arguing, 'Surely our responsibility is simply to comply with the law of the country in which we invest?' What are the implications of such diverse perspectives within the company for a systematic management approach to human rights?

Notes

1   This case study was researched and written by the author, a visiting senior lecturer at the University of Cape Town. Sasol provided payment for the case study to cover costs for the time spent on the interviews and desk research. The author has consulted to Sasol on other projects and helped them, for example, in their recent sustainable development reports, as well as in managing and facilitating their independent external stakeholder engagement processes. He has also consulted to the UN Global Compact Regional Focal Point (South Africa) on various projects. The case study is based on interviews with relevant Sasol employees and with external stakeholders, and the author was provided with access to copies of internal Sasol e-mails as well as copies of correspondence with external parties.

2   As part of its global growth strategy, the company has a 50:50 joint venture project with the National Petrochemical Company of Iran to develop new monomer and polymer production facilities at Bandar Assaluyeh in Iran. Sasol Polymers is also a significant partner in the Optimal Olefins and Petlin plants at Kertih, Malaysia.

3   Human Rights Watch, *The Curse of Gold* (New York: HRW, 2005) (see also the case study on AngloGold Ashanti in Case 2).

4   This review of Sasol's human rights related activities, undertaken as part of the NGP, is not intended to constitute a thorough, independent assessment of these activities, but rather is provided as a basis for making some key observations and for identifying possible risks and opportunities facing Sasol as it seeks to ensure effective implementation of the UNGC principles. Elements of this review draw on Sasol documents published to meet World Bank financing requirements, including in particular the *Annual Integrated Disclosure Report (February 2006)*, the *Regional Environmental and Social Assessment*, and the *Resettlement Planning and Implementation Programme*. Much of the content of these documents reflects the findings of independent third party assessments.

5   The *International Bill of Human Rights* is made up of the *Universal Declaration of Human Rights*, the *International Covenant on Economic, Social and Cultural Rights* and the *International Covenant on Civil and Political Rights*.

6   This debate gained prominence in discussions about the draft *Norms on the Responsibilities of Transnational Corporations and Other Business Enterprises with regard to Human Rights* that sought to identify what human rights apply directly to companies within their spheres of activity and influence (see also Chapter 2). These 'Draft UN Norms', written by a UN sub-commission, prompted a lively discussion, with a number of companies and business organisations protesting that the commission was seeking to shift responsibilities unduly to the private sector. Although the norms were not accepted by the UN, and do not have legal standing, some companies are using them as an assessment tool. Following the decision not to accept the UN Norms, in 2005 Secretary General Kofi Annan appointed Professor John Ruggie as his special representative on business and human rights. The report, and a lively exchange of views on it, is available at the Business and Human Rights Resource Centre, www.business-humanrights.org

7   Based on his 2006 interim report, which included a review of a survey of 65 instances of human rights abuses reported by NGOs, the UN Secretary-General's Special Representative on Business and Human Rights states that 'the extractive sector – oil, gas, and mining – utterly dominates this sample of reported abuses, with two-thirds of the total. The extractive industries also account for most allegations of the worst abuses, up to and including complicity in crimes against humanity, typically for acts committed by public and private security forces protecting company assets and property; large-scale corruption; violations of labour rights; and a broad array of abuses in relation to local communities, especially indigenous people' (J.G. Ruggie, Plenary Remarks at World Mines Ministries Forum, Toronto, 3 March 2006, available at http://www.reports-and-materials.org/Ruggie-World-Mines-Ministries-Forum-3-Mar-2006.doc (accessed July 2007)).

8   Sasol's recent commitment to a set of minimum safety, health and environmental requirements (based on the IFC's recently updated environmental and social policies and procedures) is, in part, in recognition of this development. It is interesting to note, however, that at the time of writing, of the South African financial institutions only Nedbank and the Development Bank of Southern Africa are signatories to the Equator Principles. According to a Nedbank sustainability practitioner (personal communication, August 2007), the bank has lost out on some project financing opportunities in Africa to their South African competitors who are non-signatories to the principles.

9   Office of the High Commission on Human Rights, 'The Global Compact and Human Rights: Understanding Sphere of Influence and Complicity: OHCHR Briefing Paper', Sub-Commission on the Promotion and Protection of Human Rights, Economic and Social Council, Report on the Human Rights on the Responsibilities of Transnational Corporations and Related Business Enterprises with regard to Human Rights GENERAL, E/CN.4/2005/91 (15 February 2005). In a business context the notion of complicity includes direct complicity (the company knowingly assists in the violation of human rights); beneficial complicity (the company benefits directly from the human rights abuses committed by someone else); and silent complicity (the failure of a company to question systematic or continuous human rights violations by state authorities).

10   This variation on a causation test has been applied in the US Alien Tort Claims Act case, Doe I. *et al.* v Unocal Corporation *et al.* (see A. Clapham, 'State responsibility, corporate responsibility, and complicity in human rights violations', in L. Boman-Larsen and O. Wiggen (eds), *Responsibility in World Business: Managing Harmful Side-effects of Corporate Activity* (Tokyo: UN University Press, 2004): 50–81).

11   This structured approach, developed as part of the *Human Rights and Business Project*, presents a useful set of considerations that could form part of the company's existing political risk assessment process (see http://www.humanrightsbusiness.org (accessed July 2007)).

12   Developed by the Danish Institute for Human Rights as part of the Human Rights and Business Project mentioned in endnote 11, the HRCA contains approximately 350 questions and more than 1,000 human rights indicators drawn from the Universal Declaration of Human Rights and other major treaties. The tool enables companies to identify human rights dilemmas and to detect possible human rights violations within their field of operation.

Learning from the experience of
AngloGold Ashanti
in the Democratic Republic of Congo

PAUL KAPELUS, RALPH HAMANN & ED O'KEEFE

Introduction[1]

It is a sunny highveld morning in July 2006 and Steve Lenahan is looking out over Johannesburg from the window of his office at AngloGold Ashanti (AGA), one of the world's largest gold mining companies. He is the company's corporate affairs director. The role of big business in sustainable development is on his mind as he studies the view of the city. He is thinking about how radically people's perceptions can vary. He recalls how Tony Trahar, the CEO of Anglo American (one of AGA's main shareholders) once said, 'Johannesburg, built upon the gold industry, is a shining example of sustainable development!' And yet Patrick Bond, a prominent academic, has called Johannesburg 'the world's most unsustainable city', with reference to the human rights abuses committed by mining companies during apartheid.[2]

Currently, many of the company's most pressing human rights challenges are experienced in countries such as the Democratic Republic of the Congo (DRC). These countries may be wracked by violent conflict, but their large reserves of minerals and metals exert a tremendous pull on mining companies; indeed, it is often said that it is the very presence of the minerals that is the root cause of the conflict. AGA was at the centre of such a controversy when it was revealed in mid 2005 that its staff had made payments to a militia group in the DRC accused of gross human rights abuses. Rather than attempt to deny or to cover up its complicity, the company admitted that it had erred and committed itself to learning from its mistake. At the same time, it insisted that it would not abort its plans in the DRC.

Instead, Lenahan and the AGA CEO, Bobby Godsell, have decided that the experience in the DRC be used to identify important lessons that can be applied to future investments in strife-torn environments. In the company's *Report to Society 2005*, Godsell posed the human rights question that confronts AGA: For companies like AngloGold Ashanti that seek to uphold socially responsible values, under what conditions in such societies is the continued pursuit of business activities justified, and when is it not?

The DRC context

The DRC has for many years epitomised what the Organisation for Economic Cooperation and Development (OECD) calls a 'weak governance zone':

> A weak governance zone is defined as an investment environment in which governments are unable or unwilling to assume their responsibilities. These 'government failures' lead to broader failures in political, economic and civic institutions that, in turn, create the conditions for endemic violence, crime and corruption and that block economic and social development. About 15 per cent of the world's people live in such areas, notably in sub-Saharan Africa.[3]

The DRC's human development index is among the lowest in the world. For the most part it has gone down in the period during which this index has been measured (1975 to 2003), with a slight rise in 2004.[4] The conflict that engulfed much of the country from 1996 to 2001 claimed almost four million lives and involved numerous other African countries. Parts of the DRC experienced the highest estimated conflict-related mortality rates in the world.[5]

As a result of this conflict, international investment in the DRC has been very limited. The only sectors that have experienced some investment have been extractive industries and related service providers. Given the DRC's large deposits of gold, copper, cobalt and other metals and minerals, and given the increasing global demand and the concomitant decrease in accessible deposits in more stable countries, resources companies have been the most likely to discount the political and economic risks associated with doing business in the DRC. Junior mining companies and small, unlisted companies have an even greater appetite for risk and are generally subject to less intense international scrutiny by government and civil society organisations.[6] In some cases, this increased risk has been rewarded with significant returns. As one mining company CEO observed: 'It's the holy grail of the copper industry – companies are saying: to hell with the political risk, we just have to be here!'[7]

Over and above the direct risks to the companies' employees or operations as a result of physical violence, disruptions due to destroyed or faulty infrastructure and expropriations, companies operating in weak governance zones also face a number of indirect risks associated with the international corporate responsibility movement. Companies have been accused of supplying the economic resources that provide the 'motives and means' to perpetuate conflict, especially where such resources take the form of bribes or remittances to armed groups. Such complicity in human rights abuses means they risk damaging their reputation and their relations with their stakeholders.

To guard against corporate complicity in human rights abuses, various initiatives now exist to guide companies. Some of the most prominent of these are the Voluntary Principles on Security and Human Rights and the OECD Risk Awareness Tool for Multinational Enterprises in Weak Governance Zones.[8] Related initiatives include the Extractive Industries Transparency Initiative (EITI), which seeks to enhance the disclosure of information on payment of taxes and royalties by companies in the extractive industries, and the Kimberley Process, which focuses on bringing together governments and companies to stop the trade in so-called 'blood' or 'conflict' diamonds.[9]

Figure 1: Map of the DRC showing Mongbwalu and the Ituri area

Source: AngloGold Ashanti, *Report to Society 2005.*

The AGA experience in the DRC as a 'test case'

The DRC has been a prominent test case for international efforts to break the link between corporate activity and conflict and human rights abuses. As a start, a panel of experts mandated by the United Nations Security Council has identified a number of corporations that have contributed to the coffers of 'elite networks' of rebel groups, Congo army officials and armies from other African countries. These elite networks have fought over the proceeds of natural resources extraction and used these proceeds to fund their hostilities.[10]

AGA's was one of the most prominent cases to illustrate the challenges and complexities facing companies operating in weak governance zones and in the DRC in particular. The company has a licence to explore a gold deposit in the Ituri district in the northeast (see Figure 1). The exploration area is near the town of Mongbwalu and covers an area of approximately 10,000 km². The Ituri area has been one of the most volatile in the country, even after the large-scale deployment of the UN peacekeeping force, Mission des Nations Unies en République Démocratique du Congo (MONUC), in 1999 and the establishment of a transitional government in 2003. Clashes between the DRC military and the Front des Nationalistes Intégrationnistes (FNI), the main rebel group in the area, have taken place as recently as October 2006.

In January 2005, staff of the AGA exploration team in the Ituri district made an US$8,000 payment to the FNI which controlled much of the Ituri area during the civil war and has been accused of committing extensive human rights abuses. In addition, the AGA exploration project provided the FNI with accommodation and access to transport and paid levies on cargo flown into the local airport. The payment and assistance established a relationship between AGA and the FNI and gave the FNI a certain degree of political legitimacy.

In June 2005 Human Rights Watch released a report entitled *The Curse of Gold*.[11] The report offered a detailed account of the financial and material assistance provided by AGA to the FNI. It also noted that AGA had gained permission from the militia group to enter the area, despite being warned by the UN peacekeeping force MONUC not to start operations in Mongbwalu. For many observers, this report buttressed the conclusion that corporations often act irresponsibly in weak governance zones and that they should not be permitted to operate in such areas. AGA, while contrite, argued that the interests of local communities in Ituri and the DRC in general would be better served by the company remaining in the area.

Ashanti's historic presence in the region

Gold was first discovered in the north eastern Congo in 1903 and in 1905 the Belgian colonial authorities began to exploit it through private companies. As with other mines under colonial rule, the mining companies took a paternalistic approach and provided most social services to the local community. After independence in 1960, the president of the renamed Zaire, Mobuto Sese Seko, nationalised the mines. He continued the high level of social service provision; however, much of this service was provided through external agencies such as churches. Despite this, high levels of corruption and patronage meant that few long-term economic benefits flowed to local communities.

The production of gold declined slowly over the next three decades. In the early 1990s a joint venture agreement was entered into between a DRC government company, Kilo-Moto (OKIMO)-Mindev, and the International Finance Corporation (IFC). This joint venture created a company called KIMIN. The IFC pulled out of KIMIN as the threat of violent conflict in the country increased. By 1996, KIMIN's debts were threatening the continued viability of the operation. In order to raise much needed funds the Ghanaian mining company Ashanti Goldfields Company Limited (Ashanti) was successfully invited to invest in KIMIN. Ashanti began more detailed exploration of the Mongbwalu concession in 1996.

Ashanti halted its activities around Mongbwalu in 1998 because it was recognised that the country's impending (second) civil war would make exploration activity in the region impossible. Over the next four years the war in the DRC escalated. Despite the conflict, Ashanti maintained an interest in the concession and in November 2000 it secured a majority stake in KIMIN and the company was renamed Ashanti Goldfields Kilo (AGK). However, as a result of the ongoing war, no mining and only limited exploration took place. The retrenchment of workers and a subsequent dispute over the payment of salaries led to significant tension between the company management and workers, most of whom hail from the Mongbwalu area. This tension has contributed to the atmosphere of mistrust between the mining company and local communities in the region.

As the virulence of the war in the DRC increased with foreign involvement from Uganda, Rwanda, and Zimbabwe, the United Nations published a report that linked the war to mineral resources extraction.[12] In July 2002, the Ashanti personnel left the exploration site. However, in the chaos of the conflict, some prospecting continued on the basis of personal contact between mining operators on site and the fighting factions. Towards the end of 2003, MONUC established a base in Ituri and engaged in repeated clashes with the FNI.

In 2003, AGK returned to the site. In March 2004, the self-styled president of the FNI, Floribert Njabu, returned from his base in Kinshasa to Mongbwalu and began talks with AGK. According to internal AGA documentation, he told AGK that they were welcome to return to the area, that the war was over, and that the FNI wanted to become a political party. The FNI set itself up as the authority in the area and provided 'permission' to AGK to continue exploration activities in the concession area. Accounts vary as to whether AGK actively sought permission to operate from the FNI, thereby providing political legitimacy to the militia group, or whether this 'permission' was granted without the company soliciting it.

After AGK had re-established a presence in the area, the FNI was provided with financial payments and other support, including accommodation, transport and levies for cargo flown into the area by AGK. The justification for this support remains a matter of dispute. AGA claims that AGK's support of the FNI was essential to ensure the safety of employees whose lives were threatened by the FNI. Human Rights Watch (HRW), on the other hand, claims that this support ensured AGK's control of the concession area. In its report published in mid 2005, a local resident is quoted as saying: 'Njabu [president of the FNI] now has power due to the gold he controls and [the presence of] AngloGold Ashanti.'[13]

The merger of Ashanti and AngloGold

In April 2004, Ashanti and the South African company AngloGold Limited finalised their merger. These two major mining companies became one of the largest gold mining companies in the world, AngloGold Ashanti. AGA has its headquarters in Johannesburg and its primary listing on the Johannesburg Securities Exchange. It is also listed on exchanges in Australia, New York, London, Ghana, Paris and Belgium.

Although the usual due diligence studies were undertaken prior to the merger between Ashanti and AngloGold, these seemingly did not consider the risks associated with conducting business activity in weak governance zones. The AGA experience suggests that human rights considerations play, at best, a secondary role in the negotiations for mergers and acquisitions.

After the merger the company developed a new set of business values and principles to guide its operations and exploration activities (see Table 1). These values and principles relate to ethics and governance, occupational safety and health, regional health threats, labour practices, the environment and the community. They set high standards for the company and are in line with international standards and guidelines, such as the United Nations Global Compact.[14] The question remains, however, to what extent these new business principles are embedded in the new company's procedures and culture. The inculcation of a new set of values is a complex process that takes a significant period of time,[15] and this complexity is further increased by the new company's international spread of operations, and – in some instances – their setting in weak governance zones.

Table 1: AngloGold Ashanti's business values and principles

Business values
• Anglo Gold Ashanti consistently strives to generate competitive shareholder returns. We do this by replacing profitable gold reserves and by continuously improving the performance of our key resources – our people, our assets and our product. We conduct ourselves with honesty and integrity.   • We provide our employees with opportunities to develop their skills while sharing risks and rewards in workplaces that promote innovation, teamwork and freedom with accountability. We embrace cultural diversity.   • Every manager and employee takes responsibility for health and safety; and together we strive to create workplaces which are free of occupational injury and illness.   • We strive to form partnerships with host communities, sharing their environments, traditions and values. We want the communities to be better off for Anglo Gold Ashanti's having been there. We are committed to working in an environmentally responsible way.

Principles
• We will *comply with all laws*, regulations, standards and international conventions which apply to our businesses and to our relationships with our stakeholders. Specifically, Anglo Gold Ashanti supports the Universal Declaration of Human Rights, the Fundamental Rights Conventions of the International Labour Organization (ILO) and those principles and values referred to in the United Nations Global Compact.   • Should laws and regulations be non-existent or inadequate, we will maintain the highest reasonable regional standard for that location.   • We will fully, accurately and in a timely and verifiable manner, consistently *disclose material information* about the company and its performance. This will be done in readily understandable language to appropriate regulators, our stakeholders and the public.   • We will *not* offer, pay or accept *bribes*, nor will we condone anti-competitive market practices and we will not tolerate any such activity by our employees.   • We *prohibit* our employees from *trading shares* when they have unpublished, material information concerning the company or its operations.   • We require our employees to comply with all money handling requirements under applicable law, and we further *prohibit* them from conducting any illegal money transfers or any form of *'money laundering'* in the conduct of the company's business.   • We will require our employees to perform their duties conscientiously, honestly and in ways which *avoid conflicts* between their personal financial or commercial *interests* and their responsibilities to the company.   • We will take all reasonable steps to *identify and monitor* significant *risks* to the company and its stakeholders. We will endeavour to safeguard our assets and to detect and prevent fraud. We will do this in a manner consistent with the international human rights agreements and conventions to which we subscribe.   • We will promote the application of our *principles* by *those with whom we do business*. Their willingness to accept these principles will be an important factor in our decision to enter into and remain in such relationships.

- We are committed to seeking out mutually beneficial, ethical *long-term relations* with *those with whom we do business*.
- We encourage employees to take *personal responsibility* for ensuring that our *conduct* complies with our principles. No employee will suffer for raising with management violations of these principles or any other legal or ethical concern. Although employees are encouraged to discuss concerns with their direct managers, they must, in any event, inform the group internal audit manager of these concerns. Mechanisms are in place to anonymously report breaches of this statement of principles.
- The company will take the *necessary steps* to *ensure* that all employees and other stakeholders are *informed of these principles*. If an employee acts in *contravention* of these principles, the company will take the appropriate disciplinary action concerning such contravention. This action may, in cases of severe breaches, include termination of employment. In addition, certain contraventions may also result in the commencement of civil proceedings against the employee and the referral of the matter to the appropriate enforcement bodies if criminal proceedings appear warranted.

The decision to re-enter the Ituri district

Despite continuing conflict in the Ituri area in November 2004, AGA took a decision to recommence exploration activity in Mongbwalu. Prior to this, the company consulted a range of external informants on the situation and assessed the risks and opportunities involved. Reflecting on the process that guided this decision, Lenahan states: 'The judgement, on balance, at that time, based on the views of a wide range of stakeholders, was that there was an appreciable measure of risk associated with the venture, but that it was manageable.'[16]

One management response to the decision to re-establish activities in the conflict zone was to build relations with MONUC. Views about their relationship differ. MONUC did not advise AGA in writing that it was feasible to re-enter the area, nor did it commit, in writing, to a degree of support which would enable AGA to avoid negative relationships with rebel groups. The absence of a clear commitment in writing means that the company could not rely on this crucial support and that MONUC was not accountable to AGA for providing it.

In early 2005 the leadership of the FNI was detained in Kinshasa in connection with the killing of UN peacekeepers. Further UN peacekeepers were then deployed in Mongbwalu to manage the conflict. The AGA exploration staff returned to the site at about this time and were accompanied by the Corporate Affairs and Community Development team from the AGA head office. This visit illustrates the realisation among head office managers that with the exploration team commencing its activities on site, the operations in the area may have posed significant risks to the company and that the existing systems for managing this risk may not have been adequate.

The decision of the AGA management to commence exploration activities, despite ongoing fighting in the area and the support being provided by company personnel to a rebel group, is at the heart of the difficulty subsequently experienced by the company. Company respondents argue that the decision was made following a careful risk assessment, including some level of stakeholder engagement. With hindsight, however, it is apparent that this risk assessment was inadequate. The fact that local AGA staff made payments and gave support to the FNI in early 2005 tarnished the image of the company internationally. As Lenahan notes:

> Events proved that we had got our timing wrong and that, consequently and with the benefit of retrospect, our assessment of the manageability of the risk had been (again on balance) flawed. In January 2005, our colleagues in Mongbwalu were forced to pay to the FNI a sum of $8,000. We knew, at that time and now, that this was quite obviously inconsistent with both our own business principles and commonly accepted conventions for the protection of human rights.[17]

The Human Rights Watch report and the company's response

The HRW report *The Curse of Gold* in June 2005 contained detailed information about the payment of bribes to the FNI and made serious allegations of complicity against AGA:

> As a company with public commitments to corporate social responsibility, AngloGold Ashanti should have ensured their operations complied with those commitments and did not adversely affect human rights. They do not appear to have done so. Business considerations came above respect for human rights. In its gold exploration activities in Mongwbalu, AngloGold Ashanti failed to uphold its own business principles on human rights considerations and failed to follow international business norms governing the behaviour of companies internationally. Human Rights Watch has been unable to identify effective steps taken by the company to ensure their activities did not negatively impact on human rights.[18]

HRW's fundamental concern was that AGA put business interests before human rights and compromised the company's own policy commitments to ethical business practices. Anneke van Woudenberg, the report's author, argued that AGA should not have entered the area until peace had been secured, and that any involvement in the region under the control of the FNI would give the FNI more power, political traction and, ultimately, the ability to commit more crimes against civilians.

The report and the associated international media attention prompted an unprecedented response by AGA. In a press release, the company argued:

> Firstly, yielding to any form of extortion by an armed militia or anyone else is contrary to the company's principles and values. It is not condoned by AngloGold Ashanti, under any circumstances. That there was a breach of this principle in this instance, in that company employees yielded to the militia group FNI's act of extortion, is regretted. In mitigation, it should be noted that as soon as it came to our attention we publicly acknowledged it, condemned it and said it would not happen again.
>
> Secondly, in contemplating whether to operate in a conflict zone, we believe we have a moral right to do so only if, after due consideration, we can honestly conclude that, on balance, our presence will enhance the pursuit of peace and democracy... We believe that, if our exploration programme does yield a mine, it will be of significant benefit to the DRC government and local communities, by providing revenue, employment and access to social development opportunities – and, of course, returns to our shareholders.[19]

AGA contended that the payment to the militia group was an aberration. It also insisted that it would not happen again. Lenahan maintains: 'If it becomes clear to us that local conditions have changed to the extent that it is not possible to act within the boundaries of our own business principles, we will go.'[20]

The company simultaneously defended its actions on the grounds that it had been 'given the repeated assurance of the DRC Government, at various levels, that it was confident that, with the continuing collaboration of the UN force MONUC, the peace and political processes would yield positive results in the Ituri region and beyond'.[21] However, without documentary evidence to support this claim the original charges laid by HRW could not be rebutted.

The HRW report and AGA's response led to wider discussion on the events in the DRC at an international level. Debates took place in the print media, on television, at conferences and at the 2006 United Nations Global Compact meeting in Shanghai. Journalists, NGOs and AGA wrote articles about the issues raised by AGA's questionable decision-making. The company's public engagement on the issue at an international level included, among other things, a press conference the day after the report appeared; press releases and articles written for the media; text on the AGA website and in its *Report to Society 2005* (including a mention in the CEO's statement and a dedicated case study discussion); various live and recorded electronic media interviews; detailed interviews and site visits with the *Financial Times*; numerous interactions with shareholders (primarily by e-mail); and a presentation by the AGA president, Sir Sam Jonah, to the UN General Assembly. At one of the press conferences, CEO Godsell publicly admitted that the company 'had messed up' in the DRC.[22]

This comprehensive engagement by AGA stands in contrast to the 'ignore and deny' strategy employed by other companies in similar circumstances. AGA's engagement has arguably contributed to the international debate on the role of big companies in weak governance zones, and anecdotal evidence suggests that a broad range of stakeholders take a positive view of the company's open approach to the accusations made by HRW. This engagement and debate, arising out of what some commentators anecdotally characterised as a minor side-show in the context of the DRC's broader challenges, also attests to the increased attention being paid to multinational enterprises and international corporate responsibility principles.

It may also be noted that the company did not raise an argument, as others have done in similar situations. Large multinational enterprises that have committed themselves formally to human rights principles and agreements (such as the UN Global Compact) and have prominent exposure to international shareholders, including large socially responsible investment funds, and an international network of advocacy NGOs, may be a 'better bet' for local communities' human rights than companies that are substantially smaller. From a pragmatic point of view, this argument has some force.[23]

At a local level, AGA consulted with a variety of stakeholders about their ongoing presence in the area. Lenahan notes:

> In the period immediately after January 2005, management asked every organization or leader to whom we spoke in Ituri whether, in their candid view, we should cease our activities there and go and, if not, what should we do better. The view was unanimous. We should stay, but we should ensure that we were more visible in the community and we should establish structures which ensure that our development initiatives enjoyed a reasonable degree of consensus in the surrounding communities.[24]

The results of this stakeholder engagement have been cited by AGA as the reason why the company remained in operation in Mongbwalu. Sir Sam Jonah, the AGA chairman at the time, published an article in *The Star* (Johannesburg) of 15 June 2005, which highlighted why AGA took the management decision to remain in the DRC despite the issues arising from the conflict and the risks they might pose to the company:

> AngloGold Ashanti certainly found itself with dirty hands when in January its employees at its exploration camp were forced to hand over US$8,000 (ZAR55,000) to members of the National Integrationist Front militia. Our mandate to operate derives from the transitional authority whose legitimacy is extensive. And that authority and the one that succeeds it after the elections need economic progress to sustain them. That said we still need to ensure that our presence does more good than harm.
>
> How do we think we can do that? First, our policy must firmly state that no financial or logistical assistance can be given to rebel groups. Where a situation threatens that it may be unavoidable we need to withdraw. Second, we will not initiate any contact with such groups. Where such contact takes place unavoidably at their behest its nature needs to be recorded and limited to ensure it meets the above basic constraints. Third, continued dialogue must be maintained with legitimate authorities over these matters. We will also maintain communication with relevant NGOs.
>
> And finally as we continue our local economic development activities in the region we will redouble our efforts to ensure that it is done on a non-partisan basis. We believe that continuing our activities on this kind of basis will do more for the peace process than those who would prefer to keep their hands clean by advocating an economic scorched earth approach. They might find should they succeed that they end up with far dirtier hands than ours.[25]

The required responses outlined in the article by Jonah have begun to be put in place at a local level. AGA states that its current practice in Mongbwalu is that every time there is any form of interaction with a third party, from the mayor to the local commander of the MONUC force stationed in the town, a record is made. Regularly and frequently a summary of these interactions is shared with executive management, local politicians, the United Nations and the joint venture partners, OKIMO. One of the many benefits of this record-keeping, according to AGA, is that it forces project management to reflect upon the likely consequences of their proposed actions before committing to a process:

> Before he agrees to meet a local business owner or a political party leader, the manager asks himself, 'Will I be happy for my corporate office, the UN Group of Experts on the DRC and HRW, to know about this meeting?' If the answer is positive, there's a good chance that it passes the test of consistency with our business values.[26]

AGA's community engagement

AGA has also focused more attention on its approaches to local stakeholder engagement. Prior to the HRW report, AGA had set up a community forum to act as a body to engage with the company. There are 23 different community groupings in the forum, ranging from women's groups to indigenous Bambuti (often referred to as 'pygmies', although this term is considered pejorative). Representatives are elected by the constituent groups. The forum initiates community development projects with the support of the company and oversees their implementation and management. Most of these projects are in the fields of health care, education and infrastructure development. The community forum serves as the vehicle through which foreign donor aid will be disbursed.

The establishment of a community forum is a critical step in ensuring a greater degree of communication and accountability between parties. It provides the community with more responsibility for their well-being and ensures that the mining company has a legitimate group with which to engage. However, HRW has highlighted some potential challenges to the community forum to act as an effective mechanism for stakeholder engagement.[27] For a start, the forum has to deal with historically complex relations with workers, traditional authorities, the community and artisanal miners. The process of electing people onto the forum contributed to ethnic tension and at one point the mayor had to stop the elections. Further complexities arose from the participation of previous militia personnel in the forum. Moreover, it has the potential to undermine the traditional rights of the local traditional leader, Nyali, the chief of the Kilo (the original inhabitants of the land and the beneficiaries of Belgian rule). The country's new mining code, which was established in 2003, provides traditional authorities with rights over the process and the proceeds of mining. The chief may also feel undermined by a process requiring that he use the forum to engage with the mining company.

HRW contends that the dual roles of the forum for stakeholder engagement and the disbursement of development funds will, inevitably, generate political tension. However, HRW's suggestion that two separate bodies be established to carry out these distinct roles may be impractical: not only is the mining company the dominant player in the area in both the political and economic terrain, but there is a need to reduce duplication of community representation structures. Despite – or perhaps because of – the complexities and tensions at the local level involving the mine and exploration site, the company's attempts to develop a representative forum are to be welcomed. That said, to a significant extent the forum's success will depend upon the skills and facilitation abilities of the company staff charged with engaging the forum.

The future of mining in the Ituri district

The mineral resource at Mongbwalu appears promising and AGA is willing to develop the project further. A second drill rig arrived on site in 2007 to speed up the feasibility studies. AGA now faces the challenge of rapidly developing the project while simultaneously building trust with local stakeholders and ensuring the project delivers sustainable benefits to the region and supports the strengthening of governance structures.

At a local level, AGA faces challenges on how best to make social investments in community development projects. The key issue is that there are massive expectations that AGA will deliver development and these have to be managed. The community remembers the social benefits afforded to them by previous mining companies in the area, including schools, hospitals and libraries. The crucial management issues AGA will need to address will be those faced in other mining areas with a similar history of paternalism. Here local communities may expect that as happened previously, the failure of joint ventures to keep their promises will again cause development backlogs. Initial social investments during the exploration, development and construction phases will be necessarily small as revenues are not being generated. A fund of US$50,000 has been established, and there is an agreement that 1% of profits (pre-tax) will be contributed to local sustainable development.

More generally, the limits of the company's responsibilities are unclear. In particular, in post-conflict areas with weak governance, there will be expectations that companies will need to assume responsibilities which coincide with those of local governments and civil society. Collaborative approaches will be central to negotiating these shared responsibilities success-fully.[28]

An additional local development challenge for AGA is that of artisanal mining, which has been on the increase in the Ituri region. There are approximately 100,000 miners operating in the area of the gold reserve, many of whom are former militia and are likely to be reluctant to cease mining and leave the district. The new mineral legislation recognises the status of artisanal miners but leaves their access to ore bodies up to negotiations between them and the company that holds the mineral rights. The presence of the miners increases the volatility of the situation because they have strong political allegiances and are firmly entrenched in the political dynamics of the area.

The social complexities of the area are significant. Political factions, the legacy of the war, high levels of poverty within communities, and relations with the workforce and artisanal miners are all connected. The mine, associated exploration activities and their complex inter-relationships with the various stakeholders in the area, are firmly entrenched in communities' perceptions of their long-standing suffering.

On a wider level, AGA also needs to address its role in supporting good governance in the area. The DRC's new constitution places heavy emphasis on local autonomy and more sig-nificantly, from the perspective of mining companies, cedes considerable control over mining regulation and revenues to provincial governments. In addition, extensive autonomy is granted to local governments. As with other countries where there has been decentralisation, there is an increased burden on mining companies in the DRC to help deliver public services and infra-structure on behalf of the local authority. They are often unable to meet the increased demand for such services and infrastructure occasioned by the development of mining projects, par-ticularly before they benefit from increased revenue streams associated with the projects. As experience has shown in other resource-rich states with weak governance, increased revenues and opportunities for rent-seeking can result in high levels of corruption.

The above mentioned initiative, EITI, in which AGA is an active participant, is a global multi-stakeholder initiative focused on the management of revenues and more transparent governance in resource-rich countries. Its key stipulation is that companies and host govern-ments report on and account for all payments made by companies to host governments. The actual implementation of this objective may vary from country to country, but generally there needs to be an aggregating body that receives the information from the companies and from the government. In other words, companies are not actually required to publicly report such information.[29]

The DRC government committed itself to the EITI in 2005 and a National EITI Commit-tee was set up with financial support from the government. But the EITI requirements have yet to be implemented. Instead, companies such as AGA have been prevented from publicly reporting on their payments to the government by a law that requires any such information to be vetted by the parliament. Hence, on its company website AGA currently provides figures for payments to all of the relevant host governments except those to the DRC.[30] There is thus increasing pressure on the DRC government to implement its EITI commitment and there are recent signs of some renewed momentum towards the establishment of a new multi-stakeholder EITI Committee in September 2007.[31]

Conclusions

Investing in and re-entering the DRC during the period of conflict was clearly an ill-advised decision. Though there is unlikely to be legal certainty on the company's complicity in human rights abuses, or whether the actions of the FNI are within AGA's sphere of influence, the company suffered significant damage to its reputation as a result of the adverse publicity over the payment. Arguably the risk of complicity in human rights violations could not be accurately assessed in such difficult and chaotic circumstances and there should perhaps be a precautionary principle in place to guide decisions of this nature. Such a principle would generally emphasise a more risk-averse approach, also taking into consideration the possibility of unforeseen events or circumstances. In this example, the company relied inter alia on the particular role of the UN in the area, and this reliance was arguably part of the reason why the company was exposed to extortion by the rebel group. It also seems that these risks were not given sufficient attention in the merger process between AngloGold and Ashanti, bearing in mind the complex history of interaction between Ashanti and the local communities. This experience therefore illustrates the broader importance of giving careful consideration to human rights issues and related matters of corporate responsibility when undertaking mergers and acquisitions.

The company's decision to remain in the area subsequent to the dubious payment is also difficult to assess, because so much depends on how the local and national governance system develops. There is little doubt that a mining operation such as AGA's proposed Ituri mine can provide crucial employment and income opportunities to the local population, the region and the country as a whole, provided that legitimate decision-making processes are established and supported at various levels of government. Arguably the present trajectory is more benign than when AGA made its initial decision to re-enter the region in late 2004, and the company has also shown that it can make a meaningful contribution to improved governance at various levels. At the local level, this includes, for instance, the establishment of a local decision-making forum to guide the development of the mine and the company's social investment programme. At the national level, there is much hope that the EITI can become a catalyst for greater transparency in the payment and allocation of mining-related revenues, and the recent establishment of a new, multi-stakeholder EITI Commission with representatives from government, extractive industry companies and civil society is an encouraging development.

To conclude, AGA's experiences in the DRC and the company's engaged response to the HRW report arguably made an important contribution to the international debate on the role of big extractive companies in weak governance zones. The case highlights how difficult it is to assess and manage the risk of complicity in human rights abuses in such areas. Weighing these risks against the promise of socio-economic development that large-scale investments can bring, is even more fraught. Another broader question is whether – in the context of increasing pressure on companies to invest in such resource-rich areas – the risk of complicity in human rights abuses is being adequately considered, particularly among smaller companies that are perhaps less in the spotlight than companies like AGA.

Editors' reflections and questions

AGA clearly erred in its initial transactions with the FNI and the local community. From the perspective of the UN Norms on the Responsibilities of Transnational Corporations and Other Business Enterprises with regard to Human Rights, AGA could be viewed as being complicit in both previous and ongoing human rights abuses. Recall that the draft norms include the following definition and illustration of 'complicity':

> A company is complicit in human rights abuses if it authorizes, tolerates, or know-ingly ignores human rights abuses committed by an entity associated with it, or if the company knowingly provides practical assistance or encouragement that has a substantial effect on the perpetration of human rights abuse. Four situations illustrate where an allegation of complicity might arise against a company. First, when the company actively assists, directly or indirectly, in human rights viola-tions committed by others; second, when the company is in a partnership with a Government and could reasonably foresee, or subsequently obtains knowledge, that the Government is likely to commit abuses in carrying out the agreement; third, when the company benefits from human rights violations even if it does not positively assist or cause them; and fourth, when the company is silent or inactive in the face of violations.

According to Human Rights Watch, AGA was complicit in the FNI's human rights abuses because the company knowingly ignored these abuses and provided practical assistance that may well have contributed to the perpetration of these abuses.

1. Did the actions of the FNI fall within AGA's 'sphere of influence'?

2. Assuming that abuses committed by the FNI fell within AGA's 'sphere of influence', should we conclude that AGA is or was complicit in these human rights abuses? Or, to put the question differently, is the connection between the AGA's support for the FNI and the FNI's abuses too attenuated to support a claim of 'complicity'?

3. Given the apparent ongoing conflict between the FNI and the DRC military, are AGA's subsequent actions sufficient to mitigate the effects of its previous self-con-fessed error?

4. Do the positive contributions of AGA – job creation, tax payment and the creation of a forum for local governance – outweigh the effects of its previous error?

5. What steps ought to be taken to prevent instances such as the extorted payment to the FNI from recurring?

Notes

1   Over and above the cited documents, this case study is based on interviews conducted by Paul Kapelus with Paul Holleson and Steve Lenahan of AngloGold Ashanti (in Johannesburg, 31 August 2006) and with Anneke Van Woudenberg of Human Rights Watch (in Johannesburg, 9 October 2006).

2   See R. Hamann, P. Kapelus and N. Acutt, 'Responsibility vs Accountability? Interpreting the World Summit on Sustainable Development for a Synthesis Model of Corporate Citizenship', *Journal of Corporate Citizenship*, 9, (2003): 20–36.

3   OECD (Organisation for Economic Cooperation and Development), *OECD Risk Awareness Tool for Multinational Enterprises in Weak Governance Zones* (Paris: Organisation for Economic Cooperation and Development, 2006). Available at http://www.oecd.org/dataoecd/26/21/36885821.pdf (accessed July 2008).

4   UNDP (United Nations Development Programme), *Human Development Report 2006. Beyond Scarcity: Power, Poverty, and the Global Water Crisis* (New York: UNDP, 2006). See also OECD, 'Conducting Business with Integrity in Weak Governance Zones: Issues for Discussion'. Background document for consultations that provided inputs to the OECD Risk Awareness Tool for Multinational Enterprises in Weak Governance Zones, 2005 (cited with the permission of the OECD).

5   D. Guha-Sapir and W.G. van Panhuis, 'The Importance of Conflict-related Mortality in Civilian Populations', *The Lancet*, 361 (2003): 2126–2128.

6   See OECD, 'Conducting Business with Integrity'.

7   Clive Newall, CEO of First Quantum, quoted in Global Witness, *Digging in Corruption: Fraud, Abuse and Corruption in Katanga's Copper and Cobalt Mines* (London: Global Witness, 2006).

8   On the Voluntary Principles on Security and Human Rights see http://www.voluntaryprinciples.org; on OECD, see *OECD Risk Awareness Tool*.

9   See http://www.eitransparency.org and http://www.kimberleyprocess.com (accessed July 2008).

10 UN Security Council, *Final Report of the Panel of Experts on the Illegal Exploitation of Natural Resources and Other Forms of Wealth of the Democratic Republic of the Congo* (New York: United Nations, 2002); Global Witness, 'Digging in Corruption'.

11 Human Rights Watch, *The Curse of Gold* (New York: HRW, 2005).

12 UN Security Council, *Final Report of the Panel of Experts*.

13 HRW, *The Curse of Gold*, 69.

14 See S. Reich, 'When Firms Behave "Responsibly", are the Roots National or Global?', *International Social Science Journal*, 185 (2005): 509–28.

15 For instance, see A. Sinclair, 'Approaches to Organisational Culture and Ethics', *Journal of Business Ethics*, 12, 1 (1993): 63–73.

16 S. Lenahan, Presentation to the Fifth Annual Transatlantic Dialogue on 'The Humanitarian Crises in Darfur and the DRC', October 2006, Northwestern University School of Law, Chicago.

17 Ibid.

18 HRW, *The Curse of Gold*, 2.

19 AngloGold Ashanti, news release, 'Human Rights Watch Report on AngloGold Ashanti's Activities in the DRC', 1 June 2005, available at http://www.anglogold.com/NR/rdonlyres/1BC8B7B3-6363-48B3-AE85-B315606CF248/0/2005Jun01_SAreleaseDRC.pdf (accessed July 2008).

20 Lenahan, Presentation to the Fifth Annual Transatlantic Dialogue.

21 AngloGold Ashanti, news release, 'Human Rights Watch Report'.

22 *Mail & Guardian*, 'Anglo "messed up" in the DRC,' 2 June 2005, available at http://www.mg.co.za/articlePage.aspx?articleid=242206&area=/breaking_news/breaking_news_business (accessed July 2008).

23 P.A. French, 'Inference Gaps in Moral Assessment: Capitalism, Corporations and Individuals', *International Social Science Journal*, 185 (2005): 573–84.

24 Lenahan, Presentation to the Fifth Annual Transatlantic Dialogue.

25 S. Jonah, 'Why AngloGold Must Not Desert the DRC', *The Star*, 15 June 2005: 15.

26 S. Lenahan, personal communication.

27 A. Van Woudenberg, personal communication.

28 See R. Hamann, D. Sonnenberg, A. Mackenzie, P. Kapelus and P. Hollesen, 'Local Governance as Complex System: Lessons from Mining in South Africa, Mali, and Zambia', *Journal of Corporate Citizenship*, 18 (2005): 61–73.

29 In contrast, the NGO coalition Publish What You Pay asks companies to publicly report on all their payments to governments. See http://www.publishwhatyoupay.org

30 See http://www.anglogoldashanti.com (accessed September 2007).

31 See, for instance, Publish What You Pay Coalition in the Democratic Republic of Congo, 'Final Statement of the Workshop to Build Awareness on the Extractive Industries Transparency Initiative', 2007, available at http://www.publishwhatyoupay.org (accessed September 2007).

Global Alumina's efforts

to mitigate conflict-related risks in the Republic of Guinea

JOSEF SEITZ

Introduction

The Republic of Guinea is a country endowed with rich natural resources. It has more than a third of the world's recoverable reserves of high-quality bauxite, an ore used to produce aluminium, and the world's largest untapped reserves of iron ore. Yet it remains one of the poorest countries in the world, ranked 156th on the UNDP Human Development Index. A high percentage of its population survives on a daily income of less than US$1. Most are un-employed and life expectancy barely exceeds 50 years. About 23% of the children die before reaching the age of five, and among the poorest quintile of the population the infant mortality rate is nearly 12%. [1] The country's persistent poverty flows from a range of political, social and economic problems: the absence of accountable and transparent governance, difficult political transitions, limited agricultural capacity, labour unrest, poor infrastructure, a large influx of refugees and economic stagnation. Guinea's recent political volatility can be traced to the poor health of President Lansana Conté and the absence of clear, democratic rules for succession. However, in comparison with its neighbours, the country has enjoyed relative peace. Liberia, Sierra Leone and the Côte d'Ivoire are some of the most unstable nations on the continent and their protracted civil wars have destabilised the region for the better part of the past decade.

Undeterred by these problems, Global Alumina, a company based in New York, began constructing a US$3bn alumina refinery in Guinea after a 2001 agreement with the country's government. This investment is roughly equivalent to Guinea's annual GDP of US$3.38bn in 2005. This is not only the largest foreign investment in the country; it is one of the largest such investments in the history of sub-Saharan Africa.

The company's senior vice-president for Government Relations, Haskell Sears Ward, views this investment as a crucial contribution to the country's development. However, many remain cautious or even sceptical about such a large investment in a risky environment. Can these risks, many of which are beyond the influence of the company, be adequately identified and mitigated? Can principles of corporate citizenship, including those of the UN Global Compact, contribute to improving human rights while reducing economic risks?

The company has adopted measures to mitigate socio-political risks such as the latent conflict potential within the country, as well as the spill-over of conflict from neighbouring countries. Moreover, it has attempted to minimise the endogenous risks of the project itself. It has, in particular, implemented resettlement activities in a consultative manner in the hope that such consultation will forestall any material grievances.

Alumina production and Global Alumina's project in Guinea

Bauxite is an ore containing aluminium oxide – commonly known as alumina, the primary raw material in aluminium production. Aluminium's light weight, strength, resistance to corrosion and the fact that it can be recycled make it vital in many industries and products. The global alumina market has, in recent years, been characterised by shortages in supply and a concomitant rise in demand which has pushed prices from US$160 per tonne in 2002 to highs in excess of US$500 per tonne in 2004.[2]

At 15 million tonnes per year, Guinea is the world's largest exporter of bauxite. Bauxite mining and alumina refining is responsible for more than 80% of Guinea's foreign exchange. And yet there is only one alumina refinery in the country. As a result, only a small proportion of bauxite, approximately 1.2 million tonnes per year, is transformed into alumina in Guinea. Moreover, the country produces no aluminium.

Global Alumina was established in 1998 and listed in 2004 as a public company on the Toronto Stock Exchange. The company's website describes its plans for alumina refining in Guinea as follows:

> Global Alumina is a company that intends to use the vast bauxite resources of the Re-
> public of Guinea to produce alumina for sale to the global aluminum industry. By estab-
> lishing itself in Guinea, Global Alumina will be well positioned for tremendous growth.
> The Company is developing an alumina refinery that possesses economies of scale and
> is situated in a bauxite-rich area of Guinea, a country containing one-third of the world's
> economically recoverable bauxite resources. Global Alumina expects to be one of the
> world's lowest cost producers of alumina thereby ensuring its long-term viability during
> both high and low cycles of the aluminum market.

Global Alumina's refinery (the 'project') is situated in the Sangarédi region of Guinea. This area contains some of the highest quality bauxite in the world. The refinery will have an initial capacity to produce 3 million tonnes of alumina per year, increasing ultimately to 4.5 million.[3] Global Alumina and its contractors currently employ more than 600 people, including Guineans as well as overseas staff.

The project required the creation of several large-scale infrastructure initiatives. These subsidiary projects are the refinery itself, mining operations, a coal-fired steam and power plant, a red mud disposal facility, a retention pond, an employees' village, a 14 km stretch of railroad, and various access roads in the Sangarédi region. It was also necessary to construct an alumina terminal, a marine terminal and new rail facilities at the Kamsar Port to facilitate export.

Identifying and mitigating conflict-related risks

The UN Global Compact's Business Guide identifies various steps for assessing the impact of conflict and managing risk in conflict zones:

> Conflict impact assessment and risk management constitute two different levels of activities of a company's engagement. Conflict impact analysis should be undertaken as part of the project exploration and planning stage in deciding whether to invest in a specific locality/region. These are referred to as pre-investment and pre-operational phases. Conflict impact assessment consists of an analysis of intrinsic characteristics of a proposed investment and the possible impacts (intended and unintended) they may have on existing tensions in a community or region. Understanding how a proposed investment can affect a conflict situation gives businesses a more informed method to make crucial business decisions, in particular whether to invest or not. However, even when the project is in operation, impact assessment should be carried out in the form of monitoring and additional information gathering.
>
> The decision to invest will trigger the commencement of the risk management phase, which continues throughout the lifecycle of a project. Having identified and understood the potential impacts of a given project, the company is then able to develop a strategy designed to minimize the negative consequences and maximise the positive consequences of doing business in a specific context.

Conflicts also generate costs for companies. As International Alert notes:

> Violent conflict imposes a range of costs on companies. A 'conflict-sensitive' approach to doing business – one that seeks to avoid these costs by developing informed conflict-management strategies – is therefore a strategic choice for company managers. At both a local level, through improved relationships with stakeholders, and at regional and national levels, companies can benefit from avoiding, or handling conflict more effectively through a joined-up understanding of all conflict risks and impacts.[4]

Conflict has both direct and indirect effects on a company (see Table 1). There are direct costs involved in protecting staff and property, and indirect costs in maintaining a functional operating environment.

As noted above, the project is subject to two kinds of risk. Exogenous risks relate to the broader operating environment and are not directly linked to the activities of the company, while endogenous risks flow from the activities of the project itself. The rest of this case study describes the company's responses to these two kinds of risk.[5]

Exogenous risks
Armed conflicts and refugees

The neighbouring countries of Liberia, Sierra Leone and the Côte d'Ivoire have been, and continue to be, heavy conflict zones. The conflicts have the potential to spill over into Guinea, creating massive refugee and humanitarian problems. A company might then face the following risks:

- Large proportions of the youth could take up arms and intimidate the local staff.
- Populations dislocated by conflict could lose access to their livelihood. This in turn would give rise to humanitarian crises and political instability. Threatened by starvation, people

might resort to stealing from the company or even kidnapping staff and holding them to ransom.

- The government's actions to 'pacify' an area with foreign investments could damage a company's ability to develop good local relationships and might tarnish its international reputation.[6]

That said, the project is located far from existing areas of conflict. The Sangarédi region is likely to be immune from the direct effects of the civil wars in Liberia, Sierra Leone and the Côte d'Ivoire. Moreover, in the view of numerous informants, Guineans have become attached to their peaceful life and work hard to avoid being drawn into neighbouring conflicts. The risk of internecine conflict in the region where the company is engaged is thus considered by all the interviewees to be negligible. The Compagnie des Bauxites de Guinée (CBG), the mining company that will provide the bauxite ore to the Global Alumina refinery, takes a similar view. Ward has reached the following conclusion: 'The risk of violent conflict is very low given Guinea's relative level of security in the region and the excellent history of the government's relations with CBG.'

Table 1: Direct and indirect business costs associated with conflict

Direct costs	Example
Security	Higher payments to state/private security firms; staff time spent on security management.
Risk management	Insurance, loss of coverage, specialist training for staff, reduced mobility and higher transport costs.
Material	Destruction of property or infrastructure.
Opportunity	Disruption of production, delays on imports.
Capital	Increased cost of raising capital.
Personnel	Kidnapping, killing and injury; stress; recruitment difficulties; higher wages to offset risk; cost of management time spent protecting staff.
Reputation	Consumer campaigns, risk-rating, share price, competitive loss.
Litigation	Expensive and damaging lawsuits.
Indirect costs	Example
Human	Loss of life, health, intellectual and physical capacity.
Social	Weakening of social capital.
Economic	Damage to financial and physical infrastructure, loss of markets.
Environment	Pollution, degradation, resource depletion.
Political	Weakening of institutions, rule of law, governance.

Source: International Alert, Conflict-Sensitive Business Practice: Guidance for Extractive Industries (London: International Alert, 2005), 2.

Political transition uncertainty

The current president of the Republic of Guinea, Lansana Conté, has been in power since 1984. He was re-elected for another seven years in 2003. Because of the poor state of his health, succession remains a contentious issue. The threat of an extra-constitutional resolution to succession – a military intervention – has been a matter of concern to many observers. Aside from a limited number of civil society organisations attempting to plan round tables and hold a national dialogue about the way this critical transition could be handled, few visible efforts have been made to avoid a possible political crisis.

The uncertainty surrounding the president's succession creates a significant risk for any foreign investment. His successor could, for instance, reconsider the country's commitment to prior agreements, and Global Alumina's mining concessions are no exception.

However, numerous forces oppose significant policy reversals in the wake of any change in government. For more than 40 years, Guinea has sought to attract investors to create a value-added component to bauxite mining. Under both the Sékou Touré and Conté regimes, successive governments have pressed, without success, for the development of refinery and smelting capacities in the country. Global Alumina's interest in fulfilling this national priority has received broad national support. Moreover, the company consulted all the country's major stakeholders, including the military, prior to the final agreement with the government in 2005. This broad-based consultative process contributed to the the project's unanimous approval by Guinea's national assembly in May 2005. The principal officers of the company – led by Ward – have since extended this consultative process to embrace civil society stakeholders, NGOs and international development agencies. Because of the project's importance for Guinea, the country's competing forces all came to the conclusion – after consultation – that it was in the national interest and should be allowed to succeed.

Economic inequalities

Guinea's impoverished state can lead to social unrest and strikes. As Ward notes: 'When a sack of rice consumes half of a Guinean's monthly salary there can be little prospect of political stability.'[7] In February and June 2006, union-led demonstrations and strikes were violently suppressed by the military. Ten students died during the demonstrations. Such social unrest could affect Global Alumina's construction and operation activities and lead to partial or total work stoppages.

It is, however, difficult to deny that Global Alumina's project will make a significant contribution to alleviating some of the economic hardships faced by Guineans. It will create approximately 10,000 direct jobs during the construction phase and 1 500 during its operational phase. How many of these jobs will actually go to Guineans will depend on the competencies required and the skills available. In the short term, project planners foresee that at least 50% of the construction employment opportunities will be filled by Guineans. Global Alumina has teamed up with the Canadian International Development Agency and others to offer professional training to Guineans in order to enhance their technical skills and help them make the most of the project's employment opportunities. Numerous indirect jobs will also be created during the construction and operation phases. Most of these service sector positions will be filled by Guineans.

Global Alumina has also committed itself to creating an environment in which small and medium enterprises (SMEs) and entrepreneurship can flourish. The company has established a partnership with the African Development Foundation, a US government funded entity, to provide SME training and to develop SMEs for both the construction and operation of the refinery. Global Alumina also has a requirement in its construction contracts that obliges its contractors to use local subcontractors whenever they are able to provide the required services at a competitive price and quality.

Transparency

Guinea has yet to be ranked by Transparency International but corruption permeates the entire political and economic system. The Bureau of African Affairs at the US Department of State declares:

> The Guinean Government adopted policies in the 1990s to return commercial activity to the private sector, promote investment, reduce the role of the state in the economy, and improve the administrative and judicial framework. Guinea has the potential to develop, if the government carries out its announced policy reforms, and if the private sector responds appropriately. So far, corruption and favouritism, lack of long-term political stability, and lack of a transparent budgeting process continue to dampen foreign investor interest in major projects in Guinea.[8]

Lack of transparency not only undermines the legitimacy of government decisions regarding mining concessions, but also has the potential to tarnish the company's reputation. Local authorities or decision makers may request illicit payments or indirect non-monetary advantages such as employment for family members. Nepotism and cronyism would also diminish the investing company's credibility.

Global Alumina will need to manage these issues of transparency and legitimacy carefully. Thus far they seem not to have been a problem. Ward observes: 'Despite the country's reputation for corruption, I have never been approached in nearly seven years with our project for money or other forms of a payoff as a condition for receiving a favourable decision.' Global Alumina's director general, Mamady Youla, explains the relative absence of graft in the case of Global Alumina's project in these terms: 'Guineans are very patriotic; so I showed them that the refinery is of national interest.'

Perhaps the greatest inhibitor of graft has been the company's ongoing process of consultation with local communities. Martine Forget, director of the Environmental and Social Management Unit in Sangarédi, notes: 'By integrating the population into the decision-making process, it is possible to avoid corruption – we have never had any problems here.'

The commitment to corporate transparency is manifest in the company's recruitment policy. These procedures encompass a range of basic competency tests that each job candidate must pass. By advertising these requirements, and by accepting candidates from many sources, Global Alumina avoids preferential treatment and secures enhanced credibility. Indeed, according to several company employees, Global Alumina's policies on issues of transparency have helped change the local population's attitude to bribery and corruption.

Endogenous risks

The installation of a US$3bn industrial project in one of the least developed countries in the world will have a tremendous impact on the economy, environment and social structure of the region and the country. The endogenous changes created by the project may themselves lead to conflicts that the company must anticipate in order to guarantee the long-term sustainability of its investment.

Resettlement

The Global Alumina project will have both temporary and permanent effects on the land and livelihood of local communities. The project infrastructure will take up 2050ha of land permanently. Half of this will serve as a buffer around project features or be reserved for future village expansion. This land is currently used by the local population for agriculture, grazing cattle or gathering natural resources. Approximately 500 people (63 families) live within a kilometre of the refinery and will require resettlement. An additional 3 100 inhabitants, 432 families, live on land that will be affected by the project.[9]

Global Alumina has developed a Resettlement Action Plan (RAP) in accordance with the Equator Principles and the World Bank Guidelines for resettlement and compensation. The RAP states that the 'objectives and principles on which this plan is based, not only consist of minimizing the effects of the project on local populations, but also determining how the project can improve their quality of life through a long-term integrated and sustainable socio-economic development plan'. Consultations with the public about the project and the EIA began in 2001. Global Alumina's socio-economic analysis includes the results of a detailed investigation into the administrative organisation, the regional environment, the land tenure regimes, the economic activities (agriculture, animal husbandry) and the social organisation of the affected communities.

The dialogue with the villagers is a permanent and ongoing process. Marliatou Diallo, the company liaison officer responsible for women and vulnerable persons at Global Alumina's office in Sangarédi, states:

> We come here at least once a week. The permanent contact with the villagers is essential.
> At the beginning they were sceptical. But as they realized that we were really doing what
> we had promised, their attitude changed.

After analysing the project's impact on land, people and assets, and studying alternative sites, Global Alumina began executing a detailed resettlement and compensation plan. An unexpected consequence of these plans is that Guinean government representatives now use the 'Global Alumina method' of avoiding conflicts – they require the same procedure from other companies that wish to obtain mining concessions.

Immigration

The project is expected to attract Guineans from outside the region as well as immigrants looking for work within the project zone. The population in areas around the project zone has already doubled within two years. People who had left nearby villages to receive an education or to look for work in Conakry are now returning to their home villages. This reverse migration puts pressure on host families and often makes already meagre resources even scarcer.

Global Alumina considers its ability to influence such reverse migration quite limited. However, the company is working with the villagers and regularly attempts to convince them that it is in their own interest to control immigration into the region and project area.

Environmental impact[10]

The construction and the operation of the alumina refinery and its infrastructure components will inevitably have consequences for the environment. The most significant biophysical impact will be on air quality and the quality and quantity of surface and ground water used by the villagers. There will also be impacts in the form of waste disposal, generation of noise, and changes in land use. From a human environment perspective, the greatest potential for conflict arises from the changes to land use and the corresponding need for resettlement and adjustments to livelihood activities. The company has worked to minimise the potential for conflict through its consultative efforts and by coordinating its mitigation measures with the local villagers and authorities.

Global Alumina has carried out a detailed EIA to address the environmental impact of its refinery. (The EIA was accepted by the Guinean government in May 2005.) After analysing the potential impact and possible alternatives, the company elaborated appropriate mitigation measures. The EIA led to an Environmental Action Plan (EAP). This plan goes beyond the classic and obligatory EIA and suggests that Global Alumina has taken seriously the concerns expressed by the local population during public consultations.

The company's elaboration of a detailed EIA and its transparent approach strengthened its relationship with the Guinean Ministry of Environment. The ministry now uses Global Alumina's process as an example of best practice and as a guideline for other companies. The improved relationship between the Ministry of Environment and Global Alumina has also led to an initiative in which the ministry sends some of its staff members to Global Alumina to learn more about EIA.

HIV-AIDS

During the construction phase of the refinery and its infrastructure facilities, up to 10,000 workers will be present on various sites, and 1,500 will be present during regular operations. While many of the workers will come from Guinea, others will travel from other African, European and Asian countries. Many of the workers will be single men: they represent a high-risk group for HIV-infection. The ongoing construction activities are already attracting sex workers into the villages around the construction sites. Their presence increases the risk of HIV infection within the project area and of spreading HIV beyond the region through regular contact with international workers, casual workers and truck drivers.

Besides the serious risks HIV poses for the local population, Global Alumina must face the corresponding risks for its own and its contractors' employees. It approaches AIDS prevention and treatment as one element of a more comprehensive and integrated health policy that should also include other infectious diseases as well as issues of hygiene, sexuality and childbirth. As part of this broader health policy the company thus requires its contractors to include AIDS-related action programmes for their employees.

To better integrate its own activities into existing initiatives, Global Alumina has entered into a partnership with the Guinean National Committee for the Fight against AIDS (CNLS). Mohamed Sano, the CNLS official responsible for local initiatives, confirmed that the partnership has set a series of joint objectives for data collection, education and preventive measures, treatment and monitoring.

Governance and service delivery

In Guinea, rural and urban populations have very limited access to basic services. Electricity is only available in the larger cities. Cuts are frequent and often last several days. Continuous water supply is not guaranteed and people may have to collect water from central supply stations. Waste management is non-existent and many public places and streets overflow with uncollected waste.

An obvious risk for Global Alumina is that local communities will ask the company to take over government responsibilities and gradually create a state within a state. To cope with the local population's development expectations and not fall into the trap of replacing the local government for provision of services, Global Alumina has decided not to provide free services to anyone. Payment will be required for electricity, water, rubbish removal or any other services. Furthermore, the company does not expect to provide these services directly. Instead, they will be provided by the local municipality, with organisational assistance from Global Alumina and other Guinean organisations. By creating new employment opportunities, the company hopes to put more households in a position to purchase these services.

Global Alumina's approach through the lens of the Global Compact Performance Model[11]

The UN Global Compact Performance Model helps companies and other stakeholders integrate corporate citizenship principles into company management systems. Global Alumina's approach in Guinea may be fruitfully analysed in terms of several components of this model.

- Vision: Global Alumina has developed a clear vision of its role as a responsible company regarding social, environmental and political issues. According to statements by Global Alumina employees and press articles, this vision has been driven by CEO Bruce Wrobel, whose views on corporate social responsibility are elaborated in the company's Code of Business Conduct and Ethics. The code requires employees to avoid conflicts of interest and unethical conduct, and to comply with environmental laws. It does not, however, expressly incorporate the UNGC principles.

- Leadership: The company's management emphasises the importance of the UNGC. Several employees confirmed during the author's field visit, that Global Alumina's executive management has made dialogue an essential part of the company's culture, particularly the issue of corporate responsibility.

- Empowerment: Social and environmental commitment is an essential criterion when selecting prospective employees. (Again, however, the UNGC principles are not expressly embraced in these criteria.) Individual and team performance targets with a clear reference to corporate social responsibility and a corresponding reward system are, however, not yet in place.

- Policies and strategies: Global Alumina has elaborated policies and procedures for various aspects of its activities. Recruitment must be transparent. While employment will be based on competence, the local population will be given priority in order to foster employment opportunities in the region. Another important policy document refers to health and safety issues on the construction sites. It notes that construction directors will be evaluated annually with regard to their performance on these issues. These policies have been communicated to Global Alumina's contractors. That said, the aforementioned policies and procedures exist for the most part as drafts and have not yet been finalised. An enforceable Code of Conduct could increase the impact of these policies and ensure Global Alumina's adherence to UNGC transparency principles.

- Resources: The allocation of extensive resources to manage socially and environmentally sensitive issues resulting from Global Alumina's activities is one of the company's major assets. Since its creation, Global Alumina's top management has been actively recruiting employees with a strong commitment to environmental and development issues. The appointment of senior managers such as: Ward, who has years of experience on the continent; Youla, the company's director general and former advisor to the Minister of Mines and Geology; and Jonathan Lachnit, a former NGO employee and the company official for managing resettlement and compensation issues tangibly reflects this commitment. Lachnit says he was told during his job interview with Global Alumina that they were 'looking for somebody to ensure we do things the right way'.

  Two years before starting construction activities or even defining precisely the project components and locations, Global Alumina began consultations with the local population about possible social and environmental impacts. Martine Forget, the director of the social and environmental management (UGES) unit in Sangarédi, confirmed that she was 'charged with taking into account all social and environmental considerations of the population'. The UGES unit, with about 15 employees including three expatriates working full-time on-site, prepares, implements and monitors the company's environmental, social impact and mitigation measures.

- Innovation and processes: First, Global Alumina has adopted a holistic approach to problem-solving. The company's assessment of possible impacts and risks generated by the project includes economic considerations, social and health issues, environmental impact and governance challenges. Furthermore, its intention was to anticipate any negative impact of the project as early as possible. Even after initial consultations and agreements with local communities, the company has ongoing contact with them when plans are adapted. Second, Global Alumina has established partnerships with various local institutions and international development organisations to guarantee that the refinery project does not undermine but rather contributes to the achievement of development targets. Its cooperation with USAID, the African Development Foundation and the National Committee for the Fight against AIDS has enabled the company to take into account the international development community's point of view and to better anticipate conflicts that may arise from the refinery project. Third, to its great credit Global Alumina seems to have the willingness and ability to communicate with all stakeholders. 'We were talking with everybody, even the opposition and the military', said Youla, the director general. This dialogue-oriented approach may be one reason why general support for the refinery project remains strong. Asked whether these procedures are really innovative, Youla replied: 'It is certainly not an innovative approach for the international development community. But it is, without any doubt, innovative for the private sector, and it is definitely innovative here in Guinea.'

- Impact on value chain: Global Alumina's contractors for the construction or operation phase have to align with the company's social and environmental objectives. For instance, the company has a clear policy regarding labour rights and recruitment transparency that must be accepted and supported by the contractors. Contractors also have an obligation to organise awareness raising campaigns and information sessions about HIV for their staff. For some of the companies, the AIDS prevention policies have apparently proved quite sensitive.

  As mentioned above, the way Global Alumina anticipates social problems and environmental impacts is now being used by local authorities to measure other companies' behaviour. The Ministry of Environment asks companies that apply for new mining concessions to provide an EIA similar to Global Alumina's EIA. Moreover, the way the company consults the local population serves as a model for companies implementing new concessions.

  The construction of an alumina refinery by Global Alumina has apparently triggered interest from other companies in Guinea that have been exporting, but not refining, bauxite for decades. Global Alumina's bold investment may well encourage others to move up the value chain and create additional alumina refineries.

- People satisfaction: The commitment of Global Alumina to the community and the environment of which it is a part has had a positive impact on its employees. Several employees confirmed having accepted employment at Global Alumina because they felt the company had a real commitment to social and development issues. In particular, Guinean employees were satisfied and even proud 'to work for a company that brings so many jobs to the country'. That said, a survey for measuring employee satisfaction has not yet been carried out.

- Impact on society: Initially, the local population and authorities were quite sceptical about Global Alumina and its participative consultations. When they realised, however, that their views and interests were actually being taken into account, their attitude changed. The participative consultations also changed the way people express themselves. According to some interview partners, the villagers are much more vocal today in discussing issues with other companies and local authorities.

- Reporting: Within the performance model's continuous improvement cycle, reporting is an essential way of communicating the progress made with respect to objectives and targets. Initiating a reporting process from the outset would demonstrate to shareholders and other stakeholders the company's commitment to social and environmental integrity. Global Alumina has only recently started its construction activities. Its focus has been on project planning and implementation, rather than reporting. Nevertheless, some level of reporting on sustainability issues ought to be implemented. One important step could be the publication of the EIA and in particular the RAP. A second step would be to engage in developing a sustainability report. This report would, ideally, take into consideration the principles and indicators of the Global Reporting Initiative.[12] In July 2007, the company published its first communication on progress (COP) in accordance with the Global Compact requirements.

- Unanswered questions / recommendations: A key challenge is for Global Alumina to move rapidly from the impact diagnostic phase and planning of the mitigation measures to the concrete implementation phase. Some impacts of the project may become apparent more rapidly than was initially foreseen. Given the arrival of sex workers near the work camps, for instance, the appropriate mitigation measures should already be in place.

- Further challenges relate to the broader governance of mineral resource extraction and the benefits that accrue to Guinea. For instance, a detailed land-use plan which includes all the mining activities for the near future should be elaborated by the Guinean authorities. However, Global Alumina and the other mining companies may need to help the authorities deal with this challenge.

The crisis in early 2007

Global Alumina believes that responsible and profitable business can make vital contributions to sustainable development, and that such an approach to business can mitigate some of the risks of operating in extremely poor, conflict-prone countries such as Guinea. Nevertheless the pessimists seemingly saw some of their concerns vindicated when in early 2007 a national strike broke out, aimed at forcing President Conté to resign. Martial law was declared and the Guinean army killed demonstrators, triggering further protests, widespread looting and the collapse of most economic activity, including an interruption to the export of bauxite. In a written submission to the US House of Representatives Committee on Foreign Affairs, Ward argued:

> In light of the recent crisis many people are probably asking themselves if Guinea is open for business. Although my response may seem counterintuitive to many, my answer to that question is yes. Like many countries in Africa and the developing world, Guinea is a high-risk place to do business, but the country is a hospitable destination for investors. In fact, Guinea has never expropriated or nationalized any foreign assets. And unless and until replacements can be found for gold, diamonds, ire ore and, of course, bauxite, the business climate can be tolerated much as it is in problematic petroleum producing countries. A good deal of my optimism can also be attributed to the high priority given to investors who want to create a value-added dimension to their mining projects. Yes, the roads are bad, electricity unreliable, skilled labor in short supply and political uncertainty exists. But I believe that Global Alumina's entry into Guinea represents a historic turning point for the country. One has only to observe the number of major private sector initia-tives which have been announced since the unanimous parliamentary ratification of our agreement to observe a fundamental shift in the economic environment.[13]

Ward's optimism is based on his conviction that his company has implemented a model ap-proach to responding to the country's risk profile, one which embraces measures to identify and mitigate exogenous socio-political risks – such as the strike in early 2007 – and to minimise endogenous risks that flow from the project itself. Ward notes: 'A community consultative approach has characterised our work and is a feature of every aspect of the project.'[14] While the company seems to have weathered the crisis of early 2007, it remains to be seen whether its efforts will indeed help lessen operational risks to the project in the medium and long term. Decision makers at BHP Billiton, the world's largest resources company, seem to share Ward's optimism. In April 2007, BHP Billiton bought 33.3% of the refinery for US$140m.[15]

Editors' reflections and questions

Any investment equal to a country's entire GDP is likely to entail diverse socio-economic issues. Risk management is a top priority and the case study describes how Global Alumina adopted numerous proactive measures to identify and mitigate risks related to the socio-political environment and the impacts of the project itself. However a number of questions remain:

1. To what extent can the various risks to a large project such as this be identified in an objective and credible manner? Is there any way in which contingent factors such as conflict in a neighbouring country can be assessed so as to be convincing to, say, a possible investor in the project? What factors ought to be considered when deciding whether these various risks are manageable or not?[16]

2. If you were an investor in Global Alumina, to what extent would you feel reassured that the company's efforts to mitigate the identified risks are effective and sufficient? How would you feel about these efforts if you were, for instance, a resident in a village close to the smelter site?

3. To what extent can the company improve governance in the project area or indeed the country? Given Global Alumina's economic power in Guinea, is it appropriate for the company to address problems in the political domain?

Notes

1   UNDP (United Nations Development Programme), *Human Development Report 2005* (New York: UNDP, 2005).
2   http://www.globalalumina.com/ga_new/aboutus.htm (accessed August 2007).
3   Global Alumina: Resettlement Action Plan, September 2005.
4   International Alert, *Conflict-Sensitive Business Practice: Guidance for Extractive Industries* (London: International Alert, 2005), 2. See also J. Nelson, *The Business of Peace: The Private Sector as a Partner in Conflict Prevention and Resolution* (London: International Alert, the Council on Economic Priorities, and International Business Leaders Forum, 2000).
5   The documentation for this case study was sourced from a number of institutions and a number of site visits. Global Alumina itself supplied the Resettlement Action Plan (RAP), the Environmental Impact Assessment (EIA), and partnership agreements, and other project-related information. Field visits to Sangarédi and Conakry allowed the author to meet and interview the local Global Alumina staff, villagers affected by resettlement, local authorities and representatives of the international development community. Several interviews with Global Alumina's executive management were conducted telephonically. The Global Compact 'Business Guide to Conflict Impact Assessment and Risk Management in Zones of Conflict' was used to categorise and analyse both the exogenous

and endogenous risks the project could face. Because the pre-investment risk assessment was not publicly available, the risks were evaluated, in large part, by considering the opinions of the various stakeholders.

6   International Alert, *Conflict-Sensitive Business Practice*.

7   Written submission by Haskell Sears Ward, senior vice-president, Global Alumina Corporation, to US House of Representatives Committee on Foreign Affairs, 22 March 2007, at http://foreignaffairs. house.gov/110/war032207. htm (accessed August 2007).

8   http://www.state.gov/r/pa/ei/bgn/2824.htm (accessed July 2007).

9   Global Alumina: Resettlement Action Plan, September 2005.

10   Global Alumina: Environmental Impact Assessment, January 2006.

11   C. Fussler, A. Cramer, and S. van der Vegt, *Raising the Bar: Creating Value with the United Nations Global Compact* (Sheffield: Greenleaf Publishing, 2004); see also Chapter 1.

12   See http://www.globalreporting.org (accessed July 2007).

13   Written submission by Haskell Sears Ward.

14   Ibid.

15   http://www.bhpbilliton.com/bb/investorsMedia/news/2007/bhpBillitonSecures InterestInGuinean-BauxiteProject.jsp (accessed August 2007).

16   On project-related risks, see, for instance, L. T. Wells and E. S. Gleason, 'Is Foreign Infrastructure Investment Still Risky?', *Harvard Business Review* (September/ October 1995): 1–12.

A beacon of stability in a sea of unrest –
Pharmakina in the DRC

BASTIAN BIRKENHÄGER

Introduction[1]

Michael Gebbers, 36 years old and of German origin, has spent most of his life in Bukavu, a town in the heart of Africa, in the Democratic Republic of the Congo (DRC). Bukavu lies in the epicentre of a civil war that began in 1998 and has ravaged on for a decade, during which the war and the continued internecine fighting have claimed the lives of almost four million people. Although the war officially ended in 2002, significant fighting and gross human rights offences continue to this day. Why, one might wonder, does Michael continue to live here? What keeps a family like the Gebberses from returning to the safety of their farm in Germany?

Michael returned to Bukavu, after studying in Germany and working in Belgium, to help his father, Horst Gebbers, manage Pharmakina, a pharmaceutical company that produces malaria and HIV/AIDS medication. It provides these vital medicines to the Congolese population at low cost – often by means of subsidies and other support from international aid organisations. As importantly perhaps, Pharmakina is one of very few companies in the eastern part of the DRC to have survived the turmoil of the past decade. It is now the largest employer and supports the livelihoods of some 20 000 people in the region. It thus makes a crucial contribution to the local economy in this desperately poor area.

Michael can tell many a story of the personal dangers posed to the family and the company's employees, as well as the operational risks and challenges faced in running a company in such a context. In 1996, his father spent three days hiding under a table, where he had taken refuge from fleeing army deserters who were raiding the company's factory. Though the mountains of Rwanda are within sight, the border is often closed, forcing the company to import inputs such as petrol by plane via Europe. Even now, after the 2006 election, some of the company's plantations are inaccessible due to militia activity, and the company's managers cannot prevent

146

their employees' wives and daughters from being raped by soldiers or the militia. A recent Reuters report shows that these conditions are not improving:

> Rape and brutality against women and girls are 'rampant and committed by non-state armed groups, the Armed Forces of the DRC, the National Congolese Police, and increasingly also by civilians', said Turkish lawyer Yakin Erturk. 'Violence against women seems to be perceived by large sectors of society to be normal', she added in a report after an 11-day trip to the strife-torn country. Erturk, special rapporteur for the United Nations Human Rights Council on violence against women, said the situation in South Kivu province, where rebels from neighbouring Rwanda operate, was the worst she had ever encountered. The atrocities perpetrated there by armed groups... 'are of an unimaginable brutality that goes far beyond rape', she said.[2]

In such circumstances, how can a company with large plantations and sophisticated manufacturing processes be run successfully? In the case of Pharmakina, one has to ask how can a company operating under such conditions actually expand production, increase its market share, and come to dominate the global quinine market? How can the company contribute to some degree of stability and socio-economic development in the area and at the same time avoid overt complicity in the serious human rights abuses that continue to occur in Bakuva? For Michael Gebbers, the appropriate response to these apparently irreconcilable choices is clear. If one is motivated by the desire to make a difference in people's lives, as he is, then the only way to succeed in this war-torn area is to work closely and tirelessly with and in support of the local community. As Horst Gebbers notes:

> The people here yearn for peace and security. And to work with them for this goal, this makes it worthwhile living here in Bukavu.[3]

The company in context

Pharmakina, originally called Congokina, was founded in 1942 by Belgian colonists in Bukavu, the capital of South Kivu province in the eastern part of the DRC. The aim of its founders was the industrial extraction of quinine. This anti-malaria agent, the harvested bark of the quinquina tree (*Cinchona ledgeriana*), grows readily in this area.

In 1998, the German pharmaceutical company Boehringer Mannheim, which owns Pharmakina, was bought by Hoffman La Roche. Hoffman La Roche later decided that given the deteriorating situation in the DRC and low profit margins in the sale of malaria medicines, Pharmakina was not a viable business. The company was therefore offered for sale (at low cost) to its managers, Horst Gebbers and his French colleague, Étienne Erny, who bought the company. Gebbers notes: 'I didn't need more than two minutes to decide!'[4]

Despite the civil war, which erupted in 1998, Pharmakina managers did not scale down production and wait for better times. Instead, they pursued an aggressive business strategy, even when that initially entailed incurring substantial financial losses. This strategy enabled them to corner more than a third of the world market for quinine salts.

Today Pharmakina is the biggest private employer in Bukavu, a town of more than 750 000 inhabitants. (Another 250 000 people live in the surrounding towns and villages.) The company employs 736 people full-time and almost 1 000 seasonal workers. Less than half a per cent of all its full-time employees are expatriates. Given estimates that in this region up to 30 people depend on a single income earner, the company directly supports the survival of approximately 20 000 people. The importance of Phamakina's continued existence in this desperately poor area – where most commercial activity, social services and governance have all but collapsed – cannot be overstated. Table 1 illustrates how Pharmakina represents the exception in the general decline of all economic activity in the area.

Table 1: Overview of companies' employee numbers in the South Kivu province in 1996, before the war, and in 2003, after the war

Company	Activity	Employees in 1996	Employees in 2003	Comments
Bralima	Brewery	450	250	
Chibeke	Quinquina plantation	1 200	37	
Farmers' Plantation	Tea, coffee, etc.	127	–	Closed
Gombo	Tea, quinquina plantation	332	–	Closed
Katana	Cement works	–	–	Closed
Kiliba	Sugar refinery	3 400	–	Closed
Kiringwe	Rice, palm oil press	186	–	Closed
Lemera	Tea, quinquina plantation	–	–	Closed
Mbayo	Tea, quinquina plantation	430	120	Est. 2003
Nyamulinduka	Quinquina plantation	600	–	Closed
Olive	Coffee, quinquina plantation	1 000	400	
Pharmakina	Pharmaceutical company	2 182	1 800	475 in 1999
Sipef	Coffee, quinquina plantation	638	50	
Sominki	Mining company	10 000	–	Closed
Tolinki	Roofing industry	100	35	
Uzabuco	Tobacco industry	170	–	Closed
Total		20 815	2 692	

Source: Fédération d'Entreprises Congolaises.

The company owns 31 *Cinchona* plantations (two of which are situated in neighbouring Rwanda) and farms a total of 1 300ha. These plantations produce 700 tonnes of bark a year. The company buys a further 2 000 tonnes of bark from other, mostly small-scale, growers. The bark processed in the company's factory produces a total of about 100 tonnes of quinine salts a year. The salts are trucked from Bukavu to Kigali in neighbouring Rwanda and then flown out from the airport there (providing the border is passable). Table 2 provides an overview of the land owned by Pharmakina.

Table 2: The actual land holding of Pharmakina, under a 25-year renewable lease agreement

Surface area	Land use
1 300ha	Plantations of quinquina trees *(Cinchona ledgeriana)*
600ha	Plantations of African cherry trees *(Prunus africana)*
700ha	Plantations of Eucalyptus trees for firewood supply of factory in Bukavu
200ha	Agricultural production for local market
300ha	Natural forest, not used/ reserve for medicinal plants
2 200ha	Eroded areas, roads, areas planted with *Leguminosae* for soil improvement; includes 1 000ha where *Cinchona ledgeriana* could be planted

Source: Pharmakina.

Through the acquisition of the necessary machinery from Europe (often second-hand), ready-to-use malaria tablets, syrup and ampoules for injection are now produced for the domestic market. These medicines have a higher profit margin than quinine salts. The motive for this expansion was primarily a quest for greater profitability for the enterprise. However, the vital role of relatively low-cost, reliable malaria medicines in the broader DRC context and a sense of commitment to the operation, its workers and the local community were also important imperatives for developing this processing capacity. Figure 1 shows a technician during part of the production process. The sophisticated, technology intensive nature of this operation stands in stark contrast to the dilapidated state of the infrastructure in the surrounding region, and power cuts are a frequent occurrence.

In 2005, Pharmakina began producing low-cost generic HIV/AIDS medicines. Working with Thai pharmacist Krisana Kraisintu, and with the support of the German development agency GTZ and German NGO Action Medeor, the company developed a process for providing a three-fold combination antiretroviral treatment that costs only US$12 a month. (Branded products cost US$1 000 a month.) This combination therapy – supported by international aid agencies – allows for a large-scale roll-out of treatments in the DRC and other African countries. (The international support is important, because even US$12 a month may be too much for most infected Africans and their families to cover.)[5] The treatment is provided free of charge to Pharmakina employees and their families.[6]

The production of these low-cost HIV/AIDS medicines was not motivated primarily by profits, although its commercial feasibility was carefully assessed. Rather, the company managers realised that the rapid spread of HIV in the area – driven largely by the widespread practice of rape by soldiers and the militia – was creating a further layer of humanitarian and economic hardship in the region. Pharmakina's employees were often directly affected. Hence the provision of low-cost medicines seemed to Horst Gebbers and his colleagues an obvious way to respond to a practical operational problem and to a humanitarian crisis.

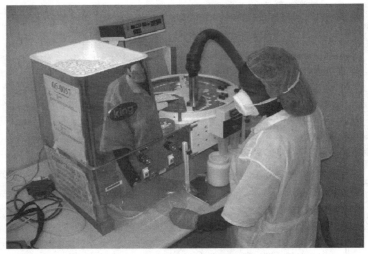

Figure 1: A stage in the anti-malaria medicine production process
(photo: Franz Stirnimann, 2007)

Employee and community relations as a matter of survival

In the literature on corporate responsibility, the term 'social licence to operate' is often used to suggest that a company needs not only the official government licences to operate but also a broader social contract with the communities surrounding a company's operations. Mining companies, for instance, emphasise the need for good community relations in order to pre-empt theft, sabotage or labour unrest. The Pharmakina experience shows that in unstable and conflict areas the social licence to operate may be crucial for survival.

The fact that the company and its operations enjoy widespread support among local communities has been a vital factor – coupled to other strategies mentioned below – in saving it from repeated plundering or total destruction. Except for the plundering in 1996 by fleeing army deserters, the company has never been directly attacked. As Horst Gebbers notes: 'There were only a few weeks in which we had to stop production.'[7] Even the militia, who are often drug-fuelled youths with extremely short-term time-horizons, seem to recognise that the Pharmakina operation ought to be spared. Local community support helps the company managers negotiate with the militia or army leaders. Achieving such insulation from direct attacks is no mean feat, given that nearby hospitals are routinely ransacked.

The fact that the company produces accessible, vital medicines for malaria and HIV/AIDS and makes these available free of charge to many community members, especially employees and their families at a dedicated health centre, contributes to the communities' appreciation of the company. Pharmakina's commitment to public health is now widely recognised within the eastern region of the DRC. For example, the regional governor, Deogracias Buhamba, stated, during a visit to Pharmakina: 'I have heard Pharmakina is taking care of people with AIDS on an anonymous basis – this is a good thing'.

Fair and transparent employment practices also help generate goodwill. The company pays decent salaries that compare favourably to those paid by the local banks and the brewery.

It recognises and regularly interacts with workers' unions. This interaction also means that Pharmakina must deal with challenges rarely encountered by other companies: for instance, a serious problem has been that workers are targeted and robbed on paydays. The company has had to make provision for making in-kind payments or finding other ways to pay wages safely, in conjunction with employee representatives. Such efforts have contributed to an excellent reputation among the surrounding communities, as captured by Aaron Musombwa, a recognised community representative, who said, 'from the beginning Pharmakina was a company with a social character'.

Pharmakina's commitment to local communities is perhaps most clearly expressed in an extensive project in support of former employees. In the late 1990s, following the management buy-out of the company, up to 1 000 employees had to be retrenched. Another reason for the retrenchment was a worldwide drop in demand for quinine salts. The new managers recognised that these layoffs would cause significant hardship not only for the affected employees (there is, of course, no social security system), but also for the local economy. Such systemic hardship could, in turn, contribute to problems for the firm in the form of violence, sabotage, extortion, theft, or destruction of plantations for the purpose of planting subsistence crops. Dedicated strategies and projects were hence developed to help the retrenched workers. These strategies were motivated by both a desire to care for the company's workers and a need to maintain 'social peace' in the region.

A first step was the establishment of a 'hardship fund'. This fund provides the means for the retrenched workers to access health facilities, pay school fees and establish small businesses. The fund also supports the cooperative ACOSYF (Association Coopérative en Synergie Féminine). ACOSYF supplies micro credits (after schooling) to individuals active in the fields of agriculture, animal husbandry, apiculture, small commerce and tailoring. One challenge at the start of this initiative was to establish a culture of repayment, considering that many local people have become accustomed to aid agencies disseminating grants. This shift in strategy – of making loans to self-regulating groups and providing training – is beginning to pay off.

Simultaneously, it was recognised that a crucial unexploited opportunity existed on company plantation land that was not needed for quinine bark production. In partnership with the GTZ, the company established a cooperative called ACAP (Association Coopérative pour l'Appui à la Population) for the retrenched workers and donated some of its unused land to this cooperative. The cooperative proved only partly successful, because only two of the original four regions used by the cooperative are still under plantation. The under-utilisation is primarily a function of the still dangerous and unstable security situation. Also, though the original idea was to encourage the new smallholders to plant cinchona trees and sell these to the company, many beneficiaries opted to plant edible crops to feed themselves. Michael Gebbers emphasises that significant time and resources were dedicated to projects such as ACAP by Pharmakina managers.

Besides ACAP, Pharmakina started a model farm called Alimenkina in 2000. Located 25km south of Bukavu, it provides a total of 135 jobs, many of which are held by former Pharmakina employees. On 370ha of previously malaria-infested land, the farm employs modern farming methods according to strict ecological controls on the basis of a commercial, but not-for-profit, model. Among other things, it produces more than 10 tonnes of fish, 10 tonnes of pork and 30 tonnes of rice annually for the local and domestic market. When interviewed, one of the former

Figure 2:   One of the fish ponds at Alimenkina
(photo: Franz Stirnimann, 2007)

employees of Pharmakina now working at Alimenkina, Dieudonné Bagaloi, acknowledged the farm's virtues, saying: 'Hopefully Alimenkina keeps going, because it creates many jobs in this area.'

Establishing and maintaining good community relations has also involved ensuring that communication channels between the company and various community groups are always open. Traditional authorities, as well as representatives of churches, local NGOs and sport associations are often invited for discussions with Pharmakina managers.

Building and maintaining relationships

Over and above demonstrating a long-term commitment to employees and local communities, Pharmakina managers have had to build relationships with diverse role-players, including heads of warring factions. Of course, managing this process can be a complicated and potentially dangerous undertaking in the DRC. However, it is a skill that Horst Gebbers, in particular, has often demonstrated, building good relations while still maintaining an overarching degree of independence. Responding to one of many (German) reporters who have interviewed him, he notes:

> As a businessman, here, you also need to have good 'beer-colleagues' [that is, good relationships with people in positions of influence] … A normal German manager would not survive more than three months here.[8]

Gebbers's long-standing friendship with King Chimanye II, monarch of Kaziba, a kingdom of about 70 000 people, situated about 50km south of Bukavu, is of particular importance. Chimanye is also a senator in Kinshasa and thus provides Pharmakina with a direct link to the national government. In return, Gebbers provides support to the kingdom, facilitates relations with GTZ and contributes to the local hospital.[9]

Maintaining good relations with national, provincial and local authorities is often complicated by the absence of legal redress for decisions taken by state officials. In such circumstances, Pharmakina managers cannot avoid providing unpaid services to the provincial governor or the chief of police in order to maintain good relations. In another interview, Gebbers admits: 'To journalists I always say, no, we are totally clean and never pay bribes, but in reality we have to live with the people here.'[10]

This strategy also applies to army deserters and rebels. To prevent them from attacking the factory or the plantations, Pharmakina managers have found themselves in a position where inviting them to drink some beer was seen as a means of averting violence and destruction. Decisions to engage in such socialising or negotiations are made on an ad hoc basis, and Pharmakina managers emphasise that they do not involve the payment of money – though medicines do change hands. Michael Gebbers notes:

> When the rebels occupied our plantations, for example, the company stopped its activities there and waited until the rebels or the militias withdrew from there before reopening the plantations. Of course, direct threats to the plant in Bukavu needed prompt reactions and so the company had to decide on a case by case basis what to do in such events. In general the intervention of a close 'friend' or someone you know helped to sort out the problem. Fortunately this didn't happen so often and the plant wasn't harmed. The rebels took power with a 'political' goal, setting up a 'government' to run the region according to their goals... So as most of the rebels motivate their engagement with political reasons and as the company is strictly a private business it was generally quite easy to convince them of our inability to support them... But, of course, if a general comes to you and asks for some medicine for his men, there is little option for you to say, 'No, we won't!'[11]

Ethical implications, let alone the wish to adhere to principles such as those of the United Nations Global Compact, do not feature explicitly in such decisions. However, they do arguably play a crucial role in the company's underlying business strategy. The two primary objectives are the survival of the company and the security of its employees. In a conflict zone marked by weak governance and appalling widespread human rights abuses, the tenth principle of the Global Compact – 'Businesses should work against corruption in all its forms, including extortion and bribery' – might be considered a luxury with limited application.

Conclusion

Pharmakina is, of course, an unusual case. It nevertheless illustrates a number of crucial lessons. Its managers have developed and implemented a number of strategies and initiatives that merged the objective of making the business profitable with a commitment to providing long-term support to employees and the surrounding communities. In some instances, short-term profits were forfeited for the purpose of fostering community development opportunities. Yet these choices were viewed as being in the long-term interests of the company. This long-term outlook has contributed to the development of good relationships with diverse groups and role-players – relationships that have provided a vital bulwark against the endemic theft and violence in the region.

The company's core business and its various community engagement efforts have also made crucial, tangible contributions to the survival of many in this extremely impoverished region. Furthermore, the company's managers hope that by demonstrating that business is possible in the area they will attract other investors to Bukava.

That said, the Pharmakina experience also illustrates that in difficult contexts such as these, strict compliance with the principles reflected in the UN Global Compact is simply impossible. Nevertheless, these principles provide an ethical framework within which companies such as Pharmakina can formulate and implement policies that enable the communities with whom they operate to survive and perhaps even flourish.

Editors' reflections and questions

In the war-torn and violent context of the eastern DRC, Pharmakina has not only been able to survive, but has actually expanded production. In so doing, the company has provided the livelihoods and the medicines that have sustained its employees and their families. Its managers have been able to do so by working closely and tirelessly with and in support of the local community. The broader community's support, in turn, has played a crucial role in securing the company's survival. It is, however, problematic to expect a company operating in this context to adhere in a straightforward manner to all of the Global Compact principles. Put yourself in the shoes of Pharmakina's owner-managers and consider the following questions:

1. Would you have stayed in the area? On the basis of which criteria would you make this decision?

2. Would you have done anything differently? What choices did Horst Gebbers and his colleagues make with which you might disagree?

3. The case shows the company managers' approach to building amenable relations with warring factions in order to ensure the survival of the company. These groups are often accused of severe human rights abuses. Is it possible to maintain 'friendly' relations with them without becoming complicit in their actions?

4. How does one choose between the risk of complicity and the virtues of providing benefits for a large number of vulnerable individuals and families in a war-torn region?

Notes

1   This case study is based in part on interviews or e-mail communication with the following people. At Pharmakina: Étienne Erny, chief executive officer; Horst Gebbers, chief operational officer; Michael Gebbers, head of Finance and Administration; Dirk Gebbers, head of Agronomy and Produc-

tion; Pierre Kafua, head of Human Resources; Elysée Mudwanga, director of Agronomy; Pontien Kizito, mechanic, representative of Union SLCC. At Alimenkina: Gauthier Mpasi, assistant to managing director; Mihigo Mahazi, worker, formerly employed by Pharmakina; Dieudonné Bagaloi, worker, formerly employed by Pharmakina. Others interviewed include: Félicité Kabonwa, coordinator ACOSYF (Association Coopérative en Synergie Féminine); Deogracias Buhamba Hamba, governor of South Kivu Province; Karl Schuler, programme leader PBF, Programme Biodiversité et Forêts, and PNKB, Parc National de Kahuzi-Biéga, GTZ; and Aaron Musombwa, chief of Logistics at CEI (Commission Electorale Indépendante), community representative.

2 Available at http://www.alertnet.org/thenews/newsdesk/L30471668.htm (accessed 17 August 2007).

3 R. Bauerdick, 'Pharmakina – ein Deutsches Unternehmen im Kongo', *Arzteblatt.de*, 23 September 2005.

4 J. Dieterich, 'Der Patriot', available at www.brandeins.de (accessed 17 August 2007).

5 No patent problem occurred, because of the World Trade Organisation (WTO) exemption of Least Developed Countries in the production of generic AIDS medicines.

6 Action Medeor, *Annual Report 2005: Medical Aid World-Wide* (Krefeld: Action Medeor, 2005).

7 Dieterich, 'Der Patriot'.

8 B. Grill, 'Kongos Kleines Wirtschaftswunder', *Die Zeit,* 14 July 2005, available at http://images.zeit.de/text/2005/29/Pharmakina.

9 Dieterich, 'Der Patriot'.

10 Ibid.

11 E-mail communication, 17 August 2007.

Preempting land-related conflicts:

The case of VCP
and eucalyptus plantations in Brazil

CLÁUDIO BRUZZI BOECHAT & ROBERTA MOKREJS PARO

Introduction[1]

Poupança Florestal (Forest Savings Account – 'the programme') is a eucalyptus plantation programme developed by Votorantim Celulose e Papel (VCP). Set in Rio Grande do Sul, the southernmost state of Brazil, this programme provides an opportunity for VCP's neighbour farmers to become partners in the production of timber. The bank, ABN AMRO Real, provides partnering farmers with loans. VCP provides seedlings and technical assistance (at no cost) to plant eucalyptus and commits itself to future purchases of the timber after seven years.

The project embraces the participation of owners of large, medium and small properties as partners in eucalyptus production. By far the largest of these is the group of small landowners, which comprises a variety of income profiles, from subsistence to commercial agriculture, mostly family-based. These small landowners are particularly vulnerable and have often lived on the verge of socio–economic exclusion and, sometimes, even extinction.

With the necessary conditions in place – access to credit, capacity building, technological resources and assistance – Poupança Florestal has sought to engage small-scale farmers (including settlers)[2] as potential business partners. The programme improves their chance of entering the market and creates new job opportunities. As importantly, it ensures greater food security, curtails unemployment related migration and enhances the sense of belonging that comes from the security of more consistent social inclusion.

The latent conflict

VCP's plan to establish a large eucalyptus plantation to supply its future pulp and paper mills in Rio Grande do Sul is faced with a number of major obstacles. Perhaps the most pressing challenge to the company comes from the Landless Workers' Movement (Movimento dos Trabalhadores Rurais Sem Terra) (MST), a social movement that vigorously defends the interests of landless rural dwellers. Rio Grande do Sul, where MST was born, has the largest concentration of landless rural workers' campsites in Brazil, and has experienced numerous land invasions by landless people. The MST's land occupations are viewed by many Brazilians as the most effective means to accelerate land reform. The movement has emerged as the most prominent exponent of the interests of both the landless and the beneficiaries of the government's recent land reform programme. It has consequently become the primary interlocutor for any discussion of new projects affecting its constituents. The conflicting interests of VCP and the MST have all the makings of a protracted internecine conflict.

VCP realised that the potential for such conflict called for a realignment of relations with the MST and that its production plans would require broad participation from the local community. For these reasons, in 2004, VCP's CEO José Luciano Penido invited Ciro Correa, a top representative from the MST, to a meeting to discuss what was needed for all parties to benefit from VCP investments in the region. The meeting was mediated by Oded Grajew, one of the founders of the World Social Forum, who is also president of the Instituto Ethos which promotes corporate social responsibility in the country.

Penido's ideas were innovative: he proposed to integrate landless and settled peasants into the production process, and to bring together novel technological and financial resources. However, Ciro Correa had to take the MST's broader political mandate into account and he indicated that he needed to consult the MST leadership before giving a definite answer to the proposed 'partnership'. However, at no stage did the MST express an official position. About a month later the message was clear: the MST did not wish to become involved. Its refusal to enter into constructive dialogue, while not officially declared, was probably the result of its opposition to large monoculture plantations. Moreover, the MST's preferred development model is at odds with large-scale agribusiness.

Looking behind the conflict

The latent conflict in Rio Grande do Sul represents a crucial challenge for Brazil's future competitiveness and development. The unequal access to property and the persistently high level of income inequality will not be easily resolved. At the same time, the resources of the region and current stagnation present a rich opportunity for business innovation.

The roots of the conflict: A persistent land concentration pattern

The current pattern of distorted land distribution in Brazil began in 1530. The Portuguese Crown distributed a vast number of lots for cultivation in exchange for one sixth of the production. Since then, the property structure has remained very concentrated. This stable pattern of land concentration is seen in the Gini Index:[3] 0.837 in 1972; 0.854 in 1978; 0.831 in 1992; 0.843 in 1998 and 0.802 in 2000.[4]

According to the Ministry of Agrarian Development, 45% of the agricultural area is concentrated in 1% of rural properties, a situation which leads, inexorably, to one of the world's most unequal income distribution patterns. These patterns hinder local development and force migration to the cities.[5] Violence and conflict in rural areas has also increased: rural populations find themselves displaced by technological modernisation and must scramble for other means of survival.[6]

A land reform process driven by conflict

The fight for land in Brazil has historically been permeated by violence. With the end of the military regime in the late 1980s, the rural workers' movement began to apply greater pressure for land title. Violence begat violence as large landowners and the government attempted to defend rural properties.[7] In 2005, 1 304 land conflicts were registered and 38 people were left dead.[8]

The lack of more aggressive state land resettlement policies encouraged important social movements, such as the MST, to use land occupation as the primary strategy for forcing the government to institute a more significant land redistribution process. As a result, between 1995 and 2001, 584 301 families gained access to land.[9] In 1996, the government established the National Programme for the Strengthening of Family Agriculture (PRONAF).

The importance of the MST in this process is broadly acknowledged, not only for bringing land reform back to the agenda, but also for strengthening the demand for special policies on family-based agriculture.[10] The MST offered an opportunity for many economically excluded groups who had no political power (such as former small farmers displaced by the large farms to marginal areas, landless workers, migrants from urban peripheries) to enter the political process effectively. MST-led land occupations became a key driver in the land reform programme.[11]

Despite the government programmes, the land reform scene has not been radically altered. Even though the government is politically aligned with social movements such as the MST, its support of land reform has been roundly criticised for not meeting its promised goals.[12] Nonetheless, property rights are just one of the constraints in the process of increasing opportunities for the rural poor. They need facilitated access to markets, credit, products, inputs and technology if their settlements are to take them beyond subsistence living.

The economic importance of small-scale farming and the socioeconomic context in Rio Grande do Sul

The importance of small landowners, especially family-based agriculture, is both economically and socially noteworthy. In the Brazilian context of scarce capital but abundant labour and land, labour-intensive family-based agriculture is an important component of local development.[13] According to PRONAF, the participation of family-based agriculture represented 10.1% of the GNP in 2003 or R$156.6bn (about US$74.6bn). Small productive units represent 85.2% of the total number of rural establishments, occupy 30.5% of the agricultural land, create 37.9% of the gross value of national agriculture, produce 50.9% of total income from agriculture and account for 77% of the labour in rural areas. The total income per hectare/year was 2.4 times higher where family work prevailed.[14]

In Rio Grande do Sul, land disputes are more intense than they are elsewhere in Brazil. The region has the highest concentration and the longest historical tradition of small property and family-based agriculture, and better politically organised farmers.[15]

In 2006, the MST became radicalised. It destroyed the eucalyptus nurseries belonging to another large pulp and paper company. Some farms now find themselves surrounded by campsites containing some hundred landless people. These campsites are comprised primarily of landless people who have claimed land, but whose claims have not yet been granted by the land reform programme. They significantly increase the fear of land invasions among the large landowners.

Figure 1: Geographical region of VCP's venture and neighbouring settlements

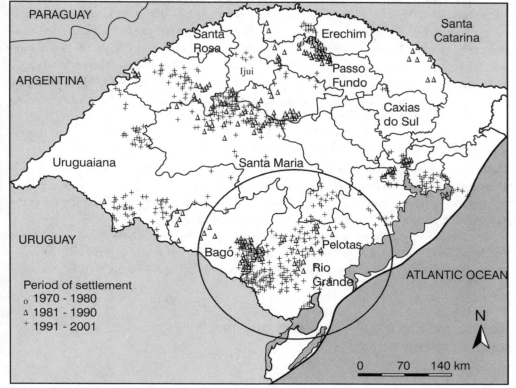

Source: SCP / DDRU.

Another unique aspect of the region is the presence of hundreds of settlements generated by the land reform programme (see Figure 1). Over the last 25 years, 4 648 families have settled (in 133 settlements). However, because access to land was not followed by the provision of the resources required to make it truly productive, the settlers can often be found living in precarious planting and housing conditions. These rural slums contribute to the region's socio-economic and political instability.

Even the traditional small-scale farmers in the region, who have already had land title for some time, find it hard to sustain their livelihoods. The southern part of Rio Grande do Sul, where VCP is expanding, is highly dependent on cattle and rice, which both suffer from price instabilities and an unfavourable tax regime. Such inhospitable conditions make Rio Grande do Sul one of the poorest regions in Brazil.

A closer look at the pulp and paper sector: Damaged reputation

The pulp and paper sector has a reputation for aggravating the agrarian conflicts in Brazil, especially in the Bahia and Espírito Santo regions.[16] In the 1970s, as the plantations expanded, small farmers, rural black communities (descendants of runaway slave communities, the *qui-lombos*) and indigenous communities were pressured into moving to marginal agricultural areas. Many lost their means of subsistence and were then driven to even more marginal existence in urban slums. The process of plantation expansion has contributed to high land concentration: in Aracruz, a single company now owns almost 40% of the territory.[17]

The expansion of eucalyptus in these regions has also contributed to a reduction in the remaining Atlantic Forest. Furthermore, non-compliance with the environmental legislation and deforestation of riparian forests and other sensitive areas has lowered the regional water table and exacerbated soil erosion. Deforestation and soil erosion have led to diminished biodiversity and limited the productivity of agricultural communities that rely on plant resources other than pulp for their livelihood.

Implications of the agrarian context for VCP

The local atmosphere of social unrest posed clear challenges for the implementation of VCP's plan to plant 100 000ha of eucalyptus. Penido, the company's CEO, frames the risk in ethical and pragmatic terms: 'How can the company grow and incorporate more land, if we run the risk of being an easy target in the clearly socially unfair Brazilian reality?'

The company's concerns were not just limited to possible land invasions. It understands that large-scale, long-term eucalyptus planting will not be viable if a significant portion of society does not see value in the company's operations: 'One cannot eat eucalyptus' is a statement often heard.

Poupança Florestal – building business linkages with local communities

The company

VCP is among the largest pulp and paper companies in Latin America. It operates in Brazil and abroad (its markets reflect a 50% foreign and 50% domestic split). The characteristics of VCP's bleached eucalyptus pulp make it suitable for producing a variety of paper types: printing and writing paper, cardboard, coated paper, carbonless paper, thermal paper and labels. It derives 38% of its income from pulp sales and 62% from paper sales. The company's integrated operations range from wood production to distribution to the final consumer. In 2005, VCP registered a net income of approximately US$1.3bn.

For decades VCP has invested heavily in research, genetic improvement and the expansion of its forest base. The pulp it uses is 100% from planted eucalyptus forests. These investments and improvements, along with its diversified array of products, have created a competitive differential for VCP. The company trades stocks on the São Paulo Stock Exchange (Bovespa) and the New York Stock Exchange (NYSE), and owns shares in other major companies from the sector such as Aracruz Celulose, Suzano Bahia Sul Papel e Celulose and Ripasa. Headquartered in São Paulo, VCP was founded in 1988 and is a subsidiary of Votorantim Participações S.A.

Planning the venture

While planning a business expansion in 2003, the company mapped worldwide the geographical areas where a new industrial park might be developed. The southern half of Rio Grande do Sul was chosen mainly for its productive advantages: good logistical conditions, land and labour availability, climate conditions and topography suitable for eucalyptus, good water supply and the high education level of (a portion of) the population. The goal was to have 100 000ha of eucalyptus planted in the area by 2011. By then VCP would have a pulp mill in the region for processing the timber.

VCP's vision for the next 15 years – a relatively short time for a business that runs in seven-year production cycles – would see the company becoming the world's biggest supplier of eucalyptus pulp. The expansion would realise a three-fold annual net income increase in pulp and paper production by 2020. This increase would translate into a four-fold increase in net income: from US$1bn in 2004, to US$4bn in 2020. As part of this plan, VCP started buying land in Rio Grande do Sul in 2004.

The traditional agribusiness model of depending as little as possible on third parties, and buying land to plant and to harvest whenever needed, had potential land concentration effects that could jeopardise the surrounding communities in Rio Grande do Sul. Smaller properties are especially vulnerable, and such vulnerability could inflame the politics of an already volatile region. In an attempt to include local farmers in the business process, VCP decided that 30% of the timber used in production should come from third party suppliers.

This 30% target would require that 30 000ha be sourced from partnerships with farmers in the local community. However, their trust would have to be earned. The local farmers were naturally suspicious of this new business in their midst and expressed concern about the reputation of eucalyptus for drying up and impoverishing the land. Another major barrier to working with the local farmers was their lack of experience in planting eucalyptus in the region. In addition, farmers would be obliged to wait some seven years until the forest could be cut and crop income realised. It was in response to these challenges that VCP created the Poupança Florestal programme.

Poupança Florestal

Implemented in 2005, Poupança Florestal facilitates the participation of the company's neighbour farmers in the eucalyptus production. VCP sought to legitimise its operations in the region by engaging the community and creating a sense of social and economic inclusion. (Box 1 gives an overview of the programme.)

Table 1: Distribution of financial resources over the production cycle

	Year 1	Year 2	Year 3	Year 4	Total
Total (R$/ha)	1 689	222	236	363	2 510
Labour (R$/ha)	1 180	124	135	280	1 719
Inputs (R$/ha)	509	98	101	83	791

Note: Values corrected by 9% a year; the loan is completely disbursed after four years, as minimal inputs are required in years 5, 6 and 7, although interest continues to accrue. Repayment does not occur until timber is harvested.
Source: VCP.

Box 1: Overview of Poupança Florestal Programme

Financing

- Financing provided by ABN AMRO Real at an interest rate of 9% per year (see Table 1 with four-year loan disbursement schedule).
- Timber guarantees the loan.
- Female head of household is signatory to the loan.
- The loan, totalling R$2 371 over four years, allows the farmer enough capital to purchase production inputs and remunerate the labour for planting eucalyptus.
- The loan amount is equivalent to VCP's own costs to plant the forest; so farmers can either hire the same company that carries out the planting for VCP, or learn how to plant themselves and use the money for something else, a tractor for example.
- The due maintenance tasks and expenditures are monitored closely by VCP.
- Agreement set for 14 years, or two cycles of eucalyptus production.
- Risks of failure (in timber delivery) would be shouldered by ABN AMRO Real and VCP. When the partnership is with land reform settlers, the risks would only be shouldered by VCP.

Alternative Income

- To avoid dependence on eucalyptus, the area planted is limited to 30% of the farmer's property. They can continue growing traditional crops (corn and rice) and raising livestock (cattle). Again, such income is critical since the timber itself cannot be harvested until the seventh year. VCP donates traditional crop seeds to settlers, and small and medium farmers.
- The net income per ha by the end of the seventh year is approximately R$4 878[18] (based on an average expected production of 280 m³/ha by the seventh year). This income should be enough to buy one hectare of land in the region (Table 2).

Technical Support and Capacity Building

- VCP provides eucalyptus seedlings (and also native forest seedlings for the reforestation of sensitive areas) at no cost. In order to guarantee productivity, VCP provides the same genetic material used in its own forests.

Table 2: Earnings calculation

	Currently: without correction	7 years: correction for 9%*
Debt (inputs & labour)	R$2 372/ha	R$4 336/ha
Selling price	R$18/m³	R$33/m³
Average expected production	280m³	280m³
Gross income	R$5040/ha	R$9213/ha
Net income	R$2668/ha	R$4878/ha

* 9% correction for selling price adjustment each year; this is the same rate as the interest.
Source: VCP.

- Emater (Technical Assistance and Rural Extension Agency) was contracted from 2005 to 2015 by VCP to provide (free) technical assistance to farmers on production operations, This assistance is offered from the initial property planning phase to planting the forest and maintenance throughout the whole cycle.
- Each plantation is regularly and closely monitored by Emater to ensure proper maintenance measures are undertaken for each phase (e.g. ant and weed control). Proper maintenance is a precondition for the release of the next instalment of the loan, and also reduces the risks of crop failure.[19]

Purchasing Terms

- After 7 years, VCP guarantees the purchase of at least 95% of the timber, for a previously established price.[20] (This price is currently set at R$18/m^3, the regional market price, corrected by 9% a year. This correction reflects the same rate as the loan.)
- If, at the time of the harvest, the market value of timber is lower than that established by contract, then the contract prevails. This provision lowers the risk for the farmer.
- VCP pays for the harvest and transportation of the timber from the farm to the pulp mill.

Agrosilviculture

- The 30% maximum land allocation to eucalyptus can be concentrated in one area, or it can be mixed with other farming activities throughout the plot of land (e.g. agrosilviculture).

Contractual Requirements

- Farmers must comply with environmental legislation.
- Farmers may not employ children or engage in forced labour.[21]

Using this model, the farmer can plant without prior financial reserves, and does not need to use their property as a guarantee for the loan. The timber produced is the guarantee. The farmer's wife acts as a signatory to the loan as a means of ensuring compliance by the farmer.

Maurik Jehee, ABN AMRO Real credit analyst, explained that VCP's intervention and continued commitment, the possibility of gaining new clients and the alignment with the bank sustainability guidelines, were the main reasons it accepted the conditions proposed by VCP. 'Besides its environmental concerns, [Poupança Florestal] has an interesting social aspect and regional development potential. Moreover, it brings the potential of new clients in a region where the bank has little penetration', said Jehee. The VCP guarantee of buying the timber and VCP's ongoing technical support mitigate the risks for the bank. At the same time, the project creates new business opportunities for a large number of individuals who would normally have difficulty in gaining access to credit on an individual basis. The financing volume is expected to reach US$30 million over seven years (i.e. by 2012) and benefit 20 000 to 25 000 farmers.

Community involvement: Inclusion of land reform settlements and traditional small-scale farmers

The programme encompasses various farmer profiles. Owners of large, medium and small properties provide the land for eucalyptus production. The region where VCP planned to expand its activities has had 4 648 families settled by the land reform programme over the last 25 years. Normally, these new landowners would, against the background of MST campsites, be viewed as potential agitators. In terms of VCP's programme, they are landowners and are viewed as potential partners.

According to ABN AMRO Real, from the initial public announcement of the programme in 2005 until the end of 2006, 312 projects had been approved. These projects represent 7 283ha of eucalyptus planted area. Another 55 were under assessment by the bank, and represent some 8 409ha. Significant growth potential remains. The main bottleneck in the approval process stems from irregularities in the property documentation of small farmers. Land regularisation is a slow process requiring government approval.

By the end of 2006,[22] about 131 families had signed agreements with VCP to join Poupança Florestal. Most of these called for planting commitments of 5–10ha each.[23] The total planted area of settled families is approximately 874ha. The majority of the projects (78%) involve small farmers and settlers. In terms of planted area, small farmers and settlers represent 47% of the total. (Table 3 shows a breakdown of VCP suppliers.) As more families join the project, the local agglomerates are able to produce a constant supply of timber on a scale that is large enough to sustain a self-sufficient organisation within the company.

Table 3: Distribution of projects by farmer type

Farmer type	Proportion of projects	Proportion of area	Number of projects	Area (ha)
Land reform settler	42%	12%	131%	873.96
Small (<100ha)	36%	35%	112%	2 549.05
Medium (101–500 ha)	18%	35%	56%	2 549.05
Large (>500ha)	4%	18%	13%	1 310.94
Total	100%	100%	312%	7 283.00

Source: ABN AMRO Real.

The partners of the programme begin by receiving Emater (Technical Assistance and Rural Extension Agency) training and in the first year receive the loan to plant the forest. By undertaking the labour activities themselves – planting, and ant and weed control – the amount designated for these activities (which is the same amount that would be paid by VCP if contractors did the work) is kept in the family as income, and can be allocated for other uses.

According to VCP's estimates, the farmer's ultimate total profit is expected to be about R$2 500 per ha.[24] (See Table 2 for details.) This profit does not reflect additional savings or potential savings in labour. The business model invites the participation of small-scale farmers, most of whom could not cover increased start-up, maintenance and logistical costs on their own. The VCP programme makes small-scale farming commercially viable and creates an opportunity for small farmers both to make a profit and to provide viable job opportunities for their families.

Property planning: Environmental compliance and mixed crops

VCP's growth strategy has also taken into consideration the need for compliance with environmental legislation. It has done so largely through such special concerns as the creation of legal land reserves and permanent protection areas. Although environmental legislation compliance should be a basic condition for the operation of any agricultural business, such compliance has been more the exception than the norm. According to VCP, while non-compliance occurs in the pulp and paper sector in Rio Grande do Sul, VCP makes environmental regulatory compliance a condition in all of its contracts with partner farmers.

The planning of plantation and preservation areas required by law occurs during the initial training phase. The trained technicians are provided by the public agency Emater.

In order to avoid dependence on eucalyptus production, and the disruption of the culture of cultivating traditional crops such as corn and rice and breeding cattle, the programme requires that 50% of the property be devoted to the farm's original staple crops. On the remaining 50% of the land, the legal minimum of 20% of the total area must be set aside for preservation and another 5% ensures permanent protection of the land surrounding bodies of water.[25] Thus, no more than 30% of the property may be allocated for eucalyptus production. The result is a mosaic very different from the monolithic plantations that usually grow across preservation areas and often have deleterious socio–economic and environmental effects.

By 2006, the permanent preservation area exceeded the original goals. As much as 55% of the programme land had been set aside for permanent preservation while 45% had been allocated for planting. The high preservation rates can be explained by the particular need to preserve sensitive zones around lakes and rivers and on slopes.

Challenges for scaling up Poupança Florestal

In order to achieve the goal of 30 000ha of eucalyptus planted by third parties, VCP must secure greater participation from the local community. As a key civil society representative of settled farmers and family-based agriculture, the MST was approached to discuss the proposal. But although the MST did not agree to any form of cooperation, it also did not articulate official *opposition* to the participation of its members in the VCP programme. Individual farmers could still join Poupança Florestal. The lack of overt opposition, and the building up of trust between VCP and its partner farmers has, in turn, increased the level of cooperation between VCP and neighbouring settlers.

The one remaining challenge is state bureaucracy. Small properties usually have irregular documentation, and the regularisation process invites additional costs and delays that may complicate the participation of small farmers in Poupança Florestal.

Challenges to building a social licence to operate

The logistics of the Poupança Florestal programme constitute only some of the hurdles VCP has needed to overcome. It also had to establish a licence to operate in the region. To secure this it had to work with the local community, attempt to resolve some of the environmental concerns about eucalyptus production, forge partnerships with public agencies and open lines of communication with other stakeholders.

Prioritising local businesses and establishing labour relations with settlers

VCP's activities on its own properties (70% of the total planned area) strengthen its licence to operate in Rio Grande do Sul by ensuring that contracts for many inputs are signed with local businesses and that local people are hired for management and operational positions. All contractors working in the plantations (including VCP's own properties) come from Rio Grande do Sul; in total, the company employs about 900 people. VCP's CEO, José Luciano Penido, says 'Less than 50 people come from other regions, and many of them come from settlements'.

The hired settlers receive special attention. Besides having all of their labour rights guaranteed, they are assisted by an employee relations team made up of people from VCP, from the third party workforce contractors, and from Emater. Proper working uniforms, transport to and from work, training, health care, hot food and toilet facilities in the fields are some of the benefits provided for the workers.

Agroforestry and eucalyptus: Controversies and joint studies

Another important aspect of the mosaic-type forest plantations is the possibility, if desired by the farmer, of technical assistance for the practice of agroforestry – planting forest with other crops or pasture on the same piece of land. The practice of agroforestry aims to produce and to maximise positive interactions between trees and crops, and is usually seen as having an important role to play in rural development and the production of sustainable agricultural systems.

However, the controversies over eucalyptus production cannot be ignored. The eucalyptus is a fast-growing tree and places significant demands on soil nutrients and water. As a result, there is an ongoing debate about its suitability for agroforestry systems.[26] It has the ability to adapt to diverse soil and water conditions due to its long and deep root system; this makes it a very competitive species, and potentially a threat to the surrounding plants. Producing eucalyptus as a cash crop thus carries a risk of desertification and biodiversity reduction. However, proponents of VCP's programme, and others like it, argue that these negative effects can be mitigated with proper management techniques.[27] With this in mind, a key component of the VCP programme is the provision of adequate technical supervision and compliance with environmental legislation. Well aware of the criticism that the introduction of eucalyptus on small properties might raise, VCP has established university partnerships to monitor the impact of eucalyptus introduction in the region.

The Federal University of Santa Maria and the Albert-Ludwigs-Universität Freiburg (Germany) have undertaken a joint study to monitor parameters such as soil, atmosphere, water (including rainfall quality and quantity inside and outside the forest), nutrients and light conditions for plantations of eucalyptus and its interaction with sorghum, soy, forage crops and native forages. Initiated in 2005, the study will carry out several measurements during the first seven-year growth period and introduce new monitoring technologies. The Universidade Católica de Pelotas, Universidade Federal de Pelotas and Universidade Federal de Santa Maria are creating fauna, flora and architectural heritage inventories and producing studies on the impact of the VCP programme. The University of São Paulo is developing a comprehensive assessment system designed to measure the impact of VCP's activities in Rio Grande do Sul on local development and sustainability.

Establishing partnerships with public agencies

The VCP's partnership with the public agency Emater (Technical Assistance and Rural Extension Agency) has been fundamental to the programme's implementation. Emater provides capacity building, training, and monitoring for the programme. Fernando Roldan Alves, the Emater employee responsible for the VCP partnership, says:

> You design a project and go see the guy and he says he wants to plant six hectares of eucalyptus trees and you go there and plant them. And you schedule a day and go there and it has all been really planted. You get there and you can see the work the [formerly] landless peasants have done. This is really great. We were not used to this kind of stuff and [Emater alone] does not have the resources needed to carry it out. That's the truth. And those six hectares must be overseen, we collect some material, we have to control it. There are five hundred hectares out there and [these fellows are] going to sell the land cheaply because [they have] no other resources. Well, now [they] can prosper. They are planting and making money that ends up being spent right here in the region.

Communication and conflict

Media criticism on the various threats posed by pulp and paper production in Rio Grande do Sul (including VCP's plantations) is commonplace.[28] These reports focus on issues such as species extinction, lack of water and jobs, and the potential for rural exodus. In an attempt to respond to these criticisms and foster debate, VCP regularly participates in meetings with the local community and conducts interviews with the press.

Invasions avoided

Thus far, VCP seems to have earned its social licence to operate. The Poupança Florestal programme appears to have been instrumental in this. In 2006, an MST-initiated occupation strategy to pressure the Brazilian government into speeding up agrarian reform has worked against many of the companies that own large tracts of land in the region. Most pulp and paper companies were affected by invasions but VCP's lands were spared because the company received 'inside information' from local settlers. For although the settlers remain linked to the MST after they acquire land, many settlers participate in the Poupança Florestal programme, either as partner farmers or hired hands. This participation seems to have engendered some degree of loyalty to VCP.

CLÁUDIO BOECHAT & ROBERTA PARO

Final comments

VCP has developed a business model tailored to the specific needs of the affected communities in Rio Grande do Sul. While the programme clearly creates livelihood opportunities for the rural poor, it would surely be enriched if the dialogue with the MST, as the strongest civil society representative of settled farmers and family-based agriculture, was enhanced.

At the same time, the programme's value to the company and the surrounding communities has been demonstrated by the greater loyalty engendered among these people. Instead of focusing on traditional security measures, the programme has lowered the potential for conflict by addressing the systemic roots of the problem: the rural poor's unmet demand for financial resources and the need for technical assistance with production.

The potential for conflict remains, however. The MST or other groups might lead new land occupations. To avoid such an eventuality, the company would be well advised to expand its existing programme and open new avenues of dialogue with farmers, workers and settlers. VCP should also engage civil society organisations and others in the broader debate over eucalyptus plantations. Some of these organisations could be drawn into joint monitoring programmes. Such partnerships would further diminish the risks to the company, enhance its social licence to operate, and generate long-term benefits for both the environment and the rural poor.

Editors' reflections and questions

Consider the traditional approaches employed by companies such as VCP in obtaining large contiguous tracts of land suitable for plantations to produce pulp and paper (or indeed any product). Now consider the alternative approach employed in the case study and its associated costs and benefits compared to the traditional method. To what extent is this new approach replicable in Brazil and elsewhere? Are there potential lessons for plantation companies operating in Africa?

1. Lack of appropriate policy and regulation on land tenure issues at national and provincial levels often aggravates land claims at a local level. This example in Brazil reflects a situation that is also common in parts of Africa. To what extent is VCP complicit in national and provincial government failure to address the high levels of inequality with respect to land ownership within its 'sphere of influence'? Does the ongoing conflict over land ownership require that VCP do more than ensure greater financial security in the local community through the programme described in the case study? Might the problem of significant land inequality – and the application of international human rights norms to private actors – require VCP to undertake its own programme of land redistribution, for instance?

2. Although VCP has succeeded, in the early stages of a very long-term programme, in securing the support of the local community, significant questions remain about the effects of pulp production on the environment. To what extent is the company responsible for limiting its plantations, over and above legal compliance, and how does this relate to its efforts to support small-scale landowners in this case study?

Notes

1   We would like to thank the following individuals for providing the interviews on which this case study is based. Maurik Jehee (credit analyst at ABN AMRO Real); Fernando Roldan Alves (technical assistant and coordinator of Poupança Florestal and Emater Technical Assistance and Rural Extension Agency); Ciro Correa (co-ordinator of the Production, Cooperation and Environment Sector, MST); Adalberto Garcia Pereira (director, Tecnoflora); Mauro Riani Fernández (co-ordinator, Poupança Florestal, VCP, Far South Unit); Arnaldo Geraldo Cardoso (forest engineer, Agrosilviculture, VCP, Far South Unit); Cristiano Antunes Souza (biologist, Environment Research, VCP, Far South Unit); Fausto Rodrigues Alves de Camargo (forest engineer, Environment and Poupança Florestal Manager, VCP, Far South Unit); Glodoaldo Arantes Ramiro (research co-ordinator, VCP, Far South Unit); João Afiune Sobrinho (operational Manager, VCP, Far South Unit); Luiz Eduardo Alves Sabbado (engineer, Forest Planning, VCP, Far South Unit); José Luciano Penido (CEO, VCP); José Maria de Arruda Mendes Filho (forest director for the Far South Operations, VCP); Luiz Henrique Ribeiro de Arruda Dias (Communication and Social Responsibility, VCP).

2   The settled peasants are former landless people who acquired small plots of land through the governmental land reform programme.

3   The Gini Index varies from 0 to 1. The closer it is to 1, the more concentrated is the attribute measured.

4   *O Brasil Desconcentrando as Terras: Índice de Gini* (Brasilia: Ministério do Desenvolvimento Agrário 2001).

5   According to the Brazilian Institute of Geography and Statistics (IBGE), from 1999 to 2001, 5.3 million people left the countryside. From 1985 to 1996, 941 000 producing units were closed, 96% of which were smaller than 100ha. M. Rossetto, 'Reforma Agrária', Ministry of Foreign Relations (2006), at http://www.mre.gov.br/cdbrasil/itamaraty/web/port/polsoc/refagra/apresent/index.htm

6   In the 1970s, the process of technological modernisation contributed to reducing the demand for rural labour. At the same time, selective credit policies favoured large producers. A.M. Buainain and D. Pires, *Reflexões sobre Reforma Agrária e Questão Social no Brasil* (Brasilia: INCRA, 2003), 47.

7   A.U. Oliveira, 'A Longa Marcha do Campesinato Brasileiro: Movimentos Sociais, Conflitos e Reforma Agrária', *Estudos Avançados,* 15, 43 (2001): 185–206.

8   Pastoral Land Commission (2006).

9   E. Teofilo and P.D. Garcia, 'Brazil: Land Politics, Poverty and Rural Development', *Land Reform: Land Settlement and Cooperatives*, 3 (2003): 19–29. Note that the estimated demand for land reform was between 3 and 4 million families by 2003.

10 See C. Guanziroli, 'Reforma Agrária e Globalização da Economia: O Caso do Brasil', *Econômica*, 1, 1 (1999); Z. Navarro, 'Mobilização sem Emancipação – as Lutas Sociais dos Sem-terra no Brasil', in B. Santos, ed., *Produzir para Viver* (Rio de Janeiro: Civilização Brasileira, 2002); and E. Veiga, 'O Brasil Rural Ainda Não Encontrou seu Eixo de Desenvolvimento', *Estudos Avançados*, 15, 43 (2001): 101–19.

11 Z. Navarro, 'Mobilização sem Emancipação'.

12 See A.U. Oliveira, 'Sociedade Brasileira Não Está Acostumada a ver Ações Políticas De Massas', (2006), Interview available at http://www.mst.org.br/biblioteca/entrevistas/ariovaldoihu.htm (accessed July 2007).

13 See Guanziroli 'Reforma Agrária'; Veiga, 'O Brasil Rural Ainda', 101–19.

14 Buainain and Pires, *Reflexões sobre Reforma Agrária*, 47.

15 Protests in this region against the effects of agriculture's modernisation led to the formation of the MST in the 1980s.

16 For example, several civil society organisations working in these regions established the Alert against the Green Desert Network (Rede Alerta Contra o Deserto Verde).

17 See M. Calazans, 'Violação de Direitos Econômicos, Sociais, Culturais e Ambientais na Monocultura do Eucalipto', available at http://www.defesabiogaucha.org/textos/texto32.pdf (accessed July 2007).

18 Corrected by 9% a year until the seventh year.

19 Eucalyptus requires particular care in the first year, and some care in the second year (ant and weed control; adding fertilisers).

20 Around 5% of the wood can be used for internal consumption (avoiding the use of native trees for that purpose), or it can be sold in the market in larger sizes for a higher price.

21 There is a commitment to enforce it among regional trade unions, and compliance is verified by Emater.

22 Information from ABN AMRO Real, 5 December 2006.

23 For example, if the average size of settlement is 20ha, and one subtracts the land for subsistence (corn, beans, cattle and sheep) and legal preservation, what is left is about 5ha for eucalyptus forests.

24 The national minimum wage is R$350 per month, and one hectare of land in the region is worth around R$2 500 to R$3 000.

25 The Brazilian Forest Code decrees the permanent protection of areas within at least 30m of the edges of bodies of water and 50m surrounding springs.

26 See K. Sungsumarn 'Why Eucalyptus is not Adopted for Agroforestry', *Reports Submitted to the Regional Expert Consultation on Eucalyptus, Volume 2,* FAO Regional Office for Asia and the Pacific, Bangkok, 4–8 October 1993, available at http://www.fao.org/DOCREP/005/AC772E/ac772e0p.htm (accessed July 2007).

27   See L. Couto and D.L. Betters, 'Short-Rotation Eucalypt Plantations in Brazil: Social and Environmental Issues', (1995), available at http://bioenergy.ornl.gov/reports/euc-braz/eucal2a.html

28   See A. Vargas and D. Cassol 'Votorantim Atinge Quilombolas no Sul do RS', *Jornal Brasil de Fato* (22 May 2006), available at http://www.brasildefato.com.br/v01/agencia/nacional/news_item.2006-05-22.1510081159 (accessed July 2007); L. Ritzel, 'Polêmica Verde', *Jornal Zero Hora* (31 July 2006), available at http://www.bracelpa.org.br/br/clipping/julho/310706/03.html (accessed September 2007). A particularly vociferous attack on such activities can be found in 'Via Campesina 'O Latifúndio dos Eucaliptos: Informações Básicas Sobre as Monoculturas de Arvores e as Indústrias de Papel' (2006), available at http://www.sof.org.br/marcha/paginas/publicacoes/cartilhaeucalipto.pdf (accessed July 2007).

Weaving sustainable partnerships in
Zanzibar:
The social fabric of women's entrepreneurship

OANA BRANZEI & MELISSA PENEYCAD[1]

> Undercapitalized sectors throughout the Third World ... buzz with hard work and inge-
> nuity. Street-side cottage industries have sprung up everywhere, manufacturing anything
> from clothing and footwear to imitation Cartier watches ... There are workshops that
> build and rebuild machinery, cars, even buses.[2]

Large or small, grassroots enterprises are important engines of sustainable development.[3] But
in certain socio-political contexts, like Tanzania, where entrepreneurial activities were delib-
erately inhibited for decades, motivating growth has required creative partnerships between
international NGOs, local communities and governmental authorities. This chapter explores
how innovative collaborations emerged and unfolded in Zanzibar, and how non-traditional
partners gradually pieced together locally appropriate role-models of sustainable enterprise.

Rekindling entrepreneurialism

During the colonial era, the British and the Germans established laws and regulations prohib-
iting indigenous populations from engaging in informal economic activities in urban areas
or gaining access to loans, credit, trading licences and permits.[4] The suppression of entrepreneurial activity worsened under two decades of socialist rule by President Julius Nyerere
(1964–1985), whose structural reforms suppressed the private sector. In 1967, the Tanganyika
African National Union formulated the Arusha Declaration, which announced the government's intention to develop a socialist society based on a set of principles known as *ujamaa*, or
the traditional African way of life. But while these policies claimed to embrace rural development and self-reliance, they ushered in state control over much of the economy. The government created state-owned crop authorities to control the production, pricing and marketing of
small farmers' produce; it also nationalised banks, insurance companies and other financial institutions, land, utilities, hospitals and educational institutions.[5] The private sector was quickly

reduced to retailing as its sole option. The government instituted Regional Trading Companies, which soon became tough competitors to private retailers. Largely controlled by Tanzanians of Asian descent, the private sector also became a target of scorn: the government 'considered private entrepreneurs to be *mabepari* (capitalist exploiters) [and any] element of business acumen or profit-seeking effort was dubbed *ulanguzi* (conmanship)'.[6] This made entrepreneurial activities both economically unattractive and socially undesirable.

Following Nyerere's resignation in 1985, his successor, Ali Hassan Mwinyi, initiated several economic and political reforms in an attempt to recover from a significant economic downturn caused by a simultaneous increase in petroleum prices and decrease in international prices for key Tanzanian exports. Mwinyi, often referred to as Mzee Rukhsa ('everything goes'), reversed many of Nyerere's socialist policies. He relaxed import restrictions and encouraged private enterprise. Whereas Nyerere frowned upon foreign aid, Mwinyi readily accepted assistance from the International Monetary Fund (IMF); this came with the requirement for structural reforms – many of which enabled a small burst of economic activity. His successor, President Benjamin Mkapa, continued the same political and economic liberalisation strategies. These nurtured an environment much more conducive to private sector initiatives.[7]

Tanzania's current president, Jakaya Kikwete, elected on 21 December 2005, clearly articulated his desire to follow through and develop a strong business road map. Since then, 'the benefits of [Tanzania's] correct economic and fiscal policies have been applauded by many, but are yet to filter down to Tanzanians'.[8]

The missing link

Since public disdain had suppressed interest in entrepreneurial activities, policy change alone could not reverse the negative image of commercial activities. Suitable role models proved necessary, if not always sufficient, to rekindle entrepreneurial pursuits. Seeing entrepreneurs at work could offer opportunities for learning – by observing, by imitating, even by failing. But finding appropriate role models was not as easy as it looked.

Despite increasing research on Tanzania (compared to other African counties, such as Ethiopia and even Kenya), and a handful of studies on Tanzanian women entrepreneurs, there is limited understanding of which policies, resources and capabilities mattered most, which combinations could best encourage new ventures to start up and grow, or how these combinations might need to change at various stages in the life cycle of an enterprise to sustain entrepreneurial development. Notably missing are longitudinal case studies, which combine ethnographic observations, business tracking, and multi-stakeholder interviews to track how entrepreneurs recognised their business acumen, how they calibrated their entrepreneurial pursuits, and how they assembled the resources needed to make their enterprises grow.

The rest of this chapter follows the evolution of the enterprise cluster around Zanzibar's key attraction, the Jozani-Chwaka Bay National Park, from the early 1960s to the present. The research was carried out through a combination of archival research, retrospective and longitudinal interviews with villagers, NGOs and policy makers, and a three-month ethnography of how the entrepreneurs are using and improving their assets. We used both primary and secondary data sources. The second author conducted retrospective and longitudinal interviews with many members of 13 different women's handicraft groups from nine villages in Zanzibar. For each enterprise, we searched through at least two to three years of newspaper, press release, magazine, trade periodical and online reports. We used a detailed research protocol to structure and focus the research and to track how various kinds of associations evolved and how they led to a variety of events that prompted women to start up businesses and make them grow, and which conditions led to success and which to failure.

Women entrepreneurship in Tanzania

In Tanzania, the kinds of businesses women run are typically small-scale food processing; brewing and catering; tailoring and batik making; beauty salons; and making decorations, pottery and baskets.[9] The more lucrative formal businesses considered to be 'suitable for men', such as large-scale food processing, bars and restaurants, tour agencies and transport, wholesale trade, manufacturing and export/import, are still much harder for women to enter. There are a few businesses available to both sexes (running retail shops and kiosks, horticulture and dealing in crops, and selling charcoal), but it is often harder for women than men to get into high value-add entrepreneurial activities.

The size of the enterprise tends to be another hurdle (see Table 1). Many women entrepreneurs start at the micro level and stay there. Only a handful of their ventures grow to small size, and very few scale up from there. Tanzanian women entrepreneurs employ an average of only 1.3 people, and they start with low levels of education and often without any business experience. They operate informally, often because they are discouraged from starting a formal venture. They also have trouble accessing appropriate forms of credit and difficulty saving start-up capital. They usually start businesses out of necessity, to provide for their immediate family. This means they tend to be both risk adverse (because they cannot afford to fail) and undiversified (they rarely own more than one business). Their scaling up often depends directly on the purchasing power of their clients. And because they have difficulties growing their enterprises and employing others, they have very limited time to get the training they need to manage their businesses successfully, or to engage in market research. Thus gains are typically restricted by local markets and low profitability.

Table 1:   Enterprise types in Tanzania

Type of enterprise	Number of employees	Amount of capital invested
Micro-enterprises	1–4	Up to TZS5m (Tanzanian Shillings) or up to US$3 990 in capital invested.[10]
Small enterprises	5–49	Between TZS5m and TZS200m or about US$3 990–US$159 590 in capital invested.
Medium enterprises	50–99	Between TZS200m and TZS800m or US$159 590–US$638 360 in capital invested.
Large enterprises	100+	TZS800m+, or more than US$638 360.

Source: Adapted from Stevenson and St-Onge (2005).[11]

Today, the micro and small-scale enterprise (MSE) sector in Tanzania is estimated to employ three to four million people or 20 to 30 percent of the total Tanzanian labour force. About one third of these, 1.16m, are women.[12] This number compares favourably with developed countries such as the US or Canada, where women also account for about one-third of the self-employed.[13]

Yet despite the similarity in the proportion, women entrepreneurs in Tanzania often approach entrepreneurial activity quite differently from women in these developed countries. Many 'have been forced into business by economic necessity, not entrepreneurial aspirations'.[14] The 'push factors' include overcoming widespread joblessness, meeting pressing economic needs or supplementing household income, and 'escaping' from household duties.[15] Table 2 lists examples of some difficulties Tanzanian women experience when going into business, and how these are commonly dealt with.

Table 2:   Constraints experienced by women micro-entrepreneurs in Tanzania, and how they deal with them

Constraints on economic activity	How a Tanzanian woman entrepreneur is likely to deal with these constraints
Reproductive role	Starting a business that allows her to combine business and household obligations, or that complements the needs of the household.
Narrow base of knowledge and skills	Starting a business that allows her to use skills she has already acquired as part of a woman's socialization process, such as food processing and personal care.
Low levels of initial start-up capital	Starting a business that requires low initial investments.
Restricted access to credit for working capital	Starting a business for which she can easily access credit from her supplier base or where she is paid in advance by her clientele. Some women entrepreneurs receive food from vendors on credit, which is common practice, and some women tailors are paid in advance by their customers.
Limited ability to absorb the cost of a failed venture	Starting a business she is certain will succeed because the market is large and has already been tested.

Source: Adapted from UDEC (2002).

A private sector development approach

Several international organisations have noticed the shortage of appropriate role models and the double trap of gender in limiting both growth and profitability for women entrepreneurs in the developing world. They have documented why women often face far greater barriers to starting and growing their cottage businesses.[16]

The typical solution for overcoming these barriers is to boost five types of livelihood asset: human, natural, financial, physical and social capital. Human capital includes such issues as

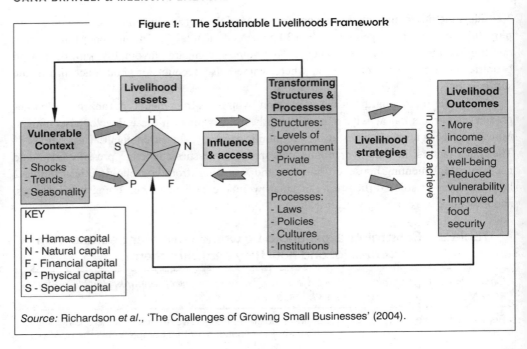

Figure 1: The Sustainable Livelihoods Framework

Source: Richardson et al., 'The Challenges of Growing Small Businesses' (2004).

drive, motivation, adequate education and appropriate technical and managerial skills. Natural capital means a woman entrepreneur's access to land, water and other natural resources she needs to conduct her business, while financial capital indicates her access to loans, cash and other forms of collateral. Physical capital is assessed in terms of appropriate facilities for conducting business and to having tools and equipment, and social capital means access to networks, associations, community and familial support. The Sustainable Livelihoods Framework (Figure 1), originally devised by the British government's Department for International Development, is now broadly used by international organisations and international donors in many African countries, including Tanzania.

When appropriately combined, these five types of livelihood asset can lessen vulnerability to shocks, trends and seasonality. They help entrepreneurs gain greater influence on structures and policies and better access to support such as micro-credit, business education, technical skills and social connections. They mobilise a self-reinforcing cycle. But finding the right balance has proved particularly difficult in rural Tanzania, in part because of the scarcity of successful small businesses to provide role models. Without a fabric of social connectivity, natural, financial, physical and human capital (in the form of training) is sometimes underutilised or wasted.

Business support services are offered by numerous private and non-governmental organisations in Tanzania, but the quality of their services varies greatly, as does their ability to reach their target audiences. For example, many business support services are available to women entrepreneurs living in urban settings and operating their businesses there but quality support services of this kind are difficult to access in rural areas. Then too, even when services such as marketing advice and management and technical training are available, women micro-entrepreneurs may not be able to afford them,[17] and in the absence of other forms of social capital such as family and community support, these services are even less likely to reach the women who need them to succeed in business.

The social fabric of entrepreneurship

Resource sharing and capability building depend on women's access to social capital. In Tanzania there are four main business associations dedicated to women entrepreneurs: the Federation of Association of Women Entrepreneurs in Tanzania (FAWETA); the Association of Women Entrepreneurs of Zanzibar (AWEZA); the Tanzania Food Processors' Association (TAFOPA); and the Artisans Development Agency of Tanzania (ADAT). But these associations generally lack the financial resources to provide their members with good quality services and staff shortages often mean they cannot reach everyone who needs them. Furthermore, some of these organisations appear exclusive or elitist. Our survey found that the majority of women entrepreneurs in Tanzania (81.3%) are in part unaware of what benefits these formal associations may offer, and some are put off by what appears to be a waste of time without any meaningful benefits (4.2%) or the high fees (2.1%).[18]

FAWETA, initiated in 1993, is the oldest women entrepreneurs' association in Tanzania. Its objectives include creating awareness about the issues facing women in business, encouraging women to establish or expand businesses, linking members with trade organisations and NGOs in order to expand market opportunities, and increasing women's participation in key decision-making activities. The organisation has 3 500 members (or about 0.2% of the estimated number of women entrepreneurs in the country), and even this membership is poorly represented on the its three-person board and the National Business Council. Although new members have to pay a one-time entrance fee of between TZS15 000 and TZS40 000 (about US$12 to US$32) depending on the size of the group, and annual group membership fees between TZS12 000 and TZS15 000 (US$9.5 to US$12), the association is strapped for resources. FAWETA relies on donor funding for its services to its members and also faces human resource limitations – it is often unable to provide proper leadership to its branches.

AWEZA, formed ten years later (2003) is much smaller; it is restricted to group membership and does not support individual entrepreneurs. Its annual fees are more affordable: TZS5 000 to TZS15 000 (US$4 to US$12) depending on the size of the group. AWEZA's goals are to work with its 56 member groups to expand existing markets and find new outlets for their wares, as well as to gradually strengthen its membership so that it can wield greater influence with the government. Yet the organisation is thus far poorly connected: it is neither a member of FAWETA, nor registered with the government of Zanzibar. Its small size, very limited resources, and its isolation limit its ability to offer a role model of entrepreneurial activities and attract new women entrepreneurs.

TAFOPA brings together 240 members across Tanzania and focuses on developing the food processing sector, which is heavily dominated by women entrepreneurs. Now registered as an NGO, TAFOPA's formation was supported by several organisations such as UNIDO (UN Industrial Development Organisation), ILO's WED (Women's Entrepreneurship Development Programme) and SIDO (the Small Industries Development Organisation of Tanzania). Its focus and connections strengthen its ability to nurture human capital. Its membership is restricted, however, to the handful who attended a technical and entrepreneurship training programme designed by SIDO and UNIDO, a programme designed specifically for food processing micro-enterprises currently managed by women entrepreneurs.

ADAT, also an NGO, was designed to provide training and support for women entrepreneurs who produce textiles and textile-related products. Started in 1996, the association now has 120 members and six board members. Its services include training courses in several crafts and the provision of raw materials at reasonable prices. ADAT is heavily dependent on donor funding.

Zanzibar: Paradise lost and found

Marketing itself as 'the Spice Island', Zanzibar attracts tourists with its natural beauty and mixed heritage of nationalities (Sumerian, Assyrian, Egyptian, Phoenician, Indian, Chinese, Portuguese, Dutch, English, Omani Arab and Shirazi Persian). The Jozani-Chwaka Bay National Park, the first and only national park in the Zanzibar archipelago (see Figure 2), lies in a shallow trough in the coral bed between the mangrove-filled bays of Chwaka and Uzi, towards the southern tip of Unguja, the largest island in the Zanzibar archipelago. The forest area is surrounded by nine villages, Bwejuu, Charawe, Cheju, Chwaka, Kitogani, Michamvi Pete/Jozani, Ukongoroni and Unjuga Ukuu.

Figure 2:   Zanzibar

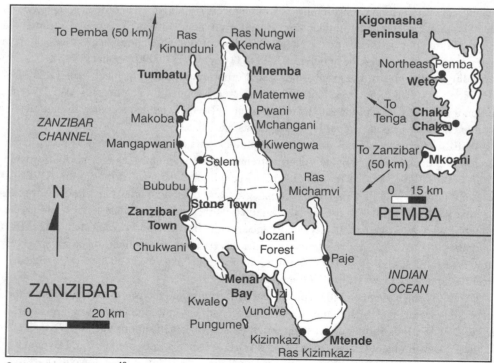

Source: 'Lonely Planet'.[19]

The Jozani forest is home to three important endemic species: the Red Colobus monkey, the Ader's duiker (a small antelope) and the Zanzibar leopard. The forest area itself is unique as it contains a mixture of coastal swamp, coral rag forest, mangrove forest and grasslands. To preserve its biodiversity, it was declared a forest reserve in the 1960s. However, commercial harvesting continued until 1990, when Jozani became a conservation area. In 1995, the Commission for Natural Resources (CNR), the predecessor to the Department of Commercial Crops, Fruits and Forestry (DCCFF), initiated the Jozani-Chwaka Bay Conservation Project by setting aside 2512 hectares of land.

At an early stage all the partners agreed that environmental protection in Zanzibar required a holistic approach to poverty alleviation. The designation 'conservation area' alone would not stop neighbouring communities from relying on the forest for wood and aggravating the serious damage caused by decades of commercial exploitation. Despite 'living in paradise', the villagers were struggling to make ends meet. Unless steps were taken to alleviate the extreme poverty in the areas, wood and plant harvesting would continue.

Partnerships for sustainable development

Several development partners, including the UN's Global Environment Facility (UN-GEF); CARE International; the Austrian government; the Ford Foundation; and the McKnight Foundation came together to support the Jozani-Chwaka Bay Conservation Project. The UN-GEF funded the biodiversity conservation component of the project, and the other four financed the income-generating activities. This funding triggered several initiatives to nurture entrepreneurial activities (see Figure 3).

JOSACA

In 1996, CARE International and its partners established the Jozani Savings and Credit Association (JOSACA), an organisation which would help begin small savings and credit groups in several villages surrounding the national park. These groups, it was hoped, would create a hub of human and social capital for different types of micro-enterprises. Once 49 savings and credit groups had become operational, CARE International pulled out. About half of the groups (24 out of 49) were not ready to survive on their own but they agreed to come together to form a new organisation called the Jozani Credit Development Organisation (JOCDO), formally registered as an NGO in October 2003.

Income generating activities

To stimulate entrepreneurial activity, CARE International in Tanzania offered group members a range of options: small-scale bee-keeping to produce honey and beeswax; mushroom growing; premium vegetable and fruit production (such as spinach, tomatoes, eggplants, sweet peppers, cucumbers and papayas) for urban markets and east coast hotels; fruit retailing (purchasing a variety of fruits from producers in bulk and reselling them in local markets for a profit); essential oil production (basil, eucalyptus and lemon grass); and handicrafts. Each group of villagers was asked to select the option that best suited their environment, skills and preferences. They were then offered appropriate training to enhance their human capital, including a

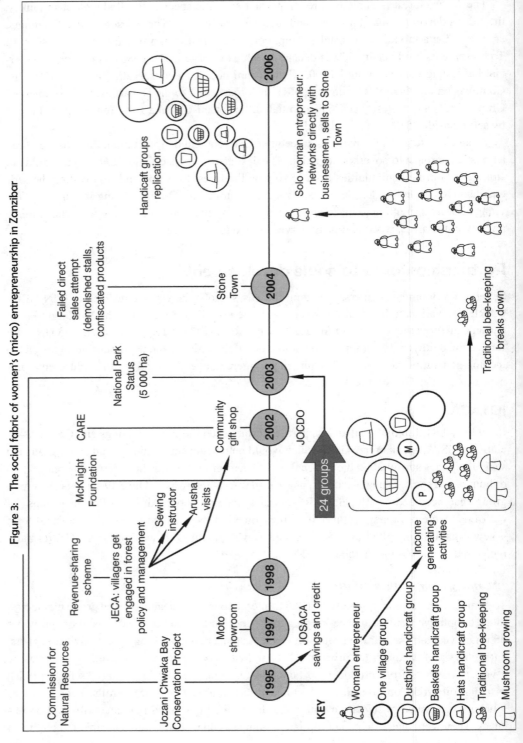

Figure 3: The social fabric of women's (micro) entrepreneurship in Zanzibar

Figure 4:   Cheju village handicraft group (photo by Melissa Peneycad)

five-week course in business management and a six-week course in money management. Each participant also received a small starter loan.

The popularity of the options varied. Mushroom growing was not particularly attractive to the villagers. Despite the market demand and the promise that their produce would be sold to tourist hotels for a good price of TZS5 000 (approximately US$4) only about 150 villagers decided to give mushrooms a try. And they soon discovered that mushroom growing was both short-lived (because the growing season is short) and inconvenient (because it required early morning and late night work and reliable transport to the market). Furthermore soil conditions were not optimal and the mycelium used to grow the mushrooms was of low quality and had to be brought in all the way from Dar es Salaam. Now, ten years later, mushroom growing has ceased altogether; not a single villager continues this activity.

Bee-keeping was particularly attractive from the start: 480 individuals chose it initially, and more than half (258) still operate in the nine villages surrounding the forest. But reliance on traditional hives and bee-keeping methods meant that the produce did not meet the quality standards for the tourist market and it was often channelled to local consumption at significantly lower prices. Many complained that it took too long to generate a profit and most of the women initially involved in this activity took up other pursuits.

Handicraft production was another popular choice amongst the women, and it quickly became their favoured activity. Woven baskets, mats and hats had been traditionally produced in the local villages surrounding the national park for years. Two organisations described in more detail below, MOTO and JECA, partnered with the villagers to facilitate local sales to tourists and then to help the women reach overseas markets. Several organisations partnered with the villagers to facilitate local sales to tourists (MOTO, JECA) and then to help the women reach overseas markets. They recommended that women form themselves into handicraft groups (see Figure 4).

MOTO

In 1997 Anje Förstle from Germany, in partnership with an organisation called solarafrica.network, established the MOTO showroom.[20] Förstle's initial intention was to display local handicrafts but MOTO came to operate as an independent agency that engaged in local community projects and provided assistance to local government institutions. It purchased wares from the village groups at attractive prices and resold them at a significant mark-up. For example, an intricately woven basket or hat fetched its producer about TZS4 000 (or US$3.18) but brought in at least three or four times that amount when resold to tourists visiting Zanzibar or overseas. MOTO supplied an increasing volume of local crafts to overseas markets and by the end of 2006 was working with about 120 members across 12 handicraft groups in five villages. Members now meet at least once a month to discuss news and problems and offer each other business training and support.

JECA

The Jozani Environmental Conservation Association (JECA) was established in 1998 to represent community interests and empower the local communities to manage the forest area. Village Conservation Committees were established in the villages adjacent to the forest. These quickly became active in conservation, education and forest-patrolling activities. One woman and one man from each committee represented their village on JECA. Community Forest Management Agreements, outlining how the forest should be used and suggesting appropriate protection activities, were signed between the government and the nine villages surrounding the forest. The committees were required to submit a report to JECA every month, and to ensure that their villages adhered to the specified activities. JECA was responsible for seeing the agreements were adhered to and met once every three months to review the situation and respond to the committees' reports.

With funding from the McKnight Foundation, JECA also sought to support local handicraft production. The association hired an instructor from Stone Town to teach villagers sewing skills. The McKnight foundation also sponsored a few villagers to go on an 'exchange programme' to Arusha (a popular tourist destination in mainland Tanzania) to learn how the locals produced their crafts and marketed them to visiting tourists.

With the help of CARE International, JECA established a Community Gift Shop as part of a broader tourism expansion plan and promised the villagers that all handicrafts and other tourist-suitable wares they produced would be purchased for resale in the gift shop. But self-sufficiency proved elusive: the gift shop was unable to sell enough products or keep the turnover rapid enough to maintain positive cash-flows.

As donor funding dried up, some villagers attempted to go it alone. Abasi Omari[21] from Chwaka village, a member of both JECA and his Village Conservation Committee, took the wares produced by the Chwaka handicraft groups to Stone Town and sold them directly to tourists and to hotel gift shops. According to Omari, he was able to sell one million Tanzanian Shillings' worth (approximately US$795) in one day. Although this was probably an exceptionally lucky occurrence, word of his success travelled quickly to neighbouring villages.

Some local traders from the Michamvi village followed his example. They set up stalls on the roadside near tourist hotels to sell goods, including handicrafts, to the tourists directly.

But the hotels complained to the government that the villagers were undermining their profits and soon the stalls were demolished and the villagers' products were confiscated. For the Michamvi villagers, the reprisal stifled innovation and left them feeling demoralised and helpless. Several similar incidents soon led to a complete ban on direct sales to tourists.

Enterprise growth in Zanzibar

In 2003, after eight years of negotiation, the Jozani-Chwaka Bay Conservation Project partners managed to persuade the government to upgrade the forest reserve (the initial 2 512ha area and an additional 2 488ha) to the status of national park. This gave fresh impetus to entrepreneurial income-generating activity across the island.

Between 2003 and 2006, the number of savings and credit groups administered by JOCDO expanded six-fold, from 24 groups in 2003 to 158 in 2006. The rapid increase was in part driven by word of mouth about the success of the scheme. The groups have spread from the nine villages surrounding the Jozani forest to a total of 28 villages across the island. Group membership ranges between 15 and 30, and over 75 percent of the members are women (see Figure 5).

The savings and credit group scheme was initially devised to support any villager wishing to obtain credit to develop a micro-enterprise. At first men turned down the idea as 'ridiculous'. Handicraft groups, however, found it appealing and useful.

Figure 5:   Cheju village savings and credit group
meeting (photo by Melissa Peneycad)

To join one had to pay an entrance fee to the group and meet certain criteria established by the group. For instance, some groups required their members to be 18 or older, environmentally sensitive inhabitants of the village, and that they demonstrate loyalty and have no prior charges of theft. To maintain one's status as a member one had to purchase shares in the group, with the price decided by the group since members were in the best position to determine their earning potential. Each group also set the minimum and maximum number of shares that could be purchased each week. Members met once a week and the process of purchasing shares continued until the amount of money available for credit reached TZS500 000 (approximately US$398). Interest rates were also determined by the group – usually between three and five per cent. New members received loans of up to TZS30 000 (approximately US$24). When early loans were successfully repaid, more money could be borrowed.

The diffusion of village savings and credit groups was accompanied by specific practices. Every three months, each group was required to submit reports to JOCDO on the standard report cards supplied, documenting money circulation statistics (money in – money out); who took out loans and why; the amount of interest collected or due; loan default rates; and fines collected.

Differentiation

As more women joined village handicraft groups, they made an effort to differentiate their businesses. Some groups produced baskets with handles and others made baskets without; some groups wove mats and hats, while some produced wastepaper baskets and purses. The differentiation was in part an outcome of learning (through the business training received from CARE, JECA, etc.), and in part a natural evolution of each group's strategy.

For example, in the village of Bwejuu, one handicraft group switched from weaving baskets with local grasses to weaving items using plastic bags that were cluttering their village and contributing to crop loss. According to this village group, they learned how to do this from an African-American woman who had visited their village a few years previously. This woman had purchased most of the goods from the village group for re-sale on international markets but she could not take everything the village group produced. The group sold the remainder of the goods to hotel gift shops.

In the village of Kitogani, some of the women in the village handicraft groups differentiated their products by making bags out of *kangas*[22] and the plastic sacks used to transport charcoal. The sack was opened up flat and then sewn in between two *kangas*, giving the bag shape and strength. Handles for the bags were fashioned out of *kangas* and zips were added. The *kangas* and the zips were purchased at local shops using money from savings and credit groups.

Going it alone

So many women had joined the handicraft business that groups naturally began to subdivide into smaller, more manageable subgroups. And despite some fears of alienation from their fellow members,[23] many of the artisans claimed they eventually wanted to start their own businesses with loan money from credit and savings groups.[24] These women were interested in livestock keeping, dairy farming, owning a small shop or producing high-quality honey for the tourist market.

Beyond entrepreneurial role models

What key lessons can be learnt from tracking the evolution of the enterprise cluster in Zanzibar? First, building role-models of sustainable entrepreneurship from scratch meant that complex forms of social capital had to be nurtured, and experimentation with various forms of pro-business associations had to be allowed at grassroots level. Simply teaching skills and bestowing resources was enough to help enterprises get started, but fell short of empowering them to survive and grow. Second, forging broad nets of partnerships helped bring together international skills through market links, capability building and policy change in ways that local entrepreneurs alone could not have foreseen, let alone manage on their own. However, once opportunities arose, villagers quickly found their own ways to market value-added crafts and negotiate their way through lucrative business activities. Third, informal and semi-formal associations trumped formal ones, both in flexibility and feasibility – enterprise and entrepreneurs developed on their own terms. CARE, JECA, MOTO and JOCDO, to name just a few of the platform associations involved, were instrumental in enabling and shaping business activities, but their interventions were not deterministic. Instead, they nourished informal ties among villagers and across villages in ways that helped the poor discover their own ability to lift themselves out of poverty, and then gradually align their skills and resources to market demand.

The idea of community-based interventions for sustainable enterprise is not new. Peredo and Chrisman have recently explained why community-based entry and buy-in are important for nurturing entrepreneurial capacity. [25] They have also advocated strengthening local networks of relationships within the context of existing social structures. However, much of the entrepreneurship theory and practice still treats local communities as exogenous forces, within which entrepreneurs act independently. Our study dovetails with a community-based view of development and illustrates the layering of social capital that typically precedes and often conditions the emergence of role-models of sustainable enterprise. Entrepreneurs and their ventures are intrinsically connected and dependent upon one another. If these interdependencies are not recognised and fostered at an early stage, isolated interventions by government officials or international organisations may fall short of achieving their full potential.

Editors' reflections and questions

This case study argues that partnerships between the Tanzanian government, local communities and several international organisations shaped the evolution of an emergent cluster of micro-entrepreneurs in the villages surrounding Zanzibar's Jozani-Chwaka Bay National Park. These partnerships gradually fostered grassroots enterprise activities by creating beneficial framework conditions and providing inspiration through relevant role-models, while at the same time adopting a flexible approach that allowed local groups of women entrepreneurs to develop their own responses. The case emphasises the importance of collective trial and error experiences, and how various forms of enterprise – individual, small group and community enterprises – benefited from one another through social networks. Informal and semi-formal associations served as platforms for entrepreneurial experimentation and shared learning. With this in mind consider the following questions:

1. The notion of partnership suggests that participants contribute complementary resources and that they are able to achieve their objectives more effectively through the partnership than through alternative, independent approaches. Was this the case in the initiatives profiled in this study? Is fostering small and micro enterprise a suitable objective and mechanism for partnerships between local people and international agencies?

2. The case mentions a number of business associations dedicated to women entrepreneurs in Tanzania, yet none of these seem to have featured significantly in the Zanzibari clusters. Why might this be the case? What are the implications for organisations such as CARE International seeking to establish partnerships in support of community-based economic development?

3. What are the costs and benefits of grassroots experimentation with enterprise activity? From the point of view of a government or international development agency, can the benefits be enhanced and the costs mitigated, and if so how?

4. A key theme in this case study is the important role played by social capital as an 'enabler' of other forms of community and household assets. The case also suggests that social capital is not always a force for women entrepreneurship. Is it possible or desirable to distinguish between 'good' and 'bad' social capital? When and how can governmental and non-governmental organisations help nurture specific types of social capital?

Notes

1   Both authors contributed equally to this chapter. The field research was conducted by Melissa Peneycad in 2006. The authors gratefully acknowledge feedback and support from Donath Olomi, director of the Entrepreneurship Centre, University of Dar es Salaam; the consultants and staff of Care Enterprise Partners of Care Canada and the consultants and staff of Care International in Tanzania; and Ally Khalfan, who at the time was completing his MBA in Finance at the Dar es Salaam University's School of Business. For an in-depth theoretical development and three more case studies of women entrepreneurship in Africa, please refer to M. Peneycad, 'An Exploration of the Relationship between Social Capital and Micro/Small-Scale Enterprise Development and Growth in Tanzania', submitted to the Faculty of Environmental Studies in partial fulfilment of the requirements for the degree of Master in Environmental Studies, York University, Ontario, Canada (2007).

2   H. de Soto, *The Mystery of Capital* (New York: Basic Books, 2000), 28.

3   International Finance Corporation (IFC), Paths out of Poverty: The Role of Private Enterprise in Developing Countries (Washington, D. C. : IFC, 2000); International Labour Organisation (ILO), The Promotion of Sustainable Enterprises, International Labour Conference, 96th Session (Geneva: ILO, 2007); WBCSD, 'Business for Development: Business Solutions in Support of the Millennium Development Goals, World Business Council for Sustainable Development Online (2005), http://www.wbcsd.org/web/publications/biz4dev-reprint.pdf (accessed 21 June 2007).

4   J. L. P. Lugalla, 'Development, Change, and Poverty in the Informal Sector during the Era of Structural Adjustments in Tanzania', *Canadian Journal of African Studies*, 31, 3 (2007): 424–51.

5   A. E. Temu and J. M. Due, 'The Business Environment in Tanzania after Socialism: Challenges of Reforming Banks, Parastatals, Taxation and the Civil Service', *The Journal of Modern African Studies*, 38, 4 (2000): 683–712.

6   Ibid. , 684.

7   B. Heilman and J. Lucas, 'A Social Movement for African Capitalism? A Comparison of Business Associations in Two African Cities', *African Studies Review*, 40, 2 (1997): 141–71.

8   J. Kikwete, 'A Business Road Map for the Challenges of the Future', *The Africa Report*, 4, 23 (2006).

9   P. Richardson, R. Howarth, G. Finnegan, G., 'The Challenges of Growing Small Businesses: Insights from Women Entrepreneurs in Africa', SEED Working Paper No. 47, Series on Women's Entrepreneurship Development and Gender Equality (WEDGE) (Geneva: ILO, 2004).

10 A Tanzanian Shilling (TZS) was valued at US$0.79795 at the time of writing. See *Oanda's Currency Converter* at http://www.oanda.com/convert/classic (last accessed 23 August 2007).

11 L. Stevenson and A. St-Onge, *Support for Growth-oriented Women Entrepreneurs in Tanzania*, (Geneva: ILO, 2005).

12 Tanzania is a medium-sized African country with approximately 37.4 million inhabitants. Source: *CIA World Factbook*, 'Tanzania', *CIA World Factbook Online* (2007), http://cia.gov/cia/publications/factbook/geos/tz.html (last accessed 15 April 2007).

13 In the US (roughly ten times the population of Tanzania) there are 7.7m women majority-owned businesses that employ over seven million individuals across the country and account for an impressive US$1.1 trillion in annual sales. See: CWBR, 'Women-Owned Businesses in the United States 2006 Fact Sheet', the Centre for Women's Business Research Online (2006), http://www.cfwbr.org/assets/344_2006nationalfactsheet.pdf (last accessed 14 April 2007). See also N. M. Carter, *Female Entrepreneurship: Implications for Education, Training and Policy* (London: Routledge, 2006); CIBC, 'Women Entrepreneurs: Leading the Charge', CIBC Resource Centre Online (2005), http://www.cibc.com/ca/pdf/women-entrepreneurs-en.pdf (last accessed 15 April 2007).

14 UDEC, 'Women Entrepreneurs in Tanzania,' (Dar es Salaam: International Labour Organization, 2002).

15 Ibid.

16 Stevenson and St-Onge, *Support for Growth-oriented Women*; ILO, *Legal Constraints to Women's Participation in Cooperatives: Country Studies from Burkina Faso, Cameroon, Ecuador, India, Le-*

sotho, Morocco, the Philippines, Tanzania, Thailand and Uruguay (Geneva: ILO, 2002); ILO, *Tanzanian Women Entrepreneurs: Going for Growth* (Geneva: ILO, 2003); and N. A. Goheer, *Women Entrepreneurs in Pakistan: How to Improve their Bargaining Power* (Geneva and Islamabad: ILO, 2003).

17 Richardson *et al.*, 'The Challenges of Growing Small Businesses'.

18 Based on 96 responses. See: ILO, *Legal Constraints*, 42.

19 http://www.lonelyplanet.com/mapshells/africa/zanzibar/zanzibar.htm (last accessed 10 August 2007).

20 http://www.solarafrica.net/activity/f-moto.html (last accessed 10 August 2007).

21 This name has been changed to ensure privacy.

22 *Kangas* are richly-patterned cloths worn by the local people.

23 Some of the women in these groups fear that if they were to become too successful on an individual level, they could be harassed or shunned by their community. Many village women cite an example of a woman in the village of Unjuga Ukuu, situated beside a major road leading to and from Stone Town. She was one of the first to begin producing differentiated products (intricately patterned baskets) and did so out of necessity as the rest of her handicraft group dissipated owing to others' lack of interest in the activity. Like everyone else, she initially sold her wares to JECA for the community gift shop but she was also visited by businessmen from Stone Town who come to purchase her goods for re-sale in their gift shops in town. Because demand continued she added other differentiated products, like figurines. Many seemed envious of her personal success, and the grapevine has it that this opportunistic entrepreneur became alienated from the community.

24 Women members of the savings and credit groups mainly use loan money to purchase salt, food for themselves and their families, and clothing.

25 A. M. Peredo and J. J. Chrisman, 'Toward a Theory of Community-Based Enterprise', *Academy of Management Review*, 31, 2 (2006): 309–28.

Who is responsible for the squatter camps?

Mining companies in South Africa and the challenge of local collaboration

RALPH HAMANN[1]

During 2003, the second largest platinum mining company in the world, Impala, planned a new open cast mine adjacent to its established mines in the area around Rustenburg, South Africa, which employed over 20 000 workers. However, it was confronted with significant resistance from residents of Luka, a small village close to the planned mine. The fact that this resistance represented a formidable challenge to the company's plans was a manifestation of the changes that had been occurring in the international mining industry, with corporate social responsibility (CSR) and related concepts gaining in currency, and – more significantly – the far-reaching changes that had occurred in South Africa since the transition to democracy in 1994. More stringent environmental legislation now governed applications for new mines, and companies were expected to show that their activities would benefit local communities.

The conflict between Impala and the Luka community was also an expression of simmering tension between local communities and the mining companies in the area (not just Impala but also the other two large platinum companies, Anglo Platinum and Lonmin, and other smaller platinum and chrome mining companies). This tension was in many ways an indictment of past approaches to CSR by these companies. The Luka villagers staunchly opposed Impala's proposed new mine on the grounds that the community had not benefited historically from the company's activities in the area and had not been adequately compensated for negative impacts, such as cracked houses and, allegedly, a degraded water supply. An overarching concern was the steady growth of informal settlements – or squatter camps – around Luka (and indeed the entire Rustenburg area), a growth that was linked at least in part to the mining companies' historical and, to a lesser extent, continuing labour recruitment and housing practices. Finally, much of the Luka residents' resentment was based on the belief that in the past Impala's communication with, and contributions to, the traditional authority – the Royal Bafokeng nation – had not benefited the community.

In response to these concerns, Impala made efforts to communicate directly with community representatives on the local government ward committee. These efforts included constructing a small office building for community meetings and interaction with the company. However, the traditional authority felt threatened by the company's engagement with the local council and ordered the destruction of the building before it could be completed (on the grounds that it had not approved the plans as owner of the land). To make matters even more difficult for the company, a more radical faction emerged within the community, identifying the resistance of the villagers as an opportunity to make more far-reaching demands of the company and threatening to derail the negotiations and embark on protest action and sabotage.

On the one hand, Impala was arguably struggling with the legacy of irresponsible mining practices and community engagement in the past. On the other, the company found it difficult to respond systematically to one of the core concerns raised by the Luka community and others – the continued growth of informal settlements and the associated deteriorating socio-economic conditions in the area. Very little could be done without some level of collaboration and coordination between the mining company, the local municipality, the traditional authority and the local communities, yet such collaboration seemed near impossible given the conflict between the groups and low levels of trust and communication. This case study analyses some of the developments that led to this intractable situation in the study area and some of the efforts the various stakeholders made to respond to it.

The historical and policy context

South Africa is endowed with the world's largest reserves of a number of minerals, such as gold, platinum and titanium, and hence the mining sector has been a crucial force in the country's industrialisation and modernisation process, including state development. Although mining contributed only about 12% of South Africa's GDP between 1950 and 1990, the country's economic dependence on the sector has been significant because of the large workforce employed on the mines, the sector's important contribution to exports, and the dominant role of a few large, diversified mining houses, including the predecessors of two of today's largest mining corporations, BHP Billiton and Anglo American.

The extent to which mining companies and industry in general, colluded with or underpinned the *apartheid* state is still a matter of debate. Most commentators agree, however, that the mining houses' activities were inextricably linked with colonial and subsequently *apartheid* policies through the migrant labour system, the primary aim of which was to ensure the supply of low-cost labour to the mines. The final report of the Truth and Reconciliation Commission goes so far as to argue that: 'The blueprint for "grand *apartheid*" was provided by the mines and was not an Afrikaner State innovation.'[2] The adverse social impacts of mining companies' practices, especially those related to the migrant labour system and the single-sex hostels, have long been documented.[3]

In the wake of the transition to democracy in the early 1990s, two kinds of institutional change took place that had implications for the evolving CSR debate in South Africa's mining industry. The first was market-related change. In the early 1990s, South Africa's capital markets were gradually re-integrated with international markets, and the mining houses came under increasing pressure to conform to international expectations. One result was organisational restructuring so as to focus on core competencies, another was that many of the large South African companies moved their primary or secondary listing to one of the main international stock exchanges, most commonly London. Market-based drivers of CSR have also gained prominence in South Africa with the publication of the King 2 code on corporate governance in 2002 and the launch of the JSE Socially Responsible Investment Index.[4]

The second kind of change was driven by the state. One of the first acts passed by the new government was the Mines Health and Safety Act of 1996, targeted at the dismal safety record of South African mines. The ultimate aim of the new government, however, was to establish an entirely new mining dispensation, which culminated in a new law promulgated in 2002. This law proclaims state sovereignty over mineral resources (private ownership was common previously) and requires all companies to renew their prospecting or mining licences. This licensing process allows the government to support previously disadvantaged South Africans in the industry under the rubric of black economic empowerment (BEE). The most prominent aspect of BEE has been the government's insistence that blacks should own significant company shares, which prompted fears of value dilution in established companies. These fears became most acute when, in July 2002, a draft government proposal stipulated that 51% of the industry be owned by blacks within 10 years, and led to a massive sell-off of shares.[5]

This intense reaction, especially by foreign investors, inspired a renewed commitment to negotiation and a search for compromises. The negotiations took place in the newly-formed Sector Partnership Committee and resulted in the 'broad-based socio-economic empowerment charter for the South African mining industry'.[6] The target that was agreed on for equity transfer was 26% within 10 years, but most importantly this was placed within a broader set of requirements by which to judge mining companies' transformation efforts. What is known as the BEE 'scorecard' includes such important CSR-related items as community development, improved employee housing and affirmative procurement (see Box 1). Companies are now assessed with respect to this scorecard in their quest for transforming their 'old order rights' into 'new order rights', and in competing for new exploration or mining licences.

The case study area

The Bushveld Complex (see Figure 1), stretches across the North West and Limpopo Provinces in the north of South Africa and contains the world's largest reserves of the platinum group of metals, as well as other metals and minerals, including chrome. It has been described as 'a geological feature unmatched anywhere on Earth, and the repository of unparalleled mineral wealth'.By about 2000, South African mines accounted for 75% of the world's platinum supply, almost all of which was produced by three companies, Anglo Platinum (a Johannesburg listed subsidiary of Anglo-American), Impala (listed in Johannesburg) and Lonmin (listed in London), in order of size by revenue.[7]

The case study area is the mining region surrounding the town of Rustenburg in the North West Province, where platinum mining first began in the late 1920s. It includes the largest and oldest mines, Anglo Platinum, Impala and Lonmin (all of which have been in production since at least the early 1980s), as well as Anglo Platinum's smaller, relatively new mine

Box 1: Scorecard for the broad based socio-economic empowerment charter for the South African mining industry

Human resource development

- Has the company offered every employee the opportunity to be functionally literate and numerate by the year 2005 and are employees being trained?
- Has the company implemented career paths for HDSA [historically disadvantaged South African] employees including skills development plans?
- Has the company developed systems through which empowerment groups can be mentored?

Employment equity

- Has the company published its employment equity plan [in accordance with the Employment Equity Act] and reported on its annual progress in meeting that plan?
- Has the company established a plan to achieve a target for HDSA participation in management of 40% within five years and is implementing the plan?
- Has the company identified a talent pool and is it fast tracking it?
- Has the company established a plan to achieve the target for women participation in mining of 10% within the five years and is implementing the plan?

Migrant labour

- Has the company subscribed to government and industry agreements to ensure non-discrimination against foreign migrant labour?

Mine community and rural development.

- Has the company co-operated in the formulation of integrated development plans [as required in local government and planning legislation] and is the company co-operating with government in the implementation of these plans for communities where mining takes place and for major labour sending areas? Has there been effort on the side of the company to engage the local mine community and major labour sending area communities? (Companies will be required to cite a pattern of consultation, indicate money expenditures and show a plan.)

Housing and living conditions

- For company-provided housing has the mine, in consultation with stakeholders, established measures for improving the standard of housing, including the upgrading

called BRPM and a mine owned by the Australian company Aquarius Platinum (both of which have been in production since 1999). Also in the area are the chrome mines of Samancor (a subsidiary of BHP Billiton) and Xstrata (listed in London). Selected statistics for the various mines in the study area, in aggregate terms by company in 2002, are provided in Table 1. This table makes it clear that a large number of mineworkers are employed in the study area. Also of the hostels, conversion of hostels to family units and promoted home ownership options for mine employees? Companies will be required to indicate what they have done to improve housing and show a plan to progress the issue over time and is implementing the plan.

- For company provided nutrition has the mine established measures for improving the nutrition of mine employees? Companies will be required to indicate what they have done to improve nutrition and show a plan to progress the issue over time and is implementing the plan.

Procurement

- Has the mining company given HDSAs preferred supplier status?
- Has the mining company identified current level of procurement from HDSA companies in terms of capital goods, consumables and services?
- Has the mining company indicated a commitment to a progression of procurement from HDSA companies over a 3–5 year time frame in terms of capital goods, consumables and services and to what extent has the commitment been implemented?

Ownership & joint ventures

- Has the mining company achieved HDSA participation in terms of ownership for equity or attributable units of production of 15 percent in HDSA hands within 5 years and 26 percent in 10 years?

Beneficiation

- Has the mining company identified its current level of beneficiation?
- Has the mining company established its base line level of beneficiation and indicated the extent that this will have to be grown in order to qualify for an offset [of equity transfer requirements]?

Reporting

- Has the company reported on an annual basis its progress towards achieving its commitments in its annual report?

Source: http://www.dme.gov.za/minerals/pdf/scorecard.pdf (accessed July 2003).

evident is the significant income of the platinum mines, owing to the rise in platinum prices since the mid 1990s. In 2002 almost half of the total workforce in the area was employed in the mining sector.[8] The unemployment rate was estimated at 26% in the 1996 census and at 32% in the 2001 census. The latter puts unemployment in some of the informal settlements scattered around the mines at about 44%.[9]

Figure 1: Map of South African platinum mining areas and mines
in 2003, showing the study area

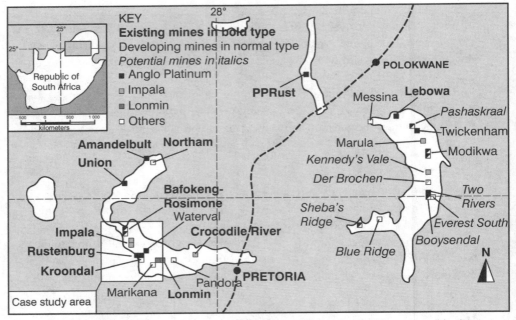

Source: Johnson Matthey, 2003, *The Expansion of Platinum Mining in South Africa*, accessible via
http://www.johnsonmatthey.com (accessed October 2003).

Table 1: Estimated employee and production figures for mines in the study area in 2002, in aggregate terms for each case study company

	Anglo Platinum	Impala	Lonmin	Aquarius	Samancor	Xstrata
Workers	21 500	28 000	25 000	1 350	4 200	1 200
Platinum group metals production (ounces – thousands)	1 560	1 900	1 500	240	N/A	N/A
Operating income (rands – millions)	3 630	6 150	3 300	400	−14	Not given

Source: Company annual reports, interviewees.

Note: These are rough estimates only, due to varying accounting systems and diverging definitions in
use in 2002 (there has been a trend towards greater uniformity in recent years). In particular, Anglo
Platinum's figures for workers exclude contract workers – a significant number – while other companies' figures include them. Aquarius employed only about 16 people directly in 2002, with most of the
mining done by contractors. The exchange rate for much of 2002 was about US$1.00=R10.00.

The first platinum mine, Rustenburg Platinum Mines (now owned by Anglo Platinum), was established near the town of Rustenburg about 75 years ago, while Impala started its operations in the late 1960s. In line with dominant historical practice in the sector, mining companies in the region employed migrant labour (from areas such as the Eastern Cape, Lesotho and Mozambique), housed workers in large single-sex hostels, and relied on the apartheid state or the Bophuthatswana government (the nominally independent Bantustan homeland that included much of the study area prior to 1994) to prevent informal settlements and community or labour protest. So, for instance, in the late 1980s, Impala Platinum reportedly employed over 40 000 employees in the area (according to various interviewees), almost all of whom were migrant workers housed in four large hostels. Until the 1990s, the large mines were therefore like industrial islands in what was still a predominantly agricultural area.

The landscape became much more industrialised and populated during the late 1990s. As one interviewee noted, 'in 1997, there was a sudden change; before, this was a quiet area, then it suddenly became industrialised'. Table 2 provides population figures from 1980 to 2005.

Table 2: Census figures and projected population in the Rustenburg local municipality

	Urban or peri-urban areas	Proportion	Non-urban	Proportion	Total
1980	103 200	73%	37 400	27%	140 600
1985	167 400	83%	33 900	17%	201 300
1991	198 600	83%	41 000	17%	239 700
1996	291 900	91%	27 600	9%	319 500
1999 [a]	335 700	92%	30 400	8%	366 100
2005 [a]	421 400	93%	31 100	7%	452 500

a   Projections
Source: These figures are adapted from Bojanala Platinum District Municipality (BPDM), 'Integrated Development Plan 2002', which in turn relies on the 1996 census. [10]

The increase during the 1990s was especially due to the promise of employment on the mines, which grew in number and increasingly employed labour through local labour brokers, rather than directly from far-off labour sending areas. Combined with less severe access and settlement control by the new government, the immigration led to the growth of informal settlements (also known as squatter camps), particularly around the mines' single-sex hostels. These settlements commonly do not have formal recognition from the landowners and do not receive basic municipal services (see Figure 2).

Informal settlements have been identified for some time as a key development challenge in the area. In an acknowledgement that local government, traditional authority and mining companies need to collaborate on the issue of informal settlements, a Housing Strategy Forum was established in 1999, comprising the local government, the Royal Bafokeng nation and

Figure 2: Growing informal settlements represent the area's most significant development challenge. These settlements are concentrated around the mine hostels – the one in the photograph being adjacent to an Anglo Platinum hostel (photo by Ralph Hamann)

all the case study companies. It commissioned the preparation of a strategy for dealing with informal settlements in the area, and reported that:

> Informal settlement takes place at a rapid rate (estimated 24.2% per annum) in the Greater Rustenburg area and to the effect that there are currently an estimated 13 600 units in informal settlements accommodating about 34 000 people. This excludes the backyard dwellings in Thlabane and surrounding areas which totals an additional estimated 11 000 units. The [growth of] informal settlements… is mainly associated with mining activities in the area. There is, however, no coordinated strategy in place to sufficiently manage the problem. In the past, initiatives launched by any of the roleplayers… were conducted on an ad hoc basis and usually with limited consultation with other parties. This resulted in uncoordinated development and unnecessary duplication of skills and facilities. [11]

The geographical spread of the informal settlements 'broadly follows the… curve created by the mineral belt'. The report underlines the role of the single-sex hostels in the growth of informal settlements.

This option [single-sex hostels] caters for the bulk of the mineworkers but not for their families. This gives rise to informal settlements being established adjacent to the mining hostels. It is generally agreed that this is not a socially preferred option. [12]

There are a number of housing initiatives under way, but the Forum argues in its report that even if these were implemented according to plan, they would not cover the backlog in all areas. Furthermore, the initiatives commonly rely on government subsidies, which exclude many mineworkers. Further problems identified include inappropriate planning, without sufficient consideration of the socio-economic needs of informal dwellers, who come from different origins and speak different languages. The deteriorating conditions in many of the informal settlements, coupled with a labour dispute between, in particular, Anglo Platinum and workers' unions, contributed to violent unrest in the late 1990s that led to the deaths of at least 60 people. In response, a Conflict Resolution Consortium (CRC) was established which, among other things, conducted a survey of Anglo Platinum's hostels to better understand the root causes of conflict. The findings are broadly representative of conditions in the hostels at the time. The survey noted that the large majority of hostel residents were immigrants to the area and that they commonly had additional accommodation in the informal settlements outside the hostels, in part because the conditions in the hostels were cramped and dangerous. It argued that '[s]ingle-sex hostel accommodation… creates an unnatural situation where a healthy community is difficult to foster. If nothing is done, informal settlements will continue to flourish'. [13]

The CRC also conducted a survey of some of the informal settlements. It found that:

- Three quarters of respondents were from outside the province.

- Almost all the dwellings in informal settlements are made from corrugated iron, cardboard, plastic, etc. In the more formal villages, many residents make backyard shacks (called *mikuku*) available for rent to mineworkers or others.

- Two thirds of the respondents had been unemployed for more than three years, with hawking and farming being common survival strategies.

- Though schools are on average only two to three kilometres from most informal settlements, they commonly use the Setswana language as the medium of instruction, thereby excluding other ethnic groups.

- Water and sanitation services are unreliable or non-existent in informal settlements. The CRC said that this posed a great health risk and danger to the people within and outside these communities. Residents had reported that during the rainy season sewage from the bushes and decomposed bodies from shallow graves were swept into the water in the dams. Apart from the health risks, this produced a very unpleasant smell and polluted the water in the dam. [14]

- Existing services or development efforts conducted by provincial or local authorities were considered by respondents insufficient and unreliable. A crucial constraint was related to the tribal ownership of land: 'The Royal Bafokeng Authority was against the District Council's provision of services to the residents of informal settlements including the erection of permanent infrastructures such as sewerage, as this would legalise their stay on the RBA land'. [15]

- Leadership structures in the informal settlements lacked legitimacy, with the majority of respondents saying that these structures were 'imposed' and ineffective.

The adverse living conditions experienced in the informal settlements were described by numerous interviewees. Susan Robinson, director of a local NGO, highlighted the vicious circle of unemployment, substance abuse, domestic violence and HIV/AIDS:

> The onset of industrialisation and all the money [that the mines] brought to the area, brought many informal settlements around the mines, but the mines do not establish infrastructure in those settlements, there is no recreation... Around the mines we have people from the Eastern Cape, from Mozambique, from Angola, from Swaziland, from Lesotho, and local Tswana people – there is such a mix, there is a lot of alienation; people cannot talk to other families; they are not part of an intact culture or established traditions... In the *kampongs* [hostels] there are many males together, without wives; there is a very high consumption of alcohol, there's nothing to do... So in the mining areas, people want to get drunk quick, to be knocked out. Here around the mines there's a big problem with homebrew, which is so toxic because they add battery acid and other chemicals to speed up fermentation. This kind of toxic homebrew acts as a hallucinogen and makes people extremely violent. The result is the complete disintegration of the family: violence against women and children, and a vicious cycle between poverty, alcohol abuse, and violence. Children in these areas... become part of the adult drinking culture; they start drinking alcohol from a very young age, in order to deal with stress and frustration. This also increases the amount of risky sexual behaviour and the prevalence of HIV/AIDS.

The picture that emerges is of an area thrust into significant demographic, institutional and economic change. A key force here is the immigration of migrant workers and those seeking jobs in the mines or attendant industries or services. In the wake of institutional changes, especially at local government level after 1994, and changing employee housing practices on the mines in the 1990s, the informal settlements that have been forming around the mines have become the main nexus of social problems in the area. The role of CSR, in its varying guises, in preventing or mitigating these developments has been very limited.

CSR and its discontents

In line with general trends in South Africa, the companies in this study traditionally understood their social responsibility in terms of *ad hoc* charitable donations to good causes, motivated by a sense that it was 'the right thing to do' (company interviewee). Apart from contributions to national business initiatives, these donations were generally for education or health initiatives in neighbouring communities, and were administered by mine managers or HR managers without dedicated policies, budgets or organisational structures. Significantly, there was no integration between this 'corporate social investment' (CSI) and companies' business plans, as noted by one company employee:

> The view that CSR is primarily CSI is a result of how things were structured, in the sense that businesses thought that they needed to pay what some people referred to as blood money, but it never needed to be part of the business processes. So in order to operate, they needed to do some charity work or CSI, but it has never been key to their own business strategy.

After 1994, the new government's policies, as expressed in the Reconstruction and Development Programme (RDP), established a culture of expectation that companies would contribute more to social development around the mines, and this expectation became more pertinent with the growth of informal settlements there. The response, particularly in the large platinum companies, was to formalise CSI with a dedicated budget (commonly pegged at about 1.0% of pre-tax profit) and a management structure that administers the funds and supports the various projects, most of which focus on education and health services and, more recently, small business development in surrounding communities (see photographs of selected CSI projects in Figures 3–5).

However, though these CSI efforts are welcome contributions to development, there are crucial limitations to this traditional interpretation of CSR as CSI. For a start, a simple reason why companies' CSI projects cannot make a significant dent in the development needs of the area is their general avoidance of informal settlements around the mines. As one mine's HR manager noted: 'No one takes care of the squatter camps'. According to most interviewees, this is due to the uncertain legal status of these settlements – the companies are unwilling to support the formalisation of informal settlements until there is an agreement between the residents and the landowners (which, in large parts of the study area, is predominantly the Bafokeng traditional authority).

A more fundamental criticism of companies' CSI efforts is that they did not have any impact on core business practices, in particular the continued reliance on migrant labour and single-sex hostels. Indeed, most mining company interviewees accepted this link between their business practices and the informal settlements. As one company's corporate affairs director said,

> You don't have to be a genius to see what the real threats are [in the area]: unemployment, crime, the disrupted social fabric created by the migrant system, and the fact that you have a lot of single men living in hostels in proximity to your operations.

Figure 3: A mobile clinic supported by Anglo Platinum (photo by Ralph Hamann)

Figure 4:   A school supported by Lonmin (photo by Ralph Hamann)

Figure 5:   A small agricultural enterprise supported by Impala (photo by Ralph Hamann)

Here it is important to note that all the companies in the study have, since the mid 1990s, decreased their reliance on single sex hostels. A mixture of internal and external motivations (including the BEE scorecard in Box 1 above) has led them to significantly reduce the numbers of workers living in these hostels.[16] However, this reduction has taken place as part of a modernisation drive motivated by an emphasis on core competencies, in which employee housing was considered expendable. In many mines, workers were given a so-called 'live-out allowance' so that they could arrange their own accommodation, but because this amount was generally very low and because wages remained low for most employment categories, many workers preferred to live in shacks in the informal settlements. The social implications of these changes to corporate employee housing policies did not feature prominently in management discussions, much less were they part of a broader CSR strategy. Hence the way the mines have reduced their reliance on single sex hostels has, paradoxically, been a further reason for the rapid growth of informal settlements in the area.

The challenge of collaboration

A further overarching reason why companies' past CSR activities have not been able to make a difference to the growing informal settlements is that they had not been part of, much less contributed to, a comprehensive coordinated and collaborative approach involving the other key role-players in the area, particularly the local government, traditional authority and local communities. This is not because of a lack of awareness, as illustrated by the establishment and the findings of the Housing Strategy Forum mentioned above. Companies have also neglected or been unable to contribute to the local municipality's Integrated Development Plan (IDP), a mechanism through which the municipality is meant to facilitate a participatory process to develop a spatial development framework and a municipal budget. One company manager noted that 'Companies must input into the IDP; but this didn't happen as well as it should have, it wasn't well managed'.

The absence of regional development coordination is not only constraining the effectiveness of companies' CSR efforts; it is a fundamental impediment to an integrated response to the problem of the growing informal settlements. For a start, the companies' CSI activities are impeded by a lack of coordination, for instance when there is no land available for the construction of low-cost housing, a big concern for company representatives. More fundamentally, improved communication structures between companies, government and community groups would allow for a more efficient and context-dependent delimitation of development roles and responsibilities. The need for a stakeholder forum has also been raised in connection with the increasingly pressing need for bulk service provision – as one mining manager noted:

> In the past, it was the responsibility of government to provide services like water and electricity; but if we sit down and wait for local government, we will not be a profitable organisation – that synergy in tri-sector partnerships is absolutely critical.

Finally, improved collaboration at the municipal level should do more to resolve or prevent conflicts between companies and local communities, such as that between Impala and the people of Luka.

Over and above isolated initiatives involving the major mining companies in some joint welfare and literary projects and a regional HIV/AIDS initiative, there have been a number of attempts to improve development coordination in the region. These have been initiated by local government or the traditional authority, as well as mining companies. For instance, between 2001 and 2003 there was an attempt by local government to convene a Joint Development Forum, in order to coordinate planning for bulk infrastructure provision and local economic development. More recent attempts have centred on particular housing initiatives and the municipality's IDP, and there have been separate joint planning efforts by the Royal Bafokeng nation. However, for the most part these initiatives have failed to bring the key role-players together for effective, collaborative plans and actions at the local level. There are three salient reasons for this.

The first is the difficulty in bringing about inter-firm collaboration in circumstances where the various parties have for a long time acted unilaterally and with very little coordination. As one mining CSR manager said; 'In Rustenburg policy implementation is more reactive, because mines have been established for a long time'. Another noted that the linear dispersion of mines along the platinum reef (see Figure 1) contributed to this insular approach among the companies: 'Rustenburg platinum occurs along a corridor and development occurs along the line of the shafts... each mine has its own area that it manages'.

The second reason is the lack of capacity and clarity within local government, partly as a result of the uncertainties about how governance jurisdiction and responsibility are shared between the elected local government and the traditional authority.[17] Significantly, the Royal Bafokeng Nation plays an important quasi-governmental role in the area as the traditional authority of the Bafokeng community, which owns most of the land in the area. The Bafokeng also own a significant stake in Impala Platinum, which is one of the reasons they are colloquially referred to as 'the richest tribe in Africa'.[18] Despite high-level efforts to establish a working relationship between the municipality and the traditional authority (which at one stage even involved a visit by President Mbeki to the area), fundamental tensions continue to thwart coordination and collaboration between them.

Furthermore, the national policy framework has only recently been set up so as to allow the local government to play a facilitative role in regional coordination. Most interviewees agree that local government is the legitimate institution to play this central role, particularly through the statutory IDP process. However, there are widespread concerns that the municipality does not have the capacity to facilitate an inclusive participation process that involves all the key role-players, especially in the context of the continuing tensions between the municipality and the Royal Bafokeng Nation.

The third reason is the role of the mining companies and the absence of high-level commitment to effective cross-sectoral collaboration, at least until relatively recently. Indeed, some of the underlying motives for companies' CSR efforts are widely recognised to have militated against collaborative approaches. Thus a key motive for the above mentioned CSI projects has been to gain competitive advantage, particularly in terms of local and national reputation. As Impala's CSI manager said: 'Every company wants to be seen to be doing much more than what the others are doing, so there is always that competition'.[19]

More fundamentally, mining company leadership's commitment to cross-sector collaboration at the local level has been limited. Companies' social managers commented that there had been insufficient senior management buy-in into previous efforts at establishing a multi-stakeholder forum, and this had resulted, for instance, in the job of company representative being delegated to low-ranking employees. According to other stakeholders, most notably some local government officials, the primary reason for this lack of commitment has been the reluctance of companies to take responsibility for social issues around the mines, especially the growth of informal settlements.

Indeed, there have been fundamental disagreements over this responsibility. For instance, at a focus group discussion facilitated for this case study research, the director for local economic development at the relevant municipality argued that the primary constraint to dealing with social problems in the area was not the lack of coordination, but rather the fact that 'mining companies have not accepted their primary responsibility for being the root cause of the informal settlements [around the mines]... through the migrant system and the single sex hostels'.

Mining company representatives responded that mining companies are, indeed, accepting some of the responsibility for housing around the mines, as evidenced by the budgets that have been allocated and the houses that are currently being built (though there was some disagreement about the extent of this commitment). Crucially, however, it was argued that mining companies would never want to accept sole responsibility for informal settlements – after all, there are informal settlements elsewhere, too – and that the responsibility for dealing with these social issues needs to be shared between business and government. Anglo Platinum's CSI manager argued the companies' case thus:

> The municipality likes to blame the mines for the informal settlements. They say that 20 percent [of residents] in the informal settlements are Anglo workers. But they [the informal settlements] are not only our responsibility... There are lots of reasons for them... It is very much a government responsibility as well... Ultimately we can't do anything without government – it's their terrain. They need to provide the land use planning and infrastructure.

More recently, some of the companies have seemed willing to accept a shared responsibility for the informal settlements, partly because of their growing understanding that informal settlements are a business risk and that there is a need to facilitate cross-sectoral collaboration to mitigate this risk. The most significant indication of this has been Anglo Platinum's commitment to establishing a tri-sector forum, premised on a step-by-step process starting with improved company internal coordination on CSR-related issues, as Anglo Platinum's local CSR manager explained in 2003:

> At the last [executive committee] meeting, we passed an agreement on [the establishment of a] tri-sector partnership in Rustenburg. We want to start with an internal company forum, including representatives from a number of company departments, where we discuss socio-economic issues, business issues, utilities, etc... The second step is to have a forum of the major producers, Impala, Lonmin, and us: the commercial forum. The objective is to get synergies on basic issues, like water, which is a major problem here in Rustenburg... The third step is the private–public forum, where we engage the Rustenburg municipality and the Bojanala district municipality... Almost parallel to that we would consolidate the social forum, where we bring in the communities, traditional leaders, NGOs, into one organised unit. Once they are organised, then we can bring business, government, and civil society together. Our timing is to reach the Joint Development Forum, the tri-sector partnership, by June next year [2004]. We have exco approval; we have a memorandum... One of my key performance areas is to ensure that we have a tri-sector partnership by June next year.

Unfortunately, at the time of writing (2007) these targets remained unmet and indeed most of the challenges and difficulties discussed above also still remained. However, there have been slow but important changes in corporate perceptions and policies on these issues, especially with regard to the growing understanding of informal settlements as a business risk. This is also reflected to some extent in companies' public reports, though more so in Lonmin's (2006) and Anglo Platinum's (2006) than in Impala's (2006). There is also an increased awareness that improved cross-sector collaboration is required, with a central role for local government. For instance, the 2006 Anglo Platinum sustainability report states that:

> One of the most notable consequences of the rate of development [in the Rustenburg area] is the recent proliferation of informal settlements and structures within the municipality (both in free-standing individual settlements and backyards). In response to these challenges, the municipality, in partnership with Anglo Platinum, embarked on a process to prepare a five- to ten-year housing strategy... The project was funded by Anglo Platinum but under the leadership and ownership of the municipality. In addition, Anglo Platinum provided technical assistance.[20]

Hence the companies have identified local government capacity as a crucial prerequisite for successful collaboration, and their representatives have alluded to targeted support to this effect, particularly for councillors. The relationship between mining companies and local government is thus potentially progressing towards a situation where some companies are providing targeted support to local government, so that it can better fulfil its statutory responsibilities and facilitate improved regional coordination. This support includes, in particular, targeted human resource development, though this needs to be undertaken sensitively and transparently to prevent allegations of corruption or cooptation. In essence, companies must learn to 'lead from behind' in facilitating more coordinated and effective responses to the development challenges in the area.

Conclusion

This case study of the Rustenburg area illustrates the crucial need in areas experiencing new mining developments, for mining companies, the local municipality and other key role-players to negotiate and collaborate in the process of developing and implementing long-term, proactive and integrated development plans for the area. This has not been the case in the Rustenburg area, with the result that it is faced with deteriorating socio-economic conditions, which also threaten the mining companies' strategic objectives. To illustrate, in mid 2007 Anglo Platinum's largest mine in Rustenburg was shut down for a week (costing the company close to 100 million rand) after 12 miners had died in that mine within the previous six months. Even more dramatically, the company's CEO, Ralph Havelstein, who had otherwise achieved notable successes with the company, resigned shortly afterwards with specific reference to safety, an unprecedented move in the South African mining industry. The relevance of this for the above discussion is that safety in the mines is, among other things, closely related to the socio-economic conditions surrounding the mines. As a mining company manager said, 'you cannot expect a worker living in a shack, without electricity or water, surrounded by shebeens and drinking, to enter the mine in the morning fit and refreshed for a long day's safe mining!'

Yet despite these increasingly important incentives, many of the challenges and difficulties constraining effective collaboration in the area remain, some of which are beyond the immediate influence of the mining companies. Most notably, the local government is the statutory authority responsible for upgrading the informal settlements and facilitating participatory, integrated development planning, but it is hampered by lack of capacity and ongoing conflicts with the influential and powerful traditional authority. Company managers are slowly learning that they need to do what they can to improve these broader local governance relationships, if they are to succeed in responding to the severe social problems around the mines.

Editors' reflections and questions

This case study emphasises the challenges of facilitating cross-sector collaboration in the complex, strained socio-economic context of a particular area in South Africa, though similar challenges exist elsewhere in South Africa and indeed in many other African countries. In the language of negotiation theory, it illustrates how difficult it can be for conflicting parties to move from an emphasis on their bargaining positions to their underlying interests, especially in the context of historical injustices, continued distrust and significantly diverging interests.

It shows how necessary it is for key stakeholders to 'step back' from particular instances of disagreement – such as the conflict between Impala and the Luka community – and to identify more systemic governance problems in the area and negotiate means of responding to them. Some of the questions worth pondering are as follows:

1. For a long time, collaboration was impeded by disagreement about who was responsible for the informal settlements and the related social problems. More recently, these challenges are commonly being referred to as a shared responsibility, but this may deteriorate into glib rhetoric unless it is translated into tangible measures. How might shared responsibility manifest itself in an area such as Rustenburg?

2. How significant are the changing incentives and pressures faced by mining companies to take greater responsibility for social problems around the mines? To what extent are they particular to the national and local context?

3. Improved collaboration between the mining companies themselves and between the companies, local government, traditional authority and civil society groups was identified by various local role-players as a prerequisite for responding to the sustainable development challenges in the area, yet this collaboration remained elusive despite various attempts to achieve it. What are the key causes of these failures and how common do you expect these challenges to be in other contexts? What are possible responses to these challenges?

4. This case study identifies limited local government capacity as a significant constraint and it also suggests that the private sector may be able to play a role in improving this capacity. How could this be achieved in an effective, unobtrusive way?

Notes

1   This case study is based on R. Hamann, 'Corporate Social Responsibility in Mining in South Africa' (Unpublished PhD thesis, University of East Anglia, Norwich, 2004). Parts of the case study have been previously published in adapted form as an article; see R. Hamann, 'Corporate Social Responsibility, Partnerships, and Institutional Change: The Case of Mining Companies in South Africa', *Natural Resources Forum*, 28, 4 (2004): 278–290. The case study research consisted of semi-structured interviews with representatives from mining companies (28 individuals), local and provincial government and traditional authorities (11), unions, NGOs, and local community organisations (10), and consultants and analysts (5). In addition to the interviews, the research consisted of participant observation, document analysis, and a facilitated group discussion involving 16 participants from mining companies, local government, traditional authority, and civil society organisations. Most of these interviews were conducted in 2003 but more recent discussions have been held with some of the original interviewees as well as others. I am grateful to the interviewees for their time and commitment to the research.

2   Truth and Reconciliation Commission of South Africa, *Truth and Reconciliation Commission of South Africa Report, 21 March 2003* (Johannesburg: TRC, 2003), available via http://www.info.gov.za/otherdocs/2003/trc/rep.pdf (accessed July 2005), 150.

3   L. Flynn, *Studded with Diamonds and Paved with Gold: Miners, Mining Companies and Human Rights in Southern Africa* (London: Bloomsbury, 1992).

4   Johannesburg Securities Exchange (JSE), *JSE SRI Index: Background and Selection Criteria* (Johannesburg: JSE, 2003).

5   Reportedly, over 52 billion rand (exchange rate R10.00 = $US1.00) was lost from the market capitalisation of South African listed mining companies within two days, with the JSE resource index falling 5% and the gold index 12% (Roger Baxter, interview).

6   See http://www.dme.gov.za/minerals/mining_charter. htm (accessed July 2003).

7   J. Reader, *Africa: A Biography of a Continent* (London: Penguin, 1998), 13.

8   Bojanala Platinum District Municipality (BPDM), 'Integrated Development Plan 2002' (Rustenburg: Bojanala Platinum District Municipality, 2002), prepared by Plan Associates, Pretoria.

9   Uncertainty about unemployment data is pervasive in South Africa. This is also due to disparate metrics, with the census counting as unemployed only those who are still actively looking for work.

10   Note that the projections have proven to be roughly correct in comparison to more recent data; see Rustenburg Local Municipality, 'Rustenburg Five-Year Integrated Development Plan, 2007–2012'.

11   'Greater Rustenburg Informal Housing Strategy 2001' (compiled for the Housing Strategy Forum by Plan Associates, Pretoria), 1.

12   Ibid., 6.

13   Conflict Resolution Consortium (CRC), Rustenburg / Anglo Platinum Conflict Stabilisation Project (Rustenburg: CRC, 2001), 57.

14   Ibid., 62.

15   Ibid., 63.

16   To illustrate, according to interviewees, in 2002 Anglo Platinum's mines in the province (including two mines outside the study area) reportedly had about 7 000 workers living in six hostels, out of a total of 24 000 employees, excluding contractors; this is a significant reduction from the initial situation, where most workers lived in hostels. Impala Platinum had about 10 000 hostel dwellers, out of 24 000 employees, whereas the majority of its initial 50 000 employees in the late 1980s were in hostels. Lonmin's Eastern Platinum mine had brought down the number of hostel dwellers from 3 000 to 1 900 (out of 4 500 employees), while Samancor still had about half of its 1 300 workers staying in hostels. Xstrata's alloys division had no hostels.

17   In this context, it should be noted that in the wake of the transition to democracy in 1994, national policy on local government has been in a state of flux, with clear structures and processes emerging only fairly recently.

18 See, for instance, A. Manson and B. Mbenga, ' "The Richest Tribe in Africa": Platinum-Mining and the Bafokeng in South Africa's North West Province, 1965–1999', *Journal of Southern African Studies*, 29, 1 (2003), 25–47.

19 However, this competitive streak seems to have diminished in recent years. One company's social manager argued that 'now we have matured' and another argued that inter-company competition had decreased due to the high platinum price and companies' long-term supply contracts with customers.

20 'Anglo Platinum Sustainability Report 2006' (Johannesburg: Anglo Platinum, 2006), 71.

CASE 8

Creating opportunities for sustainable community development:
Magadi Soda Company in Kenya

JUDY N. MUTHURI

Introduction

This case study reflects upon the experience of the Magadi Soda Company (MSC), a soda ash extracting company, operating in the Magadi division of Kenya. The study does not simply reveal conflicting company-community expectations: it demonstrates how Magadi Soda addressed such challenges by building community relationships and strengthening community participation in local governance.[1]

Corporations in developing countries are often expected to act as agents of community development and, at a local level, to 'enhance the capabilities of local people to pursue transformative and emancipatory possibilities for sustainable development'.[2] These expectations require companies to adopt novel strategies of stakeholder engagement and forms of social organisation through corporate community involvement (CCI) programmes. For a company, *community development* means making efforts to promote the long-term well-being of the host community – improving socio-economic and cultural conditions, building capacity and encouraging self-help, and empowering the community.[3] Community development interventions address various socio-economic dimensions of poverty – material deprivation, low levels of education and health, vulnerability and exposure to risk, and voicelessness and powerlessness.[4] CCI must embrace a multi-dimensional approach to community development that emphasises self-sufficiency, self-reliance and a citizenry that participates actively in local governance.[5]

Context

Magadi division is an area classified as arid and semi-arid, covering 2 749 square kilometres in Kajiado district in the Rift Valley province of Kenya. It is sparsely populated, with an estimated population of about 22 000 people.[6] The division is the poorest of seven in Kajiado district – 57% of the population live in abject poverty by Kenyan national standards.[7] The local residents are predominantly the Maasai, a semi-nomadic tribe, whose economic mainstay is livestock. The division is made up of four group ranches: Olkeri, Oldonyonyokie, Olkiramatian and Shompole. Group ranches are freehold titles to communal land under Kenya's Land Adjudication Act. Elected committees govern the ranch activities.[8] MSC has a long-term lease on the concession area (approximately 225 000 acres), an area sandwiched between the group ranches in the middle of Magadi Division.

Key actors

Magadi Soda Company

MSC was established in 1911. It became a wholly owned subsidiary of Brunner Mond Group Limited (UK) in 1924.[9] MSC is the only large corporation in Magadi division and it is Africa's foremost producer and exporter of soda ash (sodium carbonate), dredged from Lake Magadi. Soda ash is an important component in industrial and chemical processes. It is used in the manufacture of such products as detergents and glass. The company provides social amenities and infrastructure in the Magadi Township, the only company-owned town in Kenya. MSC has been and remains concerned to coexist peacefully with the community, to maintain its social legitimacy and its licence to operate, and to reduce community dependence on the company. As one MSC employee observes, good community relations are a fundamental business imperative:

> On the procurement side, we look at it as risk, in the sense that if my supplies are coming from Nairobi and Mombasa and a disgruntled community member disrupts the railway, I'll not produce because my raw materials and supplies will not have come … So we have to create a win-win situation with the community as partners.[10]

The local community

The Maasai community are a nomadic tribe with high levels of poverty and illiteracy, low income, high unemployment and a limited skills base. Such deprivation inhibits poverty alleviation programmes.[11] The community voices its requirements – the creation of sustainable livelihoods, increased employment opportunities, and participation in local governance. Its deeply entrenched cultural values and its self-identification as the 'Maasai community' of Magadi division shapes how the members participate in development and local governance processes.

The central and local government

The central government is represented by various line ministries: Education, Science and Technology; Health; Agriculture; and Tourism and Information. Their mandate is to provide services and an enabling framework for the development of their respective sectors. The local government is the Olkejuado County Council, which is made up of one nominated councillor and four elected ones. MSC pays land rates to the council. However, during the last three years the council has been trying to reclaim access to some of MSC's concession land. The company also pays royalties and taxes to the central government and is among the largest taxpayers in

Figure 1:   Local community members dredging salt from Lake Magadi workshop
(photo by Judy Muthuri)

Kenya.[12] The local and central government face significant human, logistical and budgetary constraints, which limit the efficacy of their poverty alleviation and development policies. Since the MSC plays a dominant role in the provision of social welfare and infrastructure and the government has withdrawn from providing social welfare, the local community perceives the company as its 'private government'. The councillor from Magadi ward observed:

> I must say Magadi Soda is doing a lot more than the government, and as a local community, we appreciate … what they are doing. We have some services which if we wait for the government to do, you will wait for five good years. … When we go to Magadi Soda, they are ready to assist us. They are like a small government.[13]

Civil society

The civil society actors include non-governmental organisations (NGOs), community-based organisations (CBOs) and faith-based organisations. Most CBOs suffer from resource deficits that make it difficult for them to participate in community development. Most projects implemented by civil society are funded by international and national NGOs, which possess the technical, social and financial resources to engage in community development. On the whole, community development interventions by civil society are uncoordinated and fragmented.[14]

Phase one (period prior to 2000): A paternalistic approach to CCI[15]

MSC has a history of community engagement motivated by the need to be 'a good neighbour'. Its earlier attempts at CCI, however, were 'corporate-centric', with decisions vis-à-vis social issues being at the discretion of company managers and a few community elites. Corporate-community interaction was weak, given the community's low skills base, high levels of il-literacy and strong cultural beliefs antithetical to formal work. Believing 'anyone not keeping livestock is cursed', the community relied heavily on livestock production as its economic mainstay, but the region's persistent droughts meant that this form of livelihood was regularly threatened.

However, the context within which the company operates has been changing: for instance, community members have become more educated and aware of international debates on cor-porate responsibility and indigenous communities' rights. In June 2000, the community staged a demonstration over land rights issues. The demonstrators made it plain that they believed the concession area fell within their 'ancestral right'. They also demanded that Magadi Soda address their social and economic emancipation. The community recognised a transactional element in their relationship – land for work and social services. CCI was thus no longer perceived as a privilege but as a right. An MSC Board member said:

> In one meeting, I heard a Maasai saying, 'God put this raw material here and for this rea-son it is ours. So if you have to take it you've got to pay us something'. So they began to see it as a right and the company had a responsibility to give the community employment, and participate in these and that project.[16]

MSC responded by intensifying their philanthropic giving. The outcome was escalating CCI costs and increasing community dependency. CCI became inefficient and unsustainable. To respond to this crisis of legitimacy and the growing challenge of maintaining its licence to operate, MSC had to change its CCI strategy.

Phase two (2000–2004): Participatory approach to CCI

In 2000 the company called a community leaders' meeting. The four company representatives and over 30 community leaders who attended discussed various problems and how they could be solved.[17] They explored the competencies, the capabilities and limitations, and the strengths and weaknesses of all the actors (e.g. the government, the NGOs) operating in Magadi divi-sion, and the external factors (at macro and meso levels) that contributed to unsustainable livelihoods (Table 1). This initial meeting gave rise to a formal company-community dialogue process, called SWOT (strengths, weaknesses, opportunities, threats). The SWOT deliberation process was facilitated by a respected community member – a government appointee to MSC's Board, in accordance with the Articles of Association, with a remit on community issues.[18]

The process took over a year to complete. It was the first systematic needs analysis of prob-lems facing the community and provided a platform for evaluating the roles played by other actors in community development. While the community expected the company to meet all its social needs, MSC soon realised the company 'cannot do it all'. During SWOT discussions, the facilitator skilfully encouraged the community to think in the language of 'sustainability' and not 'welfare' and, therefore, to identify other actors in Magadi who had the technical capability and competence to solve specific problems better than the company.

During the preparation of the 'community development action plan', the company and the community distinguished between social issues within (e.g. employment) and outside (e.g. security) the 'responsibility' of the company, and those problems which other actors were sufficiently competent to address. The activities identified were diverse: infrastructure development (building schools), capacity building initiatives (training water committee members in leadership and management), lobbying initiatives (lobbying central government to build more slaughterhouses or contractors to employ local labour), advocacy-related activities (enforcement of traffic act regulations, creating awareness of 'industrial discipline and work ethic' among potential MSC employees), and the promotion of best practice (indigenous knowledge about water conservation, for instance). They also identified priority social issues for the CCI programme: health, education, water, transport and infrastructure, employment and micro-business development. To ensure the continuity of the participatory process, MSC proposed the establishment of a formal dialogue structure that would be the interface between the company and the community. This is discussed in the next section.

Institutionalising community participation in CCI

The SWOT committee, consisting of community and company representatives, was mandated to implement the community development action plan. It was also given the responsibility to address issues of mutual concern, such as contracting labour from the community and conflict resolution. The community members agreed to a two-tier structure to provide a system of communication and accountability (see Figure 2). The community and MSC preferred a representative participatory approach, firstly because of the Maasai's hierarchical social ordering and their high regard for leadership, and secondly because it provided an efficient and manageable system of community engagement. They also agreed on the governing and administrative rules, the mutual responsibilities, and the procedures for the participation process, e.g. members' roles, frequency of meetings, decision rules, information dissemination and leadership, reporting and communication. The smaller SWOT committee meets monthly (and as matters arise), while the larger one is convened twice a year. The smaller committee presents progress reports to the larger one, detailing achievements and strategies for specific community interventions. The larger committee critically evaluates the suggestions and either endorses, amends or turns them down. SWOT proposals have led to task forces designed to deliver on specific activities such as the establishment of a secondary school (Patterson Memorial Secondary School), community medical care, and the promotion of ecotourism.

The SWOT committees are involved in planning, implementing and evaluating community development initiatives in Magadi division. New SWOT members are socialised into the process and are expected to adhere to generally acceptable rules of engagement. As the initiator of the participatory process, MSC facilitates the stakeholder engagement process through financial, technical and material support. The company faced challenges in institutionalising the participatory process; for example, getting the community to understand the SWOT technique and its benefits. It spent considerable energy, time and financial resources in educating the local community about the SWOT technique and its application, and informally lobbying individual members for its endorsement. Magadi Soda was unwavering on the SWOT process as its preferred technique of stakeholder engagement. Over time, it became accepted by the community as well.

Box 1: Summary of social issues diagnosis using the SWOT analysis tool

Strengths

- Magadi Soda's resource capacity, technical expertise and willingness to engage with the community.
- Actors' capabilities and competencies, e.g. Health – African Medical and Research Foundation (AMREF); Tourism – African Conservation Centre (ACC).*
- Resources available in the community, e.g. water points, health centres and hospital.
- Existing infrastructure e.g. water pipeline, railway line, three air strips, telephone lines, radio communication, trading centres with markets, good quality and well-serviced company houses.
- Other organisations that provide support service delivery, e.g. collaboration of Magadi Soda and AMREF in health care.

Weaknesses

- Human behavioural factors, e.g. encroachment on water catchment areas; vandalism of water pipes.
- Low base of skills and high level of illiteracy in the community: leading to a) marginalised or unemployed community; and b) contractor importing unskilled labour from the division.
- Local community's negative perception of and attitudes towards salaried employment.
- Social stigma about Maasai's work ethic – labelled as 'rebels', 'don't like working'.
- Pro-pastoralism local culture that is lacking in entrepreneurial spirit.
- Community's 'naïve generosity' allowing 'outsiders' to monopolise business operations.
- Weak inter-organisational network linkages and partnerships.
- MSC's stringent policies and poor communication e.g. company employment practices 'not transparent'; existence of 'nepotism and tribalism in recruitment', etc.
- Low community participation and involvement in local governance, e.g. in district road and water boards.
- Poor relations between company personnel and the local community.
- Poor maintenance of infrastructure and local amenities e.g. water pipelines, roads and public toilets.

Opportunity

- Tapping into existing resources, including:
  - existing loan boards for small-scale business resources
  - unexploited business lines e.g. slaughterhouse/farming/hardware
  - available water and sunk boreholes
  - resources within the local government such as technical experts in Olkejuado County Council departments.
- Possible knowledge management and transfer e.g. exploitation of indigenous water conservation knowledge.
- Potential of behaviour change e.g. reduction of water wastage.

* AMREF and ACC are to partner with MSC in various projects related to promoting health standards (AMREF) and opening up tourism opportunities (ACC) in Magadi division.

Threats

- Environment-related factors, e.g. harsh climatic conditions, poor geological structure, saline water, low rainfall patterns, high evaporation, tsetse fly infections.
- Existing political and legal frameworks, e.g. property rights based on communal land rights.
- Rural-urban migration towards Magadi township (potential squatter problem).
- MSC business practices, e.g. ash dust and unmarked quarries have negative effects on the local environment.
- Ambiguous roles of various government committees, e.g. water and roads committees.
- Lack of delivery services through central and local government of Kenya.
- Weak enforcement of legal statutes e.g. Traffic Act, Water Act.

Source: Summarised from various SWOT reports and minutes (2000).

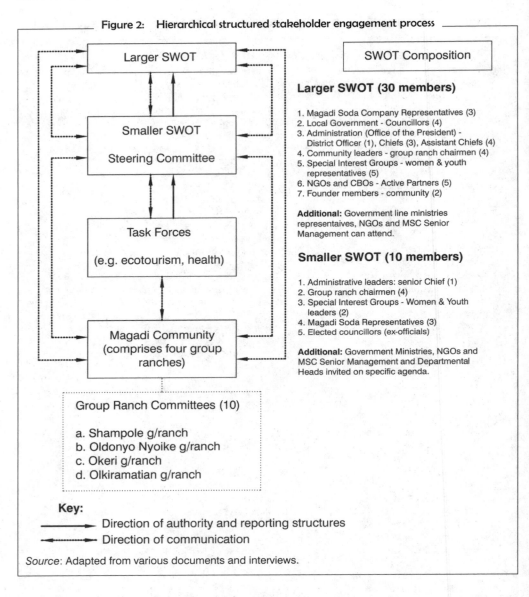

Figure 2: Hierarchical structured stakeholder engagement process

Larger SWOT

Smaller SWOT Steering Committee

Task Forces (e.g. ecotourism, health)

Magadi Community (comprises four group ranches)

Group Ranch Committees (10)

a. Shampole g/ranch
b. Oldonyo Nyoike g/ranch
c. Okeri g/ranch
d. Olkiramatian g/ranch

SWOT Composition

Larger SWOT (30 members)

1. Magadi Soda Company Representatives (3)
2. Local Government - Councillors (4)
3. Administration (Office of the President) -
   District Officer (1), Chiefs (3), Assistant Chiefs (4)
4. Community leaders - group ranch chairmen (4)
5. Special Interest Groups - women & youth
   representatives (5)
6. NGOs and CBOs - Active Partners (5)
7. Founder members - community (2)

Additional: Government line ministries representaives, NGOs and MSC Senior Management can attend.

Smaller SWOT (10 members)

1. Administrative leaders: senior Chief (1)
2. Group ranch chairmen (4)
3. Special Interest Groups - Women & Youth
   leaders (2)
4. Magadi Soda Representatives (3)
5. Elected councillors (ex-officials)

Additional: Government Ministries, NGOs and MSC Senior Management and Departmental Heads invited on specific agenda.

Key:

⟶ Direction of authority and reporting structures
⟵---- Direction of communication

Source: Adapted from various documents and interviews.

Corporate-community dialogue has been a learning experience for the company as well as the community, and this has resulted in company policies (e.g. recruitment, allocation of business stalls, transport, housing) that were previously inward-looking (benefiting mostly employees and their families) becoming more community-centred. CCI is now more structured and co-ordinated. A community relations policy based on sustainable development, capacity building and community empowerment was developed in 2001. The human resources function oversees the implementation of this policy through a community relations office that was established in 2002. New employees undergo community relations induction and are responsible for community activities as part of their performance targets.

Phase three (2005 to present): Collaborative approach to community development

To ensure sustainable community development in Magadi, the company proposed to the International Finance Corporation (IFC) the preparation of a community development plan. The IFC, at the time, was financing Magadi Soda's building of a modern soda ash processing plant in Magadi division. The plant was to enhance the company's competitive edge in the global market. This new initiative raised the community's expectations of job creation. However, since it was to be a mechanised plant, it meant few direct employment opportunities. The divergent company-community expectations created renewed tensions between them. Through the IFC's funding (US$100 000), a study was commissioned in January 2004 with the objective of reviewing the needs of the community and providing MSC and other stakeholders in Magadi with an overall framework for 'how best to take a proactive and consistent stance on community development initiatives'.[19] The study was conducted between March and November 2004 by Practical Action, a consultancy selected for its technical expertise in community development. The study applied the sustainable livelihoods framework to analyse the dimensions of poverty and define the assets base of the people in Magadi community.[20] It links Magadi division to the national policy, planning and development process. NGOs, government line ministries and community members were consulted in the data collection phases and the dissemination of study findings.

The product of the study was the *Community Development Plan (CDP)*. The CDP details the strategies necessary for the sustainable improvement of the Maasai community. It relies on a public-private-community partnership approach and marks a shift from a corporate-centric to a collective-oriented approach to tackling poverty alleviation. The CDP objectives are summarised in Table 1 (page 216).

The CDP was officially launched on 7 April 2006 with community representatives and over 21 development partners and NGOs in attendance. A number of the CDP projects are being implemented through a two-year grant from the Royal Danish embassy. These include:

- Building of a girls' dormitory at Oloika primary school to help keep girls in school who might otherwise be affected by cultural practices such as early marriages and female genital mutilation;

- Constructing a new water pipeline in Eldownyo-o-Lasho to help reduce the long distance covered by women to fetch water for both domestic and livestock use; and

- Building the local community's capacity for development, e.g. training community representatives and school head committees in management skills, etc.

Various agencies (such as MSC, Dupoto-e-Maa, Practical Action and Nidra) and the community are responsible for specific activities within the CDP projects. Significantly, the company has been able to mobilise other stakeholders in the region to harness resources and engage collectively to hasten social development in Magadi division. The CDP has helped create a new pool of resources, including government funded initiatives such as the Local Authority Transfer Fund and Constituency Development Funds. NGOs have used the CDP framework to fund-raise for projects in the region. MSC continues to champion a network governance approach that will increase societal impacts (i.e. sustainable community development) and the company's enlightened self-interest (i.e. legitimacy, lower transaction costs, enhanced reputation as a corporate citizen).

Table 1:   CDP key objectives and envisioned outputs

CDP focus area	Envisioned outputs
Development of network governance for development	The CDP is planned and implemented on a rolling basis with resources secured from a range of partners including the government, private and civil society sectors. Local stakeholders are competent in participatory development planning, project planning, monitoring, reporting and ongoing evaluation techniques. There is broadened community representation and a decision-making structure is established in the 13 sub-locations. A vibrant CDP secretariat is created to plan, coordinate and implement CDP activities. Company-stakeholder engagement is strengthened. There are operational and effective community based organisations.
Access to services	Alternative and sustainable solutions to service provision are developed. Services are enhanced and robust. New services are developed and operationalised.
Natural resources management	Approaches to the development, utilisation and management of pastoral land are sustainable. Sustainable farming solutions in Nguruman and Pakase are established. Diverse community natural resource-based enterprises are established and strengthened.

Source: Adapted from Magadi Soda Sustainability Report, 2005.[21]

Towards sustainable community development: Social investment and key milestones

Corporate social action must seek to develop human, social and economic capacities in the local community. MSC has aimed to strengthen the community's capacity for sustainable community development in order to reduce its dependence on the company.[22] The company has led by example, and has redefined its policies to reflect the centrality of the community to its business.

CCI strategies aim at strengthening the community's capital for sustainable community development, with the community playing an active role in planning, coordinating and implementing poverty reduction interventions. Some of its achievements are summarised in the following paragraphs.

Improving physical capital

The company has, on its own and in collaboration with other actors, improved public facilities in Magadi division, for example, building schools, installing water pipelines (e.g. Olekaitoriori, Sampu and Tiasilal), enhancing the quality of housing and living standards, and providing adequate infrastructure (road and rail). The community, through the SWOT approach, has played a key role in planning, designing, implementing and monitoring these initiatives. These investments have improved the socioe-conomic profiles of the community and enhanced their quality of life. MSC has supported health centres (e.g. Oloika, Entapasopia) with renovations, communication links and medical supplies. The company has built and maintained four schools, and supported all the other seven schools in the division. In collaboration with NGOs, the government and the community, MSC invested 6 006 689 Kenyan shillings (KSh) (approximately US$86 000) to build the first secondary school outside the township. This new school reduced the pressure on the Magadi township schools.

Strengthening economic capital

MSC has created business opportunities with the aim of reducing community dependence on the company and increasing the community's self-reliance. MSC continues to champion alternative and sustainable means of livelihood among the Maasai community: it promotes bee-keeping, the extraction of fresh juices, and hides and skins businesses. The company promotes entrepreneurship through skills development and has enlisted the support of other NGOs such as Practical Action and SNV-Kenya to build the community's capacity through training in business development and management. Additionally, the company provides business opportunities for the community. It has awarded cleaning contracts and scrap metal business to organised groups and associations that it has helped to establish (see Box 2, page 218). The company also supports various ecotourism projects in the region, and this support has included all of the proceeds from filming the prominent Hollywood film *The Constant Gardener* in the MSC concession area. These funds are directly managed by the local community.

Increasing human capital

Education, training opportunities and knowledge transfer within the company have enhanced the employability of community members. Likewise, the attitude of the local community to formal employment and of parents to education has changed. The parents are now more willing to invest in secondary education and take girls to school. Although the community remains relatively poor and unable to afford a good standard of health care, health standards in the community have been improved. The company continues to subsidise health care services at the 55-bed capacity company hospital, the only hospital facility in the division. In collaboration with the Ministry of Health and other health-focused NGOs such as AMREF and Rotary Doctors, MSC provides health education through awareness campaigns on HIV/AIDS and trachoma.

Multiplying social capital

This goal has been achieved through the institutionalised community participation process and the involvement of the community in planning and implementing community projects. The training and awareness creation have helped develop the community's competency and its ability to participate in development and governance in the Magadi division and in the Kajiado district. The SWOT structure now manifests wider institutional power and is recognised as the 'legitimate voice' of the Magadi division. Through SWOT, the community is able to monitor

Box 2: Case study of Magadi Multi-Purpose Cooperative Society

This community based cooperative society has a membership of 600 individuals from Magadi division. It was founded in 2004 with the purpose of uplifting the living standards of the Maasai community. Its vision is to equip the community with entrepreneurial and management skills so they can use available local resources sustainably for their own benefit.

The cooperative has benefited from a two-year township cleaning contract in addition to other maintenance and repair jobs within the civil engineering section awarded by Magadi Soda. It also provides unskilled labour and supplies building sand to both Magadi Soda and Larsen and Rourbo, the soda ash plant contractor. The community has now become an alternative source of supplies for Magadi Soda, which was hitherto not the practice. This initiative has helped the company cut down on the cost of supplies and procurement. The cooperative is an alternative source of employment for the local community

In its first year of operation, the cooperative turned a profit and paid out 100% dividends to members. The society plans to diversify and to expand their business ventures within and beyond Magadi division.

Source: Interviews with Multi-Purpose Cooperative chairman and manager, and MSC's purchasing and supplies manager in 2006.

the implementation of various development initiatives and hold actors accountable for failed or inadequate service delivery. The local community acknowledges that the SWOT process has given them a new voice. As a councillor said:

> SWOT has given us a discussion forum, whether fruitful or not fruitful, at least it's important that we air our problems. SWOT has given us a chance to prioritise and solve our problems. We solve those that we are able to and we pend [set aside] others for the future. It has also helped us not to look at Magadi Soda only but we channel our problems to others like the government and NGOs working within the local community.[23]

It seems clear that a palpable sense of community has developed within Magadi division.

Conclusions: Lessons learned

Companies in developing countries operate in complex and unpredictable environments. They must orient their CCI practices and stakeholder relationships accordingly. This case study describes the progression of CCI efforts by Magadi Soda from a paternalistic approach characterised by high transaction costs, community dependency and powerlessness, to the current practice of multi-sector collaboration that seeks to strengthen institutional mechanisms to enable communities and other actors to sustainably tackle development and poverty challenges in their locale.[24] With this change in orientation, there is an increased sense of local ownership

Figure 3: The local community attending a skills development workshop (photo by Judy Muthuri)

and self-reliance. CCI has not only become more effective, it has enhanced Magadi Soda's reputation. The community, various spheres of government and NGOs view Magadi Soda as a committed and reliable development partner. By integrating CCI into its business operations, the company has gained social and political legitimacy and a licence to operate, and has managed environmental uncertainty. Since 2000, it has won the Kenyan *Company of the Year Award* (corporate citizenship category) an impressive seven times.[25]

Corporate–community interaction and multi-sector collaboration is about sharing in the governing process where the actors jointly create rules, norms and structures that govern their relationships. For a successful collaboration, Thomson and Perry propose five dimensions that need attention:[26] *governance* (participation in decision-making), *administration* (institutionalising participatory processes), *autonomy* (reconciling individual and collective interests), *mutuality* (forging mutually beneficial relationships), and *trust and reciprocity* (relationships that generate the norms of social capital). The case study of Magadi Soda's experiences in community development offers a number of tangible illustrations of the importance of these dimensions, as summarised in Table 2 below.

Table 2: The dimensions and elements of company-stakeholder interactions in sustainable community development interventions

Dimensions [a]	Observable community development process elements
Governance	• Participation in decision making. • An ethic of collaborative problem identification, problem solving and opportunity creation. • Diverse and inclusive representation. • Equity of opportunity to participate. • Continuity of participation. • Tolerance of divergent views and respect for others' opinions.
Administration	• Structures and procedures. • Formation and strengthening of local institutions and governing structures. • Established organisational arrangements with clear rules, roles and responsibilities. • Functional communication, reporting structures and monitoring systems.
Autonomy	• Responsibility and accountability. • Ethic of 'collective responsibility'. • Open discussion. • Willingness to share and disclose information. • Continuous assessment of corporate social action and corporate-stakeholder engagement. • Reflective corporate-community interaction that promotes learning.
Mutuality	• Commitment and leadership. • Value creation for all. • Shared leadership and vision of community development. • Developed local leadership skills to champion community development.
Trust and reciprocity	• Building relationship. • Continued willingness to interact. • Honest and open interaction. • Consistency of action. • Continuity of contact.

a   Thomson and Perry, 2005.

The CCI processes depicted in this case study differ from the processes discussed in the stakeholder management literature, which implicitly views communities as 'objects' that need to be managed.[27] Magadi Soda treats communities as partners who play an active role in CCI decision-making and local governance.[28] The company goes beyond the 'affecting-affected' binary that often defines the management of corporate-stakeholder relationships and demonstrates how a company purposefully facilitates participatory governance to achieve sustainable community development.

The case study also demonstrates the significance of the participatory and collaborative approach as a means of evaluating community needs, finding solutions and creating opportunities to address community development. Participatory governance in community development helps determine the 'common good', the distribution of social benefits in the community, and the upholding of community rights and responsibilities in community development. This process addresses ongoing concerns about the 'vulnerability', 'voicelessness' and 'powerlessness' of communities in corporate-community interaction.[29] However, the process is also time consuming and resource intensive. All in all, a collective actor orientation towards building the community's capital must be cultivated in the fight to alleviate poverty and build sustainable livelihoods among deprived communities in Africa.

Editors' reflections and questions

Magadi Soda Company's efforts are exemplary in developing a more inclusive, participatory, and collaborative approach to interacting with and supporting the local community around the company's operations. It is an important example, because all too often protagonists of corporate citizenship see the company as being in the centre of a range of stakeholders, who are to be 'managed' or 'engaged with' in order to respond to social and political expectations. Instead, understanding the role of the company within a broader web or network of relationships is likely to generate more significant and long-lasting benefits, both for the community and the company. The company obviously remains a key role-player, yet the purpose and mechanisms of its interactions with the other role-players in the community are markedly different.

1. What motivated the company management's shift from a paternalistic approach to community engagement, and what is the broader significance of this?

2. The company used a well-established management tool – SWOT analysis – to facilitate a participatory interaction with the community. What are the strengths and weaknesses of this approach, and how does it compare with possible alternative approaches?

3. The structures and procedures of the SWOT committees were carefully defined. What were the benefits of this? To what extent might this design be replicable in other circumstances?

4. The Community Development Plan that was launched in April 2006 was prepared by consultants with the support of the IFC (International Finance Corporation). Does this imply that the prior participatory process implemented by MSC was unnecessary? What is the significance of the Community Development Plan for the company's relationship with its various stakeholders?

5. What are the costs and benefits of the company's collaborative approach? Was it worth it?

6. Considering the fact that it is uncommon for a private sector company to initiate the process of developing a regional development plan, to what extent does this case provide lessons for other contexts, in Africa and elsewhere?

Notes

1 The data for this study was collected between January 2005 and December 2006 using multiple methods such as archival analysis of external reports in the public domain and internal reports and minutes of meetings, interviews with 55 actors, participant observation of 12 MSC-community/

partner meetings, and three focus groups with general community members. The interview data was coded according to emergent themes using NVivo software.

2   B. Manteaw, 'From Tokenism to Social Justice: Rethinking the Bottom Line for Sustainable Community Development', *Community Development Journal* (25 May 2007), 1.

3   U. Idemudia, 'Corporate Partnerships and Community Development in the Nigerian Oil Industry: Strengths and Limitations', United Nations Research Institute for Social Development, Markets, Business and Regulation Programme, Paper No. 2 (2007).

4   The World Bank, *World Development Report 2000/2001: Attacking Poverty* (Washington, D.C.: World Bank, 2001).

5   See P. Tracey, N. Phillips, and H. Haugh, 'Beyond Philanthropy: Community Enterprise as a Basis for Corporate Citizenship', *Journal of Business Ethics,* 58 (2005): 327–44. See also J. Loza 'Business–Community Partnerships: The Case for Community Organization Capacity Building', *Journal of Business Ethics,* 53 (2004): 297–311.

6   Intermediate Technology Development Group, *Community Development Plan: A Report for Magadi Soda Company and International Finance Corporation* (2004).

7   Ministry of Planning and National Development and Central Bureau of Statistics, *Geographic Dimensions of Well-Being in Kenya. Where are the Poor? From Districts to Locations, Volume 1* (Nairobi: Ministry of Planning/Bureau of Statistics, 2003), 8.

8   See *Community Development Plan.*

9   Tata Chemicals Ltd acquired Brunner Mond Group in December 2005.

10 Interview with Purchasing and Supplies manager, MSC.

11 M.F. Hill, *Magadi: The Study of the Magadi Soda Limited* (Birmingham: The Kynoch Press, 1964); see also *Community Development Plan.*

12 In 2006, MSC was among the companies recognised by Kenya's president at the large taxpayers' awards ceremony. MSC: 'Corporate Citizenship Summary Report (2006)'.

13 Interview with councillor, Magadi ward.

14 See *Community Development Plan.*

15 For a comprehensive analysis of this process, see J. Muthuri, W. Chapple, and J. Moon, 'An Integrated Approach to Implementing Community Participation in Corporate Community Involvement: Lessons from Magadi Soda Company in Kenya', *Journal of Business Ethics* (2008, forthcoming; early online edition available).

16 Interview with MSC Board member.

17 The community leaders included the community age-group leaders (*rika*), local chiefs and assistant chiefs (administration), group ranch chairmen, councillors (elected), women leaders, youth leaders and special interest groups (e.g. the disabled).

18 See Hill, *Magadi.*

19 See *Community Development Plan,* 1.

20 For an introduction to sustainable livelihoods approaches in the context of corporate citizenship, see I. Barney, 'Business, Community Development and Sustainable Livelihoods Approaches', *Community Development Journal,* 38, 3 (2003): 255–65.

21 Magadi Soda Sustainability Report (2005), 34, available at www.magadisoda.co.ke

22 See http://www.magadisoda.co.ke/Vision.htm

23 Interview with councillor, Shompole Location.

24 See Tracey *et al.*, 'Beyond Philanthropy'. See also Loza 'Business–Community Partnerships'.

25 See Company of the Year Awards, available at http://www.kim.ac.ke/coya

26 A.M. Thomson and J.L. Perry, 'Collaboration Processes: Inside the Black Box', *Public Administration Review,* 66, 1 (2006): 20–32.

27 See E. Freeman, *Strategic Management: A Stakeholder Approach* (Boston: Pitman, 1984).

28 K. Mellah and G. Wood, 'The Role and Potential of Stakeholders in "Hollow Participation": Conventional Stakeholder Theory and Institutionalist Alternatives', *Business and Society Review,* 108, 2, (2003): 183–203.

29   See R. Hamann, P. Kapelus, D. Sonnenberg, A. Mackenzie and P. Hollesen, 'Local Governance as a Complex System', *Journal of Corporate Citizenship,* 18, 61 (2005), 73. See also P. Newell, 'Citizenship, Accountability and Community: The Limits of the CSR Agenda', *International Affairs,* 81, 2 (2005): 541–57. See also M. Prieto-Carron, M.P. Lund-Thomsen, A. Chan, A. Muro and C. Bhusan, 'Critical Perspectives on CSR and Development: What We Know, What We Don't Know, and What We Need To Know', *International Affairs,* 82, 5 (2006): 977–87.

CASE 9

Malawi Business Action Against Corruption

OONAGH FITZGERALD & JAMES NG'OMBE[1]

Introduction

Sean de Cleene frowned as he typed the last revisions to the speech he would be giving to a Lilongwe merchants' association later in the week. There was nothing he enjoyed more than explaining his initiative, Business Action Against Corruption, and the Business Code of Conduct for Combating Corruption in Malawi (the Code), to potential new partners, yet he was feeling troubled by its slow pace of adoption. He was losing sleep thinking about how to manage the delicate relationship with the government and waiting for the news that the government would be endorsing the Code.

As a founding executive director of the African Institute for Corporate Citizenship (AICC), De Cleene had successfully orchestrated the launch of a major initiative to combat corruption in Malawi by building a multi-stakeholder, cross-sectoral partnership with leaders in business, government and civil society. Although he understood the initiative needed the approbation of government and the engagement of a broad range of stakeholders, De Cleene had been adamant that, at its core, this initiative needed to be a collective *business* initiative: led, motivated and organised by Malawi business. He believed it was critical for the business community to take ownership of the initiative and to start exerting peer pressure to broaden the commitment.

In her office just down the hall, Daisy Kambalame was hurriedly piecing together the materials she would need for yet another international meeting about anti-corruption measures. As she worked, she found herself comparing the enthusiasm she knew from experience would greet her presentation on the international stage with the cautious, polite reaction she would receive when she spoke about the same initiative in Malawi. Still, she knew it was all a matter of time and persistence. By cultivating the support of key donor groups, such as the United States Agency for International Development (USAID), and international organisations, such as the United Nations Global Compact (UNGC), she knew she was bolstering the legitimacy of Business Action Against Corruption with her own government and with the big multinationals present in the country. She would describe how, under leadership from the private sector, a cross-societal coalition called the Malawi Leaders' Forum, involving representatives from government, private business, civil society, donor agencies and the media, was tackling corruption and implementing the 10th Principle of the UNGC in Malawi. Once these key supporters and a few major local companies were brought aboard, the rest of the Malawi business community could be persuaded to sign on to the Code.

Before closing down her computer Kambalame typed out a quick email response to the Canadian researcher studying their initiative:

> One of the issues that I have found most challenging but in the end helped in influencing the progress that we have made is the issue of creating partnerships. I think the success of implementing the principles will also be dependent on understanding some of the issues that arise in establishing partnerships.

Impetus for reform

Corruption had been overwhelming Malawi in recent years, to the extent that international and foreign donors and businesses were increasingly reluctant to invest in this small southern African country, leaving citizens to face a bleak and impoverished future.[2] All sectors of society had come to the realisation that non-action in the face of widespread corruption was not an option. Public and private sectors and civil society shared a common desire to position and enable Malawi to achieve its United Nations (UN) Millennium Development Goals by improving the stability, reliability and transparency of its investment climate.

The negative effects of corruption were readily apparent, but few were willing to abstain from corrupt practices, while others continued to reap personal gain from such involvement. Multi-stakeholder negotiations, which sought to bind *all* participants to collective action to eliminate corruption, seemed to provide a possible means of systematic and concerted attack on the problem. Thus, De Cleene and Kambalame of the AICC set about creating a cross-societal coalition, involving government, private business, civil society, donor agencies and the media, to tackle the corruption problem and implement the 10th Principle of the UNGC in Malawi.[3]

2005: Preparing to take collective action

In setting out to tackle a systemic, country-wide issue such as corruption, through consensual negotiation, De Cleene and Kambalame had realised they might face many difficulties. It would not be easy to reconcile legal formalities – including specific legal prohibitions, legal rights and litigation positions – with the need for cooperation, compliance discussion and informal information exchange to better understand the problem. It would take skill and patience to de-escalate self-righteous, winner-take-all attitudes, combativeness and defensiveness. It would not be easy to reconcile past, current and future business and legal risks when long-entrenched, lax business practices were being replaced by strict codes of conduct. It would be a challenge to determine how to cooperate with competitors in ethical partnerships without losing a competitive position; and to achieve the right balance between procedural perfection and common-sense solutions that could be readily implemented and applied; and it would be critical to ensure that participants were adequately trained to apply the new rules.

Both De Cleene and Kambalame also anticipated difficulties in managing political pressures and political opportunities, and in maintaining momentum over the long term. Because major instances of corruption often involved public procurement, it was almost inevitable that the fight against corruption would become politicised.[4] With the president's anti-corruption campaign being implicated in his falling out with his former party, his actions on corruption were already being challenged by his opponents as politically motivated. It would be important for De Cleene and Kambalame to keep moving forward on several fronts, building credibility and overcoming whatever setbacks might occur.

Because so many interests were at stake and there were so many risks to be faced, it was critical to develop an effective multi-stakeholder negotiation process to break the impasse and create cross-societal coalitions to find solutions that would produce system-wide reform. Such a process would allow shared ownership of the anti-corruption issue so that the initiative would not depend on the fortunes of any one person or any one sector of society but would be sustained by the deeds of many champions across Malawian society.

Harnessing a commitment to the collective interest would be necessary to overcome or at least *re-frame* self-interest in maintaining the status quo:

> Although business managers increasingly recognize that corruption is a serious business challenge, they may not always accept that they have a responsibility and key role in changing practices that have become endemic. The dilemma is to balance doing what is right against putting business operations at a competitive disadvantage ... business managers may perceive that promoting a change in accepted local business practices could jeopardise their business interests. It is often relatively easy to get business managers to acknowledge that it would be beneficial to both them and their competitors if corruption were eliminated. What is more difficult is for them to take the first steps to act together in combating corruption, for fear of losing out to each other.[5]

'Corruption is by its very nature a team sport', characterised by inappropriate influences originating from the private sector and undue benefits accruing to members of the public sector.[6] Although on one level the solution to corruption is as easy as saying 'no', this option was not workable unless people could be assured that others would also say 'no', and support each other in a collective effort to put an end to corruption. In other words, De Cleene and Kambalame recognised that business men and women might tend to view 'business as usual' as their best alternative to a negotiated agreement (or BATNA).[7] They might see the status quo as being *better and easier* than the difficult negotiating and trust-building required for collective action against corruption.

Nonetheless, it was also clear that collective approaches were well-suited to tackling corruption and improving business standards:[8]

> In practice, collective action with other companies offers an effective way to create a level playing field on which to compete and increases the impact on local business practices beyond the capacity of any one company. Knowing that other companies in your

sector or location are committed to good practice helps to build mutual confidence and the sustainability of changes in behaviour.[9]

De Cleene understood both that competing businesses shared a common interest in improving their business environment and that by working together they would have a greater impact in reducing corruption in their business sector. Acting together, companies could tackle locally relevant issues, set realisable targets and more effectively integrate anti-corruption policies and codes into their own operations and their supply and distribution chains. He was aware that Transparency International, a non-governmental organisation that was a leader in fighting corruption, had been using a coalition-building approach to bring together relevant actors to combat corruption, including representatives from government, business, academia and the professions, the media and the diversity of civil society organisations. Indeed, a growing inventory of models and best practices was available to enrich implementation of the initial action plan.[10]

From her international meetings, Kambalame was familiar with the Nigerian Convention on Business Integrity (the Convention), which relied on consensual negotiation processes to combat corruption. It was a voluntary programme, involving pledge-making by public and private sector participants, recognition and modelling of good conduct, and peer pressure through a mutual accountability network. The Convention was a declaration against corrupt business practices; it was not a legal document but represented a moral agreement between consenting parties. Its primary purpose was to encourage the establishment of a minimum standard for business integrity in Nigeria. Under the rules of the Convention, a whistleblower was granted anonymity and could present a complaint to a core group of Convention members who would then approach the company in question and ask it to appoint a senior-level ethics counsellor to work through the issue with them and to monitor compliance.

> It takes time to build confidence amongst groups of business leaders who may initially be sceptical about what can be achieved and concerned at the implications of working with competitors and others outside their normal set of relationships. Focusing on issues that have important current impacts on business and the community and then conducting a series of individual and group meetings to explore the opportunities and barriers to cooperation are essential steps leading to the formalisation of any initiative. These steps take time, but it is time well spent. Having someone who has previously been a business executive to act as a coordinator may give participants the confidence required to ensure that a process gains momentum.[11]

2005: The Malawi Leaders' Forum

The integrative negotiation process was started in earnest when De Cleene and Kambalame, through the AICC's Africa Corporate Sustainability Forum, facilitated a series of business-sponsored roundtable discussions, in partnership with the Malawi UN Global Compact. At each event, 20 to 30 leaders from business, government and civil society discussed issues related to the UNGC and the role of business in progressing towards achieving the Millennium Development Goals.

The first of these round-table discussions was held in January 2005, and focused on the newly introduced 10th Principle on Corruption.[12] Until then, the private sector had not been active in the fight against corruption despite the government's publicly declared intention in this respect, but the January 2005 meeting produced an agreement to hold a one-day Leaders' Forum on Building Alliances to Eliminate Corruption. The forum brought together leaders from government, the business sector, civil society, the media and donor organisations, and was wholly funded by private sector organisations. Having private companies fund the forum was strategically significant because experience suggested that financial contributors were 'always more likely to remain engaged, take a project seriously and demand practical results'.[13]

Experience also demonstrated that 'the *political will* to reduce corruption and to revive honesty and integrity in Government contracting is a *sine qua non* for success'.[14] Thus, it was auspicious that the president of Malawi, Bingu Wa Mutharika, opened the event, describing corruption as a major burden to society, substantially eroding the economic resources otherwise available for ensuring a country's sustainable development, and reiterating his commitment to fighting corruption. He commended the private sector for holding the event and for the active participation of a large number of company chief executive officers (CEOs), and acknowledged the support of the international donor community in the fight against corruption. Pledging his assistance, the president encouraged participants to work actively with partners from government and the broader civil society to build powerful alliances to effectively eliminate corruption in the country. The president thus helped to set the stage for a successful negotiation by publicly committing to support a collective effort, and signalling to the nation that a major societal shift was taking place.

The other keynote speakers were also chosen as strong representatives of their respective constituencies, in anticipation of developing good channels of communication. The patron of the Malawi Global Compact, Matthews Chikaonda, CEO of Press Corporation, highlighted the current government's leadership and the willingness of business to partner with government on this issue and urged concerted action to combat corruption.[15] Victor Banda, deputy director of the Anti-Corruption Bureau (ACB), and Ishmael Wadi, director of public prosecution, explained the prosecution process and the existing rules and systems designed to hold perpetrators of corruption accountable. They emphasised that the private sector could contribute to their efforts by providing information about corrupt practices in government procurement. Roderick Phiri, CEO of SDV and a member of the Malawi Global Compact Network, urged government and business leaders to form productive alliances and act as strong role models in combating corruption.[16] Fred Mzomwa, deputy director of public procurement (DPP), described how the 2003 Procurement Act decentralised government procurement to internal procurement committees for greater efficiency; but with the lack of capacity to support the new process, the DPP needed help from the private sector to identify procurement irregularities.[17] The minister for trade and private sector development, Martin Kansichi, spoke of the destructive effects of corruption on property rights, the rule of law and investment, and urged ongoing multi-sectoral cooperation to bring about a comprehensive change in societal attitudes to corruption.

The issues identified at the Leaders' Forum were wide-ranging, covering a variety of perspectives and identifying many critical needs: training and consciousness-raising for all employees in government and the private sector; a public communications campaign with announced time-bound commitments; the strengthening of professional independence and professional discipline in the legal and judicial fields; a business-to-business peer review; the joint development of common standards and guidelines for the public and private sectors; the establishment of an independent body to devise incentives, monitor systems and promote best practices; learning from anti-corruption models successfully implemented elsewhere; private-sector support for the ACB; and government targeting of bureaucratic bottlenecks that engender corrupt practice.

After discussion of the current challenges involved in fighting corruption, participants at the Leaders' Forum crafted a framework agreement, a common text to which all provided input, as *an initial action plan* for progressing towards the elimination of corruption, with the following key recommendations:

- That an independent task force be established, which would drive the action plan forward;

- That existing codes be reviewed and there be an adoption or development of a code of conduct for the private sector and state enterprise in Malawi to promote a zero-tolerance approach to corruption;

- That an independent body be formed that would build value around, or incentivise, a zero-tolerance policy on corruption – particularly as it related to the supply chain of larger companies, state enterprise and government procurement. This would include the application of a scorecard or rating model that companies would agree to respect in terms of obtaining or providing goods or services. The Nigerian Convention on Corruption model was highlighted as a potential model to be followed if it was viewed to be appropriate in the Malawian context;

- That there be a recognition of the need to strengthen corporate governance practices of both private and public sector businesses in Malawi;

- That a system be developed to publicise all major procurement contracts and transparent processes for deciding on successful bids;

- That a government working group be formed to highlight inefficiencies in the system that create loopholes for engaging in corrupt practices, and that ways be devised to eliminate such inefficiencies;

- That government should look to ratify the AU Convention on Corruption; and

- That donors should provide greater support for multi-sector alliance building initiatives that aim to eliminate corruption in the country.[18]

Consensual negotiation involving the broad range of stakeholders provided a methodology for discovering common interests, harnessing shared commitment, and building and maintaining the required anti-corruption infrastructure. Because all parties depended on each other for the successful eradication of corruption, they needed to negotiate in a way that maximised the effectiveness of each party by developing the agenda collaboratively to ensure all could prepare adequately. There was a need for shared information to achieve a common understanding of the issues. In this way they could work together to achieve practical solutions that all sides could support, and would create a web of interconnected commitments to ensure all sides were involved in and accountable for implementation.[19] At the same time, it was important to guard against the multi-stakeholder process becoming so large and unwieldy that it was incapable of taking decisive action.

The facilitator role played by De Cleene and aided by Kambalame was particularly helpful both in encouraging dialogue between sectors of Malawi society and in urging business to commit to immediate and purposeful action towards eliminating corruption. Although they had expected to stay deeply involved in the initiative as it evolved, neither had envisaged having to coordinate the anti-corruption initiative for the long term. In the days following the Leaders' Forum, once the initial glow of their success had dimmed, they began to realise they would have little choice but to assume this role at least for a while longer. Who else was there to coordinate and drive the refinement of undertakings and the implementation of action plan commitments for the foreseeable future?

2006: Reviewing progress after 15 months

It was clear to the Malawi Business Action Against Corruption task force from the outset that it would be a long-term project, requiring sustained engagement of the various sectors of Malawian society. De Cleene and Kambalame thus were left with the daunting task of channelling the moment of shared commitment of the Leaders' Forum into a longer-term implementation plan. With little in the way of human or financial resources to support the initiative, they began by setting up a working group of business, government and NGO representatives to draft a code of business conduct.

The drafting of the Code was achieved through the work of a multi-stakeholder Steering Committee[20] and a Task Force.[21] The purpose of this drafting exercise was to develop a Code of Conduct to be observed by institutions, organisations and companies operating in Malawi to ensure that they did not engage in corrupt practices. Adoption of the Code by an organisation would be a strategic decision, with the specific design and implementation being influenced by the organisation's own needs and objectives, the products or services it provided, the processes employed, and its size and structure. It was intended that the Code be used by internal and external parties to assess the organisation's performance in combating corruption. By September 2006, the Business Code of Conduct for Combating Corruption in Malawi had been completed (see Document 1) and was awaiting approval and adoption by the government of Malawi, as well as widespread adoption and implementation by Malawian businesses and other organisations.

In September 2006, independent researchers commissioned by the UNGC conducted a survey of members of the Steering Committee and Task Force to gather their views on the progress of the anti-corruption initiative. The survey posed questions about developments in implementing the initiative's goals and action plan to ascertain whether the multi-stakeholder process was bringing about cross-societal progress in fighting corruption. The survey results (see Document 2) and the researchers' conclusions and recommendations were sent to De Cleene and Kambalame in late October. The results of the survey were overwhelmingly positive, confirming that there was a continuing shared commitment by government, the business sector and civil society to work together to eradicate corruption. Respondents seemed to feel that development of the core document, the Business Code of Conduct, had been an appropriate first major project and that it had gone well, although important questions about the Code's future were still open to debate. Many thought that progress had been slow and acknowledged the difficulty in contributing effectively to the initiative while balancing their other work pressures.

Respondents recognised that the next big challenge would be obtaining widespread adoption and implementation of the Code. They had many ideas about how to publicise the Code and ensure buy-in. Responses indicating lack of knowledge about what other participants were doing suggested that ongoing communication between the various engaged sectors of society – business corporations, government agencies, the media and civil society – could be enhanced. Some responses urged greater publicity, raising the possibility of expanding the multi-stakeholder negotiation process beyond business, government and civil society leaders to engage a broader swath of Malawian society. Public consultation would probably be useful to raise awareness and increase nationwide support for the initiative, although care would need to be taken to keep the multi-stakeholder negotiation process manageable and effective.

Respondents' uncertainty about the infrastructure of the anti-corruption initiative and the specifics of its future work plan suggested that this might be a good time for the leaders to regroup, map out the next steps and set up the appropriate structures for the next phases of implementation. This strategy would be likely to involve establishing an independent agency to promote the Code and help measure compliance with it. Funding for such an agency would also have to be negotiated.

The researchers noted that the Malawi Leaders' Forum provided an excellent illustration of the use of a consensual approach in resolving a public crisis, although it was still early days to judge whether it would achieve its laudable objective of eradicating corruption.[22] For an issue of such magnitude and complexity, the commitment to the consensual negotiation process had to be long term. The round-table discussions, the Leaders' Forum and even the development of an initial action plan were only the beginning, with extensive mutual commitments being forged, long-term relationships deepening, and substantial investment in implementation expected to continue into the foreseeable future.

One year later, the project's progress boded well for the longer term survival of the initiative: a Business Code of Conduct had successfully been crafted to guide all sectors, and all the participants were still deeply committed to the goals of the initiative. The Malawi Leaders' Forum had inspired a nation to action;[23] its challenge now was not to lose momentum for the great task still ahead. By staying true to the principles of multi-stakeholder negotiation processes, this initiative could nurture ongoing involvement and participation, and continue to broaden the reach and deepen the roots of the anti-corruption movement in Malawi. A final observation by the researchers was that periodic surveying of participants in the initiative over the longer term might be a useful way to verify that the initiative continued on track, as well as to facilitate mid-course corrections if needed.

The challenge ahead

De Cleene and Kambalame were relieved by the survey results, which they had anticipated with some trepidation. They understood that it was too soon to say with certainty that the anti-corruption initiative was having an enduring impact locally, in civil society, at the company level, at the professional association level and within government. Nonetheless, they were heartened to see that participants in the initiative felt that although much remained to be done, Malawi had never been closer to coming to grips with the challenge of corruption. The UNGC identified three key conditions for successfully combating corruption:

> High level commitment from the most senior echelons of Government; investment in the building of corruption prevention infrastructure; implementation and management of such infrastructure with the aim of affecting ethical culture change.[24]

De Cleene and Kambalame knew that by creating a broad-based anti-corruption coalition they had ensured that these conditions were beginning to take hold in Malawi. It was gratifying that participants felt the initiative was on the right track and recognised that successful completion of the Code was a key early deliverable for the initiative.

The survey also raised some difficult questions about enlargement, public involvement and creation of a coordination infrastructure – areas that De Cleene and Kambalame had already sensed needed to be addressed. Although they were pleased that the Code was gradually becoming known and beginning to be accepted, they were also acutely aware both that much of the action plan remained to be accomplished and that the initiative urgently needed more resources, including a clear structure for coordinating and driving the initiative.

The action plan had called for the creation of an independent body that would promote, support and provide peer pressure for a zero-tolerance policy on corruption in big business, state enterprise and government procurement. De Cleene believed it was time to establish this independent body or risk losing significant momentum. The difficulty would be to determine how to structure the independent body, fund it and ensure its long-term leadership and survival. He knew who the key players were – in civil society, the business community, the media, the government and the legal profession – but wondered whether he could persuade them to commit to such a long-term project. He also worried that short-term political pressures or business interests might hijack a long-term national plan. He wondered what each of his contacts in business, the media, government, the NGO and donor communities would be prepared to contribute to this initiative, and what they would do to ensure it would be a success both for their own organisation and for Malawi.

De Cleene and Kambalame had discussed these questions at length, but they had not reached firm conclusions on how structure might help ensure participants' ongoing commitment to the initiative. With positive survey results behind them, however, they now felt confident they would have good support from their partners in finding the right solutions to these issues. Still, De Cleene couldn't help feeling some anxiety as he waited to hear whether the government would endorse the Code. Was it time, he wondered, to call once more on his most powerful allies to advocate for the Code's adoption?

Document 1: Excerpts from the Business Code of Conduct for Combating Corruption in Malawi (August 2006)

INTRODUCTION

The Business Code of Conduct for Combating Corruption in Malawi has been developed by a multisector steering committee that forms part of a wider Malawi Business Action Against Corruption. The Code has been developed, through private sector initiative, as a tool to assist organisations to develop effective actions in combating corruption in all its forms.

SCOPE

General

This code provides a framework for good business practices and risk management strategies for countering corruption. It is aimed at assisting organisations to:

   (i)   eliminate corrupt practices;

  (ii)   demonstrate their commitment to countering corruption; and

 (iii)   make a positive contribution to improving business standards.

DEFINITIONS

Corrupt practices include: bribery, fraud, theft, abuse of position or authority, embezzlement, extortion, influence peddling; facilitation payments.

   (i)   Bribery: promising, offering, giving or soliciting of any benefit in cash or in kind that improperly affects the actions or decisions of any person.

  (ii)   Fraud: false representation or concealment of material facts in order to part with something of value.

 (iii)   Abuse of position or authority: Use of one's vested authority to improperly benefit oneself or an entity or another person.

 (iv)   Embezzlement: This involves theft of resources by persons entrusted with the authority and control of such resources.

  (v)   Extortion: This involves coercing a person or entity to provide a benefit to himself, another person or an entity in exchange for acting (or not acting) in a particular manner.

 (vi)   Influence peddling: The practice of using one's influence with persons in authority to obtain favours or preferential treatment for another, usually in return for payment.

(vii)   Facilitation payment: These are small payments made to secure or expedite the performance of a routine or necessary action to which the payer the facilitation payment has legal or other entitlement. Also called 'facilitating', 'speed' or 'grease'.

CORRUPT PRACTICES

Corrupt practices include:

(a)   Behaviour that involves any of the following: bribery, fraud, theft, misuse of position or authority, embezzlement, extortion, influence peddling or the providing of facilitation payments;

(b)   The offering, giving, receiving, obtaining or soliciting of any advantage to influence the action of any public officer or any official or any other person in the discharge of the duties of that public officer, official or other person;

(c)   The offering, giving, acceptance or soliciting of a bribe in any form or the use of other routes or channels for the benefit of an employee or that of the employee's family, friends, associates or acquaintances;

(d) The abuse of entrusted power for private gain or any conduct or behaviour in relation to persons entrusted with responsibilities which violates their duties and which is aimed at obtaining undue advantage of any kind for themselves or for others;

(e) The unauthorised dissemination or solicitation of confidential or restricted information for reward.

PRINCIPLES FOR COMBATING CORRUPTION

- The enterprise should prohibit corrupt practices in any form whether direct or indirect.
- The enterprise should commit to the fundamental values of integrity, transparency and accountability.
- The enterprise should aim to create and maintain a trust-based and inclusive internal culture in which corruption is not tolerated.
- The enterprise shall commit to implementation of a programme to counter corruption.

REQUIREMENTS

- Development of a programme for combating corruption.
- An organisation, institution or company should develop a programme reflecting its size, business sector, potential risks and locations of operation, which should, clearly and in reasonable detail, articulate values, policies and procedures to be used to prevent corruption from occurring in all activities under its effective control.

The programme should be consistent with all laws relevant to countering corruption in all the jurisdictions in which the organisation or company operates.

Standards of conduct

Each organisation, institution or company should be committed to following practices as they relate to corrupt practices, and should put measures in place to:

- prohibit corrupt practices by any employee, agent, or any other person under the employment or authority of the enterprise;
- make corruption by an employee subject to severe disciplinary measures;
- establish a system for the recruitment of employees who are of high integrity, and systems for promotion and termination that are not arbitrary but based on fairness, openness, ability and performance;
- provide adequate safeguards to prevent abuse of powers by those engaged in the anti-corruption system and to minimise unnecessary infringements of individual rights;
- establish systems for the procurement of goods and services that are based on openness, efficiency, equity and certainty of the rules to be applied and that seek the best value for money;
- train its employees to understand and practice honest, ethical and appropriate behaviour, to avoid conflicts of interest, and to report acts of corruption;
- require the reporting of all known instances of corruption to the relevant authorities;
- require public disclosure of all its political or charitable contributions, or sponsorships;
- protect employees from repercussions for reporting corruption.

Specific programme requirements

In developing the programme for countering corruption, an organisation, institution or company should analyse which specific areas pose the greatest risk from corruption. The programme should address the most prevalent forms of corruption relevant to the organisation, institution or company, but to a minimum should cover the following areas:

Bribes

- The organisation, institution or company should prohibit the offer or acceptance of a bribe in any form or the use of other routes or channels to provide improper benefits to customers, agents, contractors, suppliers or employees of any such party or government officials.
- The organisation, institution or company should prohibit an employee from arranging or accepting a bribe from customers, agents, contractors, suppliers, or employees of any such party or from government officials, for the employee's benefit or that of the employee's family, friends, associates or acquaintances.

Political contributions

- The organisation, institution or company, its employees or agents should not make direct or indirect contributions to political parties, organisations or individuals engaged in politics, as a way of obtaining advantage in business transactions.
- The organisation, institution or company should publicly disclose all its political contributions.

Charitable contributions and sponsorships

- The organisation, institution or company should ensure that charitable contributions and sponsorships are not being used as a subterfuge for corruption.
- The organisation, institution or company should publicly disclose all its charitable contributions or sponsorships.

Facilitation payments

- Recognising that facilitation payments are a form of bribery, the organisation, institution or company should work to identify and eliminate them. Facilitation payments are payments made to secure or expedite the performance of a routine or necessary action to which the payer of the facilitation payment has legal or other entitlement.

Gifts, hospitality and expenses

- The organisation, institution or company needs to have a publicly available policy on what constitutes appropriate behaviour in relation to gifts, hospitality and expenses. This policy should prohibit the offer or receipt of gifts, hospitality or expenses whenever such arrangements could affect the outcome of business transactions and are not reasonable and bona fide expenditures.

IMPLEMENTATION REQUIREMENTS

Monitoring and review

- Management of the enterprise should monitor the programme and periodically review the programme's suitability, adequacy and effectiveness and implement improvements as appropriate. They should periodically report to the Board of Directors or shareholders, or any such appropriate body, the results of the programme review.
- The Board of Directors, shareholders, or any such appropriate body should make an independent assessment of the organisation, institution or company regarding the adequacy of the programme and make its recommendations.

CRITERIA FOR COMPLIANCE

Organisations wishing to demonstrate their compliance to the requirements of this code shall be voluntarily audited and rated on the level of compliance to this code. Such a rating system is currently being developed in Malawi and ratings will be determined by identifying process, mechanisms and practices within the organisation that enable it to comply with the requirements of the code and ensure that corrupt practices, as far as can be ascertained, are not taking place within the organisation.

Document 2:   Consolidated results of the survey of participants in the Malawi Business Action Against Corruption Task Force

In-person interviews were conducted and documented by an independent research team.[25] Not all organisations contacted responded, and not all those that did respond answered every question. The following is a consolidation of the responses received, without attribution or weighting of specific comments. The accuracy of the content of statements made by respondents was not verified. The statements are reproduced in summary form here to indicate participants' personal impressions of the initiative. Given the small sample size and nature of the questionnaire, the consolidated results are offered not as statistically significant indicators of opinion in Malawi but as informed impressions of the anti-corruption initiative at this particular point in time (October 2006). As such, the consolidated results provide some insights into the current state of the initiative as well as suggestions that may help guide it in the future.

Participants were asked to what extent their organisation had been involved in the initiative recently undertaken by the business community in the fight against corruption in Malawi. The trend of responses was to cite the Business Leaders' Forum and the involvement of most respondents in the Task Force in developing the Business Code of Conduct. In addition, two multinational companies cited their own 'risk management' programmes targeting corruption eradication within their companies through anti-fraud policies and anonymous tip-offs.

The survey asked participants what input or assistance they had provided. Some respondents who had been involved in the Task Force indicated they had contributed toward the initiative by alerting their staff to the need to be vigilant against corrupt practices. One respondent mentioned contributing to the direction, focus and mobilisation of members of the Task Force. Government participants had kept the Task Force up to date on developments within government in the fight against corruption. Additionally, comments were made on the draft Code of Conduct now awaiting adoption by the government. One respondent cited a document which had been sourced from Sweden (the Swedish International Development Cooperation Agency) which had proved useful in drafting of the Code of Conduct in reader-friendly language.

Participants were asked for their opinion as to what were the major challenges facing the initiative. The challenges cited in response were: the fact that corruption was rampant and entrenched, such that reversal would be an uphill task; the lack of punitive measures targeting offenders; the fact that participation is voluntary; integrating all sectors in the initiative and having the general business sector accept the outcome of the initiative; having the government endorse the Code of Conduct; and having a Business Conduct rating system accepted and enforced; and meeting the high expectations of Malawian society.

They were asked what in their opinion are the strengths and weaknesses of the initiative. Strengths that were mentioned by respondents were: the President's presence at the inaugural Leaders' Forum and his government's commitment to the initiative, coupled with high level support from business leaders; the enthusiasm and cooperation of members of the Task Force (noted by several respondents); that some in the private sector were already championing the cause by setting up anti-corruption systems without waiting for the results of the Task Force Code; and that there was broad support and no negativity towards the initiative. The weaknesses that respondents identified were the following: lack of expertise in the anti-corruption drive among the members of Task Force; corruption entrenched in the country (one respondent mentioned that the best intentions of the Leaders' Forum are hampered by continued corruption in high office, poor support from the judiciary, difficulty in prosecuting cases, and delays in amending laws); there are no punitive measures for non-compliance; progress towards the adoption of the Code is slow; members of the Task Force are committed to other equally pressing engagements and thus are unable to provide sufficient support and input to the initiative; and the need for more resources so as to be able to push the initiative forward. When asked about the constraints facing the initiative, respondents provided similar answers to the preceding question. An additional constraint that was identified was the lack of drafting expertise for the Code project. Another commented that there was no indication of negativity towards the initiative.

The questionnaire asked how participants hoped to help further the initiative. Some respondents answered that they would lead by example, by introducing zero-tolerance of corruption in their respective organisations and introducing senior managers to the initiative. Respondents uniformly expressed willingness and a desire to continue to assist in the implementation stage, although some noted that there were other demands on their time. Asked if the Malawi anti-corruption initiative was something they would recommend to be replicated elsewhere in the world, respondents were unanimous in saying they would. One multinational business representative said they would push for a similar approach in other countries in which they do business.

Participants were asked whether the preliminary action plan developed at the Leaders' Forum had been broken down into manageable tasks, and if so, whether there was now a detailed action plan with responsibilities assigned, timeliness, reporting and accountability. Responses varied, with some respondents saying 'no', others saying 'yes', or 'yes but it is taking time because everyone involved is busy'. Respondents clearly saw the drafting of the Business Code of Conduct as a key step in implementing the action plan. One respondent suggested that the next course of action could only be determined after the Code had been accepted and adopted by the government. Another suggested that the Code should be launched publicly to encourage companies to sign on. Other respondents commented that the Code has not been given enough publicity; that companies now need to sign on to the Code and implement it in their organisations; and that the Code will need some refinement as adoption and implementation proceed and that publicising it in the media would be useful to generate informed discussion.

The survey asked whether there is a coordinated accountability mechanism to ensure all parties live up to their commitments. Respondents answered that so far the members of the Task Force have remained on course, coordinating well and demonstrating their ongoing commitment. It was noted that it will take committed leadership to drive the initiative forward. Several respondents observed that individually some organisations have designed and implemented their own anti-corruption programmes as part of risk management.

Respondents were asked whether there is a leaders' coalition responsible for ensuring that the integrative negotiations continue, and stay on track over the long term. The responses varied with some saying 'yes, the leaders were chosen at the launch of the Forum', and others saying 'no' or 'not yet'. One respondent questioned whether the Task Force was the right vehicle to carry the message and deliver the anti-corruption initiative. Another said the future role of the Task Force had not yet been decided, beyond completing the drafting of the Business Code of Conduct. A government respondent noted the crucial role played by the African Institute for Corporate Citizenship in this initiative. A subject of some discussion at the Leaders' Forum was the creation of an independent advisory body. Participants were asked whether such an independent advisory body had been more fully defined and established and, if so, what is the membership and what are its functions. Respondents noted that this idea had not yet been acted upon. The Task Force had been mandated to draw up the Business Code and recommend it for adoption both to the Leaders' Forum and the government. Most respondents were of the view that this independent body had not yet been established and that the initiative was still looking at other comparative models and working on designing the way forward.

The questionnaire asked whether international organisations, donor organisations and foreign governments are involved effectively to support the anti-corruption effort. One respondent thought that, so far, the initiative was free of government's (financial) support – and wondered whether it would lose its independence if government funded the initiative. Another respondent noted government had provided some financial support for the initiative. Another thought the donor community was a little distant from the initiative and could do more by offering debt relief, to allow government to pay employees adequately and thereby prevent corrupt practices. It was mentioned that USAID, UNDP, SIDA-Norad, and the World Bank are currently assisting the Office of the Director of Public Procurement. Another respondent commented that the donor community was interested in, indeed keen about, the anti-corruption initiative, and that there was a possibility of obtaining funding from them if the government endorsed the Code of Conduct.

Participants were asked what steps are being taken to entrench change, so that the initiative will survive changes of leadership in various organizations and sectors. One respondent thought that this was an issue that had not yet been decided on. Another respondent felt that not enough had been done within his organisation: managers were aware of the anti-corruption initiative, but more could be done to implement anti-corruption measures. Some respondents commented that the initiative was only slowly taking root but that corrupt practices were rampant (corruption in family businesses and statutory bodies offering essential services such as water, electricity and telephones was mentioned by one respondent). Respondents also observed that civil society groups are forming to help create awareness and initiate action and that there was hope that practices in government institutions would be improving.

The survey asked whether best practices from other contexts such as integrity pacts or business integrity conventions have been adopted and, if so, whether they work well in these contexts. Respondents mentioned that the Code of Conduct had been developed with reference to existing codes and best practices from Malawi, Africa and the international community. A government respondent said he was not aware of related developments in the private sector. It was suggested by one respondent that the starting point for combating corruption in business was the need for effective risk management. Respondents cited three examples where local programmes have been developed without waiting for the Code to be launched, and which were going well: the SIDA (Swedish International Development Cooperation Agency) Anti-corruption Programme; the Unilever Anti-corruption Programme; and Illovo Risk Management (Illovo's anonymous tip-off system for employees, customers and suppliers, administered by Deloitte-Touche).

The questionnaire noted that one key problem identified at the Leaders' Forum was weak capacity in government and asked whether the causes of this problem had been identified. Some respondents considered that the problems had been identified and were being addressed by the various government organs such as the Anti-Corruption Bureau; while others thought the problems were still being identified. Some respondents remarked that there had been some noticeable efforts but that it would take time for them to have an impact. It was noted that the government has assisted the initiative up to this point, but could do more, as could the Malawi business sector. One respondent expressed concern that the courts might not be helpful in fighting corruption.

This question continued by asking whether any of six listed points were causes of lack of capacity in government: lack of adequate training; inadequate salaries; lack of a code of ethics; defects in the reward systems; and lack of independence of public servants. Responses varied considerably. Some respondents had difficulty identifying the causes, but each of the listed points was identified by at least one respondent as an underlying problem. A further question asked whether any steps have been taken to address the problems noted above. The answers varied. A government respondent indicated that measures were being taken to address identified weaknesses in training, ethics codes and independence of public servants; private sector respondents were less aware of these developments. All respondents thought the programme would need time to work.

The survey asked whether the initiative against corruption was being effectively publicised and, if so, who was responsible for the production and management of the campaign. The response was negative, with several respondents suggesting that more could be done to publicise the Code in the media, get public attention and engage the public, attract comments and demonstrate transparency. There was also a question as to whether there were anti-corruption train-the-trainer programmes for the work place and, if so, whether these programmes were supported by business or other sectors. The response was that they do not exist yet, but that this would probably be part of supporting implementation of the Code. It was also noted that some businesses have shown leadership by adopting and supporting anti-corruption practices in their operations.

A further question asked whether there were sanctions against corruption built into contracts and, if so, whether they were enforceable. A respondent commented that in companies that have adopted anti-corruption codes enforcement is through management commitment and good business management practices, and these are working well. There was also a question as to whether the prosecution function was independent and insulated from the possibility of political influence. Some respondents said 'yes', others said 'no', with one respondent mentioning the Kadwa case, concerns about the DPP and ACB, and risk of political interference. Finally, there was a question as to what steps are being taken to target the next generation through ethics training for teachers so they can teach ethics in schools. Responses suggested that education in support of the anti-corruption initiative was a good idea, to be considered seriously. One respondent thought that employees who sign the Business Code of Conduct would be likely to pass it on to the next generation. Another commented that the Business Code needs more publicity.

Editors' reflections and questions

1. Though most would agree that corruption is detrimental to sustainable development, there are also those who believe that many anti-corruption initiatives are imposing Western values and structures on indigenous economies and cultures. This case study alludes to the deep-seated nature of corruption in economic, social, and cultural systems. Without implying that this was or is the case in Malawi, some places are characterised by bureaucracies in which officials' pay is especially low in the expectation that they will be given 'facilitation payments' or other benefits by applicants. In such contexts, kickbacks are considered a legitimate and necessary component of business transactions, so any anti-corruption initiative would need to contribute to broad agreement on how to define and approach corruption. It would then need to contribute to changing mindsets, as well as deep-seated habits and administrative processes. What are the implications of such possible challenges to the initiation and facilitation of a cross-sector partnership like the one described in this case study?

2. This case study poignantly describes corruption as a 'team sport' and the concomitant need for a collaborative approach to combating corruption. It mentions that companies are reluctant to take a stand against corruption because of the competitive disadvantage they may suffer as a result. This leads to a particular form of 'collaborative advantage' that is only upheld if a minimum proportion of participants adhere to the agreements reached. In turn, this means that all participants must be sufficiently motivated to comply in the interests of long-term, shared benefit, even if this may be contrary to their short term interests. What kind of measures could contribute to establishing and maintaining this kind of motivation, and to what extent were they implemented in the Malawi example?

3. Consider the role of the roundtable discussions that eventually led to the Summit – these are likely to have made an important contribution to building trust between some of the key role-players and commitment to the process. What do these relatively informal round-table discussions say about the style of the facilitation? And is it conceivable that these may only have been possible due to the small size of the Malawi economy? To what extent might the strengths of the partnering process in Malawi be replicated in other countries or circumstances?

4. The case study ends at a vital stage in the process, with the anti-corruption code still not endorsed by the government and lingering uncertainty about how it would be implemented. Indeed, many partnerships experience significant challenges in moving from the planning or rule-making stage, described in this case study, to the subsequent implementation stage (see Chapter 3). How can this transition be best managed? In the case of the Malawi partnership, could this transition have been more proactively catered for at the outset? What is your guess on how this partnership initiative has panned out?

Notes

1 This case study was prepared in collaboration with Daisy Kambalame and Sean de Cleene of the African Institute for Corporate Citizenship (AICC) of Malawi, and with the support of Ralph Hamann of the University of South Africa (UNISA), Birgit Errath of the UNGC-New York, and Girum Bahri and Ellen Kallinowsky of the UNGC-Africa. The editorial assistance of Judy Irvine and Paul Beamish of the Ivey School of Business is also gratefully acknowledged.

2 Corruption was seen as a major impediment to achieving the UN Millennium Development Goals. On the Transparency International *Corruption Perception Index* (where the countries perceived to be the least corrupt are placed at the top of the list), Malawi slid from 42nd place in 2000 to 97th place in 2005.

3 The UNGC Principle 10 states: 'Businesses should work against corruption in all its forms, including extortion and bribery'.

4 News reports suggested that the politicisation of the fight against corruption was a serious problem, with competing allegations that prosecutions of senior opposition party members were politically motivated and that the president and members of his cabinet should also be the subject of corruption investigation, but were protected by the Anti-Corruption Bureau. See, for example P. Phiri, 'Malawi Loses US$ 40 Million in Corruption', afrol News / *The Chronicle*, 21 November 2005; UN media IRIN, 'Malawi Opposition Accuses President Mutharika of Score-Settling', Misanet / IRIN, 9 February 2006; UN media IRIN, 'Political Squabbles Hamper Governance in Malawi', afrol News / IRIN, 26 May 2006, http://www.afrol.com/; http://www.afrol.com/countries/malawi/news

5 United Nations Global Compact (UNGC), *Business against Corruption: Case Studies and Examples: Implementation of the 10th United Nations Global Compact Principle against Corruption* (New York: UNGC, April 2006). Available online at http://www.unglobalcompact.org/docs/issues_doc/7.7/BACbookFINAL.pdf (accessed 9 March 2007).

6 Ibid., 176.

7 The concept of BATNA, or 'best alternative to negotiated agreement', originated in R. Fisher and W. Ury, *Getting to Yes: Negotiating Agreement Without Giving In*, 2nd edition (New York: Penguin Books, 1991), 98 et seq.

8 UNGC, *Business against Corruption*, note 5, 133.

9 Ibid., 128.

10 Ibid., 134, 141. The *Integrity Pact* developed by Transparency International provided a practical model of consensual negotiation. It consisted of an agreement between a government department and a company bidding on a public sector procurement contract not to 'pay, offer, demand or accept bribes of any sort, or collude with competitors to obtain the contract, or while carrying it out'. Bidders were required to disclose all commissions and similar expenses paid by them to anybody in connection with the contract. Breach of the agreement would result in sanctions, ranging from 'loss or denial of contract, forfeiture of the bid or performance bond and liability for damages, to blacklisting for future contracts on the side of the bidders, and criminal or disciplinary action against employees of the Government'.

11 UNGC, *Business against Corruption*, note 5, 138.

12 The second round-table discussion was held to discuss the role of corporate governance in promoting the Millennium Development Goals, and the third and fourth round-table discussions focused on opportunity creation and sustainable development in the agriculture sector and the development of a promotional campaign for this purpose. Sponsorship for the round-table discussions was received from BP Malawi; Limbe Leaf Tobacco Company; Monsanto; Yara Malawi; Multi Choice; and Dulux Ltd. From 'Malawi Leaders' Forum on Building Alliances to Eliminate Corruption, Final Report 2005', http://www.aiccafrica.org/PDF%20files/Final%20Report%20Corruption%20Event.pdf

13 UNGC, *Business against Corruption*, note 5, 132.

14 Ibid., note 5, 137.

15 'Malawi Leaders' Forum, Final Report', note 12, 3. Chikaonda urged business to implement systems to act on the fight against corruption as a core business issue by incorporating anti-corruption clauses into managers' employment contracts. He recommended setting up an independent body

to develop incentives to back a zero-tolerance policy on corruption, particularly as it related to the supply chains of larger companies, state enterprise and government procurement.

16   Ibid., note 12, 4. Roderick Phiri argued that businesses needed to agree on a strict code of conduct, supported by internal reporting systems and improved transparency and accountability.

17   Ibid. Fred Mzomwa went on to say the establishment of an independent business lead reporting body would be a positive and welcome step forward.

18   Ibid., note 12, 1.

19   D. Ertel, 'Getting Past Yes: Negotiating as if Implementation Mattered', *Harvard Business Review* (November 2004), 65.

20   The steering committee, led by Sean de Cleene of the AICC, comprised the AICC's African Corporate Sustainability Forum; the Malawi Anti-Corruption Bureau; the Chemicals and Marketing Co. Ltd.; the Malawi Bureau of Standards; the Malawi UN Global Compact; Rab Processors Ltd.; USAID; and Yara Malawi (Ptv.) Ltd.

21   In addition to the members of the Code Steering Committee, the Malawi Business Action Against Corruption Task Force currently includes Africa Leaf; Illovo Sugar (Malawi) Ltd.; Limbe Leaf Tobacco Company Ltd.; Malawi Revenue Authority; Malswitch – Reserve Bank of Malawi; the Ministry of Trade and Private Sector Development; the Office of the Director of Public Procurement; Multi-Choice Malawi; Press Corporation Ltd.; Safetech Malawi; Dimon (Malawi) Ltd.; MSC Malawi; Africa on Line; Press Corporation Ltd.; Press Trust; Chemical and Marketing Malawi; Air Malawi; Mediterranean Shipping Company; Multi-Choice; The Society of Accountants in Malawi (SOCAM); and the United Nations Development Programme (UNDP).

22   L. Susskind and J. Cruikshank, *Breaking the Impasse: Consensual Approaches to Resolving Public Disputes* (New York: Basic Books, 1987).

23   '[W]hat the private sector has done has even motivated civil society to engage on the issue as well.' Daisy Kambalame (AICC).

24   UNGC, *Business against Corruption*, 177.

25   Interviews were conducted by James Ng'ombe with the assistance of Vales Machila.

The South African

National Anti-Corruption Forum

ODETTE RAMSINGH & KRIS DOBIE[1]

Introduction

South Africa has a past that was characterised by unequal treatment and unequal distribution of resources and services. Because the apartheid government had to limit transparency to achieve its ends, this context was a breeding ground for corruption. Now that the discriminatory past has been left behind, corruption must no longer be tolerated. This was emphasised by the then President Nelson Mandela in his opening address to parliament in 1999:

> Our hope for the future depends on our resolution as a nation in dealing with the scourge of corruption. Success will require an acceptance that, in many respects, we are a sick society. It is perfectly correct to assert that all this was spawned by apartheid. No amount of self-induced amnesia will change the reality of history. But it is also a reality of the present that among the new cadres in various levels of government you will find individuals who are as corrupt as – if not more than – those they found in government. When a leader in a provincial legislation siphons off resources meant to fund service by legislators to the people; when employees of a government institution set up to help empower those who were excluded by apartheid defraud it for their own enrichment, then we must admit that we have a sick society. This problem manifests itself in all areas of life.[2]

Since 1994 the government has made a concerted effort to further the fight against corruption through the introduction of a comprehensive legislative and regulatory framework to regulate ethical conduct and build national integrity. There was, however, early recognition of the fact that the application of a successful framework could not be the sole responsibility of government. Broad-based partnerships had to be developed to provide the necessary assistance and capacity to fight corruption. Strong components of such partnership were the business sector and civil society.

A national dialogue began in 1998 with the hosting of the Public Sector Anti-Corruption Conference, which was followed by the first National Anti-Corruption Summit in 1999. This summit led to the formation in 2001 of the National Anti-Corruption Forum (NACF), a body comprising all sectors of society and whose primary objective was to contribute to a national consensus through the coordination of sectoral strategies against corruption. However, it soon became clear that coordination and formal structures for collaboration would have to be improved if the NACF was to justify its existence. Business and civil society in particular had to find ways of coordinating their input and activities, and the forum itself had to streamline its structure to speed up decision-making and enable a focus on tangible projects. Now, in 2007, after surviving severe growing pains and adjustments, the NACF is beginning to deliver the kinds of projects that were envisaged at the outset.

Initiating a cross-sectoral approach: The origins of the NACF concept

In the hands of government

The formal fight against corruption has its origins in a cabinet decision in 1997, when a ministerial committee was mandated to consider proposals for the implementation of a national campaign against corruption focusing on the national and provincial levels of government. This committee called on the Public Service Commission (PSC)[3] to facilitate a conversation between government role-players who, through their respective mandates and activities, come into contact with corruption and the control and prosecution of corrupt practices.

This led to the first Public Sector Anti-Corruption Conference, held on 10 and 11 November 1998 in parliament in Cape Town. It was the first time in the history of South Africa that parliament had opened its doors to host a conference of this nature, and gave a clear indication of government's commitment to addressing corruption. The conference was attended by over 200 delegates from parliament, the public service, local government and organised labour in the public sector. There was also considerable interest from media and donor organisations, whose representatives attended as observers. It was at this conference that the call was made for the anti-corruption effort to become a national concern that would include all sectors of South African society.

Inviting the other sectors

Taking this call forward, the PSC arranged a series of meetings with representatives of organisations that had attended the conference and representatives from organised business, religious bodies, non-governmental organisations and the media to plan the way forward for a first National Anti-Corruption Summit. A planning committee, consisting of members of each of these sectors, was established and a final workshop of the planning committee was held on 13 April 1999, a day before the summit was due to begin. At this workshop it was agreed that 'corruption can only be addressed if it is tackled in a holistic way with all role-players working together to develop concrete action plans and programmes'.[4] Corruption was recognised as a societal issue and given a wider definition than the traditional notion of 'public sector abuse of power for personal gain'.

The first National Anti-Corruption Summit was held in parliament, Cape Town, from 14 to 15 April 1999. It was attended by 263 delegates representing government leaders, organised business, organised religion, non-governmental organisations (NGOs), the media, labour unions, academic and professional bodies and the public sector. The theme of the summit was Fighting Corruption: Towards a National Integrity Strategy.

In his keynote address, the then executive deputy president of South Africa, Thabo Mbeki, wished the conference success, expressing himself 'confident that it will not disappoint the expectations of our people whose spirit is vexed because they are the daily victims of the scourge of corruption which is a blight on our society'.[5]

The big resolution

The summit adopted various resolutions aimed at combating and preventing corruption, building integrity and raising awareness. One such resolution called for the establishment of 'a cross-sectoral task team to look into the establishment of a National Coordinating Structure with the authority to effectively lead, coordinate and monitor the national Anti-Corruption Programme'.[6] It was this resolution that would eventually lead to the formation of the NACF.

At a post-summit planning meeting the sectors agreed that the task team would comprise one person per sector, and that it would have an interim life span focusing on the setting up of the National Coordinating Structure.[7] The task team was for the duration of its existence chaired by Professor Stan Sangweni of the PSC.

Between the April 1999 summit and the creation of the NACF as national coordinating structure in March 2001, a great deal of work was done to realise the summit resolutions. Government gave effect to resolutions which led to the enactment of the Prevention and Combating of Corrupt Activities Act, the Protected Disclosures Act and the Access to Information Act, as well as the establishment of specialised commercial crimes courts and whistle-blowing hotlines. It was also during this period that the Public Sector Anti-Corruption Strategy took shape.

Business and civil society, however, found it more difficult to provide impetus to their initiatives. During this time, the business sector drafted the South African National Code for Business Conduct which, although a positive initiative, was not broadly accepted. There was a general problem of coordination. No formal structures existed to drive the initiatives forward and promote them on a national level.

The journey towards co-ordination

When the cross-sectoral task team met in March 2000, much of the discussion revolved around the potential model for the National Coordinating Structure. Strong feelings were expressed on whether it should be a statutory or advisory body. The NGO representative at the time wanted a statutory body as he believed that this would give it the necessary 'teeth' to act. Government representatives on the other hand, wanted it to be an advisory body that gives input to government on how to manage corruption. There were even fringe views wanting the establishment of a formal public/private partnership. In truth, being confronted with the task of creating this new body *ex nihilo,* cross-sectoral members were quite uncertain about how it should look. Articulating an acceptable structure was largely left up to the PSC secretariat.

After a to and fro between the secretariat and the task team, and submissions to the sectors, a draft memorandum of understanding on the establishment of the NACF was tabled at a meeting of the cross-sectoral task team held in October 2000. Two deadlines had already been missed and it had become clear that reaching consensus on the type of structure was not as easy as originally thought.[8]

A task group was appointed to flesh out the principles underpinning the choice of structure.[9] They reported back at the next meeting, held on 6 March 2001, and the memorandum of understanding was adopted, defining the NACF as an advisory body.

Preparatory stages leading to the establishment of the NACF saw government in the driving seat, with the secretariat carrying the load of not only arranging meetings, but also monitoring the content of the meetings. It was initially difficult to ensure the attendance and participation of all role-players at the meetings, and the concept was kept alive largely through the efforts of government.

The launch of the NACF

Two years after the first National Anti-Corruption Summit, after much debate and preparation, the NACF was launched in Cape Town on 15 June 2001. Ministers, high profile business and prominent civil society representatives were present. Significantly, the NACF was launched in Langa, an impoverished township of Cape Town, which underscored the need to remain mindful of the impact that corruption has on the country's developmental goals.

The NACF comprises three sectors, namely civil society, business and the public sector. Each sector is represented by ten members nominated by their respective constituencies. Significantly, nine of the ten members of the public sector are ministers or deputy ministers, with the tenth being the chairperson of the PSC. The PSC also continued to play its role as the secretariat.[10]

In terms of the memorandum of understanding, the role of the NACF is to:

1. Contribute towards the establishment of a national consensus through the coordination of sectoral strategies against corruption;

2. Advise government on national initiatives for the implementation of strategies to combat corruption; and

3. Advise sectors on the improvement of sectoral anti-corruption strategies.[11]

4. The executive committee, comprising nine members (three from each sector) was established at the inaugural meeting held a month later. The three sectors were led by: D. Mpofu, representing civil society (chairperson of the NACF); G.J. Fraser-Moleketi public sector (deputy chairperson); S. Mathuysen business sector (deputy chairperson).[12]

A slow start

After the initial enthusiasm about the idea, it took almost two years for the NACF to be launched. This initial delay might perhaps be explained by the very problem that the NACF was envisaged to overcome – there was no formal structure for collaboration on this topic.

At the time there were also no unified bodies from business or civil society to speak on the issue of corruption. Business Unity South Africa, a merger of the Black Business Council and Business South Africa, was only formed in October 2003. Business against Crime, which is currently the key business body on the forum, had been formed in 1997, but had little involvement in the early discussions. Civil society was even less organised on the issue of combating corruption.

After the drawn-out process of convening the NACF, the inaugural meeting was held promptly on 19 July 2001, but another 16 months passed before the next meeting was held in November 2002. The second was eventually convened only after the National Religious Leaders Forum raised the issue of the NACF's inactivity with President Thabo Mbeki. The president tasked Geraldine Fraser-Moleketi (minister of Public Service and Administration) with getting things moving again, and it was only after this meeting, where she took over the chair, that the NACF began gaining momentum.

Representatives from all the sectors expressed their frustration at this lull in activity. Roderick Davids of the PSC remembers this as one of the low points in the process:

> There was so much expectation and then nothing happened. Did we give birth to an organisation that was dying or dead? There was a lot of scepticism that this thing may not work because of the diversity of the role-players, and the difficulty of bringing them together and to concede to a common programme of work. The work programme was regarded as the instrument that would give us impetus and momentum, and if we couldn't meet we couldn't even discuss this.

Many offered their diagnosis of the problem. One view is that there was a serious leadership problem. At the inaugural meeting it was decided that Advocate Dali Mpofu (representing civil society) should chair the NACF, but there was little movement during his tenure. The Department for Public Service and Administration (DPSA) forwarded proposals for the rejuvenation of the NACF during this time, but received no response. The inactivity could be put down to the priorities of a busy man, but a contributing factor was the lack of accountability structures within civil society. By their very nature business and civil society are not cohesive hierarchical units in the way that government is. There is a much looser organisation of entities around specific concerns in the non-governmental sectors, which means that an individual might not be called to account by his or her constituency or leadership, as is bound to happen in government.

Specific proposals were made to improve liaison with membership. For instance, it was proposed that umbrella bodies for business and civil society should be used to facilitate interaction within and between sectors. It was also proposed that the executive committee's composition be reduced from three to two members per sector,[13] to make it easier to arrange meetings.

Business has since institutionalised its representative structures through an alliance between Business against Crime (BAC) and Business Unity South Africa (BUSA), which is the most representative body for business in South Africa. BAC has a number of project areas, including commercial crime, which also deals with corruption issues. Once a month BAC holds an Industry Alignment Forum (IAF) meeting where a broad range of business organisations are represented, including BUSA. Prior to each monthly IAF meeting, a working group that includes the business delegation at the NACF, meets to prepare feedback to the IAF on the activities of the working group and the NACF projects.

Internal communication within the civil society sector has also been improved through the creation of the Civil Society Network against Corruption (CSNAC). This group of NGOs has improved accountability and communication within the group. They are, however, only one of the ten civil society representatives on the forum, and there is concern that their communication does not reach the rest of the representatives. Ruan Kitshoff of the DPSA comments:

> We would meet with a representative from Cape Town, and then at the next meeting it would be a representative from Johannesburg, and in the discussion of issues it becomes clear that they have not communicated on the matters in the interim, which means that the discussion is still open as if no conclusion has been reached.

The problem is not only getting one representative voice, but also continuity and progress on the issues under discussion.

Picking up the pace

The next meeting of the NACF, held on 10 February 2003, demonstrated a more content-driven approach. The three sectors reported on their own initiatives to combat corruption, and sought the collaboration of the other sectors where appropriate. It was agreed that a presentation on the activities of the NACF since the 1999 Anti-Corruption Summit should be made to the Parliamentary Portfolio Committee.[14] Since parliament represents the people of South Africa, the NACF through this presentation was accounting to South Africans on what it had achieved.

Consolidating the NACF has not been an easy task. Concerns arose again about its functioning at the NACF meeting held on 5 December 2003. The Minister for Public Service and Administration as chairperson commented that while the forum had been successful in promoting itself, a number of shortcomings had been identified. Given these shortcomings it was important to review the NACF and assess its objectives. Among others, it was indicated that the forum did not achieve much due to the shortcomings of the secretariat, budgetary constraints and the forum's limited capacity. It was decided that the NACF should adopt an incremental approach to its work and look at ways of strengthening the secretariat. To take the work of the Forum forward it was agreed that a simplified message would be conveyed to the public, indicating the cost of corruption to development.[15]

To some degree the next meeting held on 17 August 2004 was a turning point in the NACF. There was robust debate, and a sense that the other sectors called government to account. At the time of the meeting media reports had broken over allegations of reported fraud by parliamentarians. The meeting decided to note the allegations and monitor the situation, but more importantly agreed that future meetings should provide space for discussion of topical issues related to corruption. Furthermore, a request for a dedicated secretariat was made to cabinet in order to strengthen and enhance this capacity.[16]

The NACF began preparing for the second National Anti-Corruption Summit. This was to be its first public event since its launch in 2001. The Summit was held from 22 to 23 March 2005 in Pretoria, and its theme was Fighting Corruption Together: Past Achievements, Future Challenges. As at the 1999 Summit, representatives from all sectors of South African society engaged with anti-corruption challenges and contributed towards a common programme of action for the immediate and long-term future.

A total of 390 delegates comprising 43 from business, 191 from the public sector, 122 from civil society and 34 representing donors and other interested parties, including the Southern African Development Community (SADC), attended the summit. Delegates adopted a wide range of resolutions centring on ethics and awareness, combating corruption, transparency, and oversight and accountability.

It was agreed to translate the resolutions into a programme of action within three months of the summit.[17] The resolutions adopted covered, among others, the following topics:

- Encouraging whistle-blowing in all sectors.
- Better coordination among anti-corruption agencies.
- Effective implementation of anti-corruption legislation.
- Encouraging post-public sector employment regulation.
- Research into ethics practices in each sector.
- Extending financial disclosures to local government.
- Raising awareness through ethics training in all sectors.
- Institutional arrangements to streamline the NACF.

Over the next few years, these resolutions would form the basis of the national fight against corruption.

The national anti-corruption programme: A programme of action

The work of the NACF was further consolidated through the development of a National Anti-Corruption Programme (NAP). A draft NAP, prepared by the secretariat in conjunction with members of the NACF, was presented at an NACF meeting on 12 May 2005. It was agreed that an implementation committee be established to oversee and monitor the implementation of NAP projects. One convener from each of the three sectors was appointed to serve on the implementation committee. The committee consists of the convenor of the Civil Society Network Against Corruption, the chief executive officer of Business Against Crime, the director-general of the Department of Public Service and Administration (chairperson) and the PSC as secretariat.[18]

At a special meeting held on 24 June 2005, the NAP[19] was adopted and launched as the two-year work programme of the NACF.[20] It serves as an important yardstick against which the public can hold stakeholders accountable. The focus of the NAP was to yield 'quick wins', to enhance the profile of the NACF and to produce results that are measurable and practical.

The NAP only focuses on joint projects. Progress on sector-specific projects relating to other resolutions is reported on a regular basis to the NACF and the implementation committee during scheduled meetings. The approach of a select number of joint projects has taken into account the need for the NACF to be modest in launching a NAP. This is largely due to limited capacity within the NACF. Fewer projects will ensure better focus and increase the potential for success. The implementation committee has therefore identified key areas of priority in the fight against corruption and believes that it would be more appropriate to tackle a few high quality projects, campaigns and initiatives than to commit itself to a long list of projects that the NACF will not be able to deliver on.

Many of the resolutions adopted at the summit affect various projects already being implemented at a sectoral level. Each sector has its own reporting mechanisms for these projects. Government showed its commitment towards the implementation of the projects of the NAP by making funds available to the amount of R4.5 million for the 2006/2007 financial year. This funding is managed by the PSC as secretariat of the NACF.

Since the development of the NAP the pace of the NACF's activities has noticeably accelerated. This is largely because activities are structured with defined time frames, and sectors are held accountable for their undertakings. Furthermore there is an expectation that the NACF must report to all provincial legislatures and parliament on its achievements.

Key current projects

In order to improve the visibility and communication of NACF activities a new website (www. nacf.org.za) and logo were recently launched. The website provides space for profiling the NACF and the work of the three sectors. In future it will also contain case studies on the combating and prevention of corruption. This will afford organisations and individuals fighting corruption an opportunity to benchmark their efforts against those of others and draw lessons from such case studies.

An Integrity Pledge was adopted and signed by the leaders of the various sectors represented on the NACF. All sectors are expected to encourage their members to sign the pledge and to popularise it within their constituencies. Signing the pledge shows a voluntary commitment by individuals to serve the country and its people with respect, dignity and integrity, and in accordance with the values and principles of the Constitution. By signing the pledge, the NACF members committed themselves to set an example through the promotion of high standards of service and ethical behaviour that are conducive to the development of the economy and the eradication of poverty.

The work of the NACF has also been characterised by some substantial projects that have ignited debate in society at large. Civil society presented a report on Apartheid Grand Corruption, sparking intense debate over whether those responsible for corruption during the apartheid era should be brought to account for such acts.

The NACF also hosted a roundtable on the Prohibition of Corrupt Persons and Businesses. The roundtable was well attended by all sectors, including academics and other interested role-players. It specifically focused on the feasibility of establishing a common database of corrupt persons and businesses for use by all sectors. The challenges of establishing such a database were deliberated and it was agreed that a committee of specialists, emanating from the roundtable, should meet to discuss and recommend an appropriate course of action for the NACF.

Legislation all over the world is written in traditional legal language which some may find difficult to understand. South Africa's Prevention and Combating of Corrupt Activities Act is no exception. For this reason, the NACF decided to popularise the act by simplifying it both in terms of language and through the use of illustrations, in the form of a guide. The NACF believes that by publishing a reader-friendly guide it has contributed in a small way to bringing legislation closer to the people.

It is clear that the NACF has evolved from a relatively inactive past to a present that displays active participation and tangible outcomes.

The difficulties of the endeavour

The task of getting three diverse sectors to work together will never be without its challenges. Representatives of the various sectors were interviewed to give their perspectives on the process. [21] The following gives a synopsis of the main themes that emerged.

Slow movement

The main area of concern was the long period of inactivity directly after the formation of the NACF. As discussed above, this was predominantly due to leadership problems and difficulties with getting the accountability structures of business and civil society in place.

Another aspect, which made it very difficult for the PSC, as secretariat, to convene the early meetings, is the seniority of some of the role-players. This was an issue in business and the public sector, but has been more problematic in the case of the latter. All the government representatives on the NACF are ministers or deputy-ministers, and trying to fit in with their diaries proved a near impossibility. Although they were well intentioned and showed great commitment from government at a political level, having so many senior politicians on board had negative administrative consequences. The issue has been raised at a number of NACF meetings, but remains unresolved. Some believe there should be fewer ministers as representatives, while others believe the ministers should delegate their representation to specific individuals who can contribute meaningfully and ensure continuity.

The issue of full diaries has been partly overcome by the secretariat sending out known meeting dates annually in advance. Nonetheless, the only time when there was a full ministerial attendance was at the first meeting.

There are, however, still frustrations, especially from business representatives, that they receive invitations to activities at an unrealistically late stage. These are often for meetings where their input is requested, but the late notification makes it impossible for them to participate. Just a little forward planning could solve this problem, and the fact that this has not happened makes them feel excluded. Business has raised this issue in the past and interviewees from this sector are of the opinion that it still needs to be successfully addressed. Secretariat representatives indicate that decisions about dates for meetings are often communicated to them at a late stage. The other point of communication breakdown could be between the business representatives on the implementation committee and their members.

Constituencies and communication

Many believe that the issue of 'constituencies' remains a challenge, especially with regard to civil society representation. How large a segment of the population is in fact represented by civil society and how successfully are they reached by the NACF?

Many of the NGOs that have an anti-corruption focus, although advocating the interests of society, do not represent communities. They do not have a large constituency base and speak largely 'for themselves'. Many have also expressed their dismay at the fact that the workers' unions have not taken up their involvement as actively as one would have wished. The South

African NGO Coalition (SANGOCO) and the National Religious Leaders Forum (NRLF) are the only active members of the forum with constituencies, but two-way communication between constituencies and representatives remains a challenge.

Hassen Lorgat of SANGOCO and chairperson of the South African chapter of Transparency International (TI-SA) admits to these difficulties. He would like to see more involvement at community level. Through TI-SA they are currently launching National Integrity Networks, which aim to mobilise communities for grassroots activism. Civil society is, however, made up of disparate interest groups and this makes it difficult to report back to constituencies. While the NACF has given civil society organisations an opportunity to focus on one key issue, the need for some level of expertise on corruption-related matters makes it difficult to involve the 'constituency NGOs'.

For some of the less well-funded civil society organisations it remains a challenge to attend the NACF meetings and therefore to contribute in a meaningful way. Kitshoff suggests that it is the responsibility of the NACF to enable these organisations to participate, not only by providing for their travel to meetings, but also by distributing information which will capacitate them and enable their meaningful contribution.

The business sector has experienced some problems of its own in getting buy-in from more businesses, and this has made a coordinated approach more difficult. Alvin Rapea, of Business against Crime, speculates that this is largely because businesses would like to see the impact that programmes are having on their bottom line. He is, however, confident that business projects launched as a result of the NACF, such as a baseline study into corruption in the private sector, will be successful in garnering more business involvement. The baseline study will show the impact that corruption has on specific industry sectors, which could provide impetus at these levels.

In contrast to the other two sectors, government is a more cohesive unit and this simplifies its internal communication and accountability. In order to reach all departments and levels of government, an Anti-Corruption Coordinating Committee, consisting of various role-players in government, meets regularly to discuss the Public Service Anti-Corruption Strategy. Some provinces have their own coordination structures, which are currently being brought into the discussions more consistently.

The secretariat

A number of representatives have expressed their concern about the functioning of the secretariat. At the time of writing officials from the PSC fulfil their roles in the secretariat in addition to their other tasks, which means that the NACF has no full-time staff members. Kitshoff stresses that the secretariat should fulfil more than just an administrative function. Like company secretaries, they should keep the members informed about current issues relevant to the work of the forum in order to inform the debate and identify future priorities.

Admill Simpson of the PSC feels, however, that these criticisms belong to a previous era of the NACF. He explains that many of the concerns about the role and capacity of the PSC as secretariat, especially the expectation that it should drive content, have been addressed through the establishment of the cross-sectoral implementation committee and the development of a NAP. Where the secretariat was previously expected to drive content, this has now become the responsibility of the sectoral convenors who serve on the implementation committee, as well as the executive committee. The secretariat, being in an independent support role, does not have the authority to act outside of such processes. Therefore any concerns about the secretariat cannot be seen in isolation from the role of the implementation committee.

Simpson suspects that there might still be some confusion in the sectors about these new responsibilities. When it comes to attending special meetings, or obtaining inputs from within the sectors, the secretariat communicates this to the implementation committee representatives. From there on it is their responsibility to communicate and coordinate with their sectors. The secretariat, however, still experiences much frustration at the apparent lack of intra-sectoral communication. In practice this means that they have to follow up on matters such as inputs into combined projects, or ensuring sufficient attendance from the sectors at events.

The National Treasury has, however, approved a budget that makes possible the appointment of two full-time PSC employees to focus on NACF matters. This should address any other capacity concerns in the secretariat.

Something for the 'man on the street'

While much has happened in terms of new legislation, anti-corruption institutions and other initiatives, particularly in the public sector, little is known about this by the 'man on the street'. Peter Just of the National Religious Leaders Forum says that people have the perception that corruption is rife in South Africa and that no one is doing anything about it. He feels that the NACF should be more vocal on issues of concern to ordinary people and build awareness of its activities through engaging with the press.

While not everyone is clear about how to achieve this, all sectors agree that there should be more awareness of the NACF and its activities among the public in general. It is felt that the NACF activities should have a tangible impact on the levels of corruption experienced by ordinary citizens. Since corruption is a societal problem, one also needs awareness of the issue amongst citizens to combat it successfully.

The contribution of the non-governmental sectors

The non-governmental players are not 'on board' the NACF merely to support government in their Anti-Corruption Strategy. All players acknowledge that civil society and business also have a responsibility to address corruption in their own sectors and still have some way to go in making this impact felt. The business representatives are currently completing a survey of corruption in the private sector that could lay the foundation for future work. Organised civil society is, however, still faced with resource and structural challenges that make this kind of activity very difficult.

Another matter that gets mentioned rather tentatively is business's lack of financial or resource contribution to the NACF and its projects. There seems to be agreement that civil society will not be able to contribute beyond its time, networks and expertise, but this is not the case with business. Many role-players expect business to bring their resources 'to the party'. This can include financial resources or, for example, making venues available for conferences, providing experts for research or hosting the website. Some business representatives feel, however, that the problem is a national one and therefore something that the taxpayer should fund. The NACF and its projects have been quite successful at attracting donor funding, to the benefit of all the sectors. Detractors feel that while this gets projects implemented, more financial commitment is needed, especially from business. There is clearly still some discussion to be had on this matter.

To talk or not to talk about controversial issues

Although it was decided at the meeting on 17 August 2004 that space should be created for discussion of topical issues, civil society in particular still feels that the NACF should be more vocal about current incidents of corruption. Alison Tilley, convenor of the Civil Society Network against Corruption, mentions that it is still difficult to talk about real life examples of corruption within the forum:

> There is a discussion about corruption, but it's very… abstract. The purpose of the Forum is to create a place where the three sectors can talk about how to create a more enabling environment to fight corruption… If you are really constrained in the quality of the discussion [because current controversies are not referred to], it impacts on the quality of your planning, which has an effect on outcomes.

That said, civil society does feel that its voice has been heard and that some difficult issues have been discussed at the NACF. These notably include the report entitled Apartheid Grand Corruption, and the current NAP project to 'establish a joint research initiative to evaluate the implementation by the Executive of resolutions made by Parliament and its committees pertaining to corruption'.

The governmental face

An underlying issue that gets mentioned is the fact that the NACF still has a somewhat governmental face, particularly with the chairperson being the minister for Public Service and Administration. The other sectors would like to see this change over time, but seem to acknowledge that they will need to achieve more maturity in their own structures before this can happen. Professor Sangweni, chairperson of the PSC, says that the intention was always to have a partnership of equals:

> We all have to maintain the equilibrium of equity in this partnership. But at the same time the government cannot abdicate its institutional responsibility to ensure that action is taken against corruption.

Are some key players missing?

Rather more striking is the inactivity of some key government players. Although the minister of Safety and Security (under whom the South African Police Services falls) and the deputy minister of Justice are members of the NACF there is very little input from them or their representatives at NACF meetings. Corruption is a problem of societal values, but it also remains a criminal problem. It has often been said that while South Africa has world class legislation and regulations, much work remains to be done to implement them. This certainly implies that these two ministries should have a keen interest in a forum such as the NACF.

An active forum

Something that everyone agrees upon is that currently the NACF is at its most active since its establishment. This activity has been largely attributed to the existence of the National Anti-Corruption Programme. This programme has linked the resolutions of the Second National Anti-Corruption Summit to specific outputs, with responsibilities allocated, time frames set and budgets assigned. The existence of the much smaller implementation committee, which consists of only one representative per sector, has facilitated quicker communication and provides necessary oversight over the projects. Furthermore, individuals have been nominated to serve on cross-sectoral task teams to implement specific projects. For many people who have been involved since the NACF's inception, this is the kind of functioning that they have been waiting for.

The nature of the projects is also significant. Many of the legislative and institutional changes in the country had already been implemented as an outcome of the first summit. The second summit had the more difficult task of deepening this work. In compiling the NAP there was a conscious decision to be modest in the tasks taken on, in order to ensure their successful implementation. These programmes also need to provide the foundation for further anti-corruption work and it was therefore important to be strategic in choosing projects that the NACF can build on incrementally. Davids stresses that the projects must deliver something tangible and sustainable.

> We must vigorously implement this anti-corruption programme to the best of our ability. We must build on that success. It will give us confidence and it will open up new opportunities. We are starting at the bottom by, for example, doing an ethics scan in schools and tertiary institutions. The outcome of this project will open up new work opportunities. It is important that the projects stem from a mandated summit. We've got a good mandate and a good foundation to build on.

Conclusion

When speaking to representatives one can sense that there is engagement from all parties in the NACF. With its beginnings as a loose grouping of well-intentioned people, it has taken a while for the initiative to come to the point where substantive projects are being implemented that will have a direct impact on corruption in South Africa. The evolution of the forum suggests that it takes a great deal more than good intentions to organise three diverse sectors to interact meaningfully and to get to a point where productive work can be achieved.

Editors' reflections and questions

The South African National Anti-Corruption Forum is an initiative that stems from the recognition that corruption is a societal problem that cannot be addressed by government alone, and that a collaborative effort is needed. However, the initial talks between the government, business, and civil society sectors were slow and difficult. Among other challenges, there was a need for business to be represented by a legitimate collective association, something that was established only at later stages. Another difficulty has been the establishment of collaborative structures that ensure credibility and sufficient buy-in from all participants on the one hand, while also facilitating timely decision-making and implementation on the other.

1. What could have been done more effectively or differently at the outset to ensure that the NACF did not go through the initial period of inactivity?

2. Considering that this is a cross-sectoral partnership, is it appropriate that the government plays such a strong role in the NACF? How can the advantages of this strong role be enhanced and its disadvantages mitigated?

3. Should business be contributing more to the NACF in terms of resources or is this an initiative that should be predominantly funded by government?

4. Should the NACF be more vocal in making statements about high-profile corruption cases, or other corruption related issues that are topical in any given period?

5. What more could be done to give the 'man on the street' a feeling that something is being done about preventing corruption?

Notes

1 This case study was commissioned by the Public Service Commission. Academic oversight was provided by Mollie Painter-Morland and peer review was provided by Ralph Hamann. The authors wish to thank the following people who were interviewed for the case study: Admill Simpson, Public Service Commission; Alison Tilley, Civil Society Network against Corruption and Open Democracy Advice Centre; Alvin Rapea, Business against Crime; Hassen Lorgat, South African NGO Coalition and Transparency International South Africa; Peter Just, National Religious Leaders Forum; Roderick Davids, Public Service Commission; and Ruan Kitshoff, Department of Public Service and Administration.

2 N.R. Mandela, 'State of the Nation' address by President Nelson Mandela to Parliament 1999. See http://www.southafrica-newyork.net/consulate/speeches/stateofnation.htm

3 The PSC is an independent body established in terms of the RSA Constitution, 1996, to provide oversight over public administration. It plays a key role in the promotion of good governance in the South African Public Service.

4 *Fighting Corruption, towards a National Integrity Strategy* (Pretoria: Public Service Commission, 1999), 68.

5   T. Mbeki, deputy president of South Africa. Key-note address to the National Anti-Corruption Summit, 14 April 1999.

6   *Fighting Corruption*, 3.

7   Minutes of the Post-NACS Consultation Meeting, 11 August 1999.

8   Although it is more time-consuming, the NACF continues to make decisions by consensus rather than voting, to prevent the alienation of any of the stakeholders.

9   Minutes of the National Anti-Corruption Cross-Sectoral Task Team, 26 October 2000.

10 *Memorandum of Understanding*, NACF, 15 June 2001.

11 Ibid.

12 Minutes of the NACF, 19 July 2001.

13 Ibid., 21 November 2002.

14 Ibid., 10 February 2003.

15 Ibid., 5 December 2003.

16 Ibid., 17 August 2004.

17 Report on the proceedings of the second National Anti-Corruption Summit, NACF, 2005, 137.

18 Minutes of the NACF, 12 May 2005.

19 Available at http://www.nacf.org.za/national-anti-corruption-programme/index.html

20 Minutes of the NACF, 24 June 2005.

21 In order to facilitate open communication, the interviews were conducted independently by Kris Dobie of the University of Pretoria, Centre for Business and Professional Ethics. Interviewees were given the option of remaining anonymous, but were in fact quite open with their views, which perhaps signals the maturity of debate at the NACF.

CASE 11

Testing the limits of
inclusive capitalism:
A case study of the South Africa HP i-community

RICARDA MCFALLS

Introduction[1]

In the run-up to the 2015 target date for achieving the Millennium Development Goals, the UN's Global Compact has targeted major corporations to play an active leadership role in promoting sustainable economic and social development. Increasingly these corporations are encouraged to do so by pursuing profit-making business opportunities that will also yield social benefits in developing countries, such as employment creation and skills development. This ideal of 'inclusive capitalism' has been popularised by C.K. Prahalad in the Bottom of the Pyramid (BOP) discourse.[2]

Under former CEO, Carly Fiorina, Hewlett-Packard (HP) embraced this concept. Motivated by a desire for 'creating breakthrough models of sustainable development, not altruism'[3] and with the support of South Africa's president, Thabo Mbeki, HP launched a three-year public/private partnership at the 2002 UN World Summit on Sustainable Development (WSSD) in Johannesburg. The project entailed establishing an i-community (inclusive community) in the Mogalakwena district of the Limpopo Province, in partnership with the province and the Mogalakwena municipality.

There were high hopes for this initiative, with HP announcing its intention 'to work with the community and use ICT to create breakthrough models of sustainable, scalable, social and economic development' that would be 'a catalyst in turning the region into a thriving, self-sustaining economic community where information and communication technologies (ICT) improve literacy, job creation, income, and access to government, education and healthcare services.'[4] Ultimately, however, the project was not as successful as initially anticipated and at the end of the three-year period, HP decided to conclude its involvement in the Mogalakwena HP i-community. According to at least one source, the project team could not demonstrate a model or acceptable timeframe for creating a profitable business model from its engagement with the community.

Despite numerous international awards being conferred on HP for the Mogalakwena project, no independent research had been undertaken on the Mogalakwena HP i-community by the end of its initial three-year partnership agreement that ended in October 2005.[5] This case explores what transpired in HP's search for such 'breakthrough models'. It reveals just how the competing logics between business realities and development imperatives are not easily reconciled, and exposes the tensions and contradictions within the model.

Project vision

The Hewlett-Packard Company (HP), a signatory to the UN Global Compact, was one of the first companies to make a public commitment, backed by a significant financial investment, to pursuing a business case for sustainable development. Fiorina, who served as CEO from 1999 to 2005, had adopted the phrase 'doing well while doing good' to describe the company's interest in profit-driven community service in her frequent speaking engagements.[6]

According to Maureen Conway (an officer at HP at the time),[7] executive interest in learning about emerging markets was heightened by the recognition that perhaps 90% of the world's population remained untouched by the company's products and services. And while there were an estimated 6.5 billion people in the world, there were only roughly 1 billion internet users. HP, like other multinationals, began to envisage future growth arising from regions such as China, Africa and India where the existing penetration of ICT is low, but where demand could potentially be high.[8] The company's investment in the i-community project would serve as a 'living laboratory'[9] in which to test new ICT solutions on an untapped market. It would be driven by commercial interests with accompanying social benefits.

Although the Mogalakwena HP i-community project was not explicitly formulated as a BOP model, it fits squarely into the inclusive capitalism paradigm. The company, under Fiorina, makes extensive references to BOP terminology in its description of the project, suggesting that it sought to test the inclusive capitalism theories promoted by Prahalad and Hart. At the same time, Prahalad and Hart identify HP as a participant in their own work.[10] The Mogalakwena HP i-community (or 'inclusive' community) initiative subsequently sought to demonstrate this ideal.

HP selected South Africa as one of two sites worldwide to promote its vision for developing 'breakthrough models of sustainable development'.[11] It selected South Africa for several pragmatic and somewhat opportunistic reasons, including the early involvement of a South African on the Palo Alto (the location of HP's head office) team; Fiorina's relationship with Mbeki; and her commitment to the WSSD, which was to be hosted by South Africa. Logistically, South Africa also offered Bottom of the Pyramid consumers in 'least developed' villages (LDVs)[12] within relatively close proximity to facilities, together with markets close to existing HP operations in Johannesburg.

The original project comprised of a combination of physical infrastructure and integrated programmes installed and executed in and around Mokopane (formerly Potgietersus). This is a middle-sized agricultural and mining town in southern Limpopo Province and the seat of the Mogalakwena municipality. The project was based in a former teachers' training college

Figure 1: An HP i-community computer lab (on the left) in Dipichi, a 'Least Developed Village' in Mogalakwena municipality. The building on the right is a second computer laboratory offering similar services, established by a competitor. (Photo by author, 12 July 2006)

in Mahwelereng, an apartheid-engineered township adjacent to Mokopane, and had additional satellite programmes located in Dipichi, another LDV, some 120 km northwest of Mokopane. These centres, known as telecentres, operated out of refurbished shipping containers (see Figure 1). In order to engage the province, municipality and broader community, additional access points (computers linked via the internet), were installed at almost two dozen sites within schools, post offices, libraries and health clinics, extending to the municipality's most northern township, Rebone.

In an effort to provide a comprehensive development solution that would integrate the use of computer technology in the complete delivery of environmental, economic, and social programmes, the initiative included a number of initiatives centred on ICT and business-related training. This included technical support and call centre certification courses, software development laboratories, and business development counselling to assist local entrepreneurs in realising their business plans by using their newly acquired skills. As many as 4 000 community members are reported to have received introductory computer training, with 96 receiving recognised technical accreditation, qualifying them for entry-level ICT service and support employment.

Part of the project sought to demonstrate how ICT might contribute to or link with other development initiatives. As a consequence, a number of resources were added to the project to demonstrate to the local community how ICT could be applied in ways that were relevant to their own lives. These included a sound studio where the community could record traditional music or capture traditional stories from elders and have it burnt onto a CD as digital culture. There was also a 'sustainable livelihoods area' displaying infrastructure solutions in water, sanitation, waste management, recycling, agriculture (drip irrigation and eco-circle farming), medicinal gardens, forestation, and alternative energy.[13]

Figure 2:   Local youth attend afternoon computer classes at HP's
            i-community, based in a refurbished shipping container, in
            Dipichi, Mogalakwena Municipality, Limpopo Province.
            (Photo by author, 12 July 2006)

It was anticipated that community members would use the i-community facilities to access additional information related to these activities and would also use the internet, computers, and other office equipment and services to develop or pursue employment opportunities. Computer laboratories erected at schools throughout the municipality could be used for similar purposes after school hours. Several of the project leaders envisioned that each of these facilities and some of the activities could be expanded into entrepreneurial ventures and operated at a profit. Under such schemes, concessionaires, who would charge usage fees, would acquire equipment and facilities from HP over time.[14]

Using the i-community as a test environment, HP's Emerging Markets Solutions Group also developed and launched a new product called the HP multi-user 441 desktop solution. HP's solution was targeted at the education market and consisted of one central processing unit (CPU) and four monitors, keyboards and mice. It ran a modified version of Linux that allows four people, using different languages, to access the internet simultaneously, send e-mail or play multi-media files, exactly as if they were working on four free-standing desktop computers. Through its configuration, which eliminates considerable redundancy, space and power requirements, as well as its use of 'open system' software (requiring no recurrent licence fees), the solution demonstrated how ICT can be much more affordable and environmentally sustainable.[15] The solution was specifically targeted at the emerging market education sector with a view to appealing to limited government budgets.

Project termination

After Fiorina left the leadership of HP in 2005 and was replaced by Mark Hurd, employees in the Palo Alto-based Emerging Markets Solutions Group (which managed the project) were dismissed as part of a sweeping cost-cutting initiative to eliminate 15 000 jobs. The South Africa-based contract employees were retained to fulfil the obligations of the partnership with the South African government and to finalise the project handover to these partners. In accordance with the Memorandum of Understanding (MOU) this was to happen at the end of October 2005. The reporting lines were redirected from California to Europe, and the project was realigned with the interests of the South African subsidiary.

At the time, the South African subsidiary was evaluating its options for fulfilling black economic empowerment (BEE) requirements mandated by the South African government. BEE guidelines require that there is black ownership of 25.1% of the shares in local companies.[16] For globally traded public companies this remains a challenge, and many such companies have put forward equivalency proposals.[17] In this case, HP put a proposal to the South African government in which the company would formally incorporate the i-community project's people and assets into a new BEE company. There were thus some encouraging signs that the project would be continued in the form of an ongoing local business, and simultaneously, that attention would shift from the short-term publicity considerations resulting from its high level international profile, to more in-depth alignment with community needs.

However, HP decided not to pursue its application with the Department of Trade and Industry, and instead to conclude its involvement in the Mogalakwena HP i-community.

On 31 January 2007, HP terminated the employment of all contractors,[18] including the director originally employed by the company to support the Mogalakwena HP i-community. The project was shutdown internally. As a part of its disengagement, the company transferred the assets to the province and municipality respectively who would assume responsibility for several of the facilities and programmes.

Findings

The insight gained from examining specific interventions may enable researchers and practitioners to move beyond generalities and identify effective methods for private sector engagement – all with a view to achieving sustainable development objectives. In this respect, an examination of the Mogalakwena i-community project shows that whereas 'inclusive capitalism' has been promoted as the latest prescription for sustainable development, there are incompatibilities between business realities and development imperatives which are difficult to reconcile.[19] In this project, two general problems arose from these incompatibilities:

- Shareholder interests continued to dominate the interests of stakeholders.[20]
- The top-down management approach exacerbated the classic North–South power dynamics, and conflicted with contemporary people-centred development principles and accepted development approaches.[21]

Shareholders over stakeholders

There were three prominent factors that led to short-term profit having precedence over the interests of other stakeholders, especially those at the base of the pyramid. At the same time these factors prevented the company from making the investments necessary to reach new markets and deliver benefits to the public:

Insufficient corporate commitment to emerging markets

Notwithstanding the fact that many employees were committed to the project, corporate commitment to serving bottom of the pyramid markets was extremely thin. According to some sources, it had never existed. While the project had support from the CEO and a narrow group within her circle, the project team had to struggle for resources to bring its 441 PC product to market, because the product divisions on whom the team was dependent did not have targets attached to the success of the product.

Any notions of institutional buy-in to the i-community strategy were dispelled in early 2005 when the employees of the Emerging Markets Solutions group were 'among the very first' to receive their employment termination notices. As for the 441 PC, a product that successfully demonstrated economic and environmental sustainability, the company discontinued its distribution. According to another senior executive, the product was considered a threat to the standard one-to-one PC to user ratios and its future was 'doomed' by a corporate culture that fostered competition among product business units. The fact that the product was developed by 'outsiders' in the Emerging Market Solutions Group rather than by the PC product division, meant that the 441 failed to gain the necessary corporate support.

Unrealistic timeframes for achieving results

Time pressures were significant at several levels. At a macro level, participants surveyed found that three years was an unrealistic timeframe in which to measure results, particularly in terms of social impact. According to one executive, this was the maximum number of years to which the company was 'comfortable with committing' on an experimental basis. As it turned out, the new management considered even that period too long.

Within the three-year timeframe, the project team was under pressure to deliver rapid, visible results, and the risk was that speed would override substance. According to Davids and colleagues, most often development fails due to lack of authentic public participation.[22] Public participation in this case was limited to a three-day 'visioning' session. The province and municipality were required, as per the MOU, to fast-track all meetings, decision-making, and regulatory approvals to expedite the launch and successful establishment of the i-community. An initial 'quick-start' phase put pressure on deliverables within the first 180 days.

Pressure for partners to perform mounted in advance of visits from the South African president each September. Then there was a requirement for progress to be seen, even if a project was only executed for purposes of the visit.

Intellectual property over social welfare

When HP publicly announced that it sought to find 'breakthrough solutions in sustainable development' that would be replicable across South Africa through an 'ecosystem of partnerships, the company effectively entered into the development arena. Thus it acquired relationships outside of those with shareholders, its primary stakeholders.[23] In this arena, the new development stakeholders were focused on measuring development outcomes. Yet it became apparent that there were differences in the way HP and its development partners viewed the role of information gathering, sharing, monitoring and assessment.

First, in the course of defining a 'breakthrough in sustainable development' and whether the project team had found one, it became clear to the author that intellectual property (IP) constraints, including those tied to social learning, placed limitations on what the team was authorised to share with other stakeholders. Any such learning had to be captured as HP IP, so that it could enhance the company's reputation as a service provider in development. Moreover, it was subsequently acknowledged that the project leaders had not established research metrics to support any breakthrough claims, and that the company had not pursued the offers of two development organisations to provide such metrics and conduct the relevant research.

One was the Canada-based International Development Research Corporation (IDRC), which was coordinating a major study in 2003 on similar ICT projects in Africa, and offered the research template to HP at no cost to enable the company to track its results. HP's participation in the survey would have contributed to a comprehensive body of knowledge on what works in using ICT for development. In the second case, HP had approached UNDP South Africa as a potential development partner. UNDP responded favourably, proposing a comprehensive social review and project-design approach[24] when it learned that sustainable development was not being addressed by the project. When issues over ownership of intellectual property arose, together with questions regarding technical and financial issues, the partnership was not consummated.

It may not always be essential to share knowledge for development to occur. Nevertheless, the failure to subject claims about 'doing well while doing good' to accepted metrics for social research (or to conduct peer reviews) calls into question the design and overall value of the intervention. At the same time it casts doubt on the organisation's stated motive for becoming involved in the project. In the context of a PPP, which involves using public funds, these actions raise normative questions about how much information should be withheld by private companies on the basis of objections about intellectual property and the conditions under which information should be disclosed.

Top-down management over people-centred development

When, because of a development project, the CEO of one of the world's largest corporations (in this case Fiorina) and the nation's president suddenly take interest in the running of a small and remote town, there are significant implications for the sustainability of the project. Whereas the infusion of high-level management attention, public relations exposure and financial resources may create urgency for implementation partners to perform, the impact on the intended beneficiaries is less certain. Because of Mokopane's enforced separate development under apartheid, many subtle issues remain hiding cautiously below the fragile surface. To overcome a history of development being used as a tool of exploitation and dehumanisation, people-centred development principles, as outlined in the Manila Declaration (1989), were incorporated in the South African Constitution of 1996. These principles insist that 'those that would assist the people with their development must recognise that it is they who are participating in support of the people's agenda, not reverse'.[25]

However, delivering a 'living laboratory' from Palo Alto, through a high powered team, into such a complex and sensitive environment, risked betraying basic notions of people-centred development. It also unwittingly created a dynamic that typified the North–South divide that the project sought to bridge. Two examples of how the engagement exacerbated this tension through a top-down approach are outlined as follows.

First, the corporation defined the project and selected the community based on company and political criteria rather than at the initiative of the community and according to its criteria. (The firm acknowledges that the community was selected on the basis of its demographics and proximity to Johannesburg.) Both HP's CEO and the Office of President directed the location and deployment of the project. Following the three-day 'visioning' session with the community, the company website described the outcome in this way:

> The i-community team chose to focus on improving information and communication technology infrastructure in Mogalakwena, increasing capacity building and technology training, ensuring cultural preservation and boosting economic development.[26]

Secondly, the project was directed by 'outsiders', rather than by representative community members. Although HP's South African subsidiary has been established for a decade, the Mogalakwena project group reported directly to Palo Alto. While the South African subsidiary benefited from the project's publicity, the parallel relationships between the company and the government were described by one respondent as 'awkward'. The project management team charged with conducting all local negotiations with the rural community was based in Johannesburg and Palo Alto, and as the project progressed, the staff members drawn from Mokopane also increasingly spent more time in Johannesburg.[27]

Local community staff members were not empowered to make many basic decisions and most questions were referred back to Johannesburg for approved responses. During a three-day visit by the author to the main centre, for example, all facilities were locked, with the exception of the PC refurbishment lab. There were no other visitors on site to benefit from the significant resources at hand.[28] With all the rooms and labs locked, the local staff members were not sure when and under what conditions local community members could access the resources. In an earlier incident, one of the project's strategic partners had hired someone to run one of the software labs, but ultimately failed to get clear guidance on when the person could access the lab, and therefore abandoned the project.

Race remains a delicate yet pervasive issue in South Africa. The racial composition of HP's project management team raised questions about HP's ability to interpret local community needs effectively, given the racial diversity of contemporary South Africa.[29]

The capacity gap

The corporation underestimated the capacity gap between corporate resources and government resources. Although the local province and municipality welcomed the investment, research findings indicate that there was not sufficient local capacity in place to accommodate the performance demands of a multinational corporation. The frequent turnover of government staff who attended team meetings, as well as the loss of key personnel at a local level, the loss of equipment, the lock-out of donated equipment, systems crashes, and many other factors all indicate that the community was inadequately equipped to support the project. A visit to the public library, where HP is reported to have donated computers, found no signs of computerisation, and there were reports that the municipality had locked away computers at its facilities, presumably for security reasons.

What can be learnt from the initiative?

This case analysis demonstrates that while the HP i-community project was effective in showcasing a range of technical solutions that might be of interest to excluded communities, the project ultimately exposed the limitations of inclusive capitalism. Admittedly, the HP i-community project went beyond the standard ICT philanthropy that typically involves simply donating equipment. In its quest for breakthrough models, HP included useful applications outside the norm for technical, computer-based applications, such as waste management, eco-circle agriculture, solar technologies, and multi-lingual curricula for schools. Thousands of local residents were also exposed to ICT, and received computer training for the first time. However, there is no evidence that these efforts contributed to lasting, sustainable, social and economic development or yielded the financial returns to the firm that are required in a private sector initiative.

Prahalad's BOP model rests on the notion that MNCs have – or are able to acquire – the social knowledge to drive sustainable development. In this case HP reverted to top-down implementation methods with an expectation of quick returns. Ultimately it handed down social development responsibilities to the local authorities without providing the capacity and technical assistance required to provide a solid foundation for such a complex initiative. As a business model, the project's financial sustainability was dependent on the sale of social services to the state (or other potential donors). Consequently, the responsibility for economic and sustainable development was not transferred to private enterprise, but remained with the government. While the use of private-sector contractors for delivery of state services is common practice, it does not in itself represent a 'breakthrough model' in the delivery of social benefit through business innovation.

Many questions are raised concerning the way in which corporate interests influence the public agenda when policy makers defer development to the private sector. These should be considered in future studies and projects of a similar kind. The business case for inclusive capitalism inherently supports the notion that the private sector is better at optimising resources than the public sector and therefore better able to deliver sustainable development. The Mogalakwena case shows that the contrary can also be true. It shows HP creating, at considerable expense to itself and augmented by public funds, a controlled environment for reaching beneficiaries on HP's terms. Had the project been driven from a beneficiary perspective, would the resources invested in boosting capacity and attendance at the public library or the planting of a medicinal garden in a central park have provided more value for the community? Local ownership and operation can make a crucial difference.[30]

Recommendations

As we have seen, the specific problems in this case arose from the general tendency of HP to revert to a short term profit-seeking orientation and a top-down management style. The inclusive capitalism model, by contrast, suggests that corporations can operate profitably by including long-term social development as a necessary condition for long-term profitability in emerging markets. It argues that such social development depends on local participation in setting goals and making decisions. Any future test of the inclusive capitalism model should therefore include the following considerations:

Setting metrics

For any model to be assessed accurately, appropriate metrics must be in place. To measure inclusive capitalism beyond profitability, the metrics must include clear indicators of social development, community involvement, and resultant market potential.

Creating mutual evaluation responsibility

The principle of partnership is that there is mutual responsibility for all elements of the project and its outcome. Consequently, partners must share the responsibility for setting success targets, and evaluating the project.

Planning properly

Reflecting on the project in its fourth year, Clive Smith, the HP i-community project director, acknowledged that projects with social content have different requirements. He recommends that corporations should allow for sufficient planning time with the community before rushing headlong into execution.[31] Ultimately, the Emerging Markets Solution Group, and later the team of contractors hired to support the initiative, had neither the full support of the corporation, nor the support of the community. As a consequence the project was abandoned.

Overcoming intellectual property constraints

In partnerships that include a component of public funding, the criteria for sharing information on social innovations with economic values must be clearly defined from the outset. Neither partner should seek to appropriate intellectual property. Social innovation must be seen as a public good.

Harnessing local knowledge

This case illustrates that multinational corporations will achieve a bottom-up approach more easily when they draw on the wealth of local knowledge and cultural understanding in their local subsidiaries. Rather than directing efforts from distant headquarters, subsidiaries should be adequately resourced, empowered, and tasked with identifying new market opportunities.

Investing for impact

For breakthroughs to be achieved, companies must be prepared to make adequate investments. They should draw on Hart's advice to build the business from the bottom up and be prepared to transfer their willingness to make large, risky investments (as they do elsewhere) to those projects targeted at the bottom of the pyramid, which cost relatively little by comparison.[32]

Strategic integration of BOP targets

At HP, in spite of the apparent initial high level of commitment from the executives, business managers remained aligned to the short-term targets demanded by Wall Street. The company was ultimately not prepared to incorporate the notion of 'breakthrough models' of sustainable development into its core strategy, as it cut products, programmes and people in pursuit of business-as-usual quarterly profits. When asked what it might take to integrate pro-poor marketing strategies into HP and other multi-national corporations, Maureen Conway, former EMSG vice president at HP, responded:

> There needs to be a focus on a five to ten year plan for penetrating emerging markets. While the early years require investment, the future years could yield incredible growth, since the traditional markets would be saturated...The fault some companies have is that they want short term return on investment – as long as that is the goal, the emerging market opportunities will go untapped.[33]

Conclusion

HP should be recognised for its effort to develop an alternative approach to sustainable development that would align with core business activities. Through the Mogalakwena HP i-community, visionary company leaders were prepared to embrace the ideal that corporations can and should have a positive role in uplifting poorer segments of the population through win-win initiatives that would ultimately generate sufficient revenues to become self-sustaining.

The early language of the BOP discourse referring to 'unlimited business opportunities in solving the world's most difficult problems' and 'eradicating poverty through profits'[34] may well have set unrealistic expectations, without meaningful precedents from which to draw, or adequate consultation to establish shared goals and the required tools with which to measure progress. The study suggests that unless there is a close fit between local needs and realities on the one hand, and the blueprint developed by the company to address those on the other, inclusive capitalism will remain misdirected, and thus difficult – if not impossible – for global companies to achieve.

Editors' reflections and questions

The case of Mogalakwena HP i-community in Limpopo Province explores what tran-spired in HP's search for a 'breakthrough model' to provide development benefits and simultaneously generate profits.

1. How representative is this case of the strengths or weaknesses of the BOP approach, considering the different circumstances that may characterise other sectors or coun-tries? Is it an outlier or a more classic BOP case?

2. What recommendations would you make to a multinational company seeking to develop business opportunities while producing benefits for social and economic development?

3. The case suggests that social innovation must be a public good. However, this might require significant investments in research and development that are less feasible for companies. How could such tensions be resolved?

Notes

1 The editors thank Claire Beswick for editing this case. This paper was originally presented at a Global Compact/UNISA/University of Washington symposium, on 'Corporate Citizenship: Is it Making a Difference?' held in Accra, Ghana in November 2006. Complete research findings are also included in the author's Master's thesis of the same title, submitted to Stellenbosch University, School of Public Management (2007). The author interviewed 18 people in connection with the Mogalakwena HP i-community between July 2006 and February 2007. Twelve were at the time current or former employees and contractors of Hewlett-Packard. The other interviews were con-ducted with prospective partners of HP, including representatives from the Council for Scientific and Industrial Research (CSIR), United Nations Development Program (UNDP), and International Development Research Centre (IDRC). Most interviews were carried out face-to-face in Johan-nesburg, Pretoria, and Mokopane, South Africa. Retired directors and officers of HP based in the United States were contacted by telephone. The author visited the Mogalakwena HP i-community in Mokopane on 12, 13, and 14 July 2006 and the Dipichi HP i-community on 12 July 2006.

2 See C.K. Prahalad and S. Hart, 'The Fortune at the Bottom of the Pyramid', *Strategy & Business*, 26 (January 2002); and, C.K. Prahalad, *The Fortune at the Bottom of the Pyramid: Eradicating Poverty through Profits* (Upper Saddle River, NJ: Wharton School Publishing, Pearson Education, 2004); and S.L. Hart, *Inclusive Capitalism: The Unlimited Business Opportunities in Solving the World's Most Difficult Problems*. (Upper Saddle River, NJ: Wharton School Publishing, Pearson Education, 2005).

3 The Hewlett-Packard Company, 'Making the Breakthrough: The Story of the Mogalakwena HP i-Community', see www.hp.com/e-inclusion/en/hp_i-community_brochure.pdf (accessed September 2006).

4 Ibid.

5 Research into public–private partnerships involving the UN Global Compact, in particular, suggests that they are subjected to very low levels of monitoring and evaluation; see P. Utting and A. Zammit, 'Beyond Pragmatism: Appraising UN-Business Partnerships' (Geneva: United Nations Research Institute for Social Development, 2006); see also Chapter 3. The scarcity of research on corporate

citizenship and the role of business in development in the African context is also discussed in R. Hamann, 'Can Business Make Decisive Contributions to Development? Toward a Research Agenda on Corporate Citizenship and Beyond', *Development Southern Africa*, 23, 2 (June 2006), 193.

6   Carley Fiorina underscores this motivation in a speech at a recognition event, the Seed of Hope Award, presented by Concern Worldwide, New York, on 4 November 2003. C.K. Prahalad also refers to 'doing well while doing good' in *The Fortune at the Bottom of the Pyramid*, 2.

7   From interview with Maureen Conway, former vice president, HP Emerging Markets Solutions (retired), by telephone from her home in New Jersey, 17 September 2006.

8   See M. Kannellos, 'HP Phases Out Group for Emerging Markets', *C-Net News.com*, 2006 available at http://www.news.com (accessed July 2007).

9   'Living laboratory' was a term used by several former top managers at HP interviewed by the author.

10 See Prahalad, *The Fortune at the Bottom of the Pyramid*, xviii; and Hart, *Inclusive Capitalism*, 73.

11 The other was located in Kuppam, India.

12 HP refers to its Least-Developed Villages (LDV) programme and identifies Dipichi, in this respect, as one of the underserved villages in the Mogalakwena district targeted for development by the South African Department of Economic Development. See http://www.hp.com/hpinfo/globalciti-zenship/gcreport/socialinvest/einclusion.html (accessed July 2007).

13 In reality, these initiatives appeared to be of little interest to the local community – with social subsidies and long-term dislocation from land there was no sign that targeted community members were keen on getting involved in agriculture, forestation etc in a significant way.

14 There was no consensus amongst the HP team members interviewed as to whether this was the ultimate aim of the project and whether it would be a successful strategy. It remained part of the ongoing research by HP into identifying a profit-driven model that was never to be completed.

15 Multi-user PCs have been manufactured to support up to 10 simultaneous users on one CPU. For schools, internet cafes, and other multi-user environments, this offers significant financial and envi-ronmental sustainability in terms of packaging, space, and power consumption. This is according to Brooke Partridge, former director of HP Emerging Markets Solutions Group and currently founder of Vitalwave Consulting, in a telephone interview on 14 September 2006. Partridge's group was responsible for the commercialisation and launch of this product in South Africa.

16 For the ICT Black Economic Empowerment Charter visit http://www.ictcharter.org.za/

17 Statement 103, issued by the Department of Trade and Industry, recognises equity equivalents, but does not stipulate what they are or how they may be earned. Also, only multinational businesses headquartered outside South Africa that have a global policy requiring that local subsidiaries be wholly owned, and that can show that they would suffer substantial commercial harm if they were to depart from that policy, may use equity equivalents. See E.N. Sonnenberg, 'South Africa: Black Economic Empowerment', International Financial Law Review (June 2007), available at http://www.iflr.com (accessed July 2007). See also Republic of South Africa, 'Broad-Based Black Eco-nomic Empowerment Act: The Codes of Good Practice, 2007' available at http://www.thedti.gov.za/bee/interpretaiveguide28june07.pdf (accessed July 2007).

18 Approximately 25 employees, according to Clive Smith, the i-community project director, inter-viewed by telephone on 23 January 2007.

19 The unit of analysis is the company.

20 The rights of shareholders were initially established in a 1919 Michigan case (*Dodge Brothers v Ford Motor Company (1919)*, 170).

21 See, I. Davids, F. Theron and K.J. Maphunye, *Participatory Development in South Africa* (Pretoria: J.L. van Schaik, 2005); OECD, Participatory Development and Good Governance (Paris: OECD, 1995), available at http://www.oecd.org/dataoecd/27/13/31857685.pdf (accessed July 2007).

22 See Davids *et al.*, *Participatory Development in South Africa*, 130.

23 The 2002 Memorandum of Understanding between Hewlett-Packard, Limpopo Province, and Mogalakwena Municipality calls for additional development partners to be identified and added to the project.

24 In 2003 UNDP South Africa programme managers conducted a preliminary project assessment of the Mogalakwena HP i-community and summarised findings in an internal UNDP report of 4

September 2003. Based on findings that the project was not aligned to 'community aspirations and the provincial development strategy', it was proposed that UNDP specialists be engaged to bring the project into line with these.

25 See Davids *et al.*, *Participatory Development in South Africa*.

26 Quote from the Hewlett-Packard company, 'Making the Breakthrough'.

27 With urban training opportunities, the situation is also indicative of the challenges in rural development, as skills migrate to the cities.

28 As explanation: Facilities were not in use as the project was in transition during 2006 and usage was to be determined by the government partners.

29 The project leaders and exclusive negotiators were white, and not originally from the province; local operations managers were town denizens and of South Asian origin; while the balance of staff was predominantly black. The Ndebele people form the largest cultural group living in the township and surroundings. Information from Mokopane Chamber of Commerce.

30 Initial positive correlation is identified in research conducted by IDRC in identifying success factors for the financial sustainability of Telecentres in Africa. See F.E. Etta and S. Parvin-Wamahiu, *The Experience with Community Tele-centres* (Ottawa: International Development Research Centre, 2003).

31 Interview with Clive Smith at HP offices Johannesburg, 21 July 2006.

32 See Hart, *Inclusive Capitalism*, 221.

33 From telephone interview with Maureen Conway, 17 September 2006.

34 See Hart, *Inclusive Capitalism* and Prahalad, *The Fortune at the Bottom of the Pyramid*.

VidaGás:

Powering health clinics and households in Mozambique with liquefied petroleum gas

COURTENAY SPRAGUE & STU WOOLMAN

Introduction[1]

In a country with 500 doctors for a population of almost 20 million, initiatives that can expand the reach of health services to rural populations are in critical demand and short supply. One major challenge: northern Mozambique's health clinics lack reliable fuel to provide lighting for surgery and routine operations. As a result, most clinics can only operate during daylight. However, accidents and births take place at all hours. Reliable fuel is also important for the immunisation of children. The storage of vaccines requires refrigeration within a fixed temperature range. Such fixed temperatures are extremely difficult to maintain with kerosene refrigerators that frequently break down. Without proper immunisation, many children will die of preventable diseases.

The absence of reliable fuel sources affects other aspects of existence in northern Mozambique. Less than 2% of households run on electricity. Many households are dependent on wood or charcoal for cooking. Burning so-called 'biomass' fuels increases the susceptibility of individuals to respiratory infections, asthma, and complications related to pregnancy (i.e., low birth weight and stillbirths).[2] In the absence of electricity or other fuel sources, the forests that supply firewood are declining. The degradation of local mangroves imperils the local commercial fishing industry – a chief income-earner for the population in northern Mozambique.

Does this concatenation of health and environmental challenges sound intractable? To mere mortals, perhaps. But take a former minister of education from Mozambique, Graça Machel, whose commitment to children's health is unshakable, and pair this two-time first lady with a visionary social entrepreneur named Blaise Judja-Sato and his sophisticated, Seattle-based NGO, VillageReach. Add a handful of Seattle philanthropists who are willing to back a new fuel source company. Throw in a Ministry of Health that, together with one dedicated Governor of the pilot province, is willing to provide state funding and eliminate state bureaucracy to improve the health of Mozambicans in the north. And, as a final ingredient, add a community foundation called FDC (Fundação para o Desenvolvimento da Comunidade), whose expert staff actually understands the complex development needs of Mozambicans. And now, you may just have a recipe for success and the solution to the absence of reliable fuel sources in northern Mozambique.

Through a Memorandum of Understanding with Mozambique's Ministry of Health (Minis-tério da Saúde or MISAU), FDC and VillageReach launched a pilot partnership project in the province of Cabo Delgado in northern Mozambique. MISAU's mandate was to identify those initiatives that would improve the health status of residents in the north. FDC would provide community partners and local experts, while VillageReach would manage the technical design and implementation of the pilot project. At the core of the project's success lay the improve-ment of the immunisation program. Such improvement required ensuring the integrity of the 'cold chain'. The cold chain encompasses the network of freezers, refrigerators and cold boxes used in the transport and storage of vaccines according to a specified temperature. Exposure to excessive heat or cold may cause a vaccine to lose its potency. Impotent vaccines must be discarded. Due to unreliable refrigerators, vaccines had often become unusable in north-ern Mozambique. VillageReach and FDC introduced an improved cold chain. They replaced decrepit kerosene refrigerators in remote health facilities in Cabo Delgado with Liquefied petroleum gas (LPG)-powered refrigerators outfitted with automatic change-over valves. The results? Read on.

The Mozambican context

At the outset, three main problems in the healthcare system in northern Mozambique were identified: (1) a lack of reliable infrastructure (roads, vehicles and electricity); (2) insufficient human resources; and (3) a lack of the necessary processes, plans, and systems to underpin health policy and practice. The result was the delivery of sub-optimal healthcare service. The partners found this array of inter-related problems required a combination of solutions. First, the initiative would have to identify a reliable source of energy to keep vaccines cold and to meet the energy needs of the clinics (e.g., sterilisation, lighting and heating). To this end, they found that LPG-powered fridges and lamps were easy for healthcare workers to use and to maintain and that a fleet of dedicated vehicles could deliver the goods. Secondly, the initiative would have to train staff to deliver medicines and supplies. The training requires a system of supervisory support whereby field teams provide feedback and mentoring to clinic employees each month. Third, the initiative would have to create a logistics platform that delivered the vaccines, medical supplies and propane to clinics on a regular basis. Nine key metrics are gathered monthly. These metrics inform the partners of the field context and help to pinpoint any problems in its constituent parts.

The initiative led to the creation of VidaGás. While the company was first established to supply public health clinics in Cabo Delgado with LPG, the company has begun to supply LPG to large commercial and industrial consumers in Cabo Delgado. In addition to supplying hotels (8), restaurants (6) and a commercial prawn operation in Pemba (the capital of the province),[3] VidaGás is now targeting small and medium enterprises and households for LPG use in urban and peri-urban areas.

VidaGás company overview

VidaGás Limitada is a limited-liability (LLC) for-profit private company, founded in 2002 by FDC and VillageReach, and based in Pemba. VidaGás' core business is to sell and distribute liquefied petroleum gas to rural, urban and peri-urban residents in northern Mozambique. Its broader social vision is to marry the Mozambican need for reliable fuel sources to a commitment to using cleaner, alternative forms of energy that will improve environmental conditions, generate employment and advance the general socio-economic development of Mozambicans.

The company's LPG distribution plant became operational in November 2002. VidaGás now distributes LPG to clinics, households and businesses.

VidaGás has expanded its operations to Nampula province and soon plans to service Zambezia province. On the back of its LPG sales and distribution network it now sells a range of other commercial products: freezers and refrigerators (for sale to health clinics, restaurants and other commercial operations); large gas ovens (for restaurants); a four burner stove; a three burner stove; a two burner stove; a single burner stove; and LPG lamps.[5]

VidaGás has thus far created 23 direct jobs and generated indirect employment in related markets. As the consumption of LPG expands, retail outlets (selling VidaGás LPG) will step in to further diversify the sale of the gas. Given the nature of LPG, the company sees women (who do most of the cooking), cooperatives of fishermen, farmers and artisans as the primary target markets for LPG.

VidaGás faces no strong competition from other suppliers of LPG. The company sells LPG in 5.5 kg cylinders. These cyclinders are more likely to be purchased for household use. The primary competition – GALP – distributes LPG in 11kg and 45kg cylinders. Moreover, GALP's distribution occurs only at its petrol or gasoline stations and through a limited number of scattered and small re-sellers. Petrogás also sells 11kg and 45kg cylinders of LPG. However, Petrogás is considering exiting the market due to insufficient sales.[6]

Despite the absence of real competition from other LPG suppliers, there is very real competition in the form of traditional biomass fuels that individuals are used to relying on for fuel. Indeed, VidaGás must overcome a number of barriers to market entry and expansion. These barriers encompass insufficient storage facilities for LPG, a weak industrial and commercial infrastructure in northern Mozambique, inadequate training of retailers in LPG use, and a lack of consumer knowledge about the benefits of LPG. The price of LPG is also an impediment, especially given the impecunity of the population.[7] The GNP of the province is estimated at US$148m (2002 data) and the GNP per capita is US$97.[8]

Liquefied petroleum gas (LPG) and its benefits

More than half the world's population – 3.2 billion people – still burn coal and biomass fuels such as wood, dung and crop residues to meet their basic energy needs ... Preventing deaths caused by polluted indoor air must no longer be delayed ... the use of cleaner fuels, such as liquefied petroleum gas, biogas or other modern biofuels, can eliminate current indoor air pollution.[9]

Autogas, propane and butane are typical names for liquefied petroleum gas. LPG is used for heating, cooking and other forms of fuel. It is, for example, compatible with internal combustion engines. LPG is often referred to as a 'green' fuel because it emits less greenhouse gas emissions than other fuels: LPG vehicles emit about 20% less CO_2 or carbon dioxide. It is also lead-free, sulphur-free, clean burning and effectively odorless. LPG is highly portable and can be packaged, stored and utilised with great ease in rural destinations.[10] The downside of LPG is that it is a fossil fuel and is therefore a non-renewable source of energy extracted from crude oil and from natural gas.

VidaGás provides reliable fuel that allows for effective vaccines, sterilisation, and lighting in 88 health clinics in Cabo Delgado. These clinics serve 1.5 million people. Its market and services have recently expanded to 163 additional clinics in the neighbouring province of Nampula. Between the two provinces, VidaGás now serves a total population of over 5 million. Most importantly, given the original purpose of the partnership initiative, participating clinics in Cabo Delgado reported a 47% increase in the number of children immunised. This increase is a direct function of the introduction of VidaGás' LPG-based cold chain and the accompanying logistics platform created by VidaGás' two NGO partners, FDC and VillageReach.[11]

The increased efficacy of the sterilisation process for medical instruments is of critical import. Each clinic houses a steam steriliser, also known as an autoclave. The autoclave uses hot steam to sterilise medical equipment. Clinic workers rely upon a propane-powered burner to heat up the steam sterilisers. As Jennifer Hannibal observes:

> If they did not have the LPG, clinic workers would gather wood and start a wood fire to heat up the sterilizer – taking valuable time away from the clinic, polluting the clinic area with wood smoke, and contributing to deforestation.[12]

Before VillageReach and FDC's involvement, the public health clinics in Cabo Delgado experienced a regular shortage of essential medicines. Most maternal deaths globally result from infection and hemorrhage due to complications in pregnancy; oral antibiotics and rehydration solutions can stave off infection and overcome the deleterious effects of blood loss.[13] However, such medicines need to be ordered, supplied and stocked. The supply chain introduced by the partners means that stocks of these essential medicines are more reliable. The reliable fuel supply, the cold chain and the improved distribution of medicines all directly support the goals of the Ministry of Health, the UN Millennium Development Goals, and ultimately, public health in Mozambique.[14]

Efficacy of the VidaGás model

> It's not difficult to get vaccines delivered to developing countries. What's difficult is delivering the vaccines throughout the country. The last mile is just as important as the first.[15]

The following indicators are used by the partners to assess the success of the project.

Refrigerator reliability. Of the 88 refrigerators in 88 clinics served in Cabo Delgado in 2005 and 2006, a nominal number of repairs were reported following the introduction of LPG. Only 2% of refrigerators required repair in 2006.[16]

Figure 1:   A typical cold chain

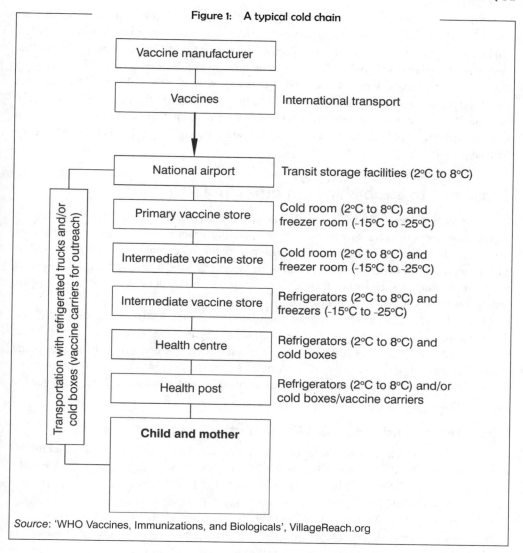

Source: 'WHO Vaccines, Immunizations, and Biologicals', VillageReach.org

Vaccine wastage rates. Quantitatively, closed-vial vaccine wastage rates are tracked to monitor effectiveness. The current 'waste' rates for Cabo Delgado LPG powered clinics are consistently low: they average below 3% for each type of vaccine. This is in keeping with World Health Organisation standards.

Data collection. Field teams gather data from healthcare workers on a monthly basis. The data is sent to the VillageReach office in Seattle where monthly reports are generated for the nine key metrics at the 251 current clinics served. The importance of accurate data – in a post-civil war context in which data systems and record-keeping fell into total disrepair – cannot be over-emphasised.[17]

Integrity of supply chain. Based upon the data provided by the clinics, medical supplies are ordered by the Ministry of Health, and transported to a MISAU warehouse shared by staff of VillageReach and FDC in Pemba. The vaccines are kept cold in LPG-powered refrigerators. Three drivers collect the supplies from the warehouse and embark on a two week mission to deliver fuel, medicines, syringes and related items to each of the 88 clinics in the province of Cabo Delgado. Similar teams are deployed to the 163 clinics in the province of Nampula. Staff members repair refrigerators and other essential equipment. Communities have also been outfitted with bicycles or motorcycles in case deliveries are urgently needed between visits by the lead drivers.[18]

Challenges to establishing a market for LPG

The long term success of LPG as a reliable fuel source for healthcare clinics will require greater economies of scale. Given the current operating structure of VidaGás, its break-even point is estimated at sales of 25 to 30 tonnes per month. The company is currently selling only 14 tonnes of LPG per month. To achieve its target of 25 to 30 tonnes, VidaGás is serving customers in Nampula. However, this expansion naturally raises the current break-even point, which now stands at 50 tonnes per month.[19]

Figure 2 (LPG sales in Mozambique from 2000) indicates a steady incline in LPG use through 2005, followed by a slight decline in 2006 'owing to upstream shipping constraints in South Africa, which supplies Mozambique'.[20] In addition to the general challenges of doing business in Mozambique – the World Bank ranks Mozambique 134th out of 178 countries in terms of the 'ease of doing business' – a range of specific impediments for LPG sales need to be overcome.[21]

Infrastructure and supply of LPG to northern Mozambique

LPG is not produced in-country. Neighbouring South Africa supplies Mozambique with LPG (produced in a natural gas separation plant). LPG is shipped overland by rail and truck to the capital of Maputo. The procurement and the delivery of all LPG imported from South Africa is coordinated by IMOPETRO (a co-operative company that operates on behalf of its members). VidaGás procures LPG through IMOPETRO by the container load (10 tonnes).[22]

The next leg of the trip is the most arduous. The distance between Maputo and Pemba (also a port) is 2,700km (1,677 miles). The physical roads between Cabo Delgado and Maputo are in poor condition. Only 10% of the roads are tarred; 60-70% of the untarred roads are barely passable. The rail network is also in a state of decay.[23] Such a weak transportation infrastructure translates into higher pricing of LPG. The price of LPG at the Maputo port is US$785 per metric tonne – significantly higher than international prices. US$15 is added by IMOPETRO to cover operational costs. Transport costs from Maputo to Pemba further increase the final price in the north. In addition, because South Africa lacks adequate physical storage space for LPG, it is unable to store large quantities. This limitation, in turn, restricts Mozambique's supply and results in fluctuations in price.[24]

While reducing Mozambique's reliance on its neighbour might appear attractive,[25] Mozambique's low GNP dramatically curtails its ability to develop large-scale distribution networks for LPG in the north and in the interior. At the same time, the relative poverty of its residents

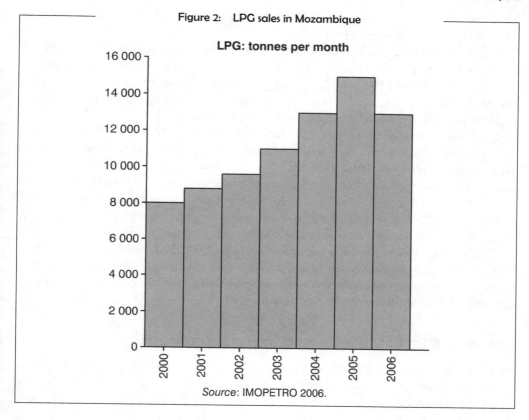

Figure 2: LPG sales in Mozambique

LPG: tonnes per month

Source: IMOPETRO 2006.

limits the capacity of VidaGás to ramp up production and distribution.[26] Although the local currency has strengthened in the last couple of years, between 1998 to 2003 it lost more than half of its value against the US dollar. According to USAID: 'This drop in the value of the currency has important implications for the use of non-traditional fuels such as LPG, which are more expensive compared to charcoal and firewood, which have traditionally been used in households especially in the poorer provinces of the country.'[27]

Consumer pricing and energy efficiency of LPG

If the aforementioned barriers can be overcome, then an untapped consumer market may well await. A 5.5 kg cylinder or container of LPG would be the optimal choice for households and provide fuel for up to two weeks. The cost of the cylinder is US$11. By comparison, an equivalent amount of charcoal costs US$33.[28]

Consumer behaviour and perceptions

USAID funded a market research study in 2005 of 400 households in Pemba, Cabo Delgado. The purpose of the survey was to gain insight into those factors that influence residents' attitudes towards cooking, lighting and heating. The survey revealed that most residents thought LPG was too expensive and that its multiple benefits were unappreciated. Most Mozambicans were concerned with LPG's suitability for cooking.[29] Product availability and safety were also deemed important considerations.

The study revealed other forms of uncertainty regarding the use of LPG. Only 36% of respondents knew that LPG was available through VidaGás. Just half of those surveyed understood that LPG could be used for cooking or lighting, and an astonishing 79% of those surveyed believed LPG to be toxic, explosive or dangerous.[30] Its price and its continued availability were cited as potential problems by 50% of respondents.

However, in spite of the negative associations attached to LPG's safety and price, 80% of respondents indicated that they would be willing to try LPG under the right conditions. Based on these findings, USAID observed: 'This points to the need for an intensive awareness campaign to make people aware of the uses and benefits of LPG.'[31] One LPG customer in Pemba, Ester Ferreira, said that she would recommend it to others because 'LPG is faster (than firewood), cleaner and more efficient'.[32] Respondents suggested a variety of methods that would expand consumers' knowledge about LPG: direct campaigning and demonstrations, as well as word of mouth through local community leaders.[33] The data suggest the need for an aggressive marketing campaign using multiple media channels (radio, cellular phone text messaging, newspapers and billboards) and the ability to make consumers aware of both the economic and the health benefits associated with LPG.

Opportunities to scale-up and increase profitability

VidaGás can achieve financial sustainability – and thus accomplish its primary goal of improved healthcare – if it is able to realise a number of complex initiatives and meet several important benchmarks.

Maritime harbour

A USAID study suggests that a new maritime harbour in Nacala, off the coast of Nampula, could be used by companies that operate in the northern region of Mozambique. USAID estimates the required investment at roughly US$1.5m. Such a harbour would reduce transport costs and increase reliability.[34]

Expansion to other northern provinces

The provinces of Nampula and Niassa have slightly higher per capita incomes than the population in Cabo Delgado. Taken together, the two provinces have a population of 4.5 million. If VidaGás were able to establish the requisite distribution and sales network in these provinces, then the 'potential for LPG sales in Nampula/Niassa could well be in the region of 100 tonnes per month'.[35]

Microfinance

The experiences of another Lusophone country may prove instructive for VidaGás. About 35 years ago, Brazilian companies wishing to penetrate the interior rural markets of Brazil with LPG began micro-finance schemes. Companies financed both the LPG stove and cylinder with an agreement that the money would be paid back to the lender within a one to two year period. Because the upfront costs of purchasing a stove and cylinder can be prohibitive, the initial financing of those set-up costs can make LPG a more attractive option. (The advantage of charcoal is that it can be purchased in small quantities. Users of LPG – mainly women – may find that the canisters are too bulky to carry or they may wish to buy a smaller quantity of gas.)[36]

Government subsidy and regulation

The Indian government subsidises LPG as a fuel for households. As of 2001, an estimated 18% of households in India (roughly 34 million households) used LPG for cooking. The Indian government offers a subsidy to low-income families at a rate of an estimated US$3 per month. This subsidy enables 4.5 million families to benefit from a cleaner, healthier fuel.[37] A subsidy is but one potentially necessary intervention on the part of the state in this public–private initiative. At the moment, Mozambique lacks the requisite legislation to regulate bottling, storage, safety, use and distribution of LPG. A legal framework governing the use of LPG is necessary to ensure consumer protection and quality control.

Conclusion

This public–private partnership initiative is already a success – if success if measured by its ability to contribute positively to the healthcare outcomes of residents throughout Cabo Delgado. However, the ultimate success of the venture rests on the sustainability of LPG as an alternative fuel. Those who might wish to replicate the achievements of VidaGás in other environments should pay particular attention to a number of critical success factors:

1. LPG has demonstrated that it is a superior product: it outperforms competitor fuels in terms of price, storage, efficiency and environmental sustainability.

2. Although the financial capital to launch this start-up venture was secured through a small number of local Seattle NGOs, larger partners emerged as the project grew. These partners included the Hunter Foundation of Scotland, the Dutch government's bilateral organisation and anonymous donors.

3. The improved supply chain designed by VillageReach and FDC has enabled VidaGás to move people and goods through a regular monthly cycle that anticipates stocks, supplies, equipment, maintenance, and other needs. Yet, as most development projects illustrate, the difference between brilliant on-paper planning and in-the-field execution can be stark. The successful implementation of the cold chain against the background of poor physical transport and infrastructure, logistical challenges, and a lack of human resources (which define the context in northern Mozambique) was nothing short of astonishing. This achievement is testimony to the vision and ingenuity of Blaise Judja-Sato and the staff of VillageReach and FDC.

4. A fourth critical success factor was the intervention of Graça Machel. In her home country, she is more famous, even more revered, than her husband, Nelson Mandela. Graça Machel brought in the strongest local partner: FDC. FDC's staff enabled VidaGás to succeed largely due to their tacit understanding of how business and politics in Mozambique actually work.

5. If VidaGás can build on its healthcare networks, then it has the potential to survive as an independent privately-held company that – in addition to making a profit – also achieves important health, employment, ecological and social-environmental goals. However, the need to make a profit to sustain the more lofty goals cannot be under-estimated. In order to survive, VidaGás and its partners must realise growth in the household cooking and heating market, as well as the medium to large scale commercial market for generators, refrigerators and freezers.

Editors' reflections and questions

The case study explores the innovations achieved by VidaGás in establishing a profitable business that supplies liquefied petroleum gas (LPG) to poor consumers in northern Mozambique. VidaGás is a company owned and controlled by two NGOs (one in Maputo and one in Seattle) that was initially established to support health clinics in the region. Based on the significant health and environmental advantages, and a feasibility study of LPG, VidaGás was established to sell LPG to small businesses and consumers in the region, with a view to creating a long term solution to fuel shortages, while delivering other social and environmental benefits. To ensure a sustainable supply of LPG in northern Mozambique, VidaGás must achieve its stated goal of becoming a revenue-generating entity within three years. This requires the establishment of a viable market and the uptake of LPG by poor consumers. Key challenges include the need to achieve economies of scale, competition with traditional sources of fuel (perceived to be less expensive), high transport costs, and the dearth of government policy and private sector incentives.

1. LPG must compete with traditionally dominant sources of fuel (such as charcoal and wood 'biomass' fuels), which have well-established markets, and around which villagers have long-held patterns of use. What are possible methods for introducing alternative fuels and making them attractive to the consumers being targeted in northern Mozambique?

2. The case illustrates the value of a partnership approach, involving government and NGO stakeholders. Could companies aiming to achieve similar objectives be successful without such support? Could such political support be considered anti-competitive?

Notes

1 This reasearch was commissioned and funded by the UN Development Program. A dozen interviews were conducted by Courtenay Sprague with VidaGás and FDC key personnel at two sites in December 2006 and January 2007: Maputo and Pemba (Cabo Delgado). These interviews were supplemented by numerous e-mail exchanges with FDC and VillageReach staff. Translation for interviews with Portuguese speakers in Pemba was kindly provided by João Rodrigues, general

manager of VidaGás. The authors are grateful to VidaGás, FDC and VillageReach staff for their co-operation.

2   World Health Organisation (WHO), *Fuel for Life: Household Energy and Health* (Geneva: WHO, 2006).

3   E-mail correspondence with VillageReach, 7 March 2007.

4   Ibid.

5   VidaGás Domestic Gas, *Proposal Document* (undated).

6   Nexant Inc. and United States Agency for International Development (USAID) 'LPG Market Assessment Study' (June 2005).

7   Ibid.

8   Ibid.

9   E. Rehfuess, C. Corvalan and M. Neira, 'Indoor Air Pollution: 4 000 Deaths a Day Must No Longer be Ignored' (Geneva: WHO, 2007).

10   LPG emits similar levels of CO2 to diesel: 'It is simply a cleaner way of burning a fossil fuel, not a way of reducing the need to drill for oil.' Scottish Environmental Protection Agency 'Green Tips' (2007), available at http://www.sepa.org.uk/publications/sepaview/html/20/green_tips (accessed July 2008). Also Conoco Phillips, 'LPG is Best Green Option' (2008) at http://www.conocophillips.co.uk/stations/autogas/Latest_News/LPG_is_best_green_option (accessed July 2008).

11   The cold chain describes the network of freezers and refrigerators and coolers or cold boxes used in the transport and storage of vaccines within a set range of 35.6°F–46.4°F (2°C–8°C). If vaccines are exposed to heat or freezing temperatures, they lose their effectiveness and become unusable. It is imperative to maintain an unbroken cold chain from the point of manufacture until the point of use. See VillageReach, 'Project Spotlight – Mozambique' (2003), available at http://newsletters.worldbank.org/external

12   E-mail correspondence with Jenny Hannibal, VillageReach, 9 February 2007.

13   A. Costello, K. Azad and S. Burnett, 'An Alternative Strategy to Reduce Maternal Mortality', *The Lancet,* 28 September 2006. Medical opinion has it that: 'It is essential that pregnant women in whom complications develop have access to the medical interventions of emergency obstetrical care. Programs to make such care more widely available involve upgrading rural health centers and referral hospitals and stocking them with the necessary drugs, supplies, and equipment, such as magnesium sulfate for eclampsia, antibiotics for infection, and basic surgical equipment for cesarean sections.': A. Rosenfield, C. Min and L. Freedman, 'Making Motherhood Safe in Developing Countries', *New England Journal of Medicine,* 356, 14 (2007): 1395–97.

14   DFID, *Reducing Maternal Deaths: Evidence and Action: First Progress Report* (London: DFID, 2005.)

15   VillageReach 'Biography of Blaise Judja-Sato' (2007), available at http://www.villagereach.org/bioblaise (accessed July 2007).

16   VillageReach, available at http://www.villagereach.org (accessed July 2007)

17   As Mozambique's government report states in its assessment of progress made toward achieving the UN Millennium Development Goals: 'There are obvious reasons for the lack of comprehensive … and reliable data … such as the occurrence of the civil war. The first comprehensive household income survey was only conducted in 1997, which perhaps is also the first reliable data point for many other development indicators (e.g. health, education and environment): *Report on the Millennium Development Goals* .

18   VillageReach website, available at http://www.villagereach.org (accessed July 2007).

19   'LPG Market Assessment Study'.

20   E-mail correspondence with Jenny Hannibal, VillageReach, 9 February 2007.

21   World Bank Group, *Ease of Doing Business Index* (2007), available at http://www.doingbusiness.org/economyrankings (accessed February 2008).

22   See 'LPG Market Assessment Study'.

23   Ibid.

24   Ibid. Sample costs associated with LPG transport from South Africa to Mozambique are as follows: The transport of a 9-tonne container from Maputo to Pemba is US$2 500. The return of the empty

container costs US$500. The costs at port are US$70 per tonne. This translates into a cost per tonne of US$407. The high cost of supplying LPG to Pemba leads to a higher cost of supply. However, according to USAID, other types of transport would not make LPG much cheaper. For example, using 18 tonne capacity tankers to transport LPG by road from Maputo to Cabo Delgado would require an estimated US$7 600, leading to a delivered cost of US$422 per tonne. The transport cost of LPG in cylinders is higher still. Galp transports 350 x 11kg capacity cylinders at a cost of about US$520 per tonne.

25   'LPG Market Assessment Study'.
26   Ibid.
27   Ibid.
28   E-mail correspondence with Jenny Hannibal, VillageReach, 9 February 2007.
29   Consumers also evaluated the product in terms of its affordability, availability, convenience, ease of use, safety and other factors: 'LPG Market Assessment Study'.
30   Ibid.
31   Ibid.
32   Interview with Ester Ferreira in Pemba, 16 January 2007.
33   'LPG Market Assessment Study'.
34   Ibid.
35   Ibid.
36   Ibid.
37   Ibid.

Aspen Pharmacare:

Providing affordable generic pharmaceuticals to treat HIV/AIDS and tuberculosis

STU WOOLMAN & COURTENAY SPRAGUE

Introduction

In 1997, the South African government lacked a comprehensive and coordinated treatment programme for HIV/AIDS. No programme appeared on the horizon.[1] The present pandemic – more than five and a half million people living with HIV/AIDS – was well beyond its incipient stages and the state was doing almost nothing to arrest its development.[2]

The private sector was no better with respect to antiretroviral medicines (ARVs). While South Africa had initiated generic drug activity – driven mainly by Aspen Pharmacare and Adcock Ingram – the price of patented anti-AIDS medicines made them prohibitively expensive for the majority of South Africa's HIV-infected population. Only the affluent and, in some cases, those persons with adequate insurance cover, were assured of access to life-saving antiretroviral drugs. Despite a well-developed pharmaceutical sector, and the obvious growing need in the market for affordable ARVs, investors showed little interest in building a generic pharmaceutical industry that would provide an answer to the country's imminent HIV/AIDS pandemic.

Ten years later, the climate has changed dramatically. South Africa possesses a free, universal, public sector HIV/AIDS treatment programme. Serious competition exists between local generic suppliers of ARVs for the government's national treatment programme. And the competition is stiffening. The World Health Organisation (WHO) notes:

> The AIDS epidemic demonstrates that the supposedly impossible can become possible. Ten years ago, no one would have believed that there would be affordable HIV-related drugs that saved lives.[3]

As Jim Yong Kim, former WHO director of HIV/AIDS observes: 'What we are seeing now is not only is treatment possible in areas like sub-Saharan Africa, but that treatment scale-up is possible. People are figuring how to scale up and they are doing it.'[4]

What prompted this change? How did we get from there to here? A significant piece of putting together the puzzle of generic treatments for infectious diseases in South Africa has been Aspen Pharmacare.

In a conservative investment climate, Stephen Saad, Aspen Pharmacare's chief executive officer, saw opportunity. In a reactionary health policy environment, Saad saw need. The opportunity: to build a major pharmaceutical manufacturer capable of supplying the South African market with brand name, generic and over-the-counter medicines at affordable prices. The need: to supply South Africans with the essential medicines required for the treatment of life-threatening, yet chronic diseases such as HIV/AIDS and tuberculosis.

Through a series of well-planned deals and calculated risks, the greatest being the US$340m acquisition of the company, SA Druggists, Saad turned Aspen Pharmacare into the largest producer of tablets and capsules in Africa. By building the largest manufacturing plant in the country, Saad put Aspen Pharmacare in a position to supply South Africa's national anti-retroviral therapy treatment programme with approximately 60% of its current requirements.

Those national requirements are daunting. As indicated, over 5.5 million South Africans are now living with HIV/AIDS; more than 600 000 individuals will require immediate access to life-extending antiretrovirals each year for at least the coming decade.[5] The government could be doing more: only an estimated 400 000 of people living with the human immunodeficiency virus who require antiretroviral therapy (ART) have access to such treatment in public clinics and hospitals.[6] According to Dorrington's current projections, some 3.5 million South Africans will die of AIDS-related infections by 2010.[7]

As the South African Department of Health has acknowledged, the solution to this grim situation – a sustainable, universal public health ART programme – depends, in part, on both lower drug prices and an uninterrupted local supply of ARVs.[8] Companies such as Aspen Pharmacare have recognised that the government's best hope for meeting public health needs over the long-term rests on the state's ability to nurture the country's nascent generics industry. (Such an industry could also supply medicines to other African countries at affordable prices.) While observing that the creation of such an industry poses an immense challenge for both government and big business, *The Economist* notes that Aspen Pharmacare provides a model for local generic firms and is currently 'doing the most to supply the market with ... generic drugs'.[9]

Access to medicines: The not so new apartheid

The global health revolution over the last 30 years can be measured in increased life expectancy – an additional four months over each calendar year – and the 'near-eradication' of treatable diseases such as malaria and tuberculosis (TB).[10] However, a majority of the world's population, about 80%, reside in the developing world. And they have not enjoyed the benefits of the health revolution.[11] For example, a child born in Sierra Leone has a life expectancy of less than half that in Japan.[12] A child born in southern Africa today has a shorter life expectancy than her grandparents.[13] To make matters worse, many people living in developing countries fall ill and die from preventable and treatable diseases.[14]

Access to essential medicines to treat HIV/AIDS, tuberculosis and other infectious diseases should lead to a decrease in morbidity and mortality rates in the developing world. However, as Jim Yong Kim cautions, 'expanding AIDS treatment is the most complex public health challenge the world has ever faced.'[15]

Recent developments in the southern hemisphere suggest that public-private partnerships of varying kinds can create sustainable ART programs. With appropriate government incentives, voluntary licences and technology transfers from multinationals, generic pharmaceutical manufacturers located in developing countries could become low-cost producers of the life-extending drugs that HIV-infected individuals require. Indeed, Aspen Pharmacare has, with some support from a Strategic Investment Programme (SIP) introduced by the Department of Trade and Industry, followed this model. So successful has Aspen been that it is not hard to imagine that Aspen could soon possess a meaningful comparative advantage as a producer of ARVs – and leverage that advantage to become a supplier of low-cost pharmaceuticals to HIV-infected individuals throughout the African continent. Aspen faces a number of sizable hurdles before it achieves such a goal.

Aspen Pharmacare: Company overview

Stephen Saad, the CEO of Aspen Pharmacare, is a pharmaceutical entrepreneur. At the age of 29, he sold his shares in the pharmaceutical group, Covan Zurich, to Adcock Ingram for US$2.85m. Saad did not rest on his laurels – or his capital. In 1997, the trio of Saad, Aspen Deputy CEO Gus Attridge and Steve Surlese created Aspen. It began as a small business, located in Durban, and worth an estimated US$7m. Based on a series of weighted risks, including the assumption of US$350 000 in debt to grow the company, Saad identified a number of niche opportunities for Aspen.

The greatest risk was the hostile takeover by Aspen of the under-performing yet colossal SA Druggists in 1999. The price tag was US$340m.[16] Based on its short but profitable track record, Aspen was able to raise the necessary capital from investors. A sceptical market assumed that Aspen would simply strip the company of its assets. And they were not far from the mark. As Saad admits: 'One of the plans we had was to sell off the manufacturing business. But I realised we would be selling the heart and lungs.'[17] Instead, Aspen sold off SA Druggists' non-core operations and invested more heavily in pharmaceutical manufacturing. It made significant investments in new facilities, while upgrading existing pharmaceutical manufacturing sites: four in South Africa and one in India. These sites house a total of nine manufacturing facilities. (A tenth plant is completed and currently being commissioned and validated.) One of these manufacturing plants, the Oral Solid Dosage (OSD) facility in Port Elizabeth, is both the largest on the African continent and the leading producer of tablets and capsules in Africa.[18]

Growing at an average rate of 40% per year, the company quickly established itself as a leading South African drug company.[19] The pre-2007 figures for the Aspen Group are annual revenues of close to US$600m and net profits of roughly US$140m. Aspen's overwhelming success parallels the increase in the domestic production and demand for generic medicines.

Voluntary licences for generic medicines: A win–win–win

A generic drug is a pharmaceutical product that is meant to be interchangeable with an innovator product (a brand name or proprietary product). It is generally (but not always) manufactured without a licence from the innovator company. It is usually (but not always) marketed after the patent on the original product expires. More importantly for our purposes: generic drugs are much cheaper to purchase than branded drugs.[20]

The use of generic drugs offers one possible remedy for the problem of access to medicines to treat HIV/AIDS, tuberculosis, malaria and an assortment of other tropical and infectious diseases ravaging populations in the developing countries. The WHO describes the important role generics can play as follows:

> Because of their low price, generic drugs are often the only medicines that the poorest can access. The Trade-Related Aspects of Intellectual Property Rights (TRIPS) agreement does not prevent governments from requiring accurate labelling or allowing generic substitution. Indeed, it is argued that competition between drug companies and generic producers has been more effective than negotiations with drug companies in reducing the cost of drugs, in particular those used to treat HIV/AIDS.[21]

Recognising these benefits, the South African Department of Trade and Industry (DTI) employed the Strategic Investment Programme to induce Aspen to invest US$29m in the manufacturing facility in Port Elizabeth.[22] This manufacturing facility is now able to produce, among other drugs, considerable quantities of generic ARVs. On the back of that investment, and government's promise of an imminent rollout of ARVs through the national public health system, Aspen secured voluntary licences from a sizeable number of multinational patent-holders to produce a broad range of ARVs.[23]

As a rule, these voluntary licence agreements contain 0 to 5% royalty charges, backward technology transfers, and technical assistance with respect to both the manufacture and the distribution of the pharmaceutical. GlaxoSmithKline (GSK) has signed seven voluntary licensing agreements for ARVs in Africa (five in South Africa and two in Kenya). GSK articulates the pharmaceutical company's perspective on voluntary licences as follows.

> Voluntary licences (VL) enable local manufacturers to produce and sell generic versions of our products. A decision to grant a VL depends on a number of factors including the severity of the HIV/AIDS epidemic in that country, local healthcare provision and the economic and manufacturing environment ... Selecting the most appropriate licencee is key. We need to be sure that the manufacturer will be able to provide a long-term supply of good-quality medicines and will implement safeguards to prevent the diversion of medicines to wealthier markets.[24]

One might well wonder why a multinational pharmaceutical company would agree to 'give away' its patented processes for the manufacture of a drug that continues to be extremely profitable. However, a genuine pecuniary interest attaches to well-enforced voluntary licences and makes them highly attractive to pharmaceutical companies. The licences ensure better resource allocation in the markets from which pharmaceutical companies derive the greater part of their profits: Europe, North America and parts of Asia. Voluntary licences eliminate the production and the marketing of high cost drugs in regions that will show little or no meaningful profit. At the same time, the voluntary licence eliminates the need for multinationals – and various states – to police the grey markets in drugs that inevitably occur when purchasers of brand name pharmaceuticals in developing countries (who benefit from differential pricing) attempt to resell the brand name product in markets in the developed world. Voluntary licences to generic manufacturers in developing countries eliminate such arbitrage and safeguard more lucrative markets.[25]

Ultimately, the benefits of voluntary licences are shared. In 2001, before South African companies started producing ARV generics, the cost of ARVs to the patient was more than US$428. Today, Aspen Pharmacare can supply triple combination therapy to the South African government at the low price of US$13 per patient, per month.[26] Everyone wins: the patient, the state, the multinational, the generic manufacturer and the healthier body politic.

Table 1: How generic drugs stack up against patented medicines

GENERIC	PATENT
Antiretrovirals	
Zidovudine 250g =US$15.50 (Aspen)	Retrovir 250g = US$42.00 (Glaxo)
Pain relief for sprained ankle	
Panamor 50mg = US$1.17 (Novartis)	Voltaren 50mg = US$5.00 (Novartis)
Bronchitis	
Adco Lintopent 200ml = US$3.80 (Adcock)	Flemeze syrup 200ml = US$4.35 (Pfizer)

Source: Financial Mail, 17 November 2006.

Voluntary licences: Co-operation not litigation

The access to and supply of affordable generic drugs is a political minefield – not solely a problem of resource allocation to be solved by correcting market inefficiencies. It is fiercely contested nationally and internationally. A short history of this charged environment will further evince just how exceptional Aspen's achievements are.

In 2001, the South African government was at an impasse with multinational pharmaceutical companies and the domestic pharmaceutical industry over patent rights. The dispute eventually took the form of a suit by the Pharmaceutical Manufacturers' Association of South Africa – filed on behalf of 39 pharmaceutical companies – to stop the Medicines and Related Substances Control Amendment Act (Medicines Act) from being implemented.[27] The applicants asserted that the Medicines Act breached both the South African Constitution and the Trade-Related Aspects of Intellectual Property Rights (TRIPS) Agreement.[28] The essence of their complaint was that the act granted the Minister of Health limitless power to disregard South Africa's patent laws. After the trial commenced in March 2001, it soon became clear that the section of the Medicines Act at the heart of the disagreement was modelled on a draft legal text prepared by the World Intellectual Property Organisation (WIPO) Committee of Experts. Due to WIPO's involvement and attendant role in TRIPS enforcement, it became impracticable for the drug companies to argue that the Medicines Act violated TRIPS.[29] Due to their weak legal position and the robust international support for South Africa's aim to provide inexpensive drugs to meet its public health epidemic, the companies dropped the law suit in April 2001. The conclusion? While the suit ultimately set no legal precedent, the outcome shifted the balance of power back, ever so slightly, toward the developing countries' right to provide essential medicines to their populations.[30]

About the same time, the Treatment Action Campaign (TAC) filed a complaint with South Africa's Competition Commission. The complaint declared that a proposed merger between SmithKline Beecham and Glaxo Wellcome would increase the new entity's market share to a degree that would result in monopoly-like pricing for a not insignificant number of ARV drugs. The Competition Tribunal rejected this assertion. The tribunal's concerns were largely dispelled by the agreement of the two merging parties to issue voluntary licences for the following medicines: anti-emetic Kytril; anti-viral Famciclovir; and antibiotics Polysporin, Cicatrin and Neosporin.[31]

In 2002, as a result of the final settlement agreements associated with a separate Competition Case (*Hazel Tau*), several existing ARV voluntary licensing agreements between Boehringer Ingelheim, GlaxoSmithKline (GSK) and Aspen had their reach extended. The licences permitted both: (a) the production and sale of Nevirapine, AZT and lamivudine (commonly known as 3TC) and the fixed dose combination of AZT and 3TC within South Africa, and (b) the production and sale of the same regimens for export to 47 countries in Africa for a royalty of no more than 5% of net sales.[32] By committing to these voluntary licences, both GSK and Boehringer Ingelheim agreed not to seek enforcement of their patents on the African continent. These agreements illustrated that voluntary licences can, in the right environment, be gainfully exploited in the service of a free, universal ART programme for those requiring AIDS treatment.

These recurring legal battles between the South African government, civil society and the pharmaceutical manufacturers often obscure both the virtues of voluntary licences and how development objectives should be achieved through means other than coercion. Voluntary licences from multinational pharmaceutical companies to local generic manufacturers demonstrate, instead, the potential for businesses to advance development and public health objectives while still achieving a profit. For example, Aspen Pharmacare is currently producing significant amounts of first and second line ARVs, as well as multi-drug resistant (MDR) tuberculosis drugs, under voluntary licences with Bristol-Myers Squibb, Eli Lilly, GlaxoSmithKline, Gilead Sciences, Boehringer Ingelheim, F. Hoffmann-La Roche Ltd., and Merck Sharpe & Dohme. As the public record demonstrates, Aspen alone has voluntary licences to produce the following 13 AIDS and TB drugs: Nevirapine; Efavirenz (Stocrin);[33] Atazanavir; Tenofovir; Tenofovir+Emcitrabine (a combination drug); Lamivudine (3TC); Zidovudine; Lamivudine+Zidovudine; Stavudine; Didanosine; Saquinavir; Capreomycin and Cycloserine. Aspen has recently reached agreement on additional voluntary licences.[34]

These agreements are not aberrations: over 90% of Aspen's requests for voluntary licences have been granted.[35] Given the growing TB epidemic in South Africa, the spectre of multi-drug and extensively or 'extreme' drug resistant TB, and the complications attached to the treatment of TB and HIV co-infection, the recent manufacturing, supply and distribution agreement between Aspen and Lupin Ltd of India to produce first and second line TB drugs, reinforces the efficacy of Aspen's aforementioned voluntary licences for ARVs.[36] Indeed, while the first agreements reflected an 'immunity of suit', the very latest agreements negotiated by Aspen embrace licensing, full technology transfer and distribution agreements. They are, essentially, wholly vertical agreements. Aspen has negotiated one such agreement with Tibotec, a subsidiary of Johnson & Johnson, for Duranavir, an ARV drug.[37]

Aspen now has 11 AIDS drugs in its stable.[38] It expects that line of products to increase.[39] In March 2005, the company announced that it had increased its production of ARVs by 30% since 2006 to cope with demand. While about half of Aspen's domestic AIDS drugs sales were to the private sector, Saad predicted significant increases in public sector volumes as more government clinics and hospitals began to treat patients. Aspen also expects significant growth across the continent: Nigeria and Uganda have already placed orders. At the time of writing, regulatory hurdles in African countries have delayed the US President's Emergency Plan for AIDS Relief (PEPFAR) orders.[40] As a result, Aspen's Stavros Nicolaou, who heads up Strategic Trade, warns that 'supplying both African governments and PEPFAR projects is still in its infancy' and that many of the Aspen generics are still in the process of being registered in various African countries.[41]

Barriers to success

Aspen faces a broad spectrum of challenges to its current market position as the leading supplier of ARVs to the state. The first was to convince the South African government that tax relief and investments should be continued. While the discontinuation of the Strategic Investment Programme had placed a question mark over the state's commitment to the creation of a viable generics industry in South Africa, the pharmaceutical sector has recently won cabinet approval to become a priority sector for growth in South Africa.[42] This victory indicates that Aspen may have met the first challenge.[43] Aspen's second hurdle involves increasing production in a way that meets the current demand for the full set of first, second and third line ARVs. Aspen's third challenge – and a marker of its success – is the presence of new competitors who threaten the company's market share. Amongst Aspen's chief local competitors in the ARV generics market are Adcock-Ingram, Sonke Pharmaceuticals (Pty) Ltd., and Cipla-Medpro.[44] Adcock Ingram, a South African subsidiary of Tiger Brands and the second largest generics' producer in the country, plans to enter the ARV market with a unique single tablet, triple-combination therapy.[45] However, according to some analysts, economies of scale; partnerships with northern multinational pharmaceutical companies; markets for generic drugs in sub-Saharan Africa; FDA approval; and black empowerment initiatives (an absolute imperative for doing business in post-apartheid South Africa)[46] suggest that Aspen has a good chance of remaining the market leader.[47]

Aspen's fourth challenge, indeed a challenge to all generic ARV manufacturers, is to ensure ongoing access to the active pharmaceutical ingredients (APIs) necessary to produce ARVs. As we have documented elsewhere, most generic manufacturers are currently dependent upon generic manufacturers of APIs in India, China, South Korea and Brazil.[48] Should the epidemic become a national health priority in India or China, requiring universal public treatment programmes, their domestic demand for APIs may exhaust the existing supply. Generic manufacturers from other nations could be left out in the cold. Aspen has attempted to insulate itself from the vagaries of API availability by purchasing the largest fine chemicals manufacturer in

South Africa and by initiating joint ventures with two Indian manufacturers of APIs – Lupin and Matrix.[49]

Aspen's fifth challenge is to negotiate the uncertainty surrounding the enforcement of international and domestic intellectual property regimes. Thus far, the company has avoided confrontation with both governments and multinationals by securing voluntary licences and technology transfers for the better part of its ARV product line. However, intellectual property (IP) and especially TRIPS-related questions hover over the generic APIs produced by India and China. For example, now that India has passed IP legislation intended to make the nation TRIPS-compliant, non-Indian manufacturers must ask whether their access to Indian APIs will be deleteriously affected. Aspen's co-operative approach to its relationships with both government and multinationals should serve it well in future negotiations.

Innovations

This analysis of Aspen Pharmacare reveals at least five potentially replicable (and unquestionably innovative) business responses to the problem of providing affordable ARVs, as part of a sustainable national ART programme, in a developing country. First, Aspen recognised that the costs of building a large-scale manufacturing plant would be more than off-set by the profits to be secured from the public demand and the private demand for ARVs in South Africa and on the rest of the continent. Second, Aspen convinced the state to provide SIP incentives to build a plant sufficiently large to meet South Africa's growing public health need for affordable, generic ARVs. Third, Aspen's ability to negotiate voluntary licences with multinational drug companies allows drugs under patent to be distributed at significantly reduced prices: these lower prices should enable the state to reach a larger number of individuals with HIV/AIDS who require treatment. Fourth, Aspen's knack for securing voluntary licences avoids putting South Africa in the politically uncomfortable position of breaking foreign patents and the legally undesirable position of weakening the state's own intellectual property regime.[50] Fifth, Aspen's joint ventures with Indian generic manufacturers Matrix and Lupin provide some assurance it will continue to possess an uninterrupted supply of the active pharmaceutical ingredients (APIs) required to manufacture ARVs.

A Department for International Development (DFID) evidence-based study of generic pharmaceutical companies suggests that business models similar to Aspen's enterprise could be replicated in other developing countries with the requisite levels of infrastructure, access to active pharmaceutical ingredients, skilled human capital, existing manufacturing plants, and appropriate government incentives.[51] (It must be noted that many African countries do not yet possess those necessary features.) The DFID report also gives backing to our claim that South Africa requires a state-sponsored socio-industrial policy that will create additional incentives for private investment in infrastructure, manufacturing and advanced training.

Figure 1: Aspen's financial highlights 2006

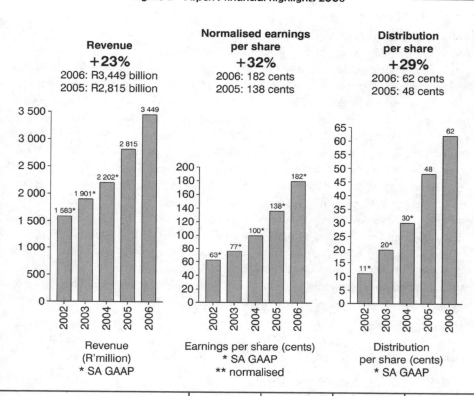

Revenue
+23%
2006: R3,449 billion
2005: R2,815 billion

Normalised earnings per share
+32%
2006: 182 cents
2005: 138 cents

Distribution per share
+29%
2006: 62 cents
2005: 48 cents

Revenue
(R'million)
* SA GAAP

Earnings per share (cents)
* SA GAAP
** normalised

Distribution
per share (cents)
* SA GAAP

Group summary	30 June 2006 R'million	Group summary R'million Change	30 June 2006 %	Compound growth*
Revenue	3 449.3	2 814.6	23	22
Normalised operating profit	1 004.1	782.9	28	26
Normalised profit after tax	626.6	468.9	34	29
Net cash from operating activities	402.4	652.8	(38)	15
Ordinary share performance				
Earnings per share – basic (cents)	185.4	54.7	239	31
Headline earnings per share (cents)	185.5	55.4	235	31
Normalised earnings per share (cents)	182.1	137.6	32	31
Distribution per share (cents)	62.0	48.0	29	54
Operating cash flow per share (cents)	116.9	191.7	(39)	15

* Compound growth represents five-year compound annual growth, calculated for the period 2002–2006.

Source: Aspen Annual Report 2006:,http://www.aspenpharma.com/Annrep_2006/financial_highlights.htm

Editors' reflections and questions

In the late 1990s, in the context of the South African government's reactionary public health policy and a conservative investment climate, Stephen Saad, Aspen Pharmacare's chief executive officer, saw the opportunity to supply the South African market with brand name, generic and over-the-counter HIV and TB medication at affordable prices. The Aspen Pharmacare case reveals a number of potentially replicable business responses to the problem of providing affordable medicines in a developing country. First, Aspen recognised that the costs of building a large-scale manufacturing plant would be more than off-set by the profits to be secured from the public and private demand for ARVs in South Africa and the rest of the continent. Second, Aspen convinced the state to provide incentives to build a plant sufficiently large to meet South Africa's growing need. Third, Aspen's ability to negotiate voluntary licences with multinational drug companies allows drugs under patent to be distributed at significantly reduced prices. This strategy avoids putting South Africa in the politically uncomfortable position of breaking foreign patents and the legally undesirable position of weakening the state's own intellectual property regime. Finally, Aspen's joint ventures with Indian generic manufacturers provide some assurance it will continue to possess an uninterrupted supply of the active pharmaceutical ingredients (APIs) required to manufacture ARVs.

However, Aspen currently faces a range of important challenges to its market position as the leading supplier of ARVs to the state. This case study raises the following questions:

1. How can Aspen increase production to meet national requirements for first, second and third line drugs in a cost-effective manner?

2. How should Aspen secure the necessary access to active pharmaceutical ingredients, especially if HIV prevalence continues to rise in countries such as China and India?

3. How can Aspen best ensure entry into markets for generic drugs in other sub-Saharan African countries?

Notes

1   Even non-South Africans are familiar with the politics attached to access to AIDS drugs in South Africa. As salon.com, the popular US website, puts it: 'the South African government's slow response to the AIDS crisis, [its] hesitations and missteps ... are well-chronicled': 'The AIDS Drug Warrior', salon.com (18 June 2001), available at http://www.salon.com

2   See UNAIDS 'Epidemiological Fact Sheet on HIV/AIDS and STIs, South Africa 2006', available at http://www.unaids.org The figures are dated 2005.

3   UNAIDS-WHO, *Guidance on Ethics and Equitable Access to HIV Treatment and Care* (Geneva: WHO, 2004).

4   S. Lafraniere, 'Poor lands treating far more AIDS patients', *New York Times,* 27 January 2005.

5   P. Barker and F. Venter, 'Setting District-Based Annual Targets for HAART and PMTCT – a First Step in Planning Effective Intervention for the HIV/AIDS Epidemic', *South African Medical Journal*, 97, 10 (2007): 916–17. According to the Department of Health, which relies on the Actuarial Society of South Africa (2000) model, 'it is estimated that by then [2009] about 1.4 million people will require ARV therapy': Government of the Republic of South Africa, 'Department of Health Operational Plan for Comprehensive HIV and AIDS Care, Management and Treatment for South Africa', (2003), available at http://www.info.gov.za/otherdocs/2003/aidsplan.pdf.

6   WHO 'Summary Country Profile for HIV/AIDS Treatment Scale-Up', (June 2005), available at http://www.who.int/3by5/countryprofiles/en

7   On the actuarial science that underpins such projections, see Bureau for Economic Research, *The Impact of HIV/AIDS on Selected Business Sectors in South Africa* (Stellenbosch: University of Stellenbosch, 2005), 11–12, citing Rob Dorrington and estimates projected by the Actuarial Association of South Africa (ASSA 2002) Model. Dorrington states: 'By 2010, despite interventions and treatments, we estimate that nearly 3.5 million South Africans will have died of HIV/AIDS related causes'. South Africa holds the dubious distinction of having the largest number of individuals currently living with the virus in a single country. See 'Joint WHO/UNAIDS Fact Sheet', No. 283 (January 2005). South Africa must also confront a growing tuberculosis (TB) epidemic, including multi-drug and extreme drug resistant TB. Indeed, TB and HIV co-infection is complicating treatment for both diseases. See Médecins Sans Frontières (MSF), 'The TB/HIV Time Bomb: A Dual Epidemic Explodes in South Africa' available from http://www.msf.org

8   According to the 'Department of Health Operational Plan', The South African government began to move in the right direction in 2004 when, at the behest of the cabinet, the Department of Health initiated a long-anticipated, free national antiretroviral treatment (ART) programme for its HIV-infected population. However, delays in the implementation of the ART programme have been widespread. The Department of Health, pressed by the threat of litigation by national activist organisations such as the Treatment Action Campaign, communicated in March of 2004 that they would need to purchase an emergency supply of antiretrovirals (ARVs) as a stop-gap measure until the formal public sector tender process for drug procurement was concluded. In May 2004, despite the emergency supply, drug shortages continued to be well-documented. Analysts observed that the South African government was in the unenviable position of possessing 'some generic medicines – sitting with the Medicines Control Council [South African equivalent of the US Federal Drug Administration] for more than a year awaiting registration' – while still being obliged 'to purchase [ARVs] from brand name sources' at considerably higher prices. On this see T. Smart, 'Antiretroviral Sources of Supply May not be Able to Meet Popular Demand'. (2005), available at http://www.redribbon.co.za

9   'Aspen's upward slope: Can South Africa's top generics manufacturer become a global giant?', *The Economist*, 6 October 2005.

10   Médecins sans Frontières (MSF), 'Fatal Imbalance 2001'. See also WHO, *World Health Report 2006* (Geneva: WHO, 2006); and WHO, *World Health Report 2000* (Geneva: WHO, 2000).

11   L. Chen and G. Berlinguer, 'Health Equity in a Globalizing World', in T. Evans, M. Whitehead, F. Diderichsen, A. Bhuiya and M. Wirth, eds, *Challenging Inequities to Health: From Ethics to Action* (Oxford: Oxford University Press, 2001).

12   For figures, see J.P. Ruger, 'Health and Social Justice', *Lancet*, 364 (2004): 1075–80; F. Dabis and E.R. Ekpini, 'HIV-1/AIDS and Maternal and Child Health in Africa', *Lancet*, 359 (2000): 2097–2104; L. Jong-wook, 'Global Health Improvement and WHO: Shaping the Future', *Lancet* 362 (2003): 2083– 88.

13   Dabis and Ekpini, 'HIV-1/AIDS', state: 'In South Africa, rates of life expectancy have dropped to 48.8 years while mortality rates have risen – largely due to opportunistic infections associated with HIV/AIDS'. See also WHO, *World Health Report 2004: Global Burden of Disease Estimates for 2002* (Geneva: WHO, 2002); UNDP, *Human Development Report 2005* (New York and Oxford: Oxford University Press, 2005). See also C. Dugger, 'Devastated by AIDS, Africa Sees Life Expectancy Plunge', *The New York Times*, 16 July 2004. A UNDP-French government-sponsored study of annual average rates of change in life expectancy at birth during four decades revealed a 'massive loss of life expectancy caused in sub-Saharan Africa in the 1990s by the HIV/AIDS pandemic': G.A. Cornia and L. Menchini, 'The Pace and Distribution of Health Improvements during the Last 40 Years: Some Preliminary Results', UNDP-French Government Sponsored Forum on Human

Development (17–19 January 2005). Wines, drawing on data released from *Statistics South Africa,* writes: 'South Africa's government reported … that annual deaths increased 57% from 1997 to 2003, with common AIDS-related diseases with tuberculosis and pneumonia fuelling much of the rise': M. Wines, 'AIDS-Linked Death Data Stir Political Storm in South Africa', *The New York Times,* 19 February 2005. For a comprehensive discussion of the impact of HIV/AIDS on mortality and morbidity rates in sub-Saharan Africa, see D.T. Jamison, R.G. Feachem, M.W. Makgoba, E.R. Bos, F.K. Baingana, K.J. Hofman and K.O. Rogo, eds, *Disease and Mortality in Sub-Saharan Africa* (Washington, DC: World Bank, 2006).

14 MSF, *Fatal Imbalance.* See also Chen and Berlinguer, 'Health Equity in a Globalizing World'.

15 See Lafraniere 'Poor Lands'.

16 The pharmaceutical industry is highly regulated with equally high barriers to entry, yet SA Druggists' credibility with doctors and pharmacists and its well-established brands counteracted these potential costs of doing business. Interview with Stavros Nicolaou, 15 December 2006.

17 S. Mzolo and S. Theobald, 'Generic Drugs: A Chance at Life', *Financial Mail* (South Africa), 17 November 2006.

18 The corporate profile of Aspen is also based on interviews conducted with Stavros Nicolaou of Aspen Pharmacare, 28 February 2006; 19 July 2006; 15 December 2006; and 9 August 2007.

19 Aspen first developed a brand-name based upon the affordability and the quality of its products. The group's product line encompasses branded, generic, over-the-counter, fast moving consumer goods, personal care, nutritional and nutriceutical products: oral contraceptives, penicillin, complementary medicines, cosmetics, hormonals, capsules, creams, ointments, lotions, liquids, powders and tinctures.

20 See WHO, *Glossary of Terms,* available at http://www.who.int/trade/glossary/story034/en

21 Ibid.

22 Interview with Stavros Nicolaou of Aspen Pharmacare, 9 August 2007. Aspen ultimately invested some US$55m in this state-sponsored, but privately funded, initiative.

23 Interviews with Stavros Nicolaou, 28 February 2006; 19 July 2006 and 15 December 2006.

24 GlaxoSmithKline, 'Corporate Social Responsibility Report 2005'.

25 See WHO *Programme on Globalization, Trade and Health*, available at http://www.who.nt/trade/glossary/story034/en

26 Mzolo and Theobald, 'Generic Drugs'

27 See Republic of South Africa (RSA), Department of Health *Briefing Document, Defending the Medicines Control Amendment Act* (2 March 2001).

28 Case No. 4183/98 (Witwatersrand High Court, filed 18 February 1998).

29 See E. t'Hoen, 'TRIPS, Pharmaceutical Patents and Access to Essential Medicines: Seattle, Doha and Beyond' (2003), *International AIDS Economics Network*, available from http://www.iaen.org/papers

30 As Rosalind Pollack Petchesky notes, 'The success of Brazil and South Africa in challenging US and corporate rigidities on patents together with the ever-tenacious transnational health and human rights NGOs, gave a green light to developing country coalitions to move aggressively on the matter of access to medicines': R.P. Petchesky, *Global Prescriptions Gendering Health and Human Rights* (New York: Zed Books, 2003), 104.

31 See *Glaxo Wellcome and SmithKline Beecham* Competition Commission (Case No. 58/AM/May, 28 July 2000).

32 See *Hazel Tau* Competition Commission (Case No. 226, September 2002).

33 The brand name in South Africa is Stocrin. In Europe and other locations, the brand name is Sustiva.

34 Interview with Stavros Nicolaou, 19 July 2006.

35 Ibid.

36 See 'Big Boost for Fight against TB' *Fin24,* 26 September 2005.

37 Tibotec also has two promising drugs in clinical phases of development: TMC-278 (Rilpivirine) and TMC-125 (Etravirine). Both drugs are experimental ARVs not yet approved by the US Food and Drug Administration.

38 Aspen's success has not gone unnoticed. Aspen was the world's first pharmaceutical manufacturer to be granted US Food and Drug Administration (FDA) approval for the manufacture of co-packed generic antiretrovirals manufactured at its world class oral solid dosage (OSD) facility. The Clinton Foundation chose Aspen as the first company in the southern hemisphere to manufacture generic ARVs for their programme. It did so, as Stavros Nicolaou notes, because it was impressed by the manner in which Aspen had positioned itself in the marketplace: Interview with Stavros Nicolaou, 15 December 2006.

39 As Saad noted: 'Antiretroviral medicines are becoming a bigger and bigger part of our production – we could never have foreseen this growth.', see T. Kahn 'Aspen to Focus on AIDS Drugs Market across 15 Countries', *Business Day,* 23 August 2005.

40 Ibid.

41 Ibid.

42 The National Industrial Policy to enhance economic growth, create employment and reduce poverty – the Accelerated and Shared Growth Initiative for South Africa (AsgiSA) – was launched in 2006. Three arguments from the pharmaceutical sector for ensuring that the sector was a central part of the policy were forwarded: 1. A deteriorating pharmaceutical trade deficit, which has worsened from a 10:1 to 20:1 ratio in the last 3 years. Health care is now the 5th largest contributor to South Africa's current account deficit. 2. Security in supply [of medicines] is critical: unarrested AIDS and TB pandemics would dent investor confidence, impact on economic growth, reduce FDI and place a further burden on social services; and 3. Export potential exists for the pharmaceutical sector, particularly for infectious diseases and other opportunities, such as drop exports: E-mail communication from Stavros Nicolaou, 13 August 2007. Interview with Stavros Nicolaou, 9 August 2007.

43 It should be noted that in the government's 2005 report on South Africa's progress in achieving the MDGs, in response to target 17 (in cooperation with pharmaceutical companies, provide access to affordable drugs in developing countries), the government states: 'Measurement of target not available for South Africa (free primary health care for all)'. While the national policy may embrace the provision of essential medicines for the South African population, this is not yet universal, nor is it accessible to many poor people, particularly for vulnerable populations such as pregnant women and HIV-infected children. According to UNICEF South Africa, each day 260 children are born infected with HIV in South Africa. This is equivalent to 94,900 children newly-infected with HIV each year. Without ARVs most of these children will die by their second birthday. In a report by South African civil society to the UN, Mellors documents that 'very few children (10%) are accessing ARV treatment', see S. Mellors, *Monitoring the Implementation of the UNGASS Declaration of Commitment: Country Report South Africa* (civil society shadow report), International Council of AIDS Service Organisations [undated]. HIV-related diseases are now responsible for 40% of child mortality cases in South Africa; rendering AIDS the largest killer of children under five in the nation. See UNICEF South Africa, *Impact on Children: Paediatric Testing and Treatment* (2006), available at http://www.unicef.org/southafrica

44 Cipla-Medpro is a joint venture between Cipla Ltd of India and Medpro Pharmaceutica, a South African generic pharmaceutical company.

45 Tiger Brands' *2005 Annual Report* outlines its intentions as follows: 'Given that the HIV and AIDS pandemic is widespread globally and expected to grow in the next five to ten years, there is clearly a viable market for ARV drugs, which will be volume driven. Worldwide there are about 40 million people currently infected with the virus. There are 25.4m people infected in sub-Saharan Africa, with six million of these residing within our borders. Adcock Ingram aims to be a key player in the ARV market ... [and] plans to formulate and strengthen key relationships and partnerships, to facilitate entry into the ARV market, are being implemented.' Available at www.tigerbrands.co.za/Investor/InvestorCentre/2005 Results/AnnualReport

46 Aspen chose not to close its factories under Saad's leadership but instead expanded manufacturing from 30% to 100% of its core business. This decision flowed in large part from consultation with and cooperation from the trade unions. Indeed, the trade unions now hold almost 17% of Aspen's shares. Aspen's new manufacturing operations, in particular its new plant in Port Elizabeth, are responsible for the creation of approximately 1 400 new jobs in the Eastern Cape (one of South Africa's poorest provinces.)

47 *Financial Mail,* 17 November 2006.

48   See C. Sprague and S. Woolman, 'Moral Luck: Exploiting South Africa's Policy Environment for an Effective National Antiretroviral Treatment Programme', *South African Journal on Human Rights,* 22 (2006): 337–79.

49   Stavros Nicolaou states that these joint ventures create a 'strategic stockpile' of APIs for Aspen. Interview with Stavros Nicolaou, 15 December 2006.

50   South Africa's enviable industrial strength and unenviable policy environment are not, generally, positions that many developing countries find themselves in. These countries will require alternative strategies.

51   See DFID, *Leveraging the Private Sector for Public Health Objectives* (London: DFID, 2004), available at http://www.eldis.org. The DFID study, which was particularly concerned with domestic production in sub-Saharan Africa, concentrated on the following factors: quality; geographical accessibility; physical availability; acceptability; affordability; the feasibility of domestic production of medicines to combat TB and malaria, as well as HIV/AIDS; government strategy; and, the domestic market.

CASE 14

Honey Care Africa:

A tripartite model for sustainable beekeeping*

OANA BRANZEI & MICHAEL VALENTE

When Kenyan-born and -raised Farouk Jiwa had launched Honey Care Africa in 2000[1], he had envisioned a business model that would tackle the constraints of subsistence farmers in rural Kenya head on.

> It was all about trying to understand the obstacles facing the farmers. Financing was clearly a problem, technology was a problem, market was a problem, government extension service was a problem. So we thought about it for a while, and asked: "How do we solve this problem for the farmer?" We looked at the sector and said, "If I was the average farmer in Kenya today with two acres of land, what would stop me from producing honey?" We then worked out how to best address each of these problems.

Agriculture in Kenya

The largest economy in East Africa, Kenya had a population of 34.7 million, a real growth rate of 5.8 per cent and purchasing power parity (PPP) of US$1,100. Two-thirds (69.6 per cent) of Kenyans lived in rural areas. Half of the population lived below the poverty line. The poorest

Richard Ivey School of Business
The University of Western Ontario   IVEY   Information
Technology

10 per cent accounted for two per cent of total household consumption; the wealthiest 10 per cent were responsible for 37.2 per cent of total household consumption. Forty per cent of the labor force, or 4.74 million Kenyans, were unemployed. Life expectancy at birth was 49 years, and the adult literacy rate was 84 per cent. The United Nations Development Programme's Human Development Index, a scale based on economic and social factors, ranked Kenya 152 out of 177 countries surveyed, compared to Canada in sixth place and the United States in eighth place.[2]

Agriculture employed 75 per cent of Kenya's labor force, contributed 16.3 per cent to the gross domestic product (GDP),[3] and generated two-thirds of foreign exchange earnings[4]. Only eight per cent of Kenya was arable land, and less than one per cent was dedicated to permanent crops — mostly the heritage of the large colonial plantations devoted to coffee, tea, cotton, sugar cane, potatoes, tobacco, wheat, peanuts and sesame. Coffee and tea were also Kenya's main export crops. The majority of the households relied on subsistence farming — small lots cultivated with corn (the basic local food), manioc, beans, sorghum and fruit. Small-scale farmers accounted for more than three-quarters of total agricultural production and over half of its marketed production.

Jiwa's idea of a socially and environmentally sustainable for-profit model that would purchase honey from small rural farmers and resell it to Kenya's urban consumers was a marked counterpoint to the three existing approaches in Kenya's agricultural sector — characterized by corruption and inefficiencies that thinned farmers' margins, disconnected them from downstream demand, and delayed reimbursement. For agricultural commodities such cotton and pyrethrum, large government-owned parastatals holding monopolistic positions often forced farmers to sell their produce at pre-set – and often rock-bottom – prices. Farmers were typically reimbursed eight to 12 months after the crop had been collected. For other commodities, such as tea, coffee and milk, produced and marketed by farmer cooperatives, corruption, mismanagement and frequent political interference meant that the farmers often waited many months to be paid for their produce. They frequently had to resort to violence to overthrow corrupt and ineffective management teams. For the so called cash crops which farmers could produce on their own, such as honey, they had to rely on a long sequence of intermediaries. Demand was limited to the number of local mid-level brokers each farmer could access. Honey changed hands at least three times through the supply chain, and farmers had limited knowledge of, and access to, the end market.

Conditions in western Kenya were ideal for producing honey and the practice had a long history in the country; however, farmers had few incentives to take on beekeeping. They were underpaid for their produce, and the cash took months to reach them. Honey was produced mostly by men, who used log hives placed on trees. Kenyan customers, increasingly disappointed with the declining quality of the local honey, were turning to imported honey, particularly from Tanzania.

Previous attempts by the Kenyan government and international donors to boost quality by introducing modern beehives had failed, due mainly to poor training and support for the beekeepers and unreliable or opportunistic market linkages that hindered the commercialization of the produce. Honey Care's solution for quality honey was also technology. Jiwa decided to equip all their suppliers with the more advanced Langstroth hives[5] (Photo: Langstroth hive; Credits: Farouk Jiwa). Langstroth hives ensured a much higher level of produce quality and were relatively simple to harvest, making commercial beekeeping popular with wider sections of the rural community, especially with women. Langstroth hives were also five times more expensive than traditional hives, but they produced a greater volume of higher quality honey which could command premium prices.

Taking the World by Swarm

By March 31, 2006, Honey Care Africa had grown to 48 full-time staff and 2,179 active honey suppliers (of which 644, or 30 per cent were women). Its supplier base was almost doubling every two years. Since June 30, 2004, Honey Care had gained 38.5 per cent additional farmers. Many of these subsistence farmers had been able to substantially increase (and often double) their income levels with only five to six extra hours of effort per month. The business model enabled small-scale beekeepers to earn KSh15,600 to KSh19,600 a year (US$200 to US$250).[6] About a third of the farmers used the additional revenues for food and medicine; about a fourth of them used them to acquire seeds and fertilizers, about a sixth paid school fees, and about a tenth channeled the money into improving housing. Approximately five per cent of the farmers used the funds they had earned through beekeeping to launch their own microenterprises[7].

Honey Care's success changed the face of beekeeping in Kenya. By 2006, 43.6 per cent of the beekeepers were women. Beekeeping now thrived in Western and Nyanza Provinces - regions not traditionally known for honey production in Kenya. The business model supported more than 22,500 Langstroth hives and 6,200 traditional hives. Of these, 3,000 hives were disbursed on microlease basis in Western Kenya through Village Banks, and 2,500 more were ongoing, involving 7,754 households in sustainable commercial beekeeping. Five Agricultural Colleges in Kenya now provided beekeeping training on a commercial but ad-hoc basis. Honey Care helped train 220 government and NGO staff, and supported the preparation and submission of the Residue Plan for Kenyan Honey to the European Union, so Kenya could now export honey to the EU (it was the 4th African country to do so). Honey Care was a founding member of the Kenya Honey Council and a key member of UNIDO Task Force on sector development in Kenya. It was closely involved in various international working groups on private sector-driven development models, including World Bank /IFC SGBI Dept, Schwab Foundation, SEED-UNEP.

Commercially, Honey Care Africa had become the leading provider of honey to the Kenyan market, with 68 per cent market share. Since 2001, its Honey Care Africa brand offered seven different types of honey (Photo: African Blossom, Credits: Farouk Jiwa). In 2003, it launched three premium honey products launched under Beekeeper's Delight Brand. In 2006, it added several types of flavored honey, including Ginger Honey, Mint Honey, and Cinnamon Honey. Honey care was now experimenting with Coffee Honey, Vanilla Honey, and Clove Honey. Its distribution reached all major supermarket chains, retail outlets, shops, hotels, lodges and restaurants in Kenya. Its packing line bottled honey for several other companies, including Premier

Food Industries. In Kenyan supermarkets a jar retails for about 220 Kenyan Shillings (US$3.25). Local competitors price their honey at 100, 120 shillings per jar. Honey Care Africa was now looking at extending its product line with innovative Base of the Pyramid offerings – honey stix (straws filled with about 6 g of honey each) who could provide a healthy source of carbohydrates to children in Kenya's sprawling slums; and honey cups (each holding about 75 g or three to four days' consumption) which were targeted for direct distribution through kiosks.

A patient loan of $500,000 from the International Finance Corporation combined with US$ 350,000 from Swiss Development Corporation for further expansion, and US$95,000 from Swisscontact supported Honey Care Africa's expansion to Tanzania. Honey Care Tanzania was run as a separate company by local partner – founder, managing director, and serial entrepreneur, Jiten Chandarana. By the end of 2006, Honey Care Tanzania had 10 collection centers established which collected honey from more than 1,000 farmers. Honey Care Africa, a 50 per cent shareholder, sourced honey and beeswax from Honey Care Tanzania. Tanzanian beekeepers had already owned traditional beehives, the expansion reconfigured the original business model to open up additional opportunities for beeswax production. By December 2005, Honey Care became the lead African exporter of beeswax (120 tonne) to the United States; growth in beeswax exports was boosted by an additional US$ 75,000 trade finance secured from United Kingdom-based Shared Interest.

Honey exports were also picking up. Honey Care Africa was distributing fair trade honey internationally through the Pangea Artisan Market and Café web portal[8]. In August 2006, in partnership with Natures Cradle Foods, Honey Care Africa brought an exotic range of fair trade honey products (*African Blossom, Highland Blend, Acacia* and *Wild Comb*) to environmental and socially-conscious consumers in Eastern United States. Honey Care was gearing up for the United Kingdom market; Canada could be next. Export growth required fairtrade certification[9]. Honey Care had already begun cooperating with the Kenyan and Tanzanian governments to develop the criteria, but the fair trade board had not yet adopted any standards.

Six years after its founding, the venture remained small in size[10], but had grown large in its impact. Honey Care's initial commitment to improving the livelihoods of the farmers led to several innovative bridges between the for-profit and NGOs. In its first three years, Honey Care had won the full support of local NGOs, international donor agencies and Kenya's governmental authorities. It then forged innovative partnerships with Africa Now, the Aga Khan Foundation, the International Finance Corporation (IFC), Care Canada, the Canadian International Development Agency's (CIDA's) Coady Institute, the U.S. Agency for International Development (USAID), the United Nations Development Programme and the European Union's Community Development Trust Fund, to name just a few.

Honey Care Africa's success against the odds helped make the case that pro-poor for-profit ventures can play an important part in sustainable agriculture across African countries and in many other developing economies. Its innovative business model had earned international acclaim. In October 2005, Honey Care Africa was named the overall winner of the Africa Small Medium and Micro-Enterprise (SMME) Award for 2005-2006. A few months earlier, Honey Care Africa was recognized by the Schwab Foundation among the world's 100 most outstanding social enterprises at the World Economic Forum in Davos. Its path-breaking business model had received several other international awards for contributing to poverty reduction and biodiversity conservation, including the UNDP Equator Initiative Prize, the Prince of Wales World Business Award and the World Bank International Development Marketplace Award. The $30,000 cash award associated

with the Equator Prize, followed shortly by a US$85,000 capacity-building grant from Project Ideas[11], hastened Honey Care's growth (Exhibit 1 lists the awards received by Honey Care since its founding five years earlier).

For Farouk Jiwa, now director and chairman of the board for Honey Care Africa (Honey Care):

> Clearly it's all about small scale producers and about giving guaranteed markets and fair prices. [...] We've got the infrastructure, we've got the farmer trust and the network group organized and we have the collection centers in place to make it easier for farmers. Going forward, it's important to remember that the model is now more valuable than the product we're producing.

Jiwa wondered whether this model would work equally well in different agricultural sectors, cultural environments or political regimes. He felt that Honey Care could, and perhaps should, play an active role in the replication of the business model. Jiwa was also interested in scaling up the model. However, as the business grew in Kenya and caught on in Tanzania, the business model was constantly facing new challenges. Honey Care's maverick approach had successfully streamlined and revamped the value chain. But its regional growth was held back in part by production (the supplier base was not going fast enough, mainly due to a shortage in suitable forms of microfinancing and constraints in scaling up Honey Care's community-centric model) and in part by competition (Honey Care's own success had spawn an entire generation of aggressive competitors, who now produced and sold quality honey at cheaper prices by taking their focus off the farmers).

A Tripartite Business Model

Honey Care's business model[12] (see Exhibit 2), based on a three-way synergistic partnership between the development sector, the private sector and rural communities, drew on the core competencies of each party and helped leverage their complementary roles and resources. Honey Care Africa sought to transfer much of the margin previously taken by intermediaries back to the rural farmer. It provided farmers with the tools required to harvest honey, purchased the honey from the farmers at guaranteed and fair prices, packaged it in marketable containers, managed the supermarket distribution and marketed the honey to Kenyan urban consumers. Honey Care Africa organized reliable collection of the honey, manufactured and helped farmers acquire hives, provided local training and technical support and, as much as possible, paid farmers in cash within 48 hours. The company facilitated individual ownership of the beehives, initially through private loans and company-sponsored plans, then through donor agencies, non-governmental organizations (NGOs) and micro-financing institutions.

Bridging the Profit Divide

Honey Care was designed as a for-profit, sustainable venture with a triple-bottom-line philosophy that would create social, environmental and economic value. Jiwa's primary objective was to work with the farmers and improve their livelihoods. But farmers had developed a chronic mistrust of corporations, large and small. They also distrusted government representatives and cooperatives, which were never there when the farmers needed them most. The farmers only trusted local NGOs, which had built close, trusting relationships with rural communities over many years. Jiwa approached many of these NGOs, but forging relationships with these organizations was not easy since significant stigma and suspicion had been associated with private sector initiatives. On the surface, the new venture's primary objectives were at odds. Honey Care Africa had strong social and environmental principles but it needed a profit to survive. NGOs, on the other hand, were purely charitable organizations, interested in sponsoring projects that would help build community self-sufficiency without asking for anything in return. And giving had its costs.

Growing up in Kenya, Jiwa had seen too many unsustainable projects. They all worked well as long as the funds from international donors kept pouring in, but as soon as funding ended, these projects quickly fell apart. NGOs in East Africa had even been publicly criticized for undertaking projects that delivered short-term relief but did not result in *sustainable* opportunities for communities[13].

Farouk Jiwa persisted. He explained how his business model would, in fact, support long-term self-sufficiency, a goal that was central for many NGOs. He identified the specific challenges that each development organization faced and thought about how the Honey Care business model would satisfy those interests. He commented on the compelling case he had to put to the NGOs:

> You have problems of implementation of agricultural projects; you have problems with sourcing the right technology and access to training. There are also issues with information dissemination and awareness creation. But by far, the biggest challenge is with ensuring some level of continuity and long-term sustainability after you exit. Honey Care is going to give you the full package. We'll start with the manufacturing of the hives, we'll go from village to village to do the demonstrations, we'll train the farmers right, focus on the economically marginalized women and youth, and we'll give all the farmers a guaranteed market for their produce and establish a prompt payment system. Above all, we'll continue to offer them a market for their produce long after the project has been wound up.

Once the complementarities became explicit, many NGOs recognized that this small for-profit company shared their goals of building long-term self-sufficiency in rural communities. They realized that Honey Care also put social impact first; commercial viability was simply a means to ensure a sustained contribution to local communities. The NGOs bought into the company's commercial model, recognizing that it could provide a guaranteed and continual stream of income for communities after initial donor funding had been exhausted. Honey Care welcomed the NGOs' endorsements; their deep relationships with rural communities in Kenya had been key to alleviating initial mistrust and providing much-needed working capital for the farmers, who could not have otherwise purchased the beehives.

Hive Ownership

Initially, the business model envisioned farmers taking out regular loans to purchase the Langstroth beehives. But that wasn't possible — interest rates were high (21 per cent), and most banks would not approve loans without collateral, which the poor rural farmers did not have. Honey Care devised a buy-back loan plan; the company would lend the hive to farmers and retain a certain percentage of the monthly revenue generated from its operation. But Honey Care's limited operational capital constrained its reach.

Many NGOs were willing to provide Honey Care with grant funding for the hives, but only if the hives were owned at the community level. Jiwa resisted. He feared that if hives were owned by groups of people, only some would bother to operate them, and if those people became frustrated and unwilling to keep at it, the investment would be wasted. Honey Care insisted that beehives be individually owned; however, the farmers could work as a group on particular activities. They could share the bee suits and the smoker. Eventually a compromise was reached. The NGOs conceded on the need for individual ownership; Honey Care agreed to support and work with existing groups.

Honey Care and the NGOs also disagreed on the basic principle of providing the hives to farmers free of charge. The NGOs were not interested in receiving money in return for the hives, but Farouk Jiwa was sensitive to the implication of giveaways. Free hives could be perceived as a discretionary asset, giving farmers no real incentive to produce honey of the quality desired. Honey Care insisted that a pay-back plan would signal to farmers that honey production was an economically viable activity that they could undertake without external help. Honey Care would retain 25 to 50 per cent of a farmer's monthly income and remit this amount to the NGO until the full cost of the hive had been recovered. This way, hive ownership in itself would become an important economic motivator: once farmers owned their hives, the economic pay-offs of honey production would almost double.

Eventually, the NGOs endorsed this position and agreed to purchase the hives for Honey Care. The firm would lend them to the farmers who could purchase the hives gradually, at their original cost. Honey Care would then place the returned funds into a savings account that could be used by the community for expanding the hive base and/or other development projects.

Joining Forces with Africa Now

The relationship between Honey Care and Africa Now[14] had been a symbiotic and model-defining one. Africa Now was one of the few NGOs interested in enabling entrepreneurial development in rural Kenya, and a vocal champion for fair treatment of small farmers. The NGO had significant experience with small-grower beekeeping in Somalia and other parts of Kenya. Rob Hale, then Africa Now's country director for Kenya, was keenly aware of the need for a business approach for overcoming the structural flaws in the existing honey supply chain.

Hale and Jiwa became good friends. Their strong personal connection and commitment to a shared goal infused all aspects of the partnership between their organizations. At the strategic level, Farouk Jiwa and Rob Hale maintained a steady and healthy tension. They constantly debated the new opportunities for providing additional services to farmers, and, in the process, collaboratively refined Honey Care's original business model. Jiwa commented:

Rob helps keep us on the straight and narrow. It's good to have somebody out there who comes from a little more on the social side of the spectrum than you are. Then we come in a slightly more on the business side of the spectrum and say "Well that's great Rob, that's wonderful, but can we actually make some money on this." So the question I ask Rob every single time is, "What are we going to do when the grant finally runs out?" and the fundamental question Rob asks me is, "What would you have done if the donors didn't have the money to start with?"

The strategic alignment also filtered down throughout the organization, affecting every aspect of Honey Care's operations. There was a tremendous amount of transparency between the two organizations. Payments to the farmers were always made in the presence of Africa Now (Photo: Africa Now Truck; Credits: Farouk Jiwa). Communication between the two organizations took place across all levels on a day-to-day, week-to-week and month-to-month basis. It quickly became an accepted norm that all major decisions of one organization would affect and involve the other.

The two firms shared operational resources, including personnel, logistical facilities and vehicles. Africa Now already had human resources on the ground in western Kenya and it assisted Honey Care to provide field services in several rural areas. Africa Now also had bases in most of Honey Care's farming areas, so Honey Care used Africa Now's facilities to conduct its administrative functions. This arrangement saved Honey Care substantial overhead expenditures when it was getting started. Furthermore, Africa Now's employees working in areas not yet serviced by Honey Care spread the word about the new business model among small-scale producers in western Kenya. Many farmers bought into the model, and Honey Care's supplier base quickly expanded. The images of Honey Care and Africa Now became inextricably linked in farmers' minds because the companies endorsed each other and shared personnel

and facilities in many communities. In fact, many of the farmers felt they were dealing with a single organization. This increased the commitment of the farmers to Honey Care.

Earning Farmer's Loyalty

Looking back, Jiwa was heartened by the firm's focus on small-scale honey-producing communities and the commitment to look after the needs of farmers. Since its founding, Honey Care had tried to be the best partner for rural Kenyan farmers. Farouk Jiwa knew that any other model, whether focused primarily on economic profit or social impact, could not have accomplished this goal. This special bond with the farmers was not only the raison d'être for the company but, as Jiwa well knew, it remained the key to its survival: any day, any season, Honey Care's viability depended on its farmer network:

> We shouldn't forget where we came from, because that's what it's all about. Being in agriculture is very fickle — a drought across the country, and we're out of business. It's as simple as that. With a steel mine or a copper mine you can just go and dig more copper, but honey is produced every single day. If the flowers don't bloom in time there is no honey. So we remember that no matter how big we become we're always going to remain very close to the edge. And the only thing that keeps us above the edge is the fact that we have good relationships with our farmers.

For the farmers, the partnerships with local NGOs and community-based organizations (CBOs) were an important signal that Honey Care was genuinely committed to Kenya's rural farming communities. But actions had to follow. As Jiwa explained, Honey Care's relationship with the farmers was equal, fair and sensible:

> I think you just go out there and speak with the farmers very honestly and without being patronizing. You explain what's in it for them and you explain what Honey Care intends on getting out of this. Above all, you listen to what they have to say and take their input seriously.

This was a very different approach from the way farmers had been treated before; government representatives would lecture farmers for two hours straight, giving them little opportunity for feedback or dialogue. Jiwa put away the podium and engaged farmers in a two-way conversation. It took him a while to break the ice, but the farmers quickly warmed up to his open, frank style. Above all, they recognized Honey Care's genuine interest in understanding and meeting their specific needs.

Money for Honey

From the outset, Honey Care implemented a money-for-honey plan. They paid farmers fair prices, on the spot, under a detailed and formal contract. No other organization had done anything like this before. Even the Coffee Board of Kenya delayed payments for eight to 12 months.

The Money for Honey proposal had gotten Jiwa the first break. DANIDA, the Danish International Development Agency, which was at the time engaged in a small development project in a semi-arid region of Kenya, agreed to fund a pilot project of 100 beehives. At harvest, Jiwa planned a public celebration which would attract other donors and investors. Only two donors showed up, but fortunately so did the *Daily Nation*, the largest circulating newspaper in East Africa, which published a full front-page article on the project.

Training and Extension Services

Immediate cash payments were needed and appreciated by the farmers, but Jiwa also knew that sustaining high-quality honey production also required initial training and on-the-ground

technical support. Governmental ministries provided some assistance through ad hoc training services, but Jiwa felt that Honey Care should provide more specific support. He initiated formal and informal training schemes that taught farmers the technical peculiarities of honey harvesting using Langstroth hives. The training covered beehive maintenance, pest control, safety and protection (e.g. bee suits), proper harvesting techniques and other activities related to the honey harvesting process. (Photo: beehive inspection training; Credits: Farouk Jiwa)

Honey Care also employed a team of project officers, who were dedicated to a small number of farmers in their neighboring communities and worked one-on-one with farmers to maximize their yield and quality. The project officers were aware of the cultural idiosyncrasies of their neighborhoods and were deeply committed to the social development of their communities. Project officers made regular visits to the farmers to see how the honey harvest was progressing. As Rob Nyambaka, Honey Care's operations director explained, they were available whenever the farmer needed advice on any aspect of the harvesting process:

> The project officer is the key: they essentially ensure that the farmer produces the honey. They also play an important role in knowing what is happening on the ground. Because most of them are from the local community and speak the language and know the culture, they are able to continuously gather the right information about the status of the projects. Whatever happens in the field, we, here at head office, will know. This helps us constantly monitor the needs of each particular community. What exactly are their problems? What exactly do they need? Project officers act as a link between Honey Care and the community. They are the Honey Care presence in the field. Whenever the communities see the project officer, they know Honey Care is in the field. This has never happened with other honey buyers. They come this season, disappear for the next six to eight months, come again for a day next season, disappear for the next six to nine months, come again for a day, disappear for another six to eight months. They simply do not have the same close relationships to the farmers as we do.

Feedback

A trusted relationship with the farmers has been pivotal to Honey Care's success from the beginning, and it had helped refine and recalibrate its business model. For example, the original business model had planned for collection centers to be located in the middle of each community. Once in the field, however, Honey Care realized how significant the distances were — the average farmer would walk about 20 kilometers to reach the closest collection center — so Honey Care switched to a mobile tent and brought the collection center to each farmer.

Early feedback also suggested that five days of intensive initial training in Nairobi conflicted with the basic demands of the farmers' lifestyles; most needed to return home after three days. Later programs were shorter and conducted closer to the farmers' homes, whenever possible. Honey Care also realized that it was difficult to convey the technical aspects of beekeeping because many of the farmers had low levels of formal education. Honey Care stripped away the technicalities and translated the training into basic and applied practices that the farmers could better remember. Wherever possible, Honey Care trainers learned to use appropriate analogies and local sayings to convey their message.

In 2004, Honey Care formalized a farmer feedback process with a simple "performance monitoring questionnaire," distributed monthly to 60 farmers selected at random from its supplier network (see Exhibit 3). The questions were designed by the farmers, through a participatory learning exercise facilitated by Honey Care's close partner, the non-governmental organization (NGO) Africa Now. The exercise involved individual farmers identifying key issues and framing the questions. The monthly questionnaire collected farmers' feedback on the firm's training, the quality of the hives and the quality of the extension services delivered by project officers, among other information. The data, carefully and timely analyzed, signaled what Honey Care was doing right and where improvement or change might help them do better. The questionnaire was also a measuring tool for Honey Care's socio-economic impact.

Going on Trust

Honey Care's entire business model relied implicitly on farmer loyalty. Honey Care did not have a monopolistic relationship with the beekeepers because many of the hives were obtained with NGO support; farmers could sell their produce to any broker. Because of the superior quality of the honey produced using Langstroth hives, other brokers were now skimming the harvest by offering KSh10 to KSh20 a kilogram more than Honey Care's KSh100 KSh per kilogram. Those farmers who had taken their hives on the buy-back plan were only receiving 50 to 75 per cent of the Honey Care rate, so selling to the higher bidder was sometimes tempting. Everyone in the field was aware of cases where farmers had taken advantage of the higher margins. These were, after all, small rural communities with incomes barely above subsistence levels, which were often pressed for cash for urgent needs. But overall, the community remained loyal to Honey Care. Lucas, one of the Honey Care farmers, commented on the situation:

> There was one member who was not being cooperative and well he was thinking of selling his honey somewhere else, so we talked about it and now he changed his mind completely. We disowned him. We told him that we'll not deal with him. If he thinks of looking for a market anywhere else, then we won't deal with him as a community. But we have changed him, and now he's all right.

Honey Care lost some farmers to ad hoc and opportunistic competitors, but many of them returned once these competitors vanished. As Jiwa explained, returning farmers developed an even greater appreciation for Honey Care's consistency and the guaranteed monthly payments that came every collection cycle:

> We're always amazed, but farmers almost always come back to us. I guess the one thing we are doing right is our level of consistency. When we tell farmers we're going to be out

there next Wednesday to collect the honey, we do it. There's no substitute for the ability to keep our promises.

Initially, the plan had been to rid Honey Care of opportunistic suppliers by providing the super (the upper portion of the Langstroth hive where the honey was stored) free of charge. The rest of the hive was owned by the farmer, but the super belonged to Honey Care. Project officers collected the filled supers and replaced them with empty ones. Although this practice reduced the chance that farmers would sell to ad hoc competitors, the process was not sustainable. As the farmer base grew, Honey Care realized that the supers were locking up a significant portion of the company's finances. Supers were distributed throughout the country, and replacing them at each harvest was costly. After carefully considering the pros and cons, Honey Care adapted its business model so that the farmer owned the entire beehive. This decision to earn the trust of the farmers, rather than limit the odds of opportunism, paid off.

The Difference Makers

At head office and in the production room employees felt they were making a difference. Jiwa diffused his vision of what Honey Care Africa stood for, one employee at a time. He would often bottle honey shoulder-to-shoulder with his employees, reminding them that packaging was essential for attracting customers. He could also be found spending time in the workshop with the carpenters or loading boxed jars onto trucks. Day after day, everyone developed a clear, deep sense of what the business model was all about. No one wanted to short-change subsistence-farming communities; they had all come from such a community and could envision the difference quality honey production could make for their friends and relatives. The sense of personal duty permeated the entire process, from the production of beehives to the distribution of the honey jars to urban supermarkets. The employees clearly understood the roles they played in the business model and looked after their specific tasks with utmost care. The carpenters assembling the beehives tasted the honey their uncles and grandfathers produced using the hives; they knew that the farmers' ability to produce high-quality honey and generate a substantial source of income depended, at least in part, on their own commitment and craftsmanship.

Jiwa wanted to keep Honey Care employees motivated every step of the way. He had seen first-hand that even the most personally invested field officers working for the Ministry of Agriculture sometimes delivered sub-par performance in rural communities. Jiwa set out to establish clearer linkages between the efforts made by project officers in the field and the quantity and quality of honey produced by the farmers. Honey Care devised an incentive program that gave project officers a bonus on top of their regular salary for every kilogram of honey produced. This bonus was awarded at the end of each year. For the first year of the plan, individual bonuses ranged from five to eight Kenyan shillings (KSh) for each kilogram that the project officers helped the farmers produce (the equivalent of 6.6 to 10.5 cents in U.S. currency. This is a third of a loaf of bread at $0.35 a sixth of a packet of sugar at $0.63, and half of a bottle of Coca Cola at $0.21[15]). The incentive plan had an unexpected positive impact on Honey Care's forecasting accuracy. Because project officers monitored local honey production closely, the firm knew in advance how much honey it would collect every month. Thus, Honey

Care could ensure sufficient cash in hand, better manage processing capacity, make informed downstream market commitments and plan distribution activities.

Scaling Up

As Jiwa reconsidered the replicability and scalability of Honey Care's business model, he recalled two of the best-known and most successful examples of sustainable agriculture in Africa: Sekem, an organic farm rooted in a strong culture and centralized logistics (see Exhibit 4); and the Kenya Tea Development Agency (KTDA), a farmer-owned and -operated cooperative focused on large-scale, low-margin crops (see Exhibit 5). He wondered how Honey Care could grow its beekeeping operations across East Africa without losing its farmer focus. A good way to expand within Kenya and Tanzania was to provide more beehives to those communities in which the company already had a strong farming presence, and then expand to neighboring communities – but collection, payment, and quality assurance bottlenecked its local growth.

Collection

With increasing numbers of farmers joining the program, the initial model of collecting from each individual producer was becoming less feasible. Honey Care was again toying with the idea of establishing collection centers. It was a typical model for Kenyan agriculture; farmers from a particular community would come together at one central location to deliver their produce and receive payment. Collection centers had their downsides, but they would enable more farmers to extract their honey and be paid in the short harvesting season. Each community would gain but individual farmers would have to bring the honey to the collection centers.

Payment

As the volume of collected honey increased, Honey Care representatives were handling significant amounts of cash, and the company had to find simpler, safer and more effective ways of managing cash payments. Cash handling could be reduced by depositing the funds right into the farmer's account of a local bank. This could allow a means of savings and allow farmers to take on other investments maybe buy more hives or other equipment through leasing mechanisms that we've developed with financial partners. The village bank network was still quite small but cell-phone banking was spreading fast throughout rural Kenya[16].

A second challenge was the time lag between Honey Care's payments to farmers and its receipts from supermarkets – usually several weeks. As volume increased, Honey Care's cash flows could not cover the entire lag. However, delaying payment to the farmers could jeopardize their hard-earned trust. But going into the field twice, once to collect the honey and then again to pay the farmer, would be expensive. Honey Care was unsure how to best reorganize the payments.

Quality Assurance

Higher volumes also meant greater stocks and longer shelf life. Honey Care had to find ways to maintain stock levels, check the heights of the fill, and prevent crystallization. There were also consequences for the bottling process, which now needed to include micro-filtration and improved honey pasteurization processes. Both would require additional investments in technology and human resources.

As beekeepers became more proficient at harvesting the honey and needed less day-to-day support from the project officers, the demand for the project officers' extension services was changing. The roles of the project officers began shifting from demonstrating the harvesting and maintenance techniques to providing advice on how to increase the purity of the honey. Project officers were acquiring new capabilities; and they now had more time for new responsibilities.

In Kenya, market share had peaked, spurring price-based competition. To maintain his market leadership at home Honey Care was turning attention to creative marketing: bi-annual campaigns featured lead producers' stories from different regions; innovation in product range and packaging sought to create additional market niches at home. International markets were beckoning, but production capacity was still lagging overseas demand. Jiwa wondered how the tripartite business model that had brought the venture international acclaim could be recalibrated and expanded to keep raising the volume of high quality honey without fracturing Honey Care's bond to rural farmers.

Exhibit 1

Selected Honey Care Awards

Bryden Alumni Award 2005–2006

Farouk Jiwa was awarded the inaugural One-to-Watch Bryden Alumni Award by York University, Toronto, Canada, in November 2005, for his work with Honey Care Africa.

Overall Winner of the Africa SMME Award for 2005–2006

The Small Medium and Micro-Enterprise (SMME) Award was presented to Honey Care Africa in October 2005, by a consortium of African businesses and the Africa Centre for Investment Analysis at the University of Stellenbosch, in Stellenbosch, South Africa.

Most Outstanding Social Entrepreneur Award

The Award was presented to Farouk Jiwa at the 2005 World Economic Forum in Davos, Switzerland, in recognition of being among the World's Top 100 Social Entrepreneurs by the Schwab Foundation for Social Entrepreneurship.

World Business Award

This award was presented to Honey Care Africa in recognition of its contribution to the Millennium Development Goals of the United Nations. In 2004, it was jointly awarded by the Prince of Wales International Business Leaders' Forum, the United Nations Development Programme (UNDP) and the International Chamber of Commerce.

Equator Initiative Prize

This award was presented to Honey Care Africa at the World Summit on Sustainable Development (WSSD) in Johannesburg, South Africa, in 2002, in recognition of the outstanding efforts to reduce poverty through the conservation and sustainable use of bio-diversity. This US$30,000 prize was jointly awarded by the UNDP, the Government of Canada, the International Development Research Centre (IDRC), the Television Trust for the Environment, the International Union for the Conservation of Nature and Natural Resources (IUCN), The Nature Conservancy, Brasilconnects and the United Nations Foundation.

Ismaili Youth Award for Excellence

This award was presented to Farouk Jiwa in 2002, by His Highness Prince Amyn Aga Khan of the Aga Khan Development Network, in recognition of excellence in entrepreneurship through Honey Care Africa.

World Bank International Development Marketplace Innovation Award

This award was presented jointly to Honey Care Africa and Africa Now in 2002 for its innovative business model and community micro-leasing scheme. This award was presented by the Small and Medium Enterprise (SME) Department of the World Bank Group/ International Finance Corporation and supported by George Soros's Open Society Institute.

Source: http://www.honeycareafrica.com/files/awards.php, accessed March 12, 2007; http://www.yorku.ca/fes/alumni/graduates.asp?recDesc=grad/mes_txt01_11.htm, accessed March 12, 2007.

Exhibit 2

HONEY CARE'S TRIPARTITE BUSINESS MODEL

Honey Care

Honey production
Hive management & harvesting
Record keeping
Demonstrations
Agro-ecological assessment
Technical beekeeping training
Training in record keeping
Supply of beekeeping equipment
Community-based extension service
Guaranteed market on contract
Honey extraction services
Honey collection from farm / centre
Cash payment on-spot
Loan payment deduction

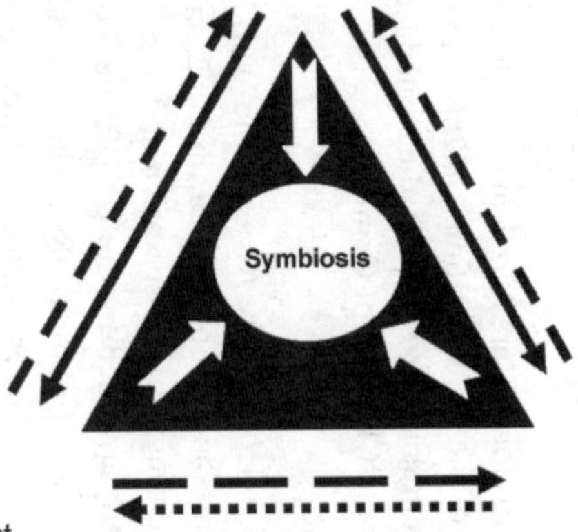

Rural Communities

Facilitate community assessment
Community organization skills
Group formation & loans
Independent monitoring & evaluation

**Development Organization
Donor Agency / MFI**

Participate in community assessment
Group formation and rules
Identify sites – individual / communal
Start beekeeping
Service loans until repayment done

Beekeeping equipment for farmers
Project planning activities
Coordination / communication
Independent monitoring & evaluation
Loan remittances from farmer
Regular monitoring reports
Project status reports
Oversee smooth exit
Publicity and public relations

Symbiosis

Exhibit 3

Performance Monitoring Questionnaire

Dear Beekeeper, we are asking you to fill in this form in order to see how Honey Care is doing, and to find ways in which we can serve you better! THIS IS YOUR CHANCE TO TELL US!

SECTION 2: BEEKEEPING DETAILS

6. Do you belong to a Beekeeping Group? (Tick Appropriate Box): Yes ☐ Group Name _____ No ☐

7. How many Hives do you have? _____ Langstroth _____ Other

8. How much time do you spend looking after your hives each month? Less than 1 Hr ☐ 1–5 Hrs ☐ More than 5 Hrs ☐

9. How much honey did you harvest last year? _____ Kg

10. How much honey did you harvest the year before? _____ Kg

11. How many honey harvests did you have in the last 12 months? _____

12. If you had NO harvests in the last 12 months, please state reason (e.g. New Beekeeper, Drought, etc)
_____

13. Have you received Beekeeping Training from Honey Care or its partners? Yes ☐ No ☐

14. If Yes, on which date? _____ *(Month and Year is sufficient)*

16. If Yes, was the Training Useful? Yes ☐ No ☐

17. Did you get any Extension Services from Honey Care or its partners in the last 12 months? Yes ☐ No ☐

18. Please rank how important the following are to help you increase honey production:

FASTER EXTRACTION AND RETURN OF SUPERS	Not Important ☐	Somewhat Important ☐	Very Important ☐
MORE FREQUENT EXTENSION SERVICES	Not Important ☐	Somewhat Important ☐	Very Important ☐
INFORMATION ON WHICH TREES / CROPS INCREASE HONEY	Not Important ☐	Somewhat Important ☐	Very Important ☐
BEEKEEPING EQUIPMENT (Bee Suit, Smokers, Hive Tools etc)	Not Important ☐	Somewhat Important ☐	Very Important ☐
MORE BEEKEEPING TRAINING	Not Important ☐	Somewhat Important ☐	Very Important ☐
MORE SUPERS	Not Important ☐	Somewhat Important ☐	Very Important ☐
MICRO-FINANCE LOANS FOR MORE HIVES	Not Important ☐	Somewhat Important ☐	Very Important ☐

OTHER (Please Specify):

SECTION 3: PERFORMANCE SATISFACTION INDEX (PSI)

19. Overall, how would you rank your satisfaction with Honey Care's Products and Services?

QUALITY OF BEE HIVE	Excellent ☐	Good ☐	Fair ☐	Need to Improve ☐
QUALITY OF BEEKEEPING KIT (e.g. Bee Suit, Smoker)	Excellent ☐	Good ☐	Fair ☐	Need to Improve ☐
BEEKEEPING TRAINING (if applicable)	Excellent ☐	Good ☐	Fair ☐	Need to Improve ☐
EXTENSION SERVICES	Excellent ☐	Good ☐	Fair ☐	Need to Improve ☐
HONEY EXTRACTION / COLLECTION SERVICES	Excellent ☐	Good ☐	Fair ☐	Need to Improve ☐
PAYMENT / LOAN DEDUCTION SERVICES	Excellent ☐	Good ☐	Fair ☐	Need to Improve ☐

ANY OTHER AREAS WE CAN IMPROVE (Please Specify): _____
_____

WHAT OTHER INFORMATION / SERVICES WOULD YOU LIKE FROM HONEY CARE? _____
_____

Exhibit 3 (continued)

SECTION 4: SOCIO-ECONOMIC AND ENVIRONMENTAL IMPACT:

20. What do you do with the money you earn from sale of honey? (*Tick as appropriate*)

BUY FOOD FOR FAMILY ☐

BUY MEDICINES ☐

BUY SEEDS, FERTILZERS, FARM TOOLS, LIVESTOCK, HIRE FARM LABOUR ☐

PAY SCHOOL FEES FOR CHILDREN ☐

BUY SCHOOL UNIFORMS / BOOKS FOR CHILDREN ☐

IMPROVE THE HOUSE ☐

START A SMALL BUSINESS ☐

SAVE ALL OR SOME OF THE MONEY ☐

BUY TREES TO PLANT NEAR THE HOUSE / APIARY ☐

HELP OTHERS IN FAMILY / COMMUNITY IN GREATER NEED ☐

BUY MORE HIVES ☐

BUY BEEKEEPING EQUIPMENT (Bee Suit, Smoker, Hive Tool etc) ☐

OTHER (Please Specify): _____

21. Would you agree or disagree with the following statements?

BEEKEPING IS GOOD FOR THE ENVIRONMENT AGREE ☐ DISAGREE ☐ DON'T KNOW ☐

BEES HELP TO INCREASE CROP YIELD AGREE ☐ DISAGREE ☐ DON'T KNOW ☐

PLANTING MORE TREES AND FLOWERS INCREASES HONEY PRODUCTION AGREE ☐ DISAGREE ☐ DON'T KNOW ☐

USING PESTICIDES AND CHEMICALS REDUCES HONEY PRODUCTION AGREE ☐ DISAGREE ☐ DON'T KNOW ☐

MY FAMILY USES HONEY REGULARLY BECAUSE IT HAS MEDICINAL PROPERTIES AGREE ☐ DISAGREE ☐ DON'T KNOW ☐

IS THERE ANYTHING ELSE YOU WANT TO TELL US? _____

Source: Honey Care Africa, personal correspondence with Farouk Jiwa, August 2006

Exhibit 4

SEKEM'S MOTHER FARM MODEL OF SUSTAINABLE AGRICULTURE

Founded in 1977, in arid Egypt, by Dr. Ibrahim Abouleish, Sekem had achieved rapid growth and international success without trade-offs in its pivotal commitment to the surrounding community and the environment. Sekem nurtured a strong culture that bound farmers together and promoted knowledge sharing and development.

The Sekem initiative (Sekem means "vitality from the sun") began by using biodynamic methods on 70 hectares of desert land, 60 kilometers outside Cairo, Egypt. With only 200,000 German marks and a network of friends and supporters, Abouleish, former head of the division of pharmaceutical research at the University of Graz in Austria, started the development of what was known as a "mother farm" in the Egyptian desert. More than 120,000 trees were planted to create both a shield from desert storms and a habitat for insects and animals. Wells were drilled at depths of more than 100 meters. Soil fertility was built up gradually using the dung of 40 cows donated by friends in Germany. In 1983, seven years after its inception, Sekem was rewarded with a crop of real organic tomatoes and carrots.

The principle at Sekem's core was fairness towards local producers and towards consumers worldwide. Initially, the idea of organic farming in the desert diffused slowly. Abouleish went from door to door, educating farmers about the benefits of organic crops and the opportunity to grow organic produce for the European market. Sekem gradually facilitated the production of organic fruits and vegetables, organic textiles and medicines from natural sources; it supplied these products directly to large supermarkets and department stores in Europe.

One of Sekem's primary goals was to support the transition of small farmers from traditional to biodynamic cultivation, both through knowledge transfers and through support services. However, despite the significantly higher margins for organic crops, farmers were initially reluctant to switch, in part because benefits were delayed by two to three years. Transitioning to organic agriculture typically took two years of zero chemical use, and regular inspection visits to ensure producer compliance. Egyptian farmers also had little trust that the European market was a feasible alternative to traditional local sales. But Abouleish guaranteed a market for all produce, at fair prices. The supplier network began growing, tentatively at first, then snowballing once word of mouth got around. Abouleish's passion caught on and inspired a strong community culture. By 1994, Sekem had attracted approximately 100 farmers.

In 1996, Sekem sponsored the Egyptian Biodynamic Association (EBDA), a non-governmental organization (NGO) that promoted biodynamic farming methods in Egypt and its neighboring region. EBDA focused on research and development, training, extension, technology transfer and many other related services. The number of farmers increased exponentially once organic growing became institutionalized. Thirty years after its founding, Sekem comprised about 180 farms and 850 farmers, who cultivated approximately 2,700 hectares all over Egypt, from Aswan to Alexandria. Each farm applied international standards in biodynamic agriculture.

The initial mother farm still housed the infrastructure required to produce, package and market all the raw materials received from small rural farmers. The mother farm continued to provide a strong, reliable linkage between rural Egyptian farmers and European chains. SEKEM had strengthened the supply chain upstream and downstream, resulting in deep and trusting relationships among its customers, suppliers and employees.

Exhibit 5

KTDA's Cooperative Alternative

One of the few successful models of sustainable agriculture in Kenya was the Kenya Tea Development Agency (KTDA), now a farmer-owned and -operated cooperative that brought together 400,000 small tea growers. KTDA, a former public institution established in 1964, has been privatized by the Kenyan government in 2000.

The cooperative intermediated between its member growers and the international bulk tea market. Upstream, KTDA provided extension services to the growers and conducted all monetary transactions as the tea leaves changed hands throughout the supply chain. Downstream, KTDA negotiated maximum prices for bulk tea with companies such as Lipton and Unilever.

KTDA oversaw the supply, production and distribution of more than 800 million kilograms of leaves per year. Small growers from around Kenya took their tea leaves to a collection center located within a few kilometers of their farms. Leaves from a dozen or so geographically proximate collection centers were then transported for processing to one of KTDA's 45 factories dispersed throughout Kenya. Processed tea leaves were then transported in bulk to the Mombasa port and shipped to Asia, the Middle East, Europe and the United States.

Within the cooperative, all major decisions were made democratically by board representatives who were elected by tea-growing communities across Kenya. Each of the 12 different districts sent one representative to the KTDA board. This representative was appointed by the three to four other factory representatives in the district. All factory representatives were elected by the small growers who sold their crop to the collection centers neighboring each factory.

KTDA's profits were fully disseminated to the tea farmers each season; very little cash was retained for factory upgrades or process improvements. The small growers were paid in two installments. The first payment was received electronically by each grower approximately one month after the leaves were delivered to the collection centre. This first installment was equal across all growers, and typically ranged between one-third and one-half of the expected market prices per bushel. For example, if KTDA expected the tea leaves to sell for KSh24 per bushel, the initial payment would be about KSh9 per bushel. The second payment occurred several months later, at the end of the year. This second installment varied among grower communities, depending on the costs incurred by each grower's collection centers and processing factory. The difference between the total revenues and the first installment, KSh15 per bushel in this example, less operating expenses, was divided evenly among the farmers in each growing community — all received the same revenue per bushel.

Before privatization, KTDA attracted about 10,000 new growers each year. The rate of growth had increased by 50 per cent after privatization, due to the incentives associated with ownership. KTDA now gained about 15,000 new members each year. This accelerated expansion had its challenges. Prior to the privatization, each extension officer had been working closely with farmers and had been responsible for up to 100 farmers. Now each extension officer worked with 800, or even 1,000 growers, and the membership kept increasing every year. KTDA board members were taking a closer look at the possible trade-offs between financial viability and social sustainability.

Editors' reflections and questions

Farouk Jiwa, the founding entrepreneur of Honey Care Africa, revitalised Kenya's national honey industry by focusing on farmers with smallholdings across the country. Central to the success was an innovative business model: a synergistic partnership between the development sector, the private sector and the rural communities that drew on the core competencies of each stakeholder. This tripartite model was combined with local manufacturing of beehives; effective beekeeping training and a community-based extension service; and a guaranteed market for smallholder farmers.

With increasing numbers of farmers joining the programme, Honey Care Africa established centrally located collection centres for farmers in each area to deliver their produce and receive payment. However, as the volume of collected honey increased it became necessary to find simpler, safer and more effective ways of managing cash payments. A second challenge was the time lag between the company's payments to farmers and its receipts from supermarkets – usually several weeks. As volume increased, the company's cash flow could not cover the entire lag but, on the other hand, delaying payment to the farmers could jeopardise their hard-earned trust. Finally, international markets beckoned, but production capacity was still lagging behind overseas demand. Jiwa wondered how the tripartite business model that had brought the venture international acclaim could be recalibrated and expanded to keep raising the volume of high quality honey without damaging the company's bond with rural farmers.

What are possible alternatives for collecting payment from farmers, apart from collection centres?

What are possible methods for overcoming the delay in payments to farmers and ensuring they are paid promptly and without interruption?

Should the business model be altered in response to existing pressures? What would be an appropriate course of action to maintain the venture's social focus and triple-bottom-line performance and to diversify the product range while increasing production capacity?

What broader lessons emerge from the Honey Care Africa experience for emerging companies in the agriculture sector in Africa? To what extent is its business model replicable?

Notes

1   Jiwa had teamed up with two Kenyan benefactors and successful businessmen, Yusuf Keshavjee and Husein Bhanji who provided the capital and gave Jiwa the freedom and flexibility to run with the idea and make it work. Yusuf Keshavjee's son, Irfan, and Husein Bhanji's wife, Shella, also became investors, and together, the Keshavjees and the Bhanjis provided the financing, while Jiwa took on the responsibility of building Honey Care Africa and managing its operations.

2   http://www.publicintegrity.org/aids/country.aspx?cc=ke, accessed January 22, 2007

3   http://www.ruralpovertyportal.org/english/regions/africa/ken/statistics.htm#agriculture, accessed March 12, 2007.

4   http://www.umsl.edu/services/govdocs/obr/obr_0008.htm, accessed on March 12, 2007

5   The Langstroth hive is split into two sections: the brood box at the bottom and the super, which sits on top. Placed between the two is a wire mesh frame called the queen excluder. This frame stops the queen bee from going up into the super to lay eggs. Instead, eggs are laid, and larvae are reared in the brood box. The only bees that can enter the super are worker bees, which store the pure honey there. Traditional and top bar hives do not have a queen excluder; the honey mixes with eggs, larvae and young bees, and the honey is bitter and of poor quality. To harvest a Langstroth hive, the beekeeper places an additional board between the queen excluder and the super. This divider is called a clearer board, and it is really a one-way trap for the bees. Worker bees move up and down between the super and the brood box throughout the day. When this trap is in place, they can find their way down to the brood box, but cannot make their way up again. During a 24-hour period, the super is thus cleared of all bees. The clearer board and the full super can then be easily removed, and a new super is placed on top of the hive. Source: http://www.honeycareafrica.com/files/faqs.php#Why, accessed March 12, 2007.

6   Schwab Foundation for Social Entrepreneurship, http://www.schwabfound.org/schwabentrepreneurs.htm?schwabid=1731, last accessed on March 12, 2007

7   Based on 1,200 farmer responses. Source: Honey Care Presentation by Farouk Jiwa, July 2006

8   http://207.145.104.124/GBO/PDF/Honey_Care.htm, last accessed on August 10, 2007.

9   Fair trade certification was an important bottleneck for exporting honey to Western countries. This certification guaranteed end-consumers that products had come from companies that incorporated social and environmental sustainability in their business functions.

10 Honey Care Africa earns annual revenues of 8.5 million Kenyan shillings (KSh), equivalent to US$110,000 (July 1, 2004 data).

11 Project IDEAS is a $1 million initiative to support innovations in small business development jointly funded by IFC's SME Capacity Building Facility and George Soros' Open Society Institute.

12 http://www.apimondia.org/apiacta/slovenia/en/jiwa.pdf, last accessed on August 10, 2007.

13 For example, in the early 1990s, several non-governmental agencies funded the installation of 10,000 water pumps in Tanzania, but did not involve local communities in their set-up or operations. Locals were not trained in how to monitor the pumps, nor held accountable for their maintenance in any way. By the mid-late 1990s, 90 per cent of the pumps became inoperable.

14 Africa Now is an international development organization tackling poverty in Africa by helping small-scale producers and promoting ethical trade. Africa Now assistance finance, training, technology and securing a fair price for their goods offers farmers a 'hand-up' rather than a 'hand-out', providing people with a future of opportunity, not charity. Source: http://www.africanow.org/, last accessed on August 10, 2007.

15 http://news.bbc.co.uk/1/hi/world/africa/4805530.stm, accessed March 12, 2007.

16 M-PESA provided an affordable, fast, convenient and safe way to transfer money by SMS anywhere in Kenya; additional details at http://www.safaricom.co.ke/m-pesa/default.asp, last accessed on August 10, 2007

A model of clean energy entrepreneurship in Africa:

E+Co's path to scale*

OANA BRANZEI & KEVIN MCKAGUE

According to the World Energy Outlook[1] some 1.6 billion people — one-quarter of the world's population — have no access to electricity. Without radical interventions, 1.4 billion people might still have no access by 2030. Four out of five people lacking access to electricity live in rural areas of the developing world. About 80 per cent of these people are located in sub-Saharan Africa and India.[2] Low-income households around the world spend about US$20 billion per year on expensive and environmentally damaging energy sources, such as kerosene, battery charging, charcoal, firewood and disposable batteries.[3] The poor often pay higher prices for traditional fuel sources (i.e. the so-called poverty premium) because modern energy technologies, such as wind and steam turbines, solar power or biofuels, which could offer cheaper and better energy sources, are often not available.

> Action to encourage more efficient and sustainable use of traditional biomass and help people switch to modern cooking fuels and technologies is needed urgently. [...] Alternative fuels and technologies are already available at reasonable cost. Halving the number of households using biomass for cooking by 2015 — a recommendation of the UN

---

* Oana Branzei and Kevin McKague wrote this case solely to provide material for class discussion. The authors do not intend to illustrate either effective or ineffective handling of a managerial situation. The authors may have disguised certain names and other identifying information to protect confidentiality.

Richard Ivey School of Business
The University of Western Ontario   **IVEY** | Information Technology

Millennium Project — would involve 1.3 billion people switching to liquefied petroleum gas and other commercial fuels. This would not have a significant impact on world oil demand and the equipment would cost, at most, $1.5 billion per year. (2006 World Energy Outlook[4])

E+Co's business model offered an unconventional solution to the twin global problems of energy scarcity and energy waste. The brainchild of Phil LaRocco and co-founder Christine Eibs-Singer[5], E+Co's business model focused on the entrepreneur — the man or woman who decides to make his or her living selling clean energy to his or her neighbors. From the beginning, E+Co's intent was to nurture and tap into a pool of local entrepreneurial talent who would be in the best position to find the optimal balance between local needs and local means and would thus deliver desirable, feasible and sustainable clean energy solutions where they were needed the most.

At its launch in 1994, E+Co's emphasis on financing local solutions that fit the needs, and the means, of each community, marked a radical departure from the top-down, grid-focused interventions by the Breton Woods institutions (i.e. the World Bank and the International Monetary Fund). Since the middle of the 20th century, these institutions had approached energy provision in developing countries by undertaking high-visibility, major power plant projects which often focused on serving the capital city or major commercial centers, and left the rural poor underserved. E+Co's market-based approach also differed from rural interventions by non-governmental groups and civil society organizations which either offered technical solutions the poor could not afford or failed to implement a financially sustainable model that could outlast short-lived donor funding.

Twelve years later, E+Co[6] had successfully championed an innovative business model to alleviate energy poverty and step the poor up the energy ladder. (Exhibit 1 summarizes the company's "energy through enterprise" approach to greener energy.) E+Co had shown how to combine investment capital and business support services to bring clean energy entrepreneurs in developing countries to a place where they can have viable, sustainable enterprises. E+Co's investee companies had been replacing the burning of firewood, kerosene, charcoal, and oil and liquid petroleum gas with cleaner, more efficient energy technologies suited to local needs and demand. Together, these companies provided more than 3.6 million of the world's poorest people with access to modern energy services and generated 2,965 jobs, while simultaneously offsetting more than 2.2 million tons of carbon dioxide (CO_2) annually. (Exhibit 2 shows a summary of E+Co's triple bottom line performance.) Just before its September 8, 2006 annual retreat, E+Co's contribution to spreading cleaner, affordable energy solutions to developing countries had been recognized by the World Renewable Energy Congress (WREC) with its prestigious 2006 Honorary Award for outstanding achievement and vision in the global renewable energy sector.

Phil LaRocco, E+Co's founder and executive director, and his team, now counting 38 employees across nine regional offices in Africa, Latin America, Asia, Europe and North America were extremely proud of the important work that E+Co had been doing: they had funded and supported 138 clean energy enterprises in 25 developing countries. E+Co's seed investments of $29 million[7] had helped leverage $114 million more from third parties to jointly fund local clean energy entrepreneurs. E+Co's portfolio included a wide range of investee enterprises, ranging from cookstove manufacturers and basic energy-efficiency companies to businesses that generated electricity from wind, geothermal, biogas, hydro and solar technologies. Almost half of E+Co's investments (49 per cent) had been channeled to African countries, including Ethiopia, Gambia, Ghana, Mali, Morocco, Senegal, South Africa, Tanzania, Uganda, and Zambia. (see Exhibit 3).

As E+Co's 2006 retreat was wrapping up, LaRocco and his team (See Exhibit 4 for E+Co's current organizational chart) were wondering how they could scale up their global impact. They felt that reaching 100 million by 2020 could bring the provision of clean energy to developing countries to a tipping point. But they knew that scaling up E+Co's enterprise-centered model thirty-fold would require at least a hundred-fold increase in the initial number of interested entrepreneurs. For example, to reach three million customers, E+Co had identified 1,173 entrepreneurs. Of these, E+Co trained 710, offered enterprise development services to 509 and invested in 138 enterprises. To reach 100 million, E+Co would need to identify 40,000 potential entrepreneurs and work closely with about half of them.

E+Co's Enterprise-Centered Alternative

Local entrepreneurs, LaRocco had argued and shown, were an important missing link in helping people in developing countries access or switch to modern cooking fuels and technologies. These entrepreneurs could best channel and utilize the global funds supporting energy projects in developing countries to meet the growing local needs for cleaner, more affordable energy. By design, E+Co's role was to identify, train, and help local entrepreneurs jumpstart cleaner energy ventures. It initially offered seed capital along with a range of enterprise development services. E+Co's seed investments ranged in size from $29,000 to $800,000. Loans were typically given against the entrepreneur's commitment and a sound business plan, with less emphasis placed on collateral (especially for the smaller start-up loans). Both financing and support services were tailored to fit local demand and then co-evolved with the needs of the entrepreneurs. Growth capital was available for follow-on investments. Since 1998, E+Co had boasted an eight per cent average internal rate of return (IRR) after write-offs and a 10 per cent weighted average IRR for repaid loans.[8] (Exhibits 4 and 5 provide an overview of E+Co's financial performance.)

Up the Modern Energy Ladder

Christine Eibs-Singer, E+Co's cofounder, explained how the model enabled communities to climb the modern energy ladder at their own pace:

> If a household is using firewood or charcoal, sure it would be great to have them use a renewable source of electricity in their hut — but the first order of business is to get them to either use that firewood or charcoal more efficiently, to substitute that firewood or charcoal for an agricultural residue briquette or to use a more efficient stove for the burning of that firewood or charcoal. If the household and community could afford it, you want to get them off the firewood or charcoal to use LPG — liquid petroleum gas — as a substitute. And later, if economically viable, their energy needs could be met by a solar

home system or a village mini-grid powered by run-of-river hydro. And so you basically want to move this population along the energy ladder, from the dirtiest to cleaner steps.[9]

E+Co's enterprise-centered model was "technology neutral" (i.e. it was not driven by one particular renewable energy technology, but rather driven by the needs and resources available to each community). Three examples of E+Co's investee enterprises in Ghana, Senegal and South Africa illustrate this step-ladder approach to cleaner energy solutions.

Anasset, Ghana

In Ghana, where many low-income households still cooked with firewood or charcoal (which was expensive, time-consuming to collect, unhealthy when used indoors and contributed to deforestation), E+Co's seed capital and enterprise development services helped Anasset profitably offer an alternative fuel source — liquid petroleum gas (LPG). Households accounted for 70 per cent of Anasset's customers and 65 per cent of its revenues; the remaining customers were commercial and institutional

consumers, such as restaurants, hospitals and schools, and those who purchased fuel for vehicles running on LPG.

Prior to working with E+Co, Anasset operated from rented premises, strategically located within the precincts of the middle-class Awudome Estates, one of the most densely populated areas of Ghana's capital city, Accra. In 2002, Anasset's owner, Seth Nanemeh, received a four-year, 7.5 per cent loan of US$38,000 from E+Co and its partner African Rural Energy Enterprise Development (AREED).[10] E+Co's assistance with growth planning helped increase Anasset's sales by 57 per cent by 2004, and almost doubled its monthly distribution of LPG, from 145,000 kilograms in 2004 to 220,000 kilograms in 2005. The seed loan also enabled Anasset to obtain an additional working capital loan from Unibank for opening a second plant at Afloa in south-eastern Ghana.

By 2006, Anasset sold 2.3 million kilograms of LPG, for annual sales of US$1.7 million and provided 26,958 households with modern energy services. Every six months it replaced the consumption of 16,174.8 tons of charcoal, or the equivalent of 114,841 tons of wood. Anasset employed 23 people with a planned expansion of 13 more jobs to staff a third plant.

Vent L'Eau pour la Vie, Senegal

In Senegal, where many local villages relied on wind-powered pumps for drinking water and subsistence agriculture, an E+Co seed loan of US $17,123 (five years, 12 per cent interest) provided working capital for a local entrepreneur, Michel Tine, to found Vent L'Eau pour la Vie or VEV (French for Wind Water for Life).

VEV pumps now delivered 44,550,000 liters of clean water per year to 8,250 households in 166 villages.[11] VEV was launched in 1992, at the end of a decade-long project funded by an Italian aid agency, LVIA. Since 1981, LVIA had installed 110 wind-powered pumps in the Thies,

Diourbel, Saint-Louis and Casamance regions of Senegal. However, without continued repair and regular maintenance, these pumps would have had the same fate as most others in Senegal, where overall fewer than 10 per cent of the pumps installed in the 1980s were still working.

Michel Tine, along with three other former LVIA employees, founded VEV to provide continued services to LVIA's former clients. The team had since grown to 13 employees and VEV had expanded its service offering to include making and installing new pumps and windmills. VEV was also designing water supply projects for rural communities and had completed 12 such projects in 2005.

New Energies, South Africa

In South Africa, where 73 per cent of energy generation came from fossil fuels and 25 per cent of all electricity was used for water heating, the appeal of greener water-heating technologies was rising quickly. Although the country is bathed in sunshine, fewer than one per cent of all households had solar thermal water heaters.[12] Yoram Gur Arie saw an opportunity to provide solar water-heating systems to large commercial institutions, such as schools, universities, hospitals, restaurants and hotels, and founded New Energies.

The biggest entry barrier was the upfront investment cost in equipment. E+Co's helped New Energies develop a sound growth plan for the company. Starting in November 2004, E+Co disbursed a total investment of $253,179, in five sequential waves. New Energies was now one of South Africa's leading suppliers of industrial solar water-heating equipment.

The Path to Scale: Demonstrate, Replicate, Institutionalize

Demonstrate

Through success stories like Anasset, VEV and New Energies, E+Co's enterprise-centered model had helped raise the profile of energy as a means to achieving global social and environmental targets, such as the Millennium Development Goals.[13] By 2006, E+Co's portfolio of investee enterprises had jointly displaced more than 450 million kilograms of firewood and charcoal, reforested more than 200 hectares of land, provided more than 140 million liters of clean water and offset 13 million tons of CO_2. E+Co had helped raise local incomes by a total of $7.4 million. It had provided training or services to 854 entrepreneurs and actively encouraged women's entrepreneurship: women were owners or co-owners of 65 per cent of E+Co's investee enterprises.

Replicate

As its portfolio of investee enterprises grew, E+Co learned to leverage its experience and impact through width and depth investing, pursuing opportunities for serial investing and broadening its partner base.

Investing for Width and Depth

E+Co's growth and sustainability plans are built on striking a balance between making investments in first-of-a-kind enterprises across a variety of clean energy sub-sectors ("investing for width") and making a number of subsequent investments in those sub-sectors that show the most promise for impact ("investing for depth").[14]

When E+Co started its quest to invest in energy entrepreneurs in emerging economies, exhaustive market research and feasibility studies were not just challenging to complete but often premature — many of E+Co's investee enterprises needed to blaze entirely new paths by creating a market for clean energy where none had existed before. Investing for width proved to be a suitable substitute for exhaustive upfront market research. Small initial investments in a wide variety of sectors helped E+Co test the waters by enabling local entrepreneurs to identify and signal which energy sectors, technologies and business models were likely to be most viable in each regional market. Some of the venture ideas were brilliant. Others did not work out. Sampling a variety of enterprises in several different sectors provided a broad platform for creating small wins and for learning from early failures.

After local enterprises had identified the most promising sectors and technologies in each region (e.g. solar hot water heating in South Africa, LPG in West Africa or photovoltaics in parts of East Africa), E+Co channeled greater investment towards those sectors by organizing specialized managed accounts, funds and affiliates that actively promoted specific types of clean energy enterprises in that region (see Exhibit 7).

Serial Investing

E+Co's model of Services+Capital (see Exhibits 1, 4 and 5) had high start-up costs yet accrued rapidly increasing economies of scope. The average cost of business development services (e.g. business plan development, feasibility studies, market assessments, risk identification and mitigation, financial modeling and ownership structuring) averaged about 40 cents on the dollar value of the loan. However, after 10 per cent to 20 per cent of E+Co's portfolio had grown to the point where the company could seek loans of more than half a million dollars, E+Co's return on these rapid-growth companies was enough to offset the high cost of business support services for a new set of initial investments. Each success story unleashed a small burst of growth: it helped provide seed investments and enterprise development services to a few more new start-ups.

Partnerships

E+Co had also been successful in forging broad partnerships with like-minded organizations, including, among many others, Greenpeace International, the Bill & Melinda Gates Foundation, the International Finance Corporation, the Multilateral Investment Fund — Inter-American Development Bank, the Rockefeller Foundation, the Citigroup Foundation, the United Nations Environment Programme, the United Nations Foundation, the U.S. Agency for International Development, the U.S. Department of Energy, the Wallace Global Fund and The Body Shop.

Institutionalize

Phil LaRocco and his team had spent several years streamlining and standardizing key elements of E+Co's operations. They were particularly proud of three achievements: a web-based Global Management System, specialized loan servicing software and a website boasting a multilingual media room. E+Co's ambitious growth planning and flexible, tightly-knit culture gave the organization additional impetus and support in its quest for expansion.

Global Management System (GMS)

Unveiled in November 2002, updated frequently, and accessible 24-7-365 with the latest information, the Global Management System (GMS) was E+Co's first line of management information and tools. GMS provided access to information on E+Co's investee enterprises, funders and all facets of operations on five continents. Standardized documents could be readily downloaded and processed. The GMS also included the most recent reports, promotional information, progress photos, periodic presentations and technology information. Logging into the GMS, everyone is greeted by Margaret Mead's well-known quote "Never doubt that a small group of thoughtful, committed citizens can change the world. Indeed it is the only thing that ever does."

Specialized Loan Servicing Software (LSS)

Because most off-the-shelf accounting and loan servicing packages did not meet E+Co's needs, Phil LaRocco had asked a specialist software developer to design a system able to manage multiple currencies, varying loan periods, differing interest rates and to automatically process and distribute invoices. The loan servicing software (LSS), launched in October 2005, was being integrated with the GMS to provide comprehensive, real-time information on each individual investment. In combination, the GMS and the LSS helped E+Co streamline many aspects of its initially boutique operations. Its investment due diligence, asset management, monitoring and evaluation templates, and accounting processes had all been standardized and simplified, which ensured more efficient operations and continued quality results.

Website

In 2005, E+Co had upgraded and expanded its English-Spanish webpage to include a media room where site visitors could download many of E+Co's tools and publications. In 2006, E+Co launched sites in Chinese, French and Portuguese.

Growth Planning

E+Co also took steps to practice what it preached. It engaged in a formal business and growth planning exercise, which helped the team chart a two-headline strategy: "Tradition of Experimentation Will Continue" and "Funds and Affiliates Approach Adopted to Tap Growth Potential". By entering markets through its traditional mode of making smaller, seed capital investments across a variety of technologies and niches, E+Co would continue to learn the market dynamics, peculiarities and players, and to realize which niches had most potential. By creating a locally grounded fund (an E+Co affiliated company), E+Co would use its seed investment experience to identify lucrative niches; greater focus, combined with the benefit of familiarity (fund investment), would attract a broader base of investors[15].

Learning Culture

Described by outside observers as "passionate, committed, inspired, innovative, flexible, creative, open, transparent, careful, calculated, humble and tenacious,"[16] E+Co's culture genuinely regarded mistakes as a valuable opportunity to improve. Everyone shared an extraordinary commitment to the company's mission and goals. E+Co's business plan was very much "a living, breathing, organic thing."[17]

A Strategy of Wedges

The 2004 World Energy Outlook of the International Energy Association (IEA) estimated that by 2030, US$7 trillion would be spent in the developing world (which would account for about two thirds of a global 60 per cent increase in energy use). The latest outlook adjusted this estimate upward by about US$3 trillion and called for a cumulative investment of just over $20 trillion (in year-2005 dollars) over 2005 to 2030. More than half of all the energy investment needed worldwide would be in developing countries.

LaRocco wondered how E+Co model could bring the provision of more efficient and sustainable use of energy to the rural poor in developing markets to a tipping point. The E+Co team estimated that they would need to serve about one to two per cent of the 1.6 billion people currently lacking access to clean, affordable energy – about 100 million customers across five continents. They were now grappling with the strategic options they had to reach this ambitious goal of a thirty-fold increase in the next 12 years.

Looking forward, Phil LaRocco thought that he could tackle the challenge of thirty-fold growth by setting several complementary strategies, which could evolve and grow independently, yet could inform and benefit one another. He summed up E+Co's efforts to scale up along three distinct wedges: 1) direct investing, 2) funds and affiliates, and 3) carbon market transactions.

Streamlining Direct Investing

Direct investing, however risky and resource-intensive, would help E+Co organization establish a growing local presence and hone its capabilities needed to identify and nurture clean enterprises in the developing world. Direct investing would also help E+Co keep a hand on the pulse of the market and better adapt the technologies available to local needs and demands. But there were at least two important bottlenecks. First, E+Co needed to build up a much larger pool of potential entrepreneurs; this would help the organization build greater breadth and greater depth. Second, E+Co needed to expand the pool of resources available to these local entrepreneurs (funds and enterprise assistance services) to get their venture ideas investment ready. If E+Co could simultaneously increase the number of entrepreneurs and keep offering them funds plus expertise, they could trigger a snowballing effect.

But LaRocco knew that his small, tightly-knit team could not directly bear the full load of the growth through direct investing. So, in partnership with the United Nations Framework Convention on Climate Change, he developed The Entrepreneur Toolkit[18] — a step by step self-screening guide that walked entrepreneurs through the early stages of the opportunity recognition and refinement process. The Toolkit quickly became a substitute for some of the initial fieldwork of our officers — it explained what clean energy entrepreneurship was all about, so it stimulated broad interest for a wide range of potential entrepreneurs[19]. It then prompted the early development of their business ideas through a series of questions and answers. The toolkit included several building-block exercises which could help an entrepreneur think about how they would turn a core but still rough business idea into a workable venture, discard bad ideas, and rework good ones into more viable models.

LaRocco felt that the toolkit had just the right balance of carrot and stick — it would cheer on those entrepreneurs who really wanted to make a difference, but would discourage those ventures that would be unfeasible, or too risky. For the entrepreneurs who gathered the most important resources (a great idea, drive and connections), E+Co staff bring could better target and deliver the most relevant support services, at the right time in the process. LaRocco was excited about the toolkit potential to gradually cut down the low value add work of the field investment officers, who could thus scale back on the time- and risk-intensive step of early recruiting and go straight into training the pre-selected entrepreneurs and the delivery of funding and growth support services.

LaRocco eagerly anticipated the official launch of the toolkit in October 2006 at the United Nations conference on climate change.[20] This resource was by no means exclusive to E+Co, nor restricted to its investee entrepreneurs — it had been designed with the end goal in mind. If successful as intended, the toolkit would not only attract better informed and better prepared entrepreneurs in these developing markets, but would also entice other potential funders to follow in E+Co's footsteps. This, in turn, would give local entrepreneurs more and better choices, and hasten the provision of market-fit, cleaner energy solutions to the poor in the developing world.

Rethinking Managed Accounts, Funds and Affiliates

E+Co would also continue to grow through managing accounts, funds and affiliates.[21] This had worked well in Latin America, particularly for the CAREC [Central American Renewable Energy and Cleaner Production Facility] Fund and the IFC/GEF [International Finance Corporation/Global Environment Facility] Managed Account.[22] As E+Co identified which of the clean energy sectors held the greatest promise in a region through direct investing, it offered investors the opportunity to zero in on those sectors with higher social, environmental and/or economic returns.

Many institutions had come to see E+Co as a partner of choice. E+Co was now working with the International Finance Corporation's Renewable Energy and Efficiency Fund and helping the World Bank's Solar Development Group to finance solar photovoltaics. Several organizations, including the World Bank and the UN, had tried to replicate E+Co's entrepreneurial spirit internally, but the results failed to materialize due to institutional inertia, difficulty to work from the bottom-up and their own burdensome systems of due diligence and paperwork.

A few years earlier LaRocco had hoped that E+Co might be able to be "cloned" by other local intermediary organizations. In the late 1990s, he gave his best support when the United Nations Foundation (UNF) attempted to replicate E+Co in different regions of the world. UNF had committed more than $8 million to the rural energy enterprise development (REED) work in Africa (A-REED), Brazil (B-REED) and China (C-REED). But the local organizations were nongovernmental organizations (NGOs) and the business DNA didn't stick; they remained, as LaRocco often put it, "grant junkies." Lots of time and money and energy were spent attempting to graft E+Co's DNA on theirs. But it seemed much harder to place business on top of development than development on top of business.

But despite these early setbacks, LaRocco had never lost the belief that cloning would work for partners who shared a pro-business approach to international development. He had never given up on the idea that local banks and financial institutions might get right into the game and invest in clean energy entrepreneurs from their own region. In his gut, LaRocco knew that well-chosen partnerships were a very promising path for getting to scale. Financial institutions, from small local self-help groups and credit unions to the major players like Citigroup and Deutsche Bank, were very important partners. These could quickly and effectively bring about scale on the fund supply side.

E+Co had started working with the Triodos Bank to structure and financially close "a fund of funds," which will invest in regional subfunds, like E+Co Africa. Triodos, LaRocco felt, was an optimal partner because they had made an explicit strategic decision that they want to focus their business activity in the clean energy sector at this fund of funds level. The European Commission had committed €80 million (of €100 total) to this Global Energy Efficiency and Renewable Energy Fund (GEEREF). The resulting mezzo stream of funding could boost E+Co's activity at the regional level and was an important step in mobilizing private investments for clean energy in developing countries.

E+Co also acted as an advisor, helper and facilitator for the Grameen Shakti's Bangladeshi Carbon Credit Biogas Project[23]. This multi-stakeholder partnership, championed by Grameen Shakti, an energy company and part of the family of Bangladeshi enterprises that includes the Grameen Bank[24], would help deliver cleaner energy to another 20,000, perhaps even 200,000, households. It also provided an opportunity to learn how to monetize and use future carbon credits to jumpstart the adoption of household biogas programs in Bangladesh. Environmental Defense, an American nonprofit, had supported some of the organizing effort, and other partners had brought intellectual property, experience and relational capital.

Playing the Carbon Market

LaRocco had watched with great interest how rapidly the increasing public, government and private sector commitment to mitigating the effects of climate change was creating new markets for carbon offsets.[25] The world carbon market was growing at 200 per cent to 300 per cent per year. In 2006 alone, a total of 1,639 megatons of carbon had been traded worldwide with a value of US$30 billion.[26] Through the Clean Development Mechanism of the Kyoto Protocol, developing countries supplied 450 megatons of carbon credits with a value of US$5 billion in 2006. The average price paid for offsetting a ton of carbon in developing countries was around US$10 per ton.[27] The thriving and growing voluntary market, in which individuals and companies voluntarily purchased carbon credits to offset their carbon footprint was now estimated at US$100 million in 2006.[28]

E+Co was poised to play a stronger role on the carbon market. Most of its investee enterprises generated high-quality carbon offsets. These could be monetized and transferred back to the entrepreneurs as either start-up capital or additional revenue stream, which would give an additional boost to E+Co's growth. Projects such as Grameen Shakti's Bangladeshi Carbon Credit

Biogas Project had helped E+Co test-pilot the carbon markets. E+Co had even experimented with some innovative approaches to aggregate the credits. But the official certification of these small-scale pools of carbon credits under the Kyoto Protocol would be too costly and administratively demanding to make the process worthwhile. Several experiments, like Honduras-based La Esperanza, had met with success and were ripe for replication in other countries:[29]

La Esperanza developed a hydroelectric project using an abandoned dam and powerhouse foundation. In 2001, E+Co supported the developers with business plan preparation assistance and a $250,000 loan for the construction of the first two powerhouses with a combined installed capacity of 1.4 megawatts (MW). In March 2004, E+Co made a $200,000 preferred share investment that allowed La Esperanza to secure financing for the second powerhouse from the Central American Bank for Economic Integration and FinnFund.

Both powerhouses started operations in June 2004. In September 2006, E+Co approved a US$800,000 loan to further increase the size of the reservoir and improve flow.

As of early 2007, La Esperanza was generating approximately 24 MW per year, and had grown to a staff of 4 managers, 23 technicians and 108 employees. The energy, distributed by the Empresa Nacional de Energía Eléctrica (ENEE) in Honduras, reached about 194 households (or an estimated 40.1 per cent of the energy produced by La Esperanza).

Aside from its economic success, La Esperanza showcased the success of renewable energy projects on the environmental and social front. The hydro energy replaced an estimated total annual expenditure of $50,807 by 90 households in San Fernando and 70 households of Santa Anita previously spent on firewood, candles and kerosene. La Esperanza's cleaner energy helped offset 19,063 tons of CO_2 annually. Thirty thousand trees were planted in 2006, through its reforestation program (3,572 in the project itself for slope stabilization, the remaining in surrounding communities). La Esperanza engaged in broad consultation with the communities, the local government and different water administration councils to jointly decide on the reforestation priorities. La Esperanza also repaired an old greenhouse, using recycled materials, to establish a tree nursery. Three thousand seeds, all collected within the land of the project, were already planted. They also started the production of fruit trees.

In August 2005, La Esperanza became one of the first small-scale projects registered under the Clean Development Mechanism of the Kyoto Protocol. With support from the Citigroup Foundation, E+Co assisted La Esperanza in assessing and quantifying its 35,000 tonnes per year of carbon emissions reductions, which were then sold to the World Bank's Community Development Carbon Fund. During 2006, an agreement was signed between E+Co and La Esperanza to pilot E+Co's Erase Your Footprint Voluntary Carbon Offset program. Under the "Generando O2" (Generating O2), E+Co would purchase 350 tons of CO_2 offsets generated by La Esperanza's Tree Planting Program, at $4 per ton.

In 2006, E+Co began taking a different angle on the carbon market — selling direct to interested third parties. E+Co had already sold 30,000 tons of carbon credits to the Klimate Neutral Group. Phil and Christine were now working on an agreement with The Body Shop whereby E+Co investee enterprises would provide 400 tons of carbon credits quarterly in lieu of interest payments on an outstanding $200,000 loan from The Body Shop.

LaRocco felt that E+Co's credits could, and should, command a premium. Their investee enterprises did more than provide cleaner energy to the world – they also helped generate great stories and grassroots role models for new generations of entrepreneurs. They were showing that climate and poverty were not just linked problems but also linked solutions for a better future. E+Co had been developing a new campaign, "Energy First", which sought to establish E+Co as the primary mover in linking cleaner energy with nutrition, health and education[30].

Looking ahead, Phil LaRocco was keen on experimenting with engaging individual investors in contributing $50 to $100 amounts to finance small enterprises serving the poor – an approach similar to Kiva's online investing business model[31] but focused on erasing one's carbon footprint (and clearing one's conscience). This approach would be a much better fit for E+Co's distributed, small-scale approach than Kyoto-based expensively certified offsets, which were often a pain to manage. And it built on its unique advantage: E+Co could offer high-quality offsets from specific countries, regions or technologies. And their field staff could monitor and verify these offsets as part of their overall social, environmental and financial impact evaluation of each enterprise.

The Tipping Point

Each wedge was vitally important to E+Co's design and mission. Taken together, these three wedges could accelerate E+Co's growth in developing countries. Higher value-add direct investing would strengthen E+Co's local presence, and expand the pool of entrepreneurial talent and clean energy solutions. Growth in funds and affiliates could leverage E+Co's experience by channelling partners' resources to market-fit, high-impact technologies. Customizing carbon market transactions and developing individual investors could give E+Co international legitimacy and fuel rapid growth.

But could this combination help E+Co achieve a thirty-fold increase in cleaner energy provision? Perhaps a tipping point would be reached even sooner — many had predicted that it would take 800 million served for microfinancing, but 100 million proved enough. And it only took 10 to 15 years for microfinancing. LaRocco felt that clean energy would be next, and was optimistic that E+Co's model would be influential in demonstrating, validating and institutionalizing the role of grassroots enterprise in this pursuit. And he was already thinking about the potential application of E+Co's model to other sectors. "Would what E+Co has done in energy work in water? Would it work in malaria bed-nets? Would it work in telecommunications?" Of course it would, LaRocco thought, but the important thing would be to help everyone else out there understand how.

The Richard Ivey School of Business gratefully acknowledges the generous support of the Schulich School of Business and the Erivan K. Haub Program in Business and Sustainability in the development of these learning materials.

Exhibit 1

E+Co Business Model

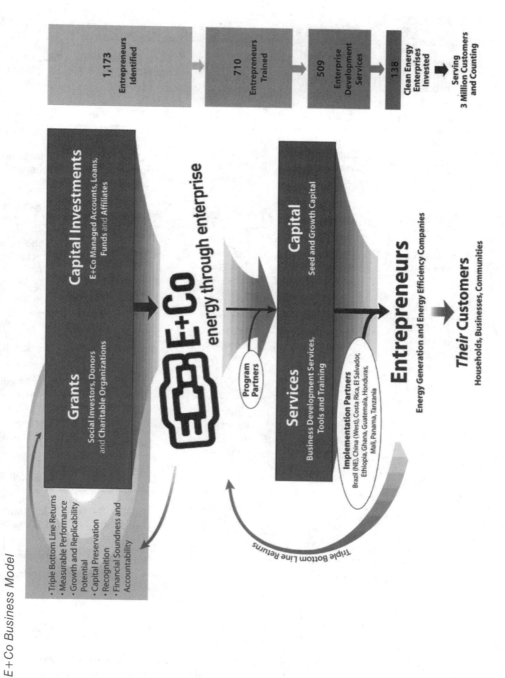

Exhibit 2

E+Co's Triple Bottom Line Performance[1]

Financial	Social and Economic		Environmental	
Investment Funds Disbursed	People with Access to Modern Energy Services	Households Served	CO_2 Offset by Enterprises Annually	CO_2 Offset (for life of project)
$14,721,633	3,607,559	721,253	2,201,780 tons	13,121,389 tons
Entrepreneur's Investment	Cumulative Clean Energy Generated	Energy Saved from Efficiency Initiatives	Value of CO_2 Offset (for life of project)	Reforested Land
$29,067,832	59,539,558 MWH	118,400 MWH	$65,606,946	228 hectares + ~220,000 trees
Leveraged from Third Parties	Jobs Supported	Improved Income	Clean Water Provided	Households with Access to Clean Water
$113,754,964	2,965	$7,394,073	140,157,750 liters	29,825
Potential Growth or Follow-On Capital	Clean Energy Enterprises	Women Ownership / Shareholding	Charcoal Displaced	Firewood Displaced
$102,838,700	138	90	257,506 tons	207,984 tons
E+Co's Portfolio Return after Write-offs	Clean Energy Employees & Customers Trained	Customers Installing Energy-Efficient Equipment	Liquid Petroleum Gas Displaced	Kerosene Displaced
8.3%	73,960	29,545	2,379,000 kg	6,045,546 L
E+Co Repayments	Entrepreneurs Identified	Entrepreneurs Receiving Services	Barrels of Oil Displaced	Dollar Value of Oil Displaced
$4,178,748	1,574	854	259,743	$14,532,621

---

1   Cumulative results through December 31, 2006. E+Co collects this information from its investee enterprises and reports it twice annually on its website, at http://www.eandco.net/.

Exhibit 3

E+Co's Investment Profile
(at December 31, 2006)

25 E+Co Countries of Operation

Bolivia, Brazil, Costa Rica, El Salvador, Guatemala, Honduras, Nicaragua, Ethiopia, Gambia, Ghana, Mali, Morocco, Senegal, South Africa, Tanzania, Uganda, Zambia, Cambodia, China, India, Malaysia, Nepal, Philippines, Thailand, Vietnam.

9 E+Co Regional Offices

Bolivia (La Paz), Brazil (Bahia), China (Kunming), Costa Rica (San José), Netherlands, Ghana (Accra), South Africa (Pretoria), Thailand (Bangkok), USA (Bloomfield, New Jersey)

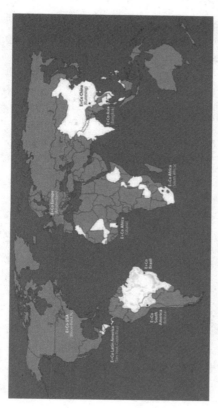

Active Investments by Technology (2006)

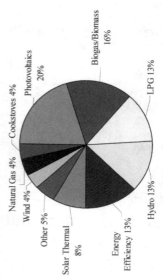

Cookstoves 4%
Photovoltaics 20%
Biogas/Biomass 16%
Natural Gas 4%
LPG 13%
Wind 4%
Other 5%
Solar Thermal 8%
Hydro 13%
Energy Efficiency 13%

Active Investments by Region (2006)

Latin America 32%
Asia 19%
Africa 49%

Exhibit 4

E+CO FINANCIAL STATEMENTS SUMMARY

ASSETS	December 04	December 05	December 06
Cash	$ 4,034,625	$ 4,293,972	$ 6,444,793
Program Loans Receivable	$ 3,742,958	$ 3,942,019	$ 5,958,279
Program Equity Investments	$ 1,505,665	$ 1,170,665	$ 1,175,665
Promises to Give	$ 7,327,778	$ 5,856,322	$ 490,532
Other Assets	$ 445,055	$ 403,429	$ 47,623
TOTAL	**$ 17,056,081**	**$ 15,666,407**	**$ 19,599,243**

LIABILITIES			
Program Loans Payable	$ 4,257,130	$ 3,871,811	$ 5,599,124
Other Liabilities	$ 184,324	$ 327,346	$ 336,188
TOTAL	**$ 4,441,454**	**$ 4,199,157**	**$ 5,935,312**

	December 04	December 05	December 06
Minority Interest in Subsidiary			$ (24,283)
Net Assets	$ 12,614,627	$ 11,467,250	$ 13,688,214

TOTAL LIABILITIES & NET ASSETS

	December 04	December 05	December 06
	$ 17,056,081	$ 15,666,407	$ 19,599,243

Statement of Activity

REVENUE & SUPPORT	December 04	December 05	December 06
Contributions	$5,593,014	$2,129,019	$4,566,994
Program Revenue	242,924	124,576	762,758
Interest Income	392,781	652,095	769,105
Other Income	203,125	7,530	533,395
TOTAL	**$6,431,844**	**$2,913,220**	**$6,542,252**

EXPENSES			
Program Service	$2,574,039	$2,332,266	$3,199,961
Management and General	513,011	743,671	746,994
Grant Procurement	259,240	285,544	398,616
Other	40,000	685,104	(10,271)
TOTAL	**$3,386,290**	**$4,046,585**	**$4,335,300**

INCREASE IN NET ASSETS			
	$3,045,554	**$(1,133,365)**	**$2,206,952**

Source: E+Co Financial Statements.

Exhibit 5

E+CO PORTFOLIO PERFORMANCE SUMMARY
(January 1998 through December 31, 2006)

Total Debt Investments made	12,953,633
Total Equity Investments made	1,768,000
Total Portfolio	**14,721,633**
Number of Equity Investments	15
Number of Debt Investments	129
Total Investments	**144**
Write offs (26 Enterprises)	1,540,548
% of Total Investments made	10.5%
Debt Portfolio After Write Offs -- (107 Investments)	**11,883,085**
Equity Portfolio After Write Offs -- (11 Investments)	**1,298,000**
Total Portfolio After Write Offs	**13,181,085**
Projected Weighted Average IRR of Equity Portfolio	6.3%
Projected Weighted Average IRR of Debt Portfolio	8.5%
Projected Weighted Average IRR of Total Portfolio After Write Offs	**8.3%**
Total Equity 100% Exited (2 Investments)	**350,000**
Weighted Average IRR for Equity Buy-Outs	**9.0%**
Total Loans 100% Repaid (27 Investments)	**2,836,177**
Weighted Average IRR for Repaid Loans	**10.5%**

Exhibit 6

E+Co's Organizational Structure[1]

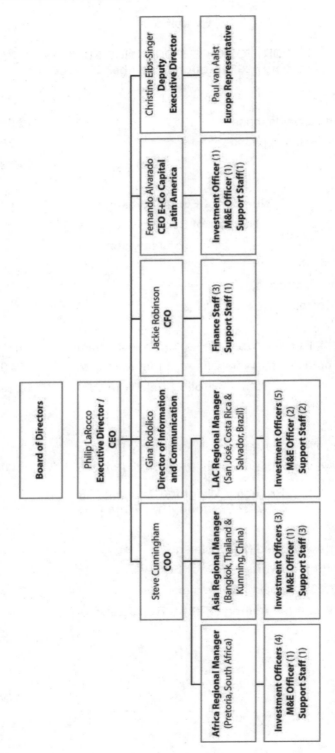

Board of Directors

Philip LaRocco
Executive Director / CEO

Steve Cunningham
COO

Gina Rodolico
Director of Information and Communication

Jackie Robinson
CFO

Fernando Alvarado
CEO E+Co Capital Latin America

Christine Eibs-Singer
Deputy Executive Director

Africa Regional Manager
(Pretoria, South Africa)

Asia Regional Manager
(Bangkok, Thailand & Kunming, China)

LAC Regional Manager
(San José, Costa Rica & Salvador, Brazil)

Finance Staff (3)
Support Staff (1)

Investment Officer (1)
M&E Officer (1)
Support Staff(1)

Paul van Aalst
Europe Representative

Investment Officers (4)
M&E Officer (1)
Support Staff (1)

Investment Officers (3)
M&E Officer (1)
Support Staff (3)

Investment Officers (5)
M&E Officer (2)
Support Staff (2)

1   Cumulative results through December 31, 2006. E+Co collects this information from its investee enterprises and reports it twice annually on its website, at http://www.eandco.net/.

Exhibit 7

Examples of E+Co's Managed Accounts, Funds and Affiliates

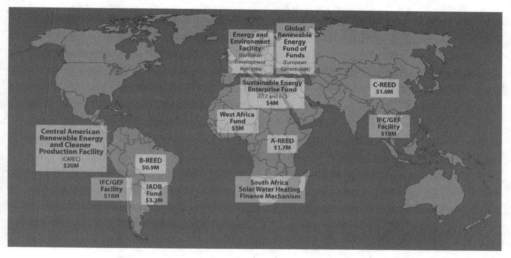

Managed Accounts

Rural Energy Enterprise Development (REED): E+Co is the manager (on behalf of the United Nations Environment Programme and others) of a €3.3 million in small and medium-size enterprise (SME) investment funds for the UN Foundation-supported Rural Energy Enterprise Development (REED) programmes in Africa (A-REED), north eastern Brazil (B-REED) and western China (C-REED).

The Sustainable Energy Facility is a mezzanine investment facility funded by International Finance Corporation/Global Environment Facility (IFC/GEF) of US$18 million for Latin America and South-East Asia: This facility came into operation in August 2005 and is being used primarily for more mature, later stage investments. Targeted projects include grid and off-grid renewable energy enterprises.

Multi-lateral Investment Fund of the Inter-American Development Bank (IADB): E+Co has managed an allocation of the Multilateral Investment Fund of the Inter-American Development Bank; a $2.2 million Venture Capital Facility and $1 million Grant Facility over an eight-year term from 1996 to 2004.

IFC SME Fund: E+Co structured and now manages a $1 million IFC and Global Environment Facility fund to support SMEs using agreed-upon criteria in which the IFC approves first investment.

Funds & Affiliates

The Central American Renewable Energy and Cleaner Production Facility (CAREC) is a US$15 million mezzanine and debt financing facility with an envisaged US$1 million technical assistance facility. CAREC is managed by E+Co Capital Latin America and reached the capitalization required for its first closing in June 2005. Investors include MIF, CABEI, B-I-O and FinnFund, with other investors in the process of preparing for the second closing at US$20 million.

Renewable Energy and Energy Efficiency Fund (REEF): E+Co prepared the initial scoping document study for the International Finance Corporation on what became the Renewable Energy and Energy Efficiency Fund. E+Co also co-managed the fund until the investors chose to retire their investment.

Exhibit 8

Advertising Campaigns (Sample Ads)

Stitch Wise:

Strategic knowledge management for pro-poor enterprise on South Africa's goldfields

MARTIN HALL

Introduction

Natalie Killassy was born into a mining family working in South Africa's goldfields, which have some of the world's deepest mine shafts.[1] Disturbed by the consequences of crippling underground injuries for miners and their families, and by the depressed economy of mining towns such as the one in which she grew up, Killassy persuaded one of South Africa's largest mining companies, AngloGold Ashanti, to allow her to use a salvage yard and the labour of paraplegic former miners only partially employed in menial work, to start a new venture that would manufacture waterproof clothing. From that simple beginning, Killassy's company – Stitch Wise – grew to become a producer of specialised underground mine safety equipment to support mine shafts and prevent rock falls, a primary cause of underground injury. Stitch Wise now dominates the South African market in this niche area. The company's workforce is mostly paraplegic, and workers own shares in it through Stitch Wise's Broad Based Black Economic Empowerment initiative. The company has diversified into other safety products as well as providing industrial training.

Since the company was founded in 1997, Stitch Wise has demonstrated the limitations of the Bottom of the Pyramid (BOP) approach.[2] While the initial support of AngloGold Ashanti was essential (substituting equipment and a labour supply for working capital), there has been a tension between large company interests in advancing corporate social responsibility and public relations, and Stitch Wise's financial viability in a competitive niche market. Rather than illustrating the value of a BOP market, Stitch Wise's ten-year history shows the potential for creating jobs and therefore income, for poor and marginalised communities through innovative enterprises that are independent of the large-scale corporate partnerships (and their interests) that are definitive of 'classic' BOP strategies.[3]

In more general terms, the case of Stitch Wise illustrates the importance of strategic knowledge management for pro-poor enterprise development. And, further, the importance and potential of enabling public policy and appropriate public institutions in countering the structural limitations to enterprise development in poor and marginalised communities.

The company

Stitch Wise was founded in 1997 at the Western Deep Mine in Carltonville, Gauteng Province. Driven by concern for the future of paraplegic ex-miners and by rising levels of unemployment and lack of opportunity, Killassy persuaded AngloGold Ashanti to give her the use of a salvage yard on the Western Deep Mine and the labour of former miners who had been seriously injured in underground accidents and who were maintained by AngloGold Ashanti in sheltered employment. Stitch Wise had no financial equity and started business making waterproof clothing using sewing machines initially donated by AngloGold Ashanti. The machines were adapted so that they could be used by operators who only had the use of their arms (Figure 1). Stitch Wise was initially owned and operated by Killassy (CEO), her husband Tim Killassy and manufacturing director, Pauline Nhlapo.[4]

The initial product line of waterproof clothing found a ready market and by 2004 Stitch Wise was manufacturing 6 000 units each month. However, Killassy was keen to get closer to the cause of underground accidents, since the motivation for founding Stitch Wise had been to address this issue. She persuaded AngloGold to let her establish an underground test facility at the Western Deep Mine. For more than a year she spent almost every day underground, collecting information on mine safety. She subsequently designed an intervention to address the problem of rock falls, the primary cause of severe injury to miners. The outcome was the development and marketing of Stitch Wise's primary product, the backfill bag. Backfill bags, which are up to 30m in length, are pumped full of graded tailings to provide roof support for

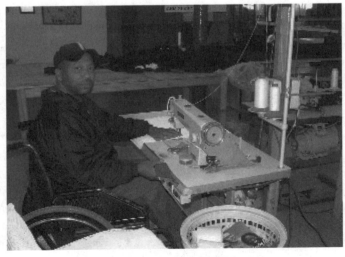

Figure 1: One of the employees at Stitch Wise
(photo by Martin Hall)

mine shafts. In 2000 AngloGold Ashanti contracted with Stitch Wise for the supply of backfill bags for their mine shafts. By 2004 Stitch Wise was manufacturing 12 000 units a year and had captured about 50% of the South African market for this aspect of mine safety equipment. The remaining market share is divided between three competitors.

Table 1: Stitch Wise income and product sales, 1997–2007

Year	Income	Product Sales	Events
1997	176 071.00	Manufacture of Crafts	
1998	404 177.00	Started Training	
1999	535 513.00	Rainwear, Personal Protective Equipment and Training	Backfill R&D started
2000	878 569.00	Rainwear and 10% AGA Backfill Bags	
2001	1 957 614.00	Rainwear and Backfill Bags	
2002	13 271 110.00	Rainwear 70% AGA Backfill Bags	
2003	19 440 784.00	Rainwear 100% AGA Backfill Bags	
2004	19 746 168.00	Rainwear 100% AGA Backfill Bags	
2005	17 676 387.00	Rainwear 100% AGA Backfill Bags	AGA tenders to reduce costs, Tebo training, and factory opened to manufacture PPE clothing
2006	24 779 915.00	Rainwear, Arm/Knee Guards, 100% Backfill Bags	
2007	36 727 074.00	Knee/Arm Guard, Backfill, Safety Nets and New Reinforced Support System	Accreditation for training, merged companies, renegotiated AGA contract for price increase

Source: Stitch Wise.

Tailings – the rock removed during excavation – have long been bagged to provide support for mine shafts. But earlier techniques were comparatively crude and less efficient than the use of wooden props. Killassy's key insight was that advanced synthetic textile technology could be used to re-engineer the backfill bag, resulting in a technology superior to the use of props (Figure 2). A key breakthrough was the development of a relationship with the Council for Scientific and Industrial Research (CSIR) in Pretoria, a parastatal organisation that supports strategic industrial research and knowledge transfer.[5] While Killassy has no engineering training herself, the partnership with the CSIR allowed her to translate her underground observations, and the former miners' deep understanding of the conditions there, into the development of a high-tech product. As a result of this partnership and her knowledge, Killassy was asked by the South African Bureau of Standards to write the national standard for this aspect of underground safety equipment.[6]

Figure 2:   Product code for the Modular Backfill Bag

HANGING

GULLY

Perfect hanging wall conditions

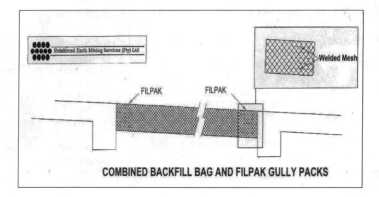

COMBINED BACKFILL BAG AND FILPAK GULLY PACKS

FILPAK ®

- Reinforcement of the backfill at either end of the backfill bag by virtue of frictional interaction between the tensile mesh reinforcement and the granular backfill
- Design procedure which enables mesh assemblies to be varied in order to meet specific stress and closure conditions in different mines and stopes
- Facility to take backfill to the edges of gullies
- Distribution of load on footwall and hanging wall with resultant absence of point loading; and, in particular, minimising damage to the footwall at gully edges
- Effecting savings in shut time and in handling and transport of materials
- Capable of functioning in either cemented or un-cemented backfill stopes
- Possible further application in dip gullies, and in any attempts at ore-pillar recovery

Source: Stitch Wise.

Stitch Wise has continued its product innovation, building on the initial relationship with the CSIR, and subsequently developing a relationship with the University of the Witwatersrand's Department of Civil Engineering. An important refinement of the initial design for backfill bags has been the design and testing of an improved front-end for the bags, comprising a gully support and better arrangements for pumping tailings into the bag. This mechanism, which considerably improves the performance of the technology, has been patented by Stitch Wise, both for the steel components and the future use of nanotextile materials.

Stitch Wise has since diversified into other aspects of mine safety. Besides being exposed to the danger of rock falls, miners work long shifts in shafts that may be less than one metre high. This results in injuries to knees and elbows, a problem not adequately addressed through the provision of safety equipment. Again building on the Stitch Wise workforce's intimate knowledge of underground conditions, Killassy and her team developed knee and elbow guards with hard outer casings and inner padding. By 2004, the company was producing 5 000 pairs of elbow guards and 13 000 pairs of knee guards each month (see Table 1).

One of the drivers of Stitch Wise's formation and its subsequent business strategy was the desire to improve the quality of life for the former miners who make up the majority of its employees. The company's mission is to 'apply the strength of our skills and diversity to business opportunities, in the common pursuit of wealth for all', and its working philosophy is that 'our staff is not disabled, but differently abled'.[7] Killassy sees her company as being built around the needs and potential of her work force. In the initial arrangement with AngloGold, the disabled former miners remained on the Western Deep payroll and Stitch Wise used income from sales to reimburse the mining company for the use of labour. This arrangement had the double benefit of serving as a substitute for working capital for Stitch Wise and mitigating a management problem for AngloGold, since the undemanding and menial nature of the sheltered employment it offered led to high levels of depression, alcoholism and associated problems among the disabled miners.

Values

True to its people-centred philosophy, Stitch Wise has placed a particular value on employee training, initially for operating the sewing equipment and then for other needs such as Adult Basic Education and Training (ABET),[8] computer literacy and HIV/AIDS prevention. Training and staff development was offered through Paragon, a subsidiary company in which Natalie and Tim Killassy had a majority share, and which was 25% owned by the Paragon Employee Trust.[9] In 2005, Stitch Wise registered with the Clothing, Textile, Footwear and Leather Sectoral Education and Training Authority (SETA), allowing access to state-provided learnerships for the development of new staff, to be employed by both Stitch Wise and other companies.[10] In an innovative response to Broad Based Black Economic Empowerment (BBBEE) requirements, employee training is linked to returns on investment in the company. Successful participation in ongoing training is indexed to dividend payments, giving a direct return on the value of enhanced skills to both the individual and the company.[11]

Killassy early recognised the reputational value of mitigating the consequences of mine injuries. In 2004, she was recognised as Sanlam's Business Owner of the Year, which provided extensive media coverage and helped her leverage more favourable arrangements with her primary clients. Other awards and public recognition have followed. She further augmented her social capital by competing successfully for recognition as an Endeavor Entrepreneur.[12] This brought a number of specific advantages. Through Endeavor, she received mentorship from a leading US-based investment advisor. Two corporate specialists spent several weeks with the company and offered a set of specific recommendations for restructuring the rather complex relationship between Stitch Wise and its subsidiary firms to improve business efficiency and effectiveness.

A tension in Stitch Wise's business model has been its relationship with the mining companies. Stitch Wise was initially – and continues to a large extent to be – dependent on the Western Deep Mine, which provided its premises, original machinery and a labour force on loan against reimbursement from sales income. With justification, AngloGold Ashanti has seen its support of Stitch Wise as a corporate social investment (CSI), and has staked this claim publicly.[13] But at the same time Stitch Wise has had to compete on price with other suppliers of mine safety equipment. Since the costs of a largely paraplegic labour force are higher because of necessary adaptations to the plant and the need for higher medical benefits, Stitch Wise pays a social premium on labour, making its margins tighter in competing for contracts. A further complication is potential market limitation because of the perception that Stitch Wise is part of AngloGold Ashanti rather than an independent and competitive manufacturer. This led Killassy initially to establish an over-complex structure of subsidiaries, with the idea that subsidiaries Paragon and Knee'Dem would be able to compete better with Harmony and Gold Fields, AngloGold's primary competitors.

This tension came to a head in 2005, in Harmony Gold's much publicised – and ultimately unsuccessful – attempt to take over Gold Fields.[14] In its case to the South African Competition Tribunal, Harmony had stated its intention to increase shareholder value in the merged company by reducing procurement costs. Killassy's primary relationship with AngloGold Ashanti was not directly threatened. If successful, however, the Harmony/Gold Fields merger could have made it more difficult for Stitch Wise to compete on price to supply the mining sector as a whole. Killassy presented a case to South Africa's Competition Tribunal on behalf of historically disadvantaged South Africans seeking to establish themselves as suppliers to the mines. She explained how their interests would be damaged by the reduced competition that would follow from the intended merger:

> Enterprises, such as those currently being set up by the Intervenors, are struggling to establish themselves in a manufacturing environment dominated by larger established companies employing able-bodied labour. The latter companies are not saddled with the higher costs and other difficulties involved in providing a suitable working environment for employees with special needs. Specially modified equipment, enhanced ablution and medical facilities, higher employee turnover and regular absenteeism for medical reasons contribute inevitably to the higher cost of establishing an enterprise of this nature. Although expensive it is a justifiable investment worthy of protection, at least for a period sufficient to become competitive.[15]

The nub of the issue was Harmony's proposal that the merged company meet its obligations to black economic empowerment by giving 'empowered suppliers' such as Stitch Wise the right to match the best price offered by the pool of suppliers as a whole, in competition. As an industry principle, this increased the tension that Stitch Wise had faced from the start in its relationship with AngloGold. Killassy argued that this was both contrary to the principles of black economic empowerment in general and particularly unfair, since the mining companies were responsible for the injuries to the miners in the first place and would be disadvantaging them a second time by disallowing the higher labour costs that were a consequence of their injuries. She argued that rather than insisting on open price competition, mining companies should enter into partnerships with black empowered suppliers to give such suppliers the opportunity to build their capacity. While the Competition Tribunal did not allow Stitch Wise's intervention, the merger was prohibited in the more general interests of maintaining competition in the mining industry.

The combination of receiving advice through the Endeavor network and presenting the case to the Competition Tribunal has led to a process of streamlining and focusing. Killassy now sees difficulties in her earlier policy of creating subsidiary structures for new product lines. Paragon, Knee'Dem and Stitch Wise have been merged, making Stitch Wise now the holding company, with three manufacturing units: Paragon (knee guards and safety equipment), Ikageng (backfill bags) and Tsebo (overalls). This is intended to achieve better vertical integration and strengthen brand value for more effective marketing, which Killassy sees as critical to reducing the company's dependence on AngloGold Ashanti. To strengthen its position further, Stitch Wise actively seeks service agreements with its clients, combining the provision of equipment with expertise in underground conditions. The company achieves this by maintaining a lead in innovation: its new products include reinforced earth technology that augments the backfill bags and a personal safety net for miners for immediate protection from rock falls.

Stitch Wise's success as a new enterprise can be measured in four ways. First, the company has been financially successful. Having started in 1997 from a base of in-kind support, by 2005 Stitch Wise had a turnover of R17.7m and a net profit of R1.2m, and by 2007 this had grown

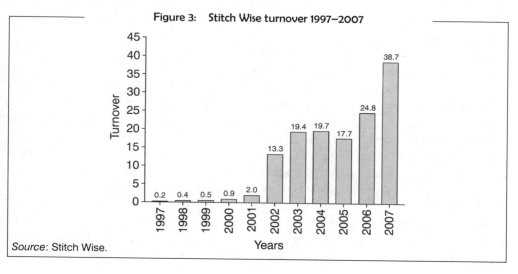

Figure 3: Stitch Wise turnover 1997–2007

Source: Stitch Wise.

to a net profit of R6m on a turnover of R38.7m. Growth is expected to continue in 2008, with a projected turnover of R58m (Figure 3).

Second, Stitch Wise has created more than 160 jobs (80 of which are for paraplegics), providing on-site training to enhance productivity and giving co-ownership of the enterprise through its employees' trust, which receives 26% of net profit.

Third, Stitch Wise has established a formidable R&D (research and development) capacity, defining the Bureau of Standards specifications for backfill bags and registering six patents for its products.

Fourth, as a result of Stitch Wise's products and services there has been a decline in the number of underground injuries from rock falls at those mines that have installed Stitch Wise's safety systems. Apart from the primary benefit to miners who work under some of the most difficult conditions in the world, there is a clear advantage both to the mining companies and to the state, which is relieved of the costs of welfare support.

Wider issues

Is Stitch Wise a one-of-a-kind enterprise, driven by a strong personality in a specialised niche? Or is this company's approach scalable or replicable in other South African mining sectors, with wider implications for economic development and countering poverty and social exclusion?

While Stitch Wise continues to anticipate growth, the market for specialised mine safety equipment in South Africa is limited. While the company will be able to strengthen its relationship with existing clients through continuing innovation and support, it is already dominant in a highly specialised niche. Because its effectiveness depends on insider knowledge of local conditions, and its product innovations depend on the former miners' experience and understanding of underground conditions, for it to replicate its approach in other countries with similar mining industries would be a challenge, particularly as these opportunities are for the most part in Latin America. Killassy is herself ambivalent about scaling up her company. On the one hand, she is rightly proud of her success and enjoys the challenge of future growth; on the other, she gets particular satisfaction from working close to the production line, with the empowered community she has created. Expansion into other locations would take her away from this immediate context.

However, Stitch Wise's history as a small and successful enterprise provides pointers to some more general aspects of pro-poor business strategies.

In the first place, its approach cannot be interpreted as a BOP strategy, and in some respects it demonstrates the limitations of BOP assumptions. BOP strategies seek to widen markets for large corporations (often, but not necessarily, multinationals) by drawing poor and excluded communities into the consumer economy, increasing the profitability of established companies and, as a collateral benefit, creating value for the poor.[16] While Stitch Wise could not have been established without being provided by AngloGold Ashanti with premises, the initial machinery and access to labour, the mining company was not motivated by a BOP strategy, and has not developed a relationship with Stitch Wise that is significantly different to its relationship with other suppliers of specialist products and services. Indeed, Stitch Wise's wider experience of working within the gold mining industry demonstrates how difficult it can be to persuade large corporations to adopt pro-poor business strategies. Harmony's insistence, as part of its takeover bid for rival Gold Fields, that it would give no more than first refusal against best price to its service providers conforms more to Bakan's view that the corporation must invariably seek short-term shareholder profit than to the BOP hope that large companies will see the benefits of doing good.[17] This is particularly striking in the case of the South African mining industry, which must counter a widespread perception of accountability for major social and economic problems in South Africa, and could thus be expected to have an interest in using the power of its supply chain to contribute to economic and social regeneration in Gauteng.

Secondly, the Stitch Wise story illustrates the limitations of CSI. While AngloGold Ashanti claimed, legitimately, that its support in starting up the enterprise was part of its CSI policy, it was slow to match this with tangible advantage to Stitch Wise as an emerging enterprise. While being praised through AngloGold's public relations division, Stitch Wise was forced to compete on price through the mine's procurement division. Although Killassy's case to the Competition Tribunal was directed at Harmony, the same criticism could fairly be levelled at AngloGold Ashanti: having created the problem of paraplegic ex-miners through the combination of underground accidents and demeaning sheltered employment, the company then stacked the odds against a successful solution by failing to recognise the tighter margins incurred by Stitch Wise through its use of a disabled labour force. By treating interventions such as these as CSI, companies such as AngloGold Ashanti may be in danger of marginalising a beneficial opportunity, rather than seeing it as part of mainstream business.

Thirdly, Stitch Wise calls into doubt easy distinctions between for-profit and social ventures. While there is a range of definitions, social ventures (or enterprises) are understood to be businesses that have 'social purpose', that seek to provide benefits for individuals or the community rather than profits for the business owner or shareholders.[18] While Killassy was – and continues to be – motivated by the promise of social improvement, Stitch Wise's success rests on her aggressive pursuit of for-profit strategies, including constant innovation, competitive pricing, locking clients into ongoing support relationships and searching continually for new markets. In other words, Stitch Wise combines clear and persistent social purpose with conventional profit-seeking and shareholder ownership. Indeed, in a community such as Carltonville, it is clear that the major source of social benefit is the creation of sustainable livelihoods.

Rather than seeking to squeeze Stitch Wise into established categories such as BOP, CSI or Social Enterprise, it is more useful to see its modus operandi as strategic knowledge management, a perspective that has yet to be applied to emerging enterprises working to develop pro-poor economic value. Recent theories of the economics of knowledge show how successful enterprises take advantage of the particular, and sometimes peculiar, characteristics of knowledge as a commodity.[19] These characteristics include the distinction between tacit knowledge, held by small groups and passed on by example or word of mouth, and codified knowledge, which can be expressed in forms that are widely disseminated (for example, in written or digital form). Knowledge is non-rivalrous (it can be used by many without being used up) and is partially non-excludable (difficult to protect from others' use). While theories of knowledge are generally applied to large high-tech enterprises and areas where economic return depends directly on the protection of intellectual property, the same characteristics apply to small-scale enterprises that depend on product and service innovation.

Thinking of Stitch Wise as a knowledge enterprise highlights aspects of the company's strategy that may be less evident through lenses such as BOP, CSI and Social Enterprise.

Firstly, the value of the paraplegic workforce's knowledge of underground mine conditions becomes evident. Rather than seeing these men as disabled workers requiring welfare support, Killassy's business strategy draws on their knowledge of the mining profession and their pride in their skill. This pool of tacit knowledge created a rich experimental environment for the company to develop additional products.

Secondly, Killassy was able to draw on formal, codified knowledge from the CSIR's laboratory to develop the backfill bag. This was critical. While her own observations underground combined with the miners' tacit knowledge, enabled her to perceive both the essential problem and a potential solution, as an emerging enterprise Stitch Wise lacked any developed R&D capacity. Through the fortuitous discovery of a matching set of interests at the CSIR, Killassy was able to put in place an effective and targeted knowledge transfer mechanism that yielded key benefits.

Thirdly, Stitch Wise shares with large corporations the problems of protecting its intellectual property. The company depends on turning knowledge into innovation and innovation into financial value. Because the key innovation, the backfill bag technology, is for all practical purposes non-excludable, Stitch Wise is driven by the need to keep improving its products and services to maintain a competitive edge.

Stitch Wise's characteristics as a knowledge enterprise can be shown diagrammatically (Figure 4). On the right is the domain of tacit knowledge, the interplay of ideas, observations and experience in the underground testing site, on the factory floor and in training sessions. On the left is the domain of formal, codified knowledge: research laboratories, the formal definition of standards, accreditation of education and training and the legal regulation of business activities. This domain is open ended, connecting to the global 'knowledge commons' of the science system. Stitch Wise functions as a knowledge broker, connecting the two domains and translating knowledge into economic value, both for the company itself, and more broadly as its own success in innovation is shared.

Seen in this way, the potential for scalability lies not so much in the specifics of Stitch Wise's products and processes (these are highly niche dependent) as in understanding how access to knowledge resources can enable innovation in pro-poor enterprises.

Poverty can be understood as a systemic trap – a set of factors that prevent communities from passing specific thresholds such as gaining access to capital, or to critical infrastructure, or obtaining relief from endemic disease.[20] This process approach to poverty can be applied on a national or continental scale, directing policy for international agencies or local governments, or at a community level, as for example in the Millennium Villages project, which depends on the identification of specific, local, circumstances that hinder economic development.[21] Stitch Wise is an example of the value of seeing poverty in process terms at a localised level. The former miners of Carltonville were locked into a self-replicating poverty trap of injury, unemployment and lack of opportunity. Stitch Wise's success has been due to Killassy's empathetic recognition of potential, and her persistence in building an effective knowledge system that has translated this potential into effective innovation and economic value. Employment, and the associated benefits of training and co-ownership in the company, may have enabled this sector of the Carltonville community to pass a critical threshold and to work towards breaking out of the poverty trap.

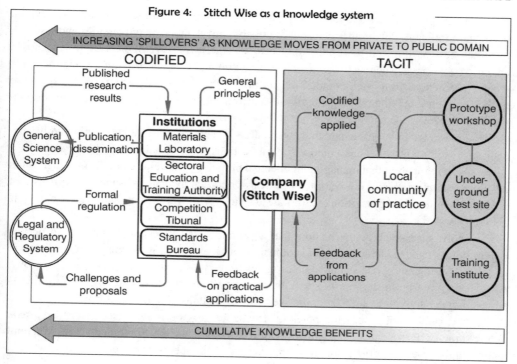

Figure 4: Stitch Wise as a knowledge system

Appropriately, Killassy's achievements as an entrepreneur have been widely recognised, and both the Sanlam award and the Endeavor network will disseminate the Stitch Wise story as a model for others. At the same time, this case illustrates the potential significance of informed public policy for enabling pro-poor enterprise development. Invariably, start-ups such as Stitch Wise will lack R&D capacity and will therefore find it difficult to turn ideas and insights into innovations that return economic value. Although Carltonville is within a few hours' drive of a cluster of major research-oriented universities and specialised, government-funded research institutions, it was happenstance that enabled Killassy to make the key link with the CSIR laboratory in Pretoria. That connection has since come to an end (the laboratory has moved on to other interests), and Killassy has had to negotiate a replacement relationship with a research group at the University of the Witwatersrand. While there is significant public investment in South African 'knowledge institutions', and while these institutions are well connected with the global science system, there are few established mechanisms for connecting formal and tacit knowledge in the way that worked for Stitch Wise. This could be corrected through innovations in public policy, enabling knowledge to be used far more extensively to open the doors for pro-poor enterprise development.

Issues and implications

Stitch Wise's successes and challenges highlight several specific issues. If the opportunities for pro-poor strategic knowledge management are be expanded, the issue of making research and development facilities available to small-scale start-ups with little or no working capital becomes significant. Put another way, how can public investments in universities and research institutes best be directed to support this kind of enterprise development? Further, should emerging enterprises such as these, which incur additional costs in providing social benefits, receive protection from open competition on price? In other words, should Killassy's case to the Competition Tribunal be generalised as a form of 'infant industry' protection through public policy?[22]

In addition, Stitch Wise's experience over a decade spent establishing its position in the specialised area of mine safety has a number of implications for pro-poor enterprises in general.

Firstly, it is apparent that managing intellectual property – the value chain from idea through development to successful innovation – can be as important to small pro-poor enterprises as it is to the larger-scale and traditional corporate activities with which knowledge management is generally associated.

Secondly, cases such as these show that corporate social investment, while offering key opportunities, can lead to complex and confusing relationships between the parent corporation and the offspring enterprise as the latter struggles for private sector competitiveness in its own right. It may not be in the interests of either the small enterprise or the larger entity that is sponsoring the activity to keep the initiative compartmentalised in the 'CSI box'.

Thirdly, public policy has the potential to enable pro-poor enterprises in critical ways. While some BOP strategies have tended to view governments as a hindrance, identifying and analysing the threshold effects that limit the success of small enterprises can turn existing and underutilised opportunities for knowledge transfer to advantage.

Conclusion

Killassy was motivated to establish Stitch Wise by the suffering caused by underground mine injuries. Over the course of a decade, she has taken her company to widespread recognition and sustained profitability. She has done so by developing technologies that have improved mine safety and creating income for a poor and marginalised community through employment, training and joint ownership in the enterprise. At the heart of the Stitch Wise business model is the strategic use of knowledge – the beneficial combination of a tacit understanding of underground conditions gleaned from the experience of ex-miners and research into new materials in specialised research laboratories. This case illustrates how the returns on intellectual capital can be as valuable in a small, pro-poor enterprise as they are in large, information-age corporations.

At the same time, underground injuries continue to plague the mining industry as a whole – despite the specific safety improvements that have resulted from Stitch Wise's systems. In 2006, AngloGold Ashanti reported 32 fatalities on its South African mines – a sharp increase, with 78% of fatal accidents due to underground rock falls. Resignations and retirements of senior executives in the Anglo American group of companies – including AngloGold Ashanti – have been attributed to this safety record. With incoming CEO Cynthia Carroll described the situation as 'simply not acceptable'. More effective safety measures would be a requirement for 'those managers who wish to make progress within the company'.[23] In reviewing their options for achieving safety objectives, AngloGold Ashanti managers could benefit by rescuing their investment in Stitch Wise from its categorisation as a CSI initiative, and seeing it as an approach that could add a wide range of value through the smart use of knowledge resources.

Editors' reflections and questions

The purpose of the Stitch Wise case study is threefold. First, it explores ways in which emerging enterprises can gain needed access to the specialised research, development and knowledge that fuels company innovation and allows them to be highly competitive. Second, it examines the tension between commercial viability and the provision of a social benefit. Third, it considers the usefulness of the 'Base of the Pyramid' model – a model which envisages beneficial relationships between large corporations and small emerging enterprises – by examining the example of Stitch Wise and its corporate clients. The author suggests it is the way these relationships are structured that may ultimately determine the success of the emerging enterprises.

One of the drivers of the formation of Stitch Wise and its subsequent business strategy was the quest to improve the quality of life for the former miners who make up the majority of its employees. The company employs disabled former miners who were initially on the payroll of AngloGold Ashanti's Western Deep Mine. Although this relationship provides benefits to Stitch Wise and its employees, as well as the mining company, it is also a source of tension in Stitch Wise's business model. Stitch Wise was initially – and continues to be – largely dependent on the Western Deep Mine, which provided its premises, the original machinery and a labour force on loan against reimbursement from sales income. Furthermore, Stitch Wise has had to compete on price with other suppliers of mine safety equipment. Since the costs of a largely paraplegic labour force are relatively high, Stitch Wise pays a social premium on labour – making its margins tighter when competing for contracts.

Natalie Killassy, founder and CEO of Stitch Wise, faces a number of critical decisions. Her company is close to meeting the requirements of the specialised South African market for safety equipment in deep mine shafts, which prompts the following questions:

1. Should Stitch Wise diversify into other products or stay with its existing product line and look to the export market for expansion? For example, should the company move into safety consultancy, offering the mines a service agreement in addition to its current products?

2. What steps could be taken to decrease Stitch Wise's dependence on Western Deep Mine?

3. Has Stitch Wise demonstrated the limitations of the Bottom of the Pyramid approach? And if so, how?

4. In what ways does Stitch Wise illustrate the importance of and potential for strategic knowledge management for pro-poor ventures?

Notes

1   Information for this study was drawn from a series of interviews with Natalie and Tim Killassy, initially under the auspices of the non-profit organisation, Endeavor South Africa, and subsequently in January, June and October 2005, March 2007 and August 2007. I am indebted to Natalie and Tim for their time and generosity in sharing information about their business and their vision.

2   There has been a tendency in some recent writing to extend the BOP concept to include all pro-poor business ventures, including those supported by philanthropy. Here, the concept is used as formulated by C. K. Prahalad and Stuart Hart in their recent works: C. K. Prahalad, *The Fortune at the Bottom of the Pyramid: Eradicating Poverty Through Profits* (New York: Wharton School Publishing, 2004); S. Hart, *Capitalism at the Crossroads: The Unlimited Business Opportunities in Solving the World's most Difficult Problems* (New Jersey: Wharton School Publishing, 2005).

3   See A. Karnani, 'Mirage at the Bottom of the Pyramid: How the Private Sector can Help Alleviate Poverty', William Davidson Institute Working Paper No. 835 (Ann Arbor: University of Michigan, 2007).

4   Pauline Nhlapo has since retired.

5   See http://www.csir.co.za for additional information.

6   See http://www.sabs.co.za/

7   www.stitchwise.co.za

8   ABET is an important aspect of South Africa's education policy that addresses the high levels of adult illiteracy that are the consequence of unequal access to an often inadequate public education system. See http://www.labour.gov.za

9   The initial set of subsidiary companies has subsequently been re-structured – see below.

10   SETAs are public bodies established by legislation. All companies pay a skills levy on their payroll, which provides for training via a SETA for their sector. Learnerships are funded by SETAs for recognised in-company training, thereby allowing companies that provide training for their staff to offset the payroll levy. The effectiveness of SETAs in meeting their obligations has been a matter of controversy.

11   Broad Based Black Economic Empowerment (BBBEE) is legislation that encourages the South African private sector to widen ownership of companies to include those denied opportunity by apartheid legislation. Initially directed to black ownership, the policy has been broadened to induce worker ('broad based') access to equity through trusts and other vehicles. Charters have been negotiated with a range of economic sectors (including the mining industry), and companies tendering for state contracts are required to have met BBBEE standards.

12   Social capital is here used in the specific sense of 'the advantage created by a person's location in a structure of relationships' (see R.S. Burt, *Brokerage and Closure: An Introduction to Social Capital* (New York: Oxford University Press, 2005). Endeavor is a US-based international organisation that seeks to advance entrepreneurship by supporting selected small and medium sized businesses. Having achieved impact in Latin America, Endeavor South Africa was inaugurated in 2004 with the selection of a first set of Endeavor Entrepreneurs that included Stitch Wise. Additional Endeavor Entrepreneurs have been selected in each subsequent years. See www.endeavor.co.za

13   See Anglo Gold *Report to Society* (Johannesburg, 2003), Section 7.1: 'Providing Jobs at Stitch Wise'.

14   See www.newratings.com/analyst_news/article_499476.html

15   Competition Tribunal of South Africa, case number 93/LMNov04. Intervenors' Statement by Stitch Wise (Pty) Ltd, Paragon Textiles (Pty)Ltd and Knee'dem (Pty) Ltd, 26 April 2005.

16   Prahalad, *Fortune at the Bottom of the Pyramid*; Hart, *Capitalism at the Crossroads*.

17   J. Bakan, *The Corporation: The Pathological Pursuit of Profit and Power* (London: Constable, 2004), sees the corporation as an 'externalizing machine', set up for the express purpose of delivering maximum returns to its shareholders. Consequently, the corporation cannot be the vehicle for 'doing good' in any sense that does not bring a return to its shareholders. Despite frequent claims that the BOP strategy was developed to alleviate poverty, the original formulations by Prahalad and Hart make it clear that this is not the case; the BOP strategy is intended to increase value to share-

holders by finding new markets that can give good returns. For example, Hart, *Capitalism at the Crossroads*, 21, 175, advocates that large corporations embrace 'radical transactiveness' in order to gain access to 'fringe stakeholders (who) may hold knowledge and perspectives that are key both to anticipating potential problems and to identifying innovative opportunities and business models for the future'. A definitive and often cited example is Hindustan Lever's strategy of marketing products in small quantities through a network of village based micro-entrepreneurs. However, South African mining companies have not adopted strategies of this type that have little relevance to their core business. Harmony Gold's argument to the Competition Tribunal that it would protect immediate shareholder value by reducing procurement costs is a model for the antithesis of a BOP strategy.

18 L. Easterly and P. Miesing, 'Social Venture Business Strategies for Reducing Poverty', in J.A.F. Stoner and C. Wankel, eds, *Innovative Approaches to Reducing Global Poverty* (Charlotte: Information Age Publishing, 2007): 3–26.

19 'Tacit' knowledge is that which is inferred, communicated by example and restricted to small groups of people who usually interact on a face-to-face basis. 'Codified' knowledge is expressed in a form that can be widely communicated without requiring face-to-face interaction – written texts, digital code, film and other forms of mass communication. See D. Foray, *Economics of Knowledge* (Cambridge: MIT Press, 2004); P. David and D. Foray, 'Economic Fundamentals of the Knowledge Society', *Policy Futures in Education*, 1, 1 (2003): 20–49; E. Von Hippel, *Democratizing Innovation* (Cambridge: MIT Press, 2005).

20 S. Bowles, S. Durlauf and K. Hoff, eds, *Poverty Traps* (Princeton: Princeton University Press, 2006); J. Sachs, J. W. McArthur, G. Schmidt-Traub, M. Kruk, C. Bahadur, M. Faye and G. McCord, 'Ending Africa's Poverty Trap', *Brookings Papers on Economic Activity*, 1 (2004): 117–240; J. Sachs, *The End of Poverty* (London: Penguin, 2005).

21 Columbia University's Millennium Villages Project is a bottom-up approach to intervene in poverty traps. Earth Institute scientists and development experts in agriculture, nutrition and health, economics, energy, water, environment and information technology are working with local communities and governments to apply a holistic package of interventions to help villages get out of extreme poverty. In 2005, work began in two Millennium Research Villages: Sauri in Kenya and Koraro in Ethiopia. The project was expanded to a further ten research villages in Ghana, Kenya, Malawi, Mali, Nigeria, Rwanda, Senegal, Tanzania, and Uganda. It is intended that this will be followed by a scale-up to national and regional levels: http://www.earthinstitute.columbia.edu/mvp/

22 For the case for infant industry protection, see H.-J. Chang, *Knocking Away the Ladder: Development Strategy in Historical Perspective* (London: Anthem Press, 2002).

23 J. Newmarch, 'All Change at Anglo', *Mail and Guardian* (Johannesburg), 3 August 2007: 1.

NOTES ON THE AUTHORS

Bastian Birkenhäger studied Tropical Forestry at Wageningen University in the Netherlands. He then worked for the FAO (Food and Agriculture Organisation) in Nepal and Sierra Leone and for GTZ (Gesellschaft für Technische Zusammenarbeit) in the Ivory Coast, in the fields of community forestry and sustainable tropical forest management respectively. Since his return to Europe Bastian has continued to work as an independent consultant, mainly on projects in Central Africa. As some of these projects deal with public-private partnerships, he has become interested in corporate citizenship.

Fleur Boulogne is a researcher in the Environmental Evaluation Unit, University of Cape Town. She is also completing her Masters degree in Sustainable Development, Planning and Management at the Sustainability Institute, Stellenbosch University. Previously, she was project coordinator of an environmental education programme at the Fairest Cape Association, South Africa. In the Netherlands, she was a senior policy advisor on European urban policy in the Ministry of the Interior and on European spatial planning projects in the Ministry of Housing, Spatial Planning and the Environment.

Claudio Bruzzi Boechat has been a teacher, researcher and project manager at the Sustainability and Corporate Responsibility Nucleus at Fundação Dom Cabral, Brazil, since 2002. His current professional activities include knowledge development in the field of Responsible and Sustainable Business Management. He is a contributor to the Globally Responsible Leadership Initiative and the UN Global Compact Principles for Responsible Management Education. He has degrees in Electrical Engineering from the Federal University of Minas Gerais and Fundação Dom Cabral, Brazil.

Oana Branzei is assistant professor of Strategy and a faculty member of the Engaging Emergent Markets and Building Sustainable Value Cross-leadership Centres at the Richard Ivey School of Business, University of Western Ontario. Prior to joining Ivey, she was part of the faculty of the Schulich School of Business at York University, Canada. Oana is a multiple research and teaching award winner, who has published in leading academic journals and has written several award-winning case studies.

Kris Dobie holds an MPhil in Workplace Ethics from the University of Pretoria. He is currently with the Ethics Institute of South Africa where his main focus is on Organisational Ethics development. He has been involved in a number of projects focusing on anti-corruption research and training, predominantly in the South African public service.

Oonagh E. Fitzgerald has been a lawyer with the federal government of Canada since 1983, as well as a manager since 1995. She has written two books, *The Guilty Plea and Summary Justice,* and *Understanding Charter Remedies,* and has also edited a collection of essays, *The Globalized Rule of Law: Relations between International and Domestic Law.* She has taught at various universities and is currently completing an Executive Masters of Business Administration at Queen's University in Canada.

Martin Hall is deputy vice-chancellor at the University of Cape Town and is affiliated to the Centre for Innovation and Entrepreneurship at UCT's Graduate School of Business. He has written on public higher education policy and the social role of universities in contributing to development, and is researching knowledge systems and knowledge flows to small enterprises that contribute to job creation and poverty alleviation.

Ralph Hamann is senior researcher in the Environmental Evaluation Unit at the University of Cape Town and associate professor extraordinary at the Sustainability Institute, Stellenbosch University. He has held research positions at the Centre for Corporate Citizenship, Unisa, and at the African Institute of Corporate Citizenship, and has consulted for various public and private sector organisations. His PhD was on CSR in mining and was conferred in 2004 by the University of East Anglia.

Jonathon Hanks is a founding director of Incite Sustainability, a consultancy that specialises in promoting sustainability practices in the public and private sectors in southern Africa. He is a senior associate of the University of Cambridge Programme for Industry and a visiting senior lecturer at the University of Cape Town's Graduate School of Business. He is currently convenor of an international ISO (International Organisation for Standardisation) Task Group developing a global standard on social responsibility (ISO 26000).

Paul Kapelus has 15 years' experience in the field of Corporate Responsibility, with a focus on mining, oil, infrastructure development, finance and telecommunications. He is the founder and former CEO of the African Institute of Corporate Citizenship, and he is currently a director at Synergy Global Consulting.

Ricarda McFalls is an International Management and Business Development specialist with more than 20 years of global IT industry experience, and has worked for the past 12 years in sub-Saharan Africa. She has recently completed a Masters degree in Sustainable Development at Stellenbosch University with a view to applying her many years of business experience in developing countries to promoting business practices and development policies supportive of a sustainability agenda.

Kevin McKague is a senior research fellow with the Institute for Research and Innovation in Sustainability at York University, Canada, and is founding president of the Foundation for Sustainable Enterprise and Development (FSED). He has consulted on major International Finance Corporation (IFC) projects, among others, and he has held posts at the IFC and the Schulich School of Business. Kevin is co-author of *Creating Sustainable Local Enterprise Networks*, published in the MIT/Sloan Management Review and has developed over 50 best-practice case studies.

Judy N. Muthuri is pursuing doctoral studies at the International Centre for Corporate Social Responsibility (ICCSR), Nottingham University Business School. She received her Masters of Research degree with distinction from ICCSR. She also holds an MBA from the University of Nairobi and a Bachelor of Education degree from Kenyatta University. Her areas of interest are corporate social strategy, corporate community involvement and CSR in developing countries.

Roberta Mokrejs Paro has been working as a researcher for the Andrade Gutierrez Center of Corporate Responsibility and Sustainability at Fundação Dom Cabral since the end of 2005. Before that, she worked in systems analysis applied to sustainability at Lund University, and on corporate social responsibility at the Ethos Institute of Business and Social Responsibility. She has a degree in Agricultural Engineering from the University of the Estate of São Paulo and a master's degree in Sustainability and Environmental Science from Lund University.

James Ng'ombe is a publisher and trader in educational books, a writer of fiction, drama, children's literature and school textbooks, and an educator and trainer of journalists. One of Malawi's most distinguished and prolific authors, he has published numerous works on political themes, including the novels *Sugarcane with Salt* (1989) and *Madala's Children* (1996). Since 1995 Dr Ng'ombe has been managing director and co-proprietor of Jhango Heinemann, formerly Jhango Publishing House. He previously managed educational publishers Dzuka Publishing and he was executive director of the Malawi Institute of Journalism.

Ed O'Keefe is a Director of Synergy Global Consulting, a consultancy which supports organisations to understand, manage and improve their relations with society. He has over ten years' experience in managing the social impacts of large-scale development projects in over 20 countries, with a focus on the extractive industries. He is a trained ISO 14001 lead auditor and leads numerous external assessments and audits of community relations management systems. His dissertation for his MA in Rural Development was based on his work on relationships between a gold mine and communities in the Kyrgyz Republic. He has formerly worked with the British Department for International Development (DFID) in Uganda, and for the conservation NGO Fauna & Flora International.

Melissa Peneycad has recently completed her Master of Environmental Studies at York University, Toronto, Ontario. Her graduate research explored equitable solutions to poverty alleviation, with a focus on women's entrepreneurship and the mutual relationship between social capital and enterprise development and growth in East Africa. Melissa is an alumna of the Care Enterprise Partners MBA Internship Program 2006, and currently works as a consultant and client service manager with TerraChoice Environmental Marketing in Ottawa, Ontario.

Odette Ramsingh is director-general in the Public Service Commission and her work revolves around the research, investigation, monitoring and evaluation of the South African Public Service. She has an MBA from the University of Cape Town; a BA and LLB from the University of Natal; a Senior Executive Programme Certificate from the Harvard Business School; and an MA in Governance and Development from the University of Sussex, UK.

Josef Seitz has 17 years experience as an expert in the fields of Environment and Sustainable Business Development. Working for the German development agency GTZ, he has advised the government of Morocco and the private sector in Argentina, among others. In 2005, he became regional coordinator for the Life Environment Programme of the European Commission in France. In 2006, he founded Global21, a consulting company that focuses on the interface between business, environment and development (www.global21.eu).

Courtenay Sprague is a faculty member at the Graduate School of Business and a doctoral student in the Development Studies Department at the University of the Witwatersrand. Most of her work lies at the interface between research and policy and is focused on understanding the development needs of poorer or marginalized groups. She has held programme and research posts at Carnegie Corporation and Harvard University for four years each. She has also conducted work for UNAIDS, and produced research commissioned by the ILO (International Labour Organisation), UNDP, Human Rights Watch, the Treatment Action Campaign, and USAID. Her recent research has focused on access to antiretroviral therapy for vulnerable groups; health equity; social determinants of health; and women's health. She holds a BA degree in political science from Michigan State University (USA), and a double MA degree in international relations and in natural resource management from Boston University (USA).

Mike Valente is an assistant professor in Strategy and Sustainability at the Faculty of Business, University of Victoria, having completed his PhD in Strategic Management and Business Sustainability at the Schulich School of Business. His areas of interest are the resource-based view of the firm and institutional theory in the context of sustainable development, corporate social responsibility and social entrepreneurship. Mike has received numerous awards, including the Governor General's Gold Medal Award.

Stu Woolman holds degrees in Philosophy from Wesleyan University (BA) and Columbia University (MA) and in Law from Columbia Law School (JD) and the University of Pretoria (PhD). Professor Woolman is the editor-in-chief and primary author of *Constitutional Law of South Africa*, the most influential and widely-cited treatise on the subject. He has practised law in Washington, DC, and New York City and is currently a public law consultant with Ashira (Pty) Ltd in Johannesburg. Prior to joining the Department of Public Law and the Centre for Human Rights at the University of Pretoria in 2002, he taught law at Columbia Law School and the University of the Witwatersrand. He has also worked on the UN Human Rights Committee and the Goldstone Commission.